Strategic Innovation Management

Strategic Innovation Management

Joe Tidd and John Bessant

WILEY

Registered office
John Wiley & Sons Ltd, The Atrium, Southern Gate, Chichester, West Sussex, PO19 8SQ, United Kingdom

For details of our global editorial offices, for customer services and for information about how to apply for permission to reuse the copyright material in this book please see our website at www.wiley.com.

Library of Congress Cataloging-in-Publication Data

Tidd, Joseph, 1960-
  Strategic innovation management / Joe Tidd, John Bessant.
     pages cm
   Includes index.
  ISBN 978-1-118-45723-8 (pbk.) — ISBN 978-1-118-86333-6 (ebk)
  1. Management—Technological innovations. 2. Strategic planning. I. Bessant, J. R. II. Title.
  HD30.2.T4956 2014
  658.4'063—dc23

                                                                     2013047070

ISBN 978-1-118-86322-0 (ebk)

A catalogue record for this book is available from the British Library

Set in 10/12 Sabon LT Std by Thomson Digital, India

Contents

About the Authors

Joe Tidd is a physicist with subsequent degrees in technology policy and business administration. He is Professor of Technology and Innovation Management at SPRU (Science & Technology Policy Research), University of Sussex, UK and Visiting Professor at University College London, Cass Business School, Copenhagen Business School and Rotterdam School of Management. He was previously Head of the Management of Innovation Specialisation and Director of the Executive MBA Programme at Imperial College, and Deputy Director and Director of Studies at SPRU www.sussex.ac.uk/spru/jtidd.

He has worked as policy adviser to the CBI (Confederation of British Industry) and as a researcher for the International Motor Vehicle Program at the Massachusetts Institute of Technology (MIT), which identified lean production. He has worked on research and consultancy projects for consultants Arthur D. Little, Capgemini and McKinsey, and technology-based firms, including American Express Technology, Applied Materials, ASML, BOC Edwards, BT, Marconi, National Power, NKT Holding, Nortel Networks, Petrobras and Pfizer, and international agencies such as UNESCO. He is the winner of the Price Waterhouse Urwick Medal for contribution to management teaching and research, and the Epton Prize from the R&D Society. He is a director of MBA Authors Ltd and a founding partner of Management Masters LLP, academic services and licensing companies. He is also Managing Editor of the *International Journal of Innovation Management* www.worldscinet.com/ijim/ijim.shtml, the official journal of the International Society of Professional Innovation Management (ISPIM) www.ispim.org/index.php. He has written eight books and more than 60 papers on the management of technology and innovation, and has more than 7,000 citations on Google Scholar.

John Bessant, who was originally a chemical engineer, has been active in the field of research and consultancy in technology and innovation management for over 25 years. He currently holds the Chair in Innovation and Entrepreneurship at the University of Exeter and has visiting appointments at the universities of Luxembourg, Erlangen-Nuremberg, Queensland University of Technology and the National University of Ireland. In 2003, he was elected a Fellow of the British Academy of Management and served as a Panel Member in the 2001 and 2008 Research Assessment Exercises in the United Kingdom. He holds Fellowships from the Advanced Institute for Management Research in the United Kingdom and the Schöller Foundation in Germany and has acted as adviser to various national governments and international bodies, including the United Nations, the World Bank and the OECD.

He is the author of 15 books and many articles on innovation and has lectured and consulted widely around the world. Clients have included Toyota, Novo Nordisk, Lego, Morgan Stanley, Coloplast, Corus, Danfoss, GSK, Grundfos, Hewlett-Packard and Kumba Resources.

Preface

Welcome to the first edition of *Strategic Innovation Management*, a new addition to our established best-selling texts *Managing Innovation* (fifth edition, 2013) and *Innovation and Entrepreneurship* (second edition, 2011).

Innovative firms grow twice as fast, both in employment and sales, as firms that fail to innovate. We know that those organizations that are consistently successful at managing innovation outperform their peers in terms of growth, financial performance and employment, and that the broader social benefits of innovation are even greater.

However, managing innovation is not easy or automatic. It requires skills and knowledge which are significantly different from the standard management toolkit and experience, because most management training and advice is aimed to maintain stability. As a result, most organizations either simply do not formally manage the innovation process or manage it in an ad hoc way. We argue that successful strategic innovation management is much more than managing a single aspect, such as creativity, research and development or product development. Here we continue to promote an integrated approach, which deals with the interactions between changes in markets, technology and organization.

Like our other texts, we aim to provide a practical yet rigorous and evidence-based approach to managing innovation in a wide range of contexts, including manufacturing, services, small to large organizations and the private, public and third sectors. However, we have developed *Strategic Innovation Management* to be more accessible to non-specialist courses and users.

In particular, this text has been designed to be fully integrated with our all-new open Innovation Portal:

www.innovation-portal.info

We have developed this resource for those, like us, who teach, study and practise the management of innovation. We're regularly adding to the function and contents of the Portal, but already it has the following open resources:

- 70 case studies, by chapter, theme and tags
- 40 media clips, both video and audio
- 75 innovation tools, by task, theme or alphabetically
- 50 activities for student seminars and assessments
- Question and test-bank of 300 Q&A
- Instructor resources, including suggested course outlines, content and PowerPoint packs.

The online Forum allows everyone to participate and contribute to the Innovation Portal, and we look forward to building this shared open resource with you.

We would like to acknowledge the extensive feedback, support and contributions from users of our other texts, our own colleagues and students, the team at Wiley and the growing community of innovation scholars and professionals who have contributed directly to this new text, in particular the generous participants in the workshops we ran in London, Manchester, Helsinki, Rotterdam and Barcelona.

Joe Tidd and John Bessant
March 2014

Acknowledgements

We would like to thank all those colleagues and students at SPRU, CENTRIM, Exeter, Imperial, UCL and elsewhere, who have provided feedback on our work. We are also grateful for the more formal input provided by various anonymous reviewers whose comments and suggestions helped develop this new text, and the experience and expertise shared by the participants in the professional faculty workshops held in London, Manchester, Helsinki, Rotterdam, Barcelona and Dar es Salaam, in particular the events for ISPIM (International Society for Professional Innovation Management) and UNESCO (United Nations Educational, Scientific, and Cultural Organization).

Thanks are also due to Emma Taylor, Dave Francis, Stefan Kohn, Philip Cullimore, Fabian Schlage, Helle-Vibeke Pedersen, Francisco Pinheiro, Melissa Clark-Reynolds, Armin Rau, Catherina van Delden, Simon Tucker, Girish Prabhu, Richard Philpott, David Simoes-Brown, Alastair Ross, Suzana Moreira, Michael Bartl, Roy Sandbach, Lynne Maher, Helen King, Patrick McLaughlin, David Overton, Michelle Lowe, Gerard Harkin, Dorothea Seebode, John Thesmer, Tim Craft, Bettina von Stamm and Kathrin Moeslein for their help in creating case studies and podcast/video material for the text and website. Particular thanks are due to Anna Trifilova for her help in background research and assembling many of the web-based cases.

As always we're really grateful for the help and support of the extended team at Wiley, who have practised what we preach with their seamless cross-functional working, especially Steve Hardman, Sarah Booth, Juliet Booker, Georgia King, Song Yee Lyn, and Tim Bettsworth.

How to Use This Book

Features in the Book

INNOVATION IN ACTION 5.1

Hidden Innovation

In 2006, the UK organization NESTA published a report on 'The Innovation Gap' in the United Kingdom, and laid particular emphasis on 'hidden innovation' – innovation activities that are not reflected in traditional indicators such as investments in formal R&D or patents awarded. In research focusing on six widely different sectors which were not perceived to be innovative, the report argued that innovation of this kind was increasingly important, especially in services, and a subsequent study looked in detail at six 'hidden innovation' sectors: oil production, retail banking, construction, legal aid services, education and the rehabilitation of offenders. The study identified four types of hidden innovation:

- Type I: Innovation that is identical or similar to activities that are measured by traditional indicators, but which is excluded from measurement (e.g. the development of new technologies in oil exploration).
- Type II: Innovation without a major scientific and technological basis, such as innovation in organizational forms or business models (e.g. the development of new contractual relationships between suppliers and clients on major construction projects).
- Type III: Innovation created from the novel combination of existing technologies and processes (e.g. the way in which banks have integrated their various back-office IT systems to deliver innovative customer services such as Internet banking).
- Type IV: Locally developed, small-scale innovations that take place under the radar, not only of traditional indicators but often also of many of the organizations and individuals working in a sector (e.g. the everyday innovation that occurs in classrooms and multidisciplinary construction teams).

Source: Derived from National Endowment for Science, Technology and the Arts (NESTA), 2006, *The Innovation Gap* and 2007, *Hidden Innovation*, www.nesta.org

Innovation In Action:
Real-life case studies
contextualize the
topics covered

Influencing the Process

It's all very well putting a basic process for turning ideas into reality in place. But it doesn't take place in a vacuum; it is subject to a range of internal and external influences which shape what is possible and what actually emerges. In particular, innovation needs:

- Clear strategic leadership and direction, plus the commitment of resources to make this happen. Innovation is about taking risks, about going into new and sometimes completely unexplored spaces. We don't want to gamble – simply changing things for their own sake or because the fancy takes us. No organization has resources to waste in that scattergun fashion: innovation needs a strategy. But, equally, we need to have a degree of courage and

Deeper Dive explanations of innovation concepts and ideas are available on the Innovation Portal at **www.innovation-portal.info**

Deeper Dives, **for more in-depth analysis of specific topics**

Web Resources

Innovation Portal

The **Innovation Portal** at **www.innovation-portal.info** houses all the online resources for the book. This fully searchable resource contains a wealth of material including a complete compendium of **videos, audio clips, cases, activities** and a fully searchable **innovation toolkit,** and is an essential resource for anyone wishing to deepen their understanding of innovation concepts. Signposts to this material can be found in the relevant book chapters wherever you see the icon boxes as shown below:

Audio Clip of an interview with Richard Reed of Innocent Smoothies exploring some of these issues is available on the Innovation Portal at **www.innovation-portal.info**

 Video Clips of several social entrepreneurs are available on the Innovation Portal at **www.innovation-portal.info**

Activity to help you think about architectural and component innovation is available on the Innovation Portal at **www.innovation-portal.info**

 Case Studies of the changing music industry and the dimming of the light bulb are available on the Innovation Portal at **www.innovation-portal.info**

Tools to enable policy deployment, including 'how/why' charts, are available on the Innovation Portal at **www.innovation-portal.info**

Additional Resources for Instructors

The authors have compiled an extensive range of resources to help lecturers teach their innovation courses including a teaching guide and course outline that provides a template for courses, seminars and assessments built around specific themes, together with linked media such as lecture slides, seminar exercises, cases, tools and assessments. There is also a comprehensive test bank and shorter quizzes to help test student understanding. All this material can also be accessed via the **Innovation Portal** at **www.innovation-portal.info**.

PART I

FOUNDATIONS OF MANAGING INNOVATION

Chapter 1

What Is Innovation – And Why Does It Matter?

LEARNING OBJECTIVES

By the end of this chapter you will develop an understanding of:

- what 'innovation' and 'entrepreneurship' mean – and how they are essential for survival and growth
- innovation as a series of changes which create some kind of value
- types of innovation – incremental/radical and component/system
- innovation as a process of change.

What Is Innovation?

Innovation is everywhere. You don't have to look very far before you see the magic word on advertising hoardings, company websites, on TV and in the press. And it's not just in the world of commercial products and services – much of the discussion in the public sector these days is all about how innovation is the way forward. For example. . .

The word 'innovation' comes from the Latin, *innovare*, and is all about change. Perhaps a more helpful definition in terms of what we actually have to manage is that innovation is

the process of creating value from ideas.

And as we'll see in this book, there are plenty of directions in which we can do this. We can change the

Case Studies exploring these companies, together with many other examples of innovation, are available on the Innovation Portal at **www.innovation-portal.info**

INNOVATION IN ACTION 1.1

Meeting the Innovation Challenge

'We always eat elephants . . .' is a surprising claim made by Carlos Broens, founder and head of a successful toolmaking and precision engineering firm in Australia with an enviable growth record. Broens Industries is a small/medium-sized company of 130 employees which survives in a highly competitive world by exporting over 70% of its products and services to technologically demanding firms in aerospace, medical and other advanced markets. The quote doesn't refer to strange dietary habits but to their confidence in 'taking on the challenges normally seen as impossible for firms of our size' – a capability which is grounded in a culture of innovation in products and the processes which go to produce them.

Despite a global shift in textile and clothing manufacture towards developing countries, the Spanish company Inditex (through its retail outlets under various names including Zara) has pioneered a highly flexible, fast-turnaround clothing operation with over 2000 outlets in 52 countries. It was founded by Amancio Ortega Gaona, who set up a small operation in the west of Spain in La Coruna – a region not previously noted for textile production. The first store opened there in 1975. It now has over 5000 stores worldwide and is the biggest clothing retailer; significantly, it is also the only manufacturer to offer specific collections for northern and southern hemisphere markets. Central to the Inditex philosophy is close linkage between design, manufacture and retailing. Its network of stores constantly feeds back information about trends which are used to generate new designs. The stores also experiment with new ideas directly on the public, trying samples of cloth or design and quickly getting back indications of what is going to catch on. Despite the network's global orientation, most manufacturing is still done in Spain, and it has managed to reduce the turnaround time between a trigger signal for an innovation and responding to it to around 15 days.

At the other end of the scale Kumba Resources is a large South African mining company which makes another dramatic claim: 'We move mountains.' In its case the mountains contain iron ore and the huge operation requires large-scale excavation – and restitution of the landscape afterwards. Much of Kumba's business involves complex large-scale machinery – and its ability to keep it running and productive depends on a workforce able to contribute their innovative ideas on a continuing basis.

People have always needed artificial limbs and the demand has, sadly, significantly increased as a result of high-technology weaponry, such as mines. The problem is compounded by the fact that many of those requiring new limbs are also in the poorest regions of the world and so are unable to afford expensive prosthetics. The chance meeting of a young surgeon, Dr Pramod Karan Sethi, and a sculptor, Ram Chandra, in a hospital in Jaipur, India, led to the development of a solution to this problem: the Jaipur Foot. This artificial limb was developed using Chandra's skill as a sculptor and Sethi's expertise and is so effective that those who wear it can run, climb trees and pedal bicycles. It was designed to make use of low-tech materials and be simple to assemble. For example, in Afghanistan craftsmen hammer the foot together out of spent artillery shells, while in Cambodia some of the foot's rubber components are scavenged from truck tyres. Perhaps the greatest achievement has been to do all of this for a low cost. The Jaipur Foot costs only $28 (£17) in India. Since 1975, nearly one million people worldwide have been fitted with a Jaipur limb and the design is being developed and refined, for example using advanced new materials.

products and services which we offer, the ways we create and deliver those offerings, the markets we offer them to and the underlying models about how we do what we do.

Of course, there are differences in the novelty of the changes we introduce. For example, updating the styling on a car is not the same as coming up with a completely new concept car which has an electric engine and is made of new composite materials as opposed to steel and glass. Similarly, increasing the speed and accuracy of a lathe is not the same thing as replacing it with a computer-controlled laser forming process. There are degrees of novelty in these, running from minor, incremental improvements right through to radical changes which transform the way we think about and use them. Sometimes these changes are common to a particular sector or activity, but sometimes they are so radical and far-reaching that they change the basis of society, for

Activity to help you compile a list of innovations and try to classify them in terms of the themes in this section (incremental or radical, products or service, etc.) – classifying innovation – is available on the Innovation Portal at **www.innovation-portal.info**

example the role played by steam power in the Industrial Revolution or the huge changes resulting from today's communications and computing technologies.

And innovation is often like Russian dolls: we can change things at the level of components or we can change a whole system. For example, we can put a faster transistor on a microchip on a circuit board for the graphics display in a computer. Or we can change the way several boards are put together in the computer to give it particular capabilities – a games box, an e-book, a media PC. Or we can link the computers into a network to drive a small business or office. Or we can link the networks to others on the Internet. There's scope for innovation at each level – but changes in the higher-level systems often have implications for lower down. For example, if cars – as a complex assembly – were suddenly designed to be made out of plastic instead of metal it would still leave scope for car assemblers – but would pose some sleepless nights for producers of metal components.

Activity to help you think about architectural and component innovation is available on the Innovation Portal at **www.innovation-portal.info**

Figure 1.1 illustrates the range of choices, highlighting the point that such change can happen at component or sub-system level or across the whole system. . .

Innovation and Value

All of these are about making *changes*, and doing so not for the sake of change itself but in order to create *value*. Value may be defined in terms of creating a product or service which others find useful and which they value. In business terms they are prepared to pay for it to

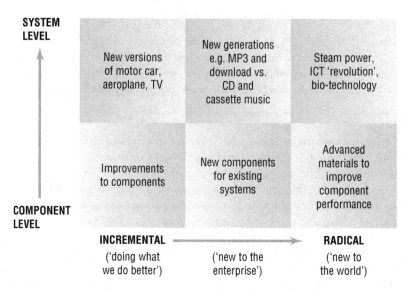

FIGURE 1.1   Types of innovation

express how much they value it – and this provides the economic underpinning for innovation. Entrepreneurs use new ideas to create 'value propositions' – it is cheaper, you can have it faster, it is of higher quality, it has more features, etc. – which they hope people in the marketplace will value enough to make a purchase.

But value isn't only commercial – innovation can also be about creating social value. Take the case of Dr Venkataswamy, an eye surgeon in India who retired after a long career working in one of the best eye hospitals there. He used his retirement to follow through a long-held passion: to try to bring good-quality eye care, specifically cataract surgery, to the millions of Indians who were unable to afford it in a country where public health care is still limited. His efforts were focused around finding new ways of delivering such surgery and in particular cutting the costs from an average of $300 (£180) per operation to $30 (£18). Over many years he developed an alternative, through his Aravind Eye Clinics, which is now able to provide care at an average cost of $25 (£15) – a social innovation which has literally transformed the lives of millions.

Case Study on Aravind Eye Clinics, together with others describing similar innovations in health care, is available on the Innovation Portal at **www.innovation-portal.info**

Activity to explore different ways of creating value through innovation and to identify actual examples of such innovations is available on the Innovation Portal at **www.innovation-portal.info**

Innovation and Competition

All of our examples are also about using changes to create a competitive edge. Let's be clear about what we mean by the word 'competition'. In some cases it is rivalry between firms for markets, and innovation helps provide the difference, making something faster, cheaper, with more features, etc. But 'competition' of a different kind drives the public sector – competing against the challenge of limited resources, for example providing high-quality health care to a growing and ageing population without raising taxes. Or it is the underlying 'competition' against illiteracy through education innovation, or against limited mobility by transport innovation. There is even the equivalent of a competition going on in the world of law and order: criminals are constantly seeking new ways to commit crime, and policing is having to innovate to keep pace with or, better, get ahead of this.

Case Study detailing a report on cybercrime and how it is becoming a rapidly moving innovation battleground is available on the Innovation Portal at **www.innovation-portal.info**

And in the third sector – of charities, voluntary workers and humanitarian agencies – the need for innovation is clear. Here 'competition' may be about competing with the problems posed by an earthquake and how to replace communications, access to shelter, food or water with viable alternatives before starvation and disease have a major impact. Or about competing as fundraisers for a share of people's disposable income.

Case Studies of innovation by humanitarian agencies are available on the Innovation Portal at **www.innovation-portal.info**

Innovations don't come from thin air. They are driven by a quest for opportunity or a response to threat. It's a bit like Darwin's model of the survival of the fittest, in which organizations find ways of coping with competitive and hostile environments. But the big difference is that there is an element of deliberate rather than random variation – innovation involves conscious experimentation.

Activity to help you explore possible sources of strategic advantage through innovation is available on the Innovation Portal at **www.innovation-portal.info**

If we look at the pattern of innovation in a particular sector, we will see that it is a mixture of occasional radical change (doing something different) punctuating long periods of incremental (doing what we do but better) change. There are times where experiment is high risk and much longer periods when the variation is stabilized and improved upon. We can see this if we look back over different sectors – for example, the music industry grew up on the back of innovations like radio and the gramophone. For a long time it was concentrated on a mature industry which rode successfully several changes in distribution format (vinyl, cassettes, CDs) before the digitalization revolution sparked by the invention of the mp3 player led to massive disruption. Similarly, the light bulb developed by Edison, Swann and others dominated lighting for over a century but has now given way to massive shifts in the industry on the back of the move to solid state electronics.

Case Studies of the changing music industry and the dimming of the light bulb are available on the Innovation Portal at **www.innovation-portal.info**

Activity to help you explore sector patterns of innovation is available on the Innovation Portal at **www.innovation-portal.info**

Innovation and Entrepreneurship

A key idea associated with making changes is the *entrepreneur*. This is an individual or group who sees an opportunity and takes the risk of trying to exploit it. If they succeed, they gain an edge – and then others notice what they are doing and start to imitate. One of the important theorists on innovation was Joseph Schumpeter, one-time finance minister of Austria, and his core ideas relate to the importance of entrepreneurship.[1]

Case Studies describing several social entrepreneurs are available on the Innovation Portal at **www.innovation-portal.info**

Entrepreneurs come in all shapes and sizes – from the lone genius who battles single-handed to bring his/ her idea to fruition (James Dyson) to the start-up team whose creative interchange helps shape something new (Larry Page and Sergey Brin of Google, Bill Gates and Paul Allen at Microsoft, the Angry Birds team at Rovio) through to social entrepreneurs like Dr Venkataswamy of Aravind, Devi Shetty (the Henry Ford of heart surgery in India) or Muhammad Yunus (the Nobel prizewinning founder of Grameen Bank).

But 'entrepreneurs' are also part of any large established organization, trying to propose and introduce changes which will renew its products, services or operating processes. Their

Video Clips of several social entrepreneurs are available on the Innovation Portal at **www.innovation-portal.info**

names may not be so familiar but they work on the inside trying to renew what the organization offers and the ways it creates and delivers those offerings.

And – as we've seen – the motivation for entrepreneurship varies from those who are trying to create commercial value to those with more of a social concern.

This idea of entrepreneurship driving innovation to create value – social and commercial – across the lifecycle of organizations is central to this book. Table 1.1 gives some examples.

TABLE 1.1 Entrepreneurship and Innovation

Stage in lifecycle	Start-up	Growth	Sustain/scale	Renew
Creating wealth	Individual entrepreneur exploiting new technology or market opportunity	Growing the business through adding new products/ services or moving into new markets	Building a portfolio of incremental and radical innovation to sustain the business and/or spread its influence into new markets	Returning to the radical frame-breaking kind of innovation which began the business and enables it to move forwards as something very different
Creating social value	Social entrepreneur, passionately concerned to improve or change something in their immediate environment	Developing the ideas and engaging others in a network for change – perhaps in a region or around a key issue	Spreading the idea widely, diffusing it to other communities of social entrepreneurs, engaging links with mainstream players like public sector agencies	Changing the system – and then acting as an agent for the next wave of change

Innovation and Knowledge

One last point is worth making here: the key role played by knowledge in innovation. The ability to make the kind of changes we looked at above depends on creating or acquiring and then deploying knowledge to create value. Essentially, what organizations know and have learnt is a core asset which they can leverage. This may be technology or it may be understanding of markets, and the knowledge involved may be in explicit or tacit form. But the evidence is clear: paying attention to creating, capturing and using knowledge is critical in innovation. One indicator of just how important it has become is the sheer scale of investment in R&D, which is currently running at $1500 billion (£920 billion) per year! We'll look closely at this theme in the book, not least because in such a knowledge-rich world the challenge is increasingly one of managing flows of knowledge around an increasingly global and networked space. This challenge is often given the label 'open innovation'. We'll return to it later in the book.

Activity to help you explore the importance of knowledge-based innovation is available on the Innovation Portal at **www.innovation-portal.info**

Why Does Innovation Matter?

As we've already seen, innovation is about survival and growth – if we don't change then competitive forces may threaten our future. But on the positive side there are real opportunities for those able to manage the process well. For example, in its regular survey of 'innovation leaders' in 25 sectors of the economy, the consultancy Innovaro reports not only that these companies outpace their competitors on a year-by-year basis but also that this has a marked effect on their share price. In the period 2003 to 2013, they regularly outperformed the average share price index on the NASDAQ, Dow Jones and FTSE markets, and in 2009, when other companies' share prices grew on average by between 40 and 70%, the Innovation leaders' average growth was 130%.

It's also important for whole economies – as the economist William Baumol pointed out: 'Virtually all of the economic growth that has occurred since the eighteenth century is ultimately attributable to innovation.'[2] Not for nothing do regional and national governments spend a great deal of money trying to stimulate and support innovation in different ways.

But part of the problem is that innovation involves a moving target – simply being able to manage it effectively today is no guarantee of long-term success since technologies, markets, regulations and other elements are constantly changing. So successful innovators are concerned to develop 'dynamic capability' to change their approaches. The risk is clear if organizations fail to keep pace: there are plenty of examples of major corporations which began with an innovative flourish but ended up beaten by their failure to innovate fast enough or in the right directions. The examples

Case Study of Fujifilm that explores this challenge is available on the Innovation Portal at **www.innovation-portal.info**

of great photographic pioneers Kodak and Polaroid are graphic reminders that competitive advantage doesn't always last, even if you are a major spender on R&D and have powerful marketing skills.

To Whom?

Innovation is about survival and growth, so simply leaving things to chance is not a great approach. Instead, individuals and organizations need to take innovation seriously; it has to be more than just a slogan. And that means having some clear idea of where and how making changes can take us forward – a 'strategy' and some idea of how we will implement that strategy, how we will make innovation happen.

But innovation also matters to a range of what we might call 'policy agents' – organizations which have a broader concern with innovation. These include:

- governments (local and national): innovation creates economic growth, jobs, etc., so fostering innovation becomes a key issue
- trade and sector bodies: their interest is in stimulating innovation to make for sector health and competitiveness
- supply chain 'owners': any supply network is only as strong as its weakest link, so it makes sense for firms to try to manage their supply systems and upgrade them.

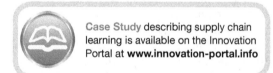

Case Study describing supply chain learning is available on the Innovation Portal at **www.innovation-portal.info**

Innovation matters to all of these players but their concern leads us in two complementary directions. For the individual enterprise it is about how to organize and manage the process – and policy agents can create an environment which helps this directly (e.g. through advice or money) or indirectly (e.g. through favourable tax or other policies). But there is a second and increasingly important level, which is about *systems*. Innovation is a multiplayer game and needs different bits of the network to work together – in supply chains, regional clusters, industrial sectors, etc. There's growing interest in such systems of innovation – local, regional and national – and how policy agents can help develop them.

Innovation Isn't Easy!

Coming up with good ideas is what human beings are good at; our brains are fitted with this facility as standard. But taking those ideas forward is not quite so simple – and the evidence is clear. Most new ideas, and most entrepreneurs carrying them, fail. It takes a particular mix of energy, insight, belief and determination to push against these odds – and even more judgement to know when to stop banging against the brick wall and move on to something else.

While the road for an individual entrepreneur may be very rocky with a high risk of hitting potholes, running into roadblocks or careering off the edge it doesn't get any easier if you are a large established company. It's a disturbing thought, but the majority of companies have a lifespan significantly less than that of a human being. Even the largest firms can show worrying signs of vulnerability, and for the smaller firm the mortality statistics are bleak.

Many small and medium-sized enterprises (SMEs) fail because they don't see or recognize the need for change. They are inward looking, too busy fighting fires and dealing with today's crises to worry about storm clouds on the horizon. Even if they do talk to others about the wider issues, it is very often to people in the same network and with the same perspectives, for example the people who supply them with goods and services or their immediate customers. The trouble is that by the time they realize there is a need to change it may be too late.

But it isn't just a small firm problem – there is no guaranteed security in size or in previous technological success. Take the case of IBM, a giant firm which can justly claim to have laid the foundations of the IT industry and one which came to dominate the architecture of hardware and software and the ways in which computers were marketed. But such core strength can sometimes become an obstacle to seeing the need for change – as proved to be the case when, in the early 1990s, the company moved slowly to counter the threat of networking technologies – and nearly lost the business in the process. Thousands of jobs and billions of dollars were lost and it took years of hard work to bring the share price back to the high levels which investors had come to expect.

A common problem for successful companies occurs when the very things which helped them achieve success – their 'core competence' – become the things which make it hard to see or accept the need for change. Often the response is what is sometimes called 'not invented here' – the new idea is recognized as good but in some way not suited to the business.

(A famous example of this was the case of Western Union, which, in the nineteenth century, was probably the biggest communications company in the world. It was approached by one Alexander Graham Bell, who wanted it to consider helping him commercialize his new invention. After mounting a demonstration to senior executives, he received a written reply which said that '. . . after careful consideration of your invention, which is a very interesting novelty, we have come to the conclusion that it has no commercial possibilities . . . We see no future for an electrical toy.'[3] Within four years of being invented, there were 50 000 telephones in the United States and within 20 years five million. Over the next 20 years, the company which Bell formed grew to become the largest corporation in the United States.)

Sometimes the pace of change appears slow and the old responses seem to work well. It appears, to those within the industry, that they understand the rules of the game and that they have a good grasp of the relevant technological developments likely to change things. But what can sometimes happen here is that change comes along from *outside* the industry – and by the time the main players inside have reacted, it is often too late.

For example, in the late nineteenth century there was a thriving industry in New England based on the harvesting and distribution of ice. In its heyday, it was possible for ice harvesters to ship hundreds of tons of ice around the world on voyages that lasted for as long as six months – and still have over half the cargo available for sale. By the late 1870s, the 14 major firms in the Boston area of the United States were cutting around 700 000 tons per year and employing several thousand people. But the industry was completely overthrown by the new developments which followed from the invention of refrigeration and the growth of the modern cold storage industry. The problem is that the existing players often fail to respond fast enough to the new signals coming from outside their industry – as was the case for many of the old ice industry players.[4]

Of course, for others these conditions provide an opportunity for moving ahead of the game and writing a new set of rules. Think about what has happened in online banking, call-centre linked insurance or low-cost airlines. In each case the existing stable pattern has been overthrown, disrupted by new entrants coming in with new and challenging business models. For many managers, business model innovation is seen as the biggest threat to their competitive position, precisely because they need to learn to let go of their old models as well as learn new ones. By the time they do so they may well have been overtaken by newcomers for whom this is the only business model and one they are well placed to exploit.

Case Study of Marshalls, a UK family business that has been operating for over 100 years and is still growing through its commitment to innovation and its agile approach to management, is available on the Innovation Portal at **www.innovation-portal.info**

It's not all doom and gloom, though. There are also plenty of stories of new firms and new industries emerging to replace those which die. And in many cases the individual enterprise can renew itself, adapting to its environment and moving into new things. Consider the company Stora in Sweden, which was founded in the twelfth century as a timber cutting and processing operation but which is still thriving today – albeit in the very different areas of food processing and electronics.

Can We Manage Innovation?

The first point here is to recognize that there is something to be managed. Innovation is not simply a random process but rather a sequence of planned experimentation. This is the difference between the Darwinian idea of survival of the fittest and the way innovation works; in the latter case the variation is planned and designed. It is still risky and may not succeed but it is a purposive activity.

And we know something about this sequence of planned experimentation. It involves a process of searching for possible opportunities (generating variation), selecting a particular one (selection) and then implementing it (propagation). Making this happen involves a set of behaviours which, over time, become learnt and embedded – ways of searching, ways of selecting, ways of implementing. These represent distinctive patterns of behaviour which shape the way innovation is managed.

At the outset – a start-up business – there won't necessarily be a clear pattern but a series of experiments, a bit like a child learning to walk for the first time. But there is learning from experience and from failure so that over time the start-up entrepreneur learns to manage the process and can repeat the trick, starting up other ventures or introducing other innovations to grow his/her business. By the time we look at the business in a mature state it has 'routinized' a lot of this, with structures and formal processes in place for searching (market research or R&D), selecting and allocating resources for innovation projects and project management systems for taking ideas through to reality.

Of course, it's also not a case of 'one size fits all'. There will be different patterns depending on the size of the organization and the sector in which it operates, for example. Small organizations have little structure and limited resources, so their 'process' for managing innovation may be informal, whereas giant pharmaceutical corporations need a range of structures and procedures to enable innovation to happen in a coordinated fashion. Service sector businesses work closely with customers and emphasize search behaviours which try to articulate and use insights around their needs – whereas high-tech businesses may be more concerned with formal scientific R&D and behaviours which enable that to work well. And whole industries have lifecycles associated with them. We can see the car industry now as a mature sector with a history of over a hundred years, whereas nanotechnology and applied genetics are still in their infancy. Innovation in new sectors tends to focus on product/service offerings as the main target, whereas in more mature sectors it shifts to the ways we create and deliver those offerings, for example can we make them cheaper or faster?

Success in innovation, be it as an individual first-timer or a global corporation, is not just about having a good idea and assembling the resources (people, equipment, knowledge, money, etc.) to make it happen. It's also about having the capabilities to manage them – and these are the hardest to get a handle on – but they make or break the process. So what is involved – and how do we know?

Over the past hundred years a wide range of studies have attempted to answer these questions. Researchers have looked at case examples, at sectors, at entrepreneurs, at big firms and small firms, at success and failure. Practising entrepreneurs and innovation managers in large businesses have tried to reflect on the 'how' of what they do. The key messages come from the world of *experience*. What we've learnt comes from the laboratory of practice rather than from some deeply rooted theory.

The Case for Strategic Innovation Management

One final point in this chapter. We've seen that innovation matters and that in order to survive and grow organizations need to pay attention to managing the process. This is of concern not only to those directly involved but also to a wider gallery of players – governments, supply chain owners, trade and sector agencies – who have a concern that innovation happens and happens effectively. And we have begun to see that there is something – a process of finding opportunities, choosing projects and implementing them – which is common to innovation and needs to be managed. We need to learn and develop the capability to do this.

But innovation takes place in a changing world. New technologies emerge, new markets appear, financial, legal, social rules change. So organizations not only have to innovate to survive and grow but also need to innovate in the ways they approach this problem of managing the process. For example, at the beginning of this century the Internet was still in its infancy and we had only just begun to see its potential role in changing the way innovation happened. Now we are in a world where increasingly products and services are delivered in virtual space and where markets are increasingly focused around social networks and communities. The potential for information flow across this world is huge: Facebook with over one billion members would qualify as the world's third largest country by population! All of these changes have an impact on what we can do in our search, select and implement process, and so organizations have had to learn new tricks to take on board these new challenges.

Table 1.2 gives an idea of these challenges.

Throughout this book we'll look at the idea of 'dynamic capability' – learning and building capability not just to organize and manage innovation but also to step back and review how we do this. And having taken a step back to review, implementing changes in the ways we make innovation happen – new or different ways and letting go of some of the older ones.

TABLE 1.2   Challenges in the Innovation Context[5]

Context change	Indicative examples
Acceleration of knowledge production	OECD estimates that around $1500 billion is spent each year (public and private sector) on creating new knowledge – and hence extending the frontier along which 'breakthrough' technological developments may happen.
Global distribution of knowledge production	Knowledge production is increasingly involving new players, especially in emerging market fields like the BRIC (Brazil, Russia, India, China) nations – so there is a need to search for innovation opportunities across a much wider space. One consequence of this is that 'knowledge workers' are now much more widely distributed and concentrated in new locations (e.g. Microsoft's third-largest R&D centre employing thousands of scientists and engineers is now in Shanghai).
Market expansion	Traditionally much of the world of business has focused on the needs of around one billion people since they represent wealthy enough consumers. But the world's population has just passed the seven billion mark and population, and by extension market, growth is increasingly concentrated in non-traditional areas, like rural Asia, Latin America and Africa. Understanding the needs and constraints of this 'new' population represents a significant challenge in terms of market knowledge.
Market fragmentation	Globalization has massively increased the range of markets and segments so that these are now widely dispersed and locally varied – putting pressure on innovation search activity to cover much more territory, often far from 'traditional' experiences – such as the 'bottom of the pyramid' conditions in many emerging markets[6] or along the so-called long tail – the large number of individuals or small target markets with highly differentiated needs and expectations.

(continued)

TABLE 1.2 (Continued)

Context change	Indicative examples
Market virtualization	The emergence of large-scale social networks in cyberspace poses challenges in market research approaches (e.g. Facebook with one billion members is technically the third-largest country in the world by population). Further challenges arise in the emergence of parallel world communities (e.g. Second Life now has over six million 'residents', while World of Warcraft has over 10 million players).
Rise of active users	Although users have long been recognized as a source of innovation, there has been an acceleration in the ways in which this is now taking place (e.g. the growth of Linux has been a user-led open community development). In sectors like the media, the line between consumers and creators is increasingly blurred (e.g. YouTube has around 100 million videos viewed each day but also has over 70 000 new videos uploaded every day from its user base).
Growing concern with sustainability issues	Major shifts in resource and energy availability prompting search for new alternatives and reduced consumption. Increasing awareness of the impact of pollution and other negative consequences of high and unsustainable growth. Concern over climate change. Major population growth and worries over our ability to sustain living standards and manage expectations. Increasing regulation on areas like emissions and our carbon footprint.
Development of technological and social infrastructure	Increasing linkages enabled by information and communications technologies around the Internet and broadband have enabled and reinforced alternative social networking possibilities. At the same time the increasing availability of simulation and prototyping tools has reduced the separation between users and producers.

Source: Bessant, J. and T. Venables, *Creating wealth from knowledge: Meeting the innovation challenge* 2008, Cheltenham: Edward Elgar, pp 6–7.

Summary

- Innovation is about growth – about recognizing opportunities for doing something new and implementing those ideas to create some kind of value. It could be business growth; it could be social change. But at its heart is the creative human spirit, the urge to make change in our environment.

- Innovation is also a survival imperative. If an organization doesn't change what it offers the world and the ways in which it creates and delivers its offerings, it could well be in trouble. And innovation contributes to competitive success in many different ways. It's a *strategic* resource to getting the organization where it is trying to go, be that delivering shareholder value for private sector firms, providing better public services or enabling the start-up and growth of new enterprises.

- Innovation doesn't just happen. It is driven by *entrepreneurship*. This powerful mixture of energy, vision, passion, commitment, judgement and risk-taking provides the power behind the innovation process. It's the same whether we are talking about a solo start-up venture or a key group within an established organization trying to renew its products or services.

- Innovation doesn't happen simply because we hope it will. It's a complex process which carries risks and needs careful and systematic *management*. Innovation isn't a single event, like the light bulb going off above a cartoon character's head. It's an extended process of picking up on ideas for change and turning them into effective reality. The core process involves four steps: recognizing opportunities, finding resources, developing the venture and capturing value. The challenge comes in doing this in an organized fashion and in being able to repeat the trick.

Further Resources

More detailed discussion of these themes can be found in our companion books, *Managing Innovation: Integrating technological, market and organizational change*, now in its fifth edition, and *Innovation and Entrepreneurship*, now in its second edition. Peter Drucker's famous *Innovation and Entrepreneurship* provides an accessible introduction to the subject, but perhaps relies more on intuition and experience than on empirical research.[7] And there are several other textbooks including those by Goffin and Mitchell,[8] Trott,[9] Schilling[10] and Dodgson, Salter and Gann.[11]

There are several compilations and handbooks covering the field, the best known being *Strategic Management of Technology and Innovation*, containing a wide range of key papers and case studies, though with a very strong US emphasis.[12] A more international flavour is present in Dodgson and Rothwell[13] and Shavinina.[14]

Case studies of innovation provide a rich resource for understanding the workings of the process in particular contexts. Good compilations include those of Baden-Fuller and Pitt,[15]

Nayak and Ketteringham[16] and Von Stamm,[17] while other books link theory to case studies, for example Tidd and Hull[18] with its focus on service innovation. Several books cover the experiences of particular companies, including 3M, Corning, DuPont, Toyota and others.[19–22]

Various websites offer news, research, tools, etc., for example AIM (www.aimresearch.org) and NESTA (www.nesta.org.uk).

References

1. Schumpeter, J. (2006) *Capitalism, Socialism and Democracy*, 6th edn. London: Routledge.

2. Baumol, W. (2002) *The Free-Market Innovation Machine: Analyzing the growth miracle of capitalism*. Princeton: Princeton University Press.

3. Bryson, B. (1994) *Made in America*. London: Minerva.

4. Utterback, J. (1994) *Mastering the Dynamics of Innovation*. Boston: Harvard Business School Press.

5. Bessant, J. and T. Venables (2008) *Creating Wealth from Knowledge: Meeting the innovation challenge*. Cheltenham: Edward Elgar.

6. Prahalad, C. K. (2006) *The Fortune at the Bottom of the Pyramid*. Upper Saddle River, NJ: Wharton School Publishing.

7. Drucker, P. (1985) *Innovation and Entrepreneurship*. New York: Harper & Row.

8. Goffin, K. and R. Mitchell (2010) *Innovation Management*, 2nd edn. London: Pearson.

9. Trott, P. (2011) *Innovation Management and New Product Development*, 5th edn. London: Prentice-Hall.

10. Schilling, M. (2005) *Strategic Management of Technological Innovation*. New York: McGraw-Hill.

11. Dodgson, M., A. Salter and D. Gann (2008) *The Management of Technological Innovation*, 2nd edn. Oxford: Oxford University Press.

12. Burgelman, R., C. Christensen and S. Wheelwright (eds) (2004) *Strategic Management of Technology and Innovation*, 4th edn. Boston: McGraw-Hill.

13. Dodgson, M. and R. Rothwell (eds) (1995) *The Handbook of Industrial Innovation*. Edward Elgar: London.

14. Shavinina, L. (2003) *International Handbook on Innovation*. New York: Elsevier.

15. Baden-Fuller, C. and M. Pitt (1996) *Strategic Innovation*. London, Routledge.

16. Nayak, P. and J. Ketteringham (1986) *Breakthroughs: How leadership and drive create commercial innovations that sweep the world*. London: Mercury.

17. Von Stamm, B. (2003) *The Innovation Wave*. Chichester: John Wiley & Sons, Ltd.

18. Tidd, J. and F. Hull (eds) (2003) *Service Innovation: Organizational responses to technological opportunities and market imperatives*. London: Imperial College Press.

19. Leifer, R., D. McDermott and G. C. O'Connor (2000) *Radical Innovation*. Boston: Harvard Business School Press.

20. Kanter, R. (ed.) (1997) *Innovation: Breakthrough thinking at 3M, DuPont, GE, Pfizer and Rubbermaid*. New York: Harper Business.

21. Graham, M. and A. Shuldiner (2001) *Corning and the Craft of Innovation*. Oxford: Oxford University Press.

22. Kelley, T., J. Littman and T. Peters (2001) *The Art of Innovation: Lessons in creativity from Ideo, America's leading design firm*. New York: Currency.

Deeper Dive explanations of innovation concepts and ideas are available on the Innovation Portal at **www.innovation-portal.info**

Quizzes to test yourself further are available online via the Innovation Portal at **www.innovation-portal.info**

Summary of online resources for Chapter 1 –
all material is available via the Innovation Portal at
www.innovation-portal.info

Cases	**Media**	**Tools**	**Activities**	**Deeper Dive**

Cases	Media	Tools	Activities	Deeper Dive
• Kumba Resources	• Suzana Moreira, moWoza	• Strategy toolkit	• Classifying innovation	• Technological trajectories
• Jaipur Foot	• Simon Tucker, The Young Foundation	• SWOT analysis	• Architectural and component innovation	
• Zara	• Melissa Clark-Reynolds, Minimonos		• Creating value through innovation	
• Aravind Eye Clinics			• Strategic advantage through innovation	
• Cybercrime report			• Sector patterns of innovation	
• Humanitarian innovation			• Knowledge-based innovation	
• The changing music industry			• Rich pictures	
• The dimming of the light bulb				
• Eastville Stores (social entrepreneurship)				
• Fujifilm				
• Marshalls				
• Supply chain learning				

Chapter 2

Innovation Strategy

Why Strategy?

As we saw in the previous chapter, innovation is about creating value through change. But simply changing things in random directions can be risky – if we don't know where we are going we may well end up somewhere else! So central to effective innovation management is a clear sense of direction: where and how is innovation going to help us move forward?

The other reason why an innovation strategy is a good idea is the resource question – even the best-endowed organization can't do everything and so we need to be clear about what we'll spend our scarce resources on and why.

> Activity to help you think about sources of strategic advantage through innovation is available on the Innovation Portal at **www.innovation-portal.info**

Innovation strategy can give us a roadmap for change – but it's important to remember that we are dealing with an uncertain future. We don't know if our technology will actually work, we can't be sure that the market we expect will actually be there, we may be surprised by the actions of competitors or governments – in fact, the only thing we can be sure of is that things will be unpredictable. So having a map for where we are trying to go is helpful, but we need to recognize that it is open to change. It's less an accurate GPS-backed picture of a well-laid-out superhighway and more a case of a rough sketch to help us find a way through the jungle. And as we move forward through that unknown forest, we may need to change direction and adjust our plans to cope with surprises and roadblocks on the way.

Case Study of Marshalls illustrating the changes, and the need for a strategic approach to managing, over its hundred-year history is available on the Innovation Portal at **www.innovation-portal.info**

Strategy is also about making clear a vision for the future – and sharing this with others who can help shape the direction and support the journey. Whether it is mobilizing enthusiasm amongst investors, convincing the Board to back a business case or aligning the efforts of employees in a focused innovation programme, the underlying need is for a clearly articulated strategy.

What's in an Innovation Strategy?

Putting an innovation strategy together involves three key steps, pulling together ideas around core themes – and inviting discussion and argument to sharpen and shape them. These are:

- Strategic analysis – what could we do?
- Strategic selection – what are we going to do, and why?
- Strategic implementation – how are we going to make it happen?

Let's look at each of these in more detail in the following sections:

Strategic Analysis

Strategic analysis begins with an exploration of innovation space – where could we innovate and why would it be worth doing so? A useful place to start is to build some sense of the overall environment, to explore the threats and opportunities currently present and the likely changes to these in the future. Typically, questions here can relate to technologies, to markets, to the underlying political trends, to emerging customer needs, to competitors and to social and economic forces. It's also useful to add to this map some sense of who the players are in the environment – the particular customers and markets, the key suppliers, and the number and type of competitors.

Within this framework it's also important to reflect on what resources the organization can bring to bear: what are its relative strengths and weaknesses and how can it build and sustain a competitive advantage?

(It's important to remember that these are tools to help start a discussion – not accurate measuring devices. There are real limitations to how much we can know about an environment which is complex, interactive and constantly changing, and there are often wide differences about where the strengths and weaknesses actually lie.)

Having explored this environment, we need to understand the range of possibilities – where could we innovate to our advantage? What kinds of opportunities exist for us to create something different and capture value from bringing those ideas into the world?

Activity to help you map and explore your innovation environment – rich pictures – is available on the Innovation Portal at **www.innovation-portal.info**

Tools to help you map and explore your innovation environment – especially tools to help develop innovation strategy – are available on the Innovation Portal at **www.innovation-portal.info**

Sometimes it is about completely new possibilities, such as exploiting radical breakthroughs in technology. For example, new drugs based on genetic manipulation have opened a major new front in the war against disease. Mobile phones, PDAs and other devices have revolutionized where and when we communicate. Even the humble windowpane is the result of radical technological innovation – almost all the window glass in the world is made these days by the Pilkington float glass process, which moved the industry away from the time-consuming process of grinding and polishing to get a flat surface

Equally important is the ability to spot where and how new *markets* can be created and grown. Alexander Bell's invention of the telephone didn't lead to an overnight revolution in communications – that depended on developing the market for person-to-person communications. Henry Ford may not have invented the motor car but in making the Model T – 'a car for Everyman' at a price most people could afford – he grew the mass market for personal transportation. And eBay justifies its multi-billion-dollar price tag not because of the technology behind its online auction idea but because it created and grew the market.

Innovation isn't just about opening up new markets. It can also offer new ways of serving established and mature ones. Low-cost airlines are still about transportation – but the innovations which firms like Southwest Airlines, easyJet and Ryanair have introduced have revolutionized air travel and grown the market in the process. One challenging new area for innovation lies in the previously underserved markets of the developing world – the four billion people who earn less than $2 (£1.20) a day. The potential for developing radically different innovative products and services aimed at meeting the needs of this vast population at what C. K. Prahalad calls 'the bottom of the pyramid' is huge, and the lessons learnt may impact on established markets in the developed world as well.[1]

And it isn't just about manufactured products; in most economies the service sector accounts for the vast majority of activity, so there is likely to be plenty of scope. Lower capital costs often mean that the opportunities for new entrants and radical change are greatest in the service sector. Online banking and insurance have become commonplace, and they have radically transformed the efficiencies with which those sectors work and the range of services they can provide. New entrants riding the Internet wave have rewritten the rulebook for a wide range of industrial games, for example Amazon in retailing, Google in advertising and Skype in telephony. Others have used the Web to help them transform business models around things like low-cost airlines, other travel services and the music business.

TABLE 2.1   Dimensions for Innovation[2]

Dimension	Type of change
'Product'	Changes in the things (products/services) which an organization offers
'Process'	Changes in the ways in which these offerings are created and delivered
'Position'	Changes in the context into which the products/services are introduced
'Paradigm'	Changes in the underlying mental models which frame what the organization does

Source: Francis, D. and J. Bessant (2006), *Targeting innovation and implications for capability development.* *Technovation* **25**: 171–183. Reproduced by permission of Elsevier.

Exploring Innovation Space

One approach to finding an answer to the question of where we could innovate is to use a kind of 'innovation compass' exploring different possible directions.

Innovation can take many forms but we can map the options along four dimensions (see Table 2.1):

For example, a new design of car, a new insurance package for accident-prone babies and a new home entertainment system would all be examples of product innovation. And change in the manufacturing methods and equipment used to produce the car or the home entertainment system, or in the office procedures and sequencing in the insurance case, would be examples of process innovation.

Sometimes the dividing line is somewhat blurred, for example a new jet-powered sea ferry is both a product and a process innovation. Services represent a particular case of this where the product and process aspects often merge. For example, is a new holiday package a product or a process change?

Innovation can also take place by repositioning the perception of an established product or process in a particular user context. For example, an old-established product in the United Kingdom is Lucozade, originally developed as a glucose-based drink to help children and invalids in convalescence. These associations with sickness were abandoned by the brand owner, Beechams (now part of GlaxoSmithKline), when it re-launched the product as a health drink aimed at the growing fitness market, where it is now presented as a performance-enhancing aid to healthy exercise. In similar fashion, Häagen Dazs created a new market for ice cream, essentially targeted at adults, through position innovation rather than changing the product or core manufacturing process.

Sometimes opportunities for innovation emerge when we reframe the way we look at something. Henry Ford fundamentally changed the face of transportation not because he invented the motor car (he was a comparative latecomer to the new industry) or because he developed the manufacturing process to put one together (as a craft-based specialist industry car-making had been established for around 20 years). His contribution was to change the underlying model from one which offered a hand-made specialist product to a few wealthy customers to one which offered a car for Everyman at a price he/she could afford. The ensuing shift from craft to mass production was nothing short of a revolution in the way cars (and later countless other products and services) were created and delivered. Of course, making the new approach work in practice also required extensive product and process innovation, for example in component design, in machinery building, in factory layout and particularly in the social system around which work was organized.

Case Study of the Model T Ford is available on the Innovation Portal at **www.innovation-portal.info**

Case Studies of Lego, Adidas and Threadless are available on the Innovation Portal at **www.innovation-portal.info**

Recent examples of 'paradigm' innovation – changes in mental models – include the shift to low-cost airlines, the provision of online insurance and other financial services, and the repositioning of drinks like coffee and fruit juice as premium 'designer' products. Another big shift is towards 'mass collaboration', which builds on social networks and communities. Companies like Lego and Adidas are reinventing themselves by engaging their users as designers and builders rather than as passive consumers. Paradigm change is also emerging around sustainability with growing concerns about global warming and the limited availability of key resources like energy and materials.

Table 2.2 gives some examples of innovations mapped onto this '4Ps' model.

TABLE 2.2   Some Examples of Innovations Mapped on to the 4Ps Model

Innovation type	Incremental – do what we do but better	Radical – do something different
Product – what we offer the world	Windows 7 and 8 replacing Vista and XP – essentially improving on existing software idea New versions of established car models (e.g. the VW Golf essentially improving on established car design) Improved performance incandescent light bulbs CDs replacing vinyl records – essentially improving on the storage technology	New to the world software (e.g. the first speech recognition program) Toyota Prius – bringing a new concept: hybrid engines. Tesla – high-performance electric car. LED-based lighting, using completely different and more energy-efficient principles Spotify and other music-streaming services – changing the pattern from owning your own collection to renting a vast library of music
Process – how we create and deliver that offering	Improved fixed-line telephone services Extended range of stockbroking services Improved auction house operations	Skype and other VOIP systems Online share trading eBay Toyota Production System and other 'lean' approaches

(continued)

TABLE 2.2   (*Continued*)

Innovation type	Incremental – do what we do but better	Radical – do something different
	Improved factory operations efficiency through upgraded equipment Improved range of banking services delivered at branch banks Improved retailing logistics	Online banking and now mobile banking in Kenya and the Philippines – using phones as an alternative to banking systems Online shopping
Position – where we target that offering and the story we tell about it	Häagen Dazs changing the target market for ice cream from children to adults Airlines segmenting service offering for different passenger groups – Virgin Upper Class, BA Premium Economy, etc. Dell and others segmenting and customizing computer configuration for individual users Online support for traditional higher education courses Banking services targeted at key segments – students, retired people, etc.	Addressing underserved markets (e.g. Tata Nano aimed at emerging but relatively poor Indian market with car priced around $2000 (£1200)) Low-cost airlines opening up air travel to those previously unable to afford it – create new market and also disrupt existing one Variations on the 'One laptop per child' project (e.g. Indian government $20 (£12) computer for schools) University of Phoenix and others building large education businesses via online approaches to reach different markets 'Bottom of the pyramid' approaches using a similar principle but tapping into huge and very different high-volume/low-margin markets (e.g. Aravind eye care, Cemex construction products)
Paradigm – how we frame what we do	Bausch & Lomb – moved from 'eye wear' to 'eye care' as its business model, effectively letting go of the old business of spectacles, sunglasses (Raybans) and contact lenses, all of which were becoming commodity businesses. Instead, the company moved into newer high-tech fields like laser surgery equipment, specialist optical devices and research into artificial eyesight Dyson redefining the home appliance market in terms of high-performance engineered products	Grameen Bank and other microfinance models – rethinking the assumptions about credit and the poor iTunes platform – a complete system of personalized entertainment Cirque de Soleil – redefining the circus experience Amazon, Google, Skype – redefining industries like retailing, advertising and telecoms through online models

(*continued*)

TABLE 2.2	(Continued)	
Innovation type	**Incremental – do what we do but better**	**Radical – do something different**
	Rolls-Royce – from high-quality aero engines to becoming a service company offering 'power by the hour' IBM from being a machine maker to a service and solution company – selling off its computer making and building up its consultancy and service side	Linux, Mozilla, Apache – moving from passive users to active communities of users co-creating new products and services

Each of these 4Ps of innovation can take place along an axis running from incremental through to radical change; the area indicated by the circle in Figure 2.1 is the potential innovation space within which an organization can operate.

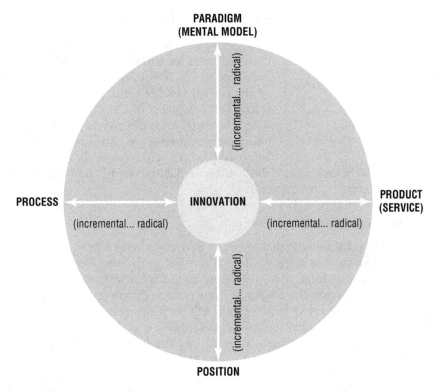

FIGURE 2.1   Exploring innovation space

Activity of an interactive test where you can explore and map different innovations to the 4Ps Analysis framework is available on the Innovation Portal at **www.innovation-portal.info**

Tools giving a description of the 4Ps approach together with a variety of other tools to help with this kind of exploration, for example Blue Ocean strategy and competitiveness profiling, are available on the Innovation Portal at **www.innovation-portal.info**

Video Clip of Finnegan's Fish Bar showing the ideas applied to a simple food business is available on the Innovation Portal at **www.innovation-portal.info**

Tools to help with strategic selection, including decision matrix, portfolio methods and bubble charts, are available on the Innovation Portal at **www.innovation-portal.info**

We can use the model to look at where the organization currently has innovation projects – and where it could move in the future. For example, if the emphasis has been on product and process innovation, there may be scope for exploring more around position innovation – which new or underserved markets could we play in? Or around defining a new paradigm, a new business model with which to approach the marketplace.

We can also compare maps for different organizations competing in the same market – and use the tool as a way of identifying where there may be relatively unexplored space which will offer significant innovation opportunities. By looking at where other organizations are clustering their efforts we can pick up valuable clues about how to find relatively uncontested space and focus our efforts on these – as the low-cost airlines did with targeting new and underserved markets for travel.

Strategic Selection

The issue here is choosing out of all the things we could do which ones we will do – and why? We have scarce resources so we need to place our bets carefully, balancing the risks and rewards across a portfolio of projects. There are plenty of tools to help us do this, from simple financial measures like payback time or return on investment through to complex frameworks which compare projects across many dimensions. Table 2.3 gives an overview. (We'll look more closely at this toolkit and the different ways we can make decisions under uncertainty in Chapter 9.)

Strategic Competencies and Capabilities

But we also need to consider here that we don't have completely free choice. First of all we need to recognize that there is a degree of what is called 'path dependency' – what we accumulate in the way of knowledge and other resources (i.e. what we can, and cannot, do). For example, if we see an opportunity for nuclear power as a new energy source this may be an interesting possibility – but pretty hard for us to achieve if we are in the business of ice cream selling! This 'resource-based' view looks from the inside out and suggests some of the ways in which we could deploy our particular strengths to our advantage.[3] (We discuss this theme in more detail in the next chapter.)

Strengths could be in the form of specific technological knowledge – maybe we own a patent on a key idea or have a lot of experience in a particular area. 3M, for example, has over

TABLE 2.3 Approaches to Project Selection

Selection approach	Advantages	Disadvantages
Simple 'gut feel', intuition	Fast	Lacks evidence and analysis, may be wrong
Financial measures (e.g. return on investment or payback time)	Fast and uses some simple measurement	Doesn't take account of other benefits which may come from the innovation – learning about new technologies, markets, etc.
Multidimensional measures (e.g. decision matrix)	Compares on several dimensions to build an overall 'score' for attractiveness	Allows consideration of different kinds of benefits but level of analysis may be limited
Portfolio methods and business cases	Compares between projects on several dimensions and provides detailed evidence around core themes	Takes a long time to prepare and present

BOX 2.1: PRAHALAD AND HAMEL

One view of resources – the 'core competencies' theory of Prahalad and Hamel – uses the metaphor of a tree. The deep roots (core competencies) allow for growth of a strong trunk and limbs (core businesses) with smaller branches (business units) yielding leaves, flowers and fruit (products and services).

one hundred years of research around the problem of coating surfaces with different materials and has been able to build its business from applying that knowledge. Intel's core competence is around the expensive and precise technologies of semiconductor manufacturing which it has built up over fifty years, while Honda's expertise lies in a deep understanding of engines and transmission of power – in cars, boats, lawnmowers and, its original starting point, motorbikes.

Of course, competencies may become superseded by shifts in the technological area. Sometimes they can destroy the basis of competitiveness (competence

Activity designed to help you explore competency mapping is available on the Innovation Portal at **www.innovation-portal.info**

Case Studies of 3M and Corning giving examples of competence building are available on the Innovation Portal at **www.innovation-portal.info**

Case Studies of Kodak and Fujifilm, both of which faced significant challenges and have been trying to redeploy their core technological knowledge into new markets, and Philips Lighting, which is using novel solid state lighting technologies to enhance its already strong position in the global lighting market, are available on the Innovation Portal at **www.innovation-portal.info**

Case Study of Tesco and its approach to building a deep understanding of its customers and their changing needs is available on the Innovation Portal at **www.innovation-portal.info**

destroying) but they can also be reconfigured to enhance a competitive position (competence enhancing). A famous study by Tushman and Anderson gives a wide range of examples of these types of change.[4]

But it isn't just technical knowledge – Google's expertise is based on not only a powerful search engine but also using the data that helps it build to offer services in advertising. Major retailers like Tesco and Wal-Mart have a rich and detailed understanding of customers and their shopping preferences and behaviour.

Strengths can also come from specific capabilities, things which an organization has learnt to do to help it stay agile and able to move into new fields. Virgin as a group of companies is represented across many different sectors but the underlying approach is essentially the original entrepreneurial one which Richard Branson used when setting up his music business.

BOX 2.2: DISADVANTAGES OF CORE COMPETENCIES

There is a downside to building core competencies and capabilities: when the environment changes, it is often difficult to let them go. So much has been sunk into investments related to them and the underlying mindset of the organization is committed deeply to them – and so there is a risk that they turn to what Dorothy Leonard calls 'core rigidities'.[5] For example, one explanation for the fall of Polaroid from a key player and technological leader in the photography business to Chapter 11 bankruptcy is that it was unable to let go of its core models for the business.

There is a fuller version of this case available on the Innovation Portal at **www.innovation-portal.info**.

Strategic Positioning

We also need to think about where and how we position ourselves – and that requires an understanding of how we fit into wider systems and where we could create competitive advantage through innovation. Michael Porter's model is a useful one here, looking at innovations in terms of how they can change the competitive position amongst a network of other organizations.[6]

Tool to help you with competency mapping – identifying innovative capabilities – based on research by Richard Hall – is available on the Innovation Portal at **www.innovation-portal.info**

Key questions in this kind of approach are:

- What are the key competitive forces?
- What are the barriers to entry – can anyone come into the game or are most potential competitors kept

out because of high costs, need for specialized knowledge, etc.?

- What is the likely threat from substitutes and different ways of delivering value in this game?
- What is the relative power of key players – customers, suppliers, regulators – and how can that shape the game?

Tool developed by Porter – the 'five forces' model – is available on the Innovation Portal at **www.innovation-portal.info**

All of these and other frameworks are useful in choosing what to do and providing a strategic rationale. They relate to how we can position ourselves in respect of the wider competing context.

Strategic Posture: How are we going to play the game?

Another part of that choice comes from the approach we choose to take – being, for example, a first mover or a fast follower? There are many different 'postures' we could adopt but we need to make sure that there is alignment between the approach we choose to take and our underlying ability to deliver on it. For example, if we want to be first movers, leading the market with new ideas, we will need a strong R&D capability. Equally, if we decide to be a fast follower then we need to have good antennae to pick up on key trends and the agility to move quickly to do something about them, by acquisition, by fast development, etc. Innovation in Action 2.1 gives an example.

Strategic Implementation

Having explored what we could do and decided what we are going to do, the third stage in innovation strategy development is to plan for implementation. Thinking through what we are going to need and how we will get these resources, who we may need to partner with, what likely roadblocks we may find on the way – all of these questions feed into this step.

Of course, it isn't a simple linear process. In practice, there will be plenty of discussion of these issues as we explore options and argue for particular choices, But that's the essence of strategy – a conversation and a rehearsal, imagining and thinking forward about uncertain activities into the future.

To help do this we have a number of tools, again ranging from the simple to the complex. We could, for example, make a simple project plan which sets out the sequence of activities we need to carry out to make our innovation come alive. That would help us identify which resources we needed and when and might also highlight some of the potential trouble spots so we could think through how we might deal with them. Many tools add a dimension of 'what if. . .?' planning to such project models – trying to anticipate key difficulties and take a 'worst case' view so suitable contingency plans can be made.

Tools to help you with this kind of planning including FMEA, potential problem analysis and project management are available on the Innovation Portal at **www.innovation-portal.info**

Activity designed to help you explore strategic planning for implementation is available on the Innovation Portal at **www.innovation-portal.info**

INNOVATION IN ACTION 2.1

Diversity of Strategic Games for Innovation

The MINE (Managing Innovation in the New Economy) research programme at Ecole Polytechnique in Montreal, Canada, together with SPRU, University of Sussex, conducted qualitative and quantitative studies to gain an understanding of the diversity of strategies for innovation. Almost 925 chief technology officers (CTOs) and senior managers of R&D (from Asia, North and South America, and Europe) across all industrial sectors of the economy responded to a global survey. The survey tool is available at www.minesurvey.polymtl.ca. Respondents come from firms such as Intel, Synopsys, Motorola, IBM Global Services, Novartis and Boeing. Executives were asked what competitive forces impact on innovation, what value-creation and -capture activities are pursued in innovating and what strategies and practices are used.

Games of innovation involve many interdependent players, persist over time and are strategically complex. Games are distinct, coherent scenarios of value creation and capture involving activities of collaboration and rivalry:

- Each involves a distinct logic of innovative activities that is largely contingent on product architectures and market lifecycle stage.
- They follow persistent trajectories, bound by some basic economic and technical forces and thus tend to fall into a small number of natural trajectories.
- They result in differing levels of performance. Market-creation games involve radical innovations, grow fast and display high variations in profitability. By contrast, market-evolution games are characterized by process innovations, a slower pace of growth, but good profitability.
- However, games are not fully determined by their contexts, but allow degrees of strategic freedom to interact with members of relevant ecosystems and to adopt collaborative and competitive moves to expand markets.

Clustering analyses led to the identification of seven distinct and stable groups each containing at least 100 firms that create and capture value in similar ways. Each game is characterized by statistically different value-creation and -capture activities:

- patent-driven discovery
- cost-based competition
- systems integration
- systems engineering and consulting
- platform orchestration
- customized mass production
- innovation support and services.

Source: Miller, R. and S. Floricel (2007) Special Issue, *International Journal of Innovation Management*, **11** (1).

It's also worth thinking through and challenging the underlying strategic concept – the business case for doing whatever it is we have in mind. Once again, building a business case or thinking through the underlying business model provides a powerful way of making our assumptions explicit and opening them up for discussion and challenge. (We'll look in detail at the role of business models as a way of capturing value in Chapter 14, but the tools for working with these ideas are very helpful at this early strategic planning stage.)

Tools to help with this activity – business model innovation and developing the business case – are available on the Innovation Portal at **www.innovation-portal.info**

Activity to help you explore some of the challenges in preparing and presenting a strategic business case – Dragons' Den – is available on the Innovation Portal at **www.innovation-portal.info**

Strategy at Different Levels

Strategy is often seen as something which is done by the top management team in an established organization or by the core entrepreneurial team in a start-up. But if it is to work then everyone else needs to understand the overall roadmap and feel comfortable and committed to it. There's a lot of talk about 'strategic vision' – but underneath the hype there is a really important point. If others can't see what you see (no matter how exciting and rich in potential it may be) then they aren't likely to buy in to that strategy. There's a need to build and share a compelling vision and to allow people to explore it for themselves, raising concerns and questions, adding their ideas and suggestions.

And that raises the big issue of communicating and sharing a strategy throughout the organization. It's perhaps easier for a small start-up, though even here there are people outside – venture capitalists, potential partners, etc. – who need to understand and support the vision. In larger, established organizations it's critical to give people a clear sense of direction but also to ensure that they understand and are committed to it. Many studies of innovation highlight the critical role of 'top management commitment' – and in part that means making sure that strategy is not simply some exciting words but that the resources and support throughout the organization to make it happen are also there.

There's another reason why clear and communicated innovation strategy is important. While a few leaders may be in a position to set the overall direction, the actual implementation of the strategy is likely to involve many smaller projects. Ensuring that there is alignment of these so that they all create value and move the organization in the same direction is a critical part of strategy implementation.

For example, we know that there is huge potential for employees to contribute to incremental innovation, especially around the processes on which they work. Research regularly shows that this effect can have a huge cumulative impact. For example, Toyota's position over decades as the world's most productive carmaker is largely a result of its commitment to *kaizen*. This is a process of continuous incremental innovation engaging the vast majority of the workforce – on average it receives one idea per worker per week and implements almost all of these. That's a powerful innovation engine – but it only

Case Studies of policy deployment in action are available on the Innovation Portal at **www.innovation-portal.info**

Tools to enable policy deployment, including 'how/why' charts, are available on the Innovation Portal at **www.innovation-portal.info**

works if all those individual activities by thousands of employees are aligned and focused towards a common strategy goal.[7]

The solution to this is to make use of approaches which have been termed 'policy deployment' (sometimes called 'hoshin planning'), essentially devolving the top-level innovation strategy to lower levels in the organization and allowing people at those levels to make the decisions. This provides a strategic focus within which they can locate their multiple small-scale innovation activities. But it requires two key enablers: the creation of a clear and coherent strategy for the business and the deployment of it through a cascade process which builds understanding and ownership of the goals and sub-goals.

INNOVATION IN ACTION 2.2

Policy Deployment

Policy deployment is a characteristic feature of many Japanese kaizen systems and may help explain why there is such a strong track record of strategic gains through continuous improvement. In such plants, overall business strategy is broken down into focused three-year mid-term plans (MTPs); typically, the plan is given a slogan or motto to help identify it. This forms the basis of banners and other illustrations, but its real effect is to provide a backdrop against which efforts over the next three years can be focused. The MTP is specified not just in vague terms but with specific and measurable objectives, often described as 'pillars'. These are, in turn, decomposed into manageable projects which have clear targets and measurable achievement milestones, and it is to these that workplace innovation activities are systematically applied.

For example, a major Japanese producer of forklift trucks and related machinery employing around 900 staff and producing three main product lines (industrial trucks, construction equipment and other new products) uses this approach.

Strategy is now focused on the 'Aggressive 30' programme, reflecting the 30 years since the plant was set up. Total productive maintenance (TPM) and indirect cost reduction are the key themes. Typical targets within the plan are:

- 1.5 times increase in overall productivity
- breakdown reduced to 10% of current levels
- streamline production flow by 30%
- reduction in new product development/introduction time of 50%.

To deliver these they have a nine-pillar structure to the programme within which the total cost of waste is calculated and broken down into 46 areas, each of which becomes the target for improvement activity.

Kaizen operates in both top-down and bottom-up modes. Each work group studies its 'waste map' and identifies a series of projects, which are led by section managers. Each section has specific targets to achieve, for example increase machine availability from 49% to 86% or cut work in progress from 100 to 20 vehicles.

Each waste theme is plotted on a matrix, with the other axis being a detailed description of the types and nature of waste arising. This matrix gives a picture of the project targets which are then indicated by a red (unsolved) or a green (solved) dot. Importantly, projects completed in one year can be revisited and the targets increased in subsequent years to drive through continuous improvement.

Making things visible is a key theme. The use of the matrix charts with their red and green dots everywhere is a constant reminder of the overall continuous improvement programme. Also each project is painted a shocking pink colour as it is completed so that it is clear on walking through the factory where and what has been done – often sparking interest and application elsewhere but at least reminding on a continuing basis.

Dynamic Capability

One of the problems in innovation strategy is that it can easily look simple. The process we've been describing – of strategic analysis, selection and implementation – seems straightforward and logical. Unfortunately, the world doesn't work like that and the evidence is clear: simple models of strategy that assume a rational process and easy availability of information don't work very well. Instead, we need to see the process as one of incremental learning, probing and exploring, with the actual strategy being constantly adjusted and refined.

Equally, our ability to move is constrained by many forces: the underlying trajectory and our prior commitments (path dependency), the patterns of innovation within a particular sector or the local or national innovation system. So models which emphasize strategic positioning and achieving competitive advantage may not always be appropriate, and these days there is much discussion of the idea that competitive advantage is only ever transient, that it won't last.

Our approach in this book is to follow a helpful direction set by David Teece and colleagues around the idea of 'dynamic capability'.[8] This sees three key components of an innovation strategy:

● competitive and national positions (technology and intellectual property, as well as its customer base and upstream relations with suppliers)

- technological paths (the strategic alternatives available to the firm, and the attractiveness of the opportunities which lie ahead)
- organizational and managerial processes (the set of routines which define 'the way we do things around here').

The core role in innovation management is 'appropriately adapting, integrating and re-configuring internal and external organizational skills, resources and functional competencies towards a changing environment' (p. 537). In other words, strategic innovation management is all about constantly reviewing and reconfiguring routines and asking three key questions:

Of the routines which we have:

- Which should we do more of, enhance and develop?
- Which should we do less of, or even stop?
- Which new routines do we need to learn and embed to cope with new features of our innovation environment?

We'll look at this theme of dynamic capabilities in more detail in the next chapter.

Summary

- Innovation involves uncertainty and risk, and no one has infinite resources. So it makes sense to have a clear sense of direction and a framework within which to make decisions about the changes our organization will make.

- Innovation strategy is not about writing a document or report so much as having a framework for discussion and alignment.

- Innovation strategy is not a detailed plan and an uninterrupted, linear progression so much as a flexible learning process.

- At the heart of an innovation strategy are three core questions:

  ○ Analysis – what could we do?
  ○ Selection – what are we going to do (and why)?
  ○ Implementation – how are we going to do it?

- There is a core role for leadership in innovation strategy to provide vision, direction and sometimes to stretch the organization in terms of its goals.

- Innovation strategy needs to be shared and communicated so that everyone in the organization understands and can contribute.

- Innovation strategy is about building the capability to work in a complex and changing environment. So it is about building routines – capability – to make innovation happen, but it is also about being able to adapt and change those routines as the world shifts. This is 'dynamic capability'.

- Dynamic capability involves working with the organization's paths, processes and positions.

Further Resources

Comprehensive and balanced reviews of the arguments and evidence for product leadership versus follower positions are provided by G. J. Tellis and P. N. Golder: *Will and Vision: How latecomers grow to dominate markets* (McGraw-Hill, 2002) and *Fast Second: How smart companies bypass radical innovation to enter and dominate new markets* (Jossey-Bass, 2004) by Costas Markides. More relevant to firms from emerging economies, and our favourite text on the subject, is Naushad Forbes and David Wield's *From Followers to Leaders: Managing technology and innovation* (Routledge, 2002), which includes numerous case examples.

For recent reviews of the core competence and dynamic capability perspectives, see David Teece's *Dynamic Capabilities and Strategic Management: Organizing for Innovation and Growth* (Oxford University Press, 2011), Joe Tidd's (editor) *From Knowledge Management to Strategic Competence* (Imperial College Press, 3rd edition, 2012) and Connie Helfat's *Dynamic Capabilities: Understanding strategic change in organizations* (Blackwell, 2006).

Lockett, Thompson and Morgenstern (2009) provide a useful review in 'The development of the resource-based view of the firm: A critical appraisal', *International Journal of Management Reviews*, **11** (1), as do Wang and Ahmed (2007), 'Dynamic capabilities: A review and research agenda', *International Journal of Management Reviews*, **9** (1). Davenport, Leibold and Voelpel provide an edited compilation of leading strategy writers in *Strategic Management in the Innovation Economy* (John Wiley & Sons, Ltd, 2nd edition, 2006), and the review edited by Robert Galavan, John Murray and Costas Markides, *Strategy, Innovation and Change* (Oxford University Press, 2008) is excellent. On the more specific issue of technology strategy, Vittorio Chiesa's *R&D Strategy and Organization* (Imperial College Press, 2001) is a good place to start.

The renewed interest in business model innovation, that is how value is created and captured, is discussed in *Strategic Market Creation: A new perspective on marketing and innovation management*, a review of research at Copenhagen Business School and Bocconi University, edited by Karin Tollin and Antonella Carù (John Wiley & Sons, Ltd, 2008). There was a special issue of the journal *Long Range Planning* on innovative business models, volume **43** (2 & 3), 2011, and a compilation of articles re-published in the *Harvard Business Review* on Business Model Innovation (2012).

References

1. Prahalad, C. K. (2006) *The Fortune at the Bottom of the Pyramid*. Upper Saddle River, NJ: Wharton School Publishing.

2. Francis, D. and J. Bessant (2006) Targetting innovation and implications for capability development, *Technovation*, **25**: 171–183.

3. Prahalad, C. and G. Hamel (1990) The core competence of the corporation, *Harvard Business Review*, **68** (3): 79–91.

4. Tushman, M. and P. Anderson (1987) Technological discontinuities and organizational environments, *Administrative Science Quarterly*, **31** (3): 439–465.

5. Leonard, D. (1992) Core capabilities and core rigidities: A paradox in new product development, *Strategic Management Journal*, **13**: 111–125.

6. Porter, M. (1984) *Competitive Advantage: Creating and sustaining superior performance*. New York: Free Press.

7. Bessant, J. and D. Francis (1999) Developing strategic continuous improvement capability, *International Journal of Operations and Production Management*, **19** (11): 1106–1119.

8. Teece, D. (2009) *Dynamic Capabilities and Strategic Management*. Oxford: Oxford University Press.

Deeper Dive explanations of innovation concepts and ideas are available on the Innovation Portal at **www.innovation-portal.info**

Quizzes to test yourself further are available online via the Innovation Portal at **www.innovation-portal.info**

**Summary of online resources for Chapter 2 –
all material is available via the Innovation Portal at
www.innovation-portal.info**

Cases	**Media**	**Tools**	**Activities**	**Deeper Dive**

Cases	Media	Tools	Activities	Deeper Dive
• Marshalls	• Finnegan's Fish Bar	• Rich pictures	• Strategic advantage through innovation	• Research themes in innovation strategy
• Model T Ford		• PEST	• Rich pictures	• Innovation strategies in the real world
• Lego		• SWOT	• 4Ps analysis	
• Adidas		• Five forces model	• Competency mapping	
• Threadless		• 4Ps analysis	• Strategic planning for implementation	
• 3M		• Competitiveness profiling	• Dragons' Den	
• Corning		• Blue Ocean strategy		
• Kodak		• Decision matrix		
• Fujifilm		• Portfolio methods		
• Tesco		• Bubble charts		
• Policy deployment		• Competency mapping		
• Philips Lighting		• FMEA		
		• Potential problem analysis		
		• Project management		
		• Business model innovation		
		• Business case development		
		• Policy deployment		
		• How/why charts		

Chapter 3

Identifying Strategic Capabilities

LEARNING OBJECTIVES

By the end of this chapter, you will be able to:

- understand the differences between resources, capabilities and dynamic capabilities
- identify the tangible and intangible resources which contribute to capabilities
- assess how capabilities contribute to competitive advantage.

The Resource-Based View

Every organization is unique by virtue of its history, experience, processes and products, market position and organizational culture. The challenge is to make this uniqueness the source of sustainable competitive advantage. The resource-based view of strategy is concerned with identifying and building on such strengths or capabilities. The most influential business analysts promoting and developing the notion of 'core competencies' have been Gary Hamel and C. K. Prahalad.[1] Their basic ideas can be summarized as follows:

- The sustainable competitive advantage of firms resides not in their products but in their core competencies: 'The real sources of advantage are to be found in management's ability to consolidate corporate-wide technologies and production skills into competencies that empower individual businesses to adapt quickly to changing opportunities' (p. 81).
- Core competencies feed into more than one core product, which in turn feed into more than one business unit. They use the metaphor of the tree:

  ○ End products = Leaves, flowers and fruit
  ○ Business units = Smaller branches

○ Core products = Trunk and major limbs
○ Core competencies = Root systems.

Examples of core competencies include Sony in miniaturization, Philips in optical media, 3M in coatings and adhesives and Canon in the combination of the precision mechanics, fine optics and microelectronics technologies that underlie all their products (Table 3.1). Examples of core products include Honda in lightweight, high-compression engines and Matsushita in key components in videocassette recorders.

At one level the identification of competence appears to pose few difficulties.

However, for core competence to be a tool of strategic analysis what is also required is a means for firms to analyse rigorously their own and their competitors' competencies. Yet, despite all the effort and attention, Coyne, Hall and Clifford,[2] writing in *The McKinsey Quarterly* in early 1997, note how elusive core competencies remain: 'Few managers we have talked to could claim to have utilised core competence to achieve success in the marketplace, and even fewer to have built a core competence from scratch . . . Indeed, most were uncertain as to exactly what qualifies a core competence . . . it is like a mirage: something that from a distance appears to offer hope . . . but turns to sand when approached' (p. 41).

Our own experience in working with the concept of core competence supports their view.

Case Study of Marshalls illustrating the building-up of competencies over a sustained period is available on the Innovation Portal at **www.innovation-portal.info**

Competencies disappear all too easily under close examination. A careful scrutiny of competence claims reveals, all too often, that they are neither firm-specific nor sustainable, that they convey neither value to the customer nor generic qualities to the firm.

Distinguishing Capabilities from Resources

Dynamic capabilities are central to innovation strategy and yet despite twenty years' development and many theoretical contributions, the conceptualization, operationalization and application of the resource-based and dynamic capabilities' views of strategic management remains problematic. For instance, there is no consensus definition of dynamic capabilities.[3]

Resource-Based View

The resource-based view (RBV) of strategy proposes that competitive advantage is primarily driven by a firm's valuable, rare, inimitable and non-substitutable *resources*.[4] The underlying assumption is that resources are heterogeneous across organizations and that this heterogeneity can sustain competitiveness over time.

Resources are stocks of available factors that are *owned, controlled* or *accessed on a preferential basis* by the firm.[5] Resources are primarily *having* (stock) rather than *doing* (flow) forms.[6] 'Having' resources can be tangible, like location, material, building, inventory,

TABLE 3.1   Innovation in Action: Core Competencies at Canon

Product	Competencies		
	Precision mechanics	**Fine optics**	**Microelectronics**
Basic camera	X	X	
Compact fashion camera	X	X	
Electronic camera	X	X	
EOS autofocus camera	X	X	X
Video still camera	X	X	X
Laser beam printer	X	X	X
Colour video printer	X		X
Bubble jet printer	X		X
Basic fax	X		X
Laser fax	X		X
Calculator			X
Plain paper copier	X	X	X
Colour copier	X	X	X
Laser copier	X	X	X
Colour laser copier	X	X	X
Still video system	X	X	X
Laser imager	X	X	X
Cell analyser	X	X	X
Mask aligners	X		X
Stepper aligners	X		X
Excimer laser aligners	X	X	X

Source: Prahalad, C. and G. Hamel (1990) The core competencies of the corporation. *Harvard Business Review*, May–June, 79–91 Table: Core competencies at Canon". Reproduced with permission.

According to Christer Oskarsson[7]:

'In the late 1950s . . . the time had come for Canon to apply its precision mechanical and optical technologies to other areas [than cameras] . . . such as business machines. By 1964 Canon had begun by developing the world's first 10-key fully electronic calculator . . . followed by entry into the coated paper copier market with the development of an electrofax copier model in 1965, and then into . . . the revolutionary Canon plain paper copier technology unveiled in 1968 . . . Following these successes of product diversification, Canon's product lines were built on a foundation of precision optics, precision engineering and electronics. . .

The main factors behind . . . increases in the numbers of products, technologies and markets . . . seem to be the rapid growth of information technology and electronics, technological transitions from analogue to digital technologies, technological fusion of audio and video technologies, and the technological fusion of electronics and physics to optronics. (pp. 24–26)

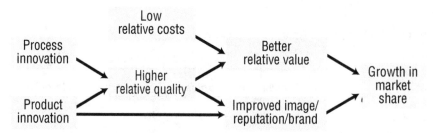

FIGURE 3.1   Relationship between innovation and performance in fast-moving consumer goods

Source: Clayton, T. and Turner, G. (2012) Brands, innovation and growth. In Tidd, J. (ed.) *From Knowledge Management to Strategic Competence: Measuring technological, market and organizational innovation.* Imperial College Press, London. Copyright Imperial College Press/World Scientific Publishing Co.

machinery and low-cost employees, or less tangible like employee skills, patents, databases, licences, brand and copyright.

These resources are normally available to most firms, tradable in the market and exogenous. In contrast, 'doing' resources, or capabilities, are more firm-specific, less tradable in the market and more difficult to imitate. Examples of 'doing' resources are capabilities incorporated in organizational and managerial processes like product development, technology development and marketing (Figure 3.1).

Dynamic Capabilities

Capabilities refer to the organization's potential for *doing*, or carrying out a specific activity or set of activities. Such capabilities tend to consist of a combination or configuration of resources. At the most basic level these can be the *basic operational or functional activities* of the firm, for example design, manufacturing or sales capability. These typically contribute directly to the creation of value from current processes, products and services (Figure 3.2). For example, Zara has successfully integrated design, clothing manufacture and IT to create a capability to introduce new clothing designs more rapidly and frequently than its competitors.

Case Study of Zara providing a more detailed view of building up competencies and capabilities around 'fast fashion' is available on the Innovation Portal at **www.innovation-portal.info**

At a higher level, *dynamic capabilities* include abilities to improve, adapt, and innovate.[8] Dynamic capabilities are dedicated to the modification of operational capabilities and lead, for example, to changes in the firm's products or production processes.[9] For example, TSMC has, over successive technology generations, continued to develop a dynamic capability in semiconductor manufacture based on deep codified scientific knowledge, tacit knowledge of materials manufacturing and cumulative experience and learning (Innovation in Action 3.1).

David Teece's original definition as 'the firm's ability to integrate, build, and reconfigure internal and external competences to address rapidly changing environments' is rather broad and difficult to operationalize, so many authors have since offered their own definitions of

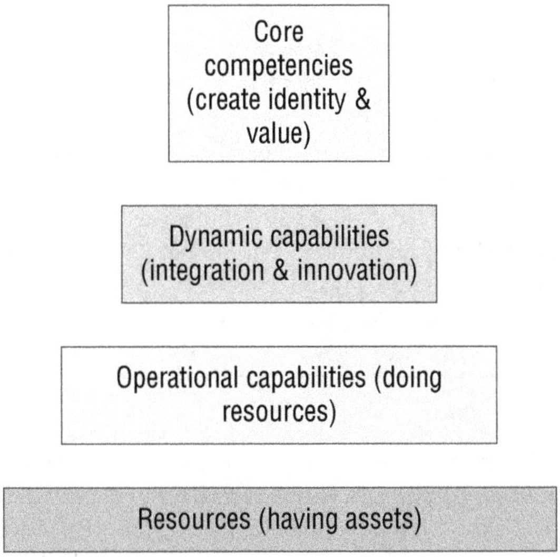

FIGURE 3.2   Resource base of the company: A hierarchical classification

INNOVATION IN ACTION 3.1

Taiwan Semiconductor Manufacturing Company (TSMC)

TSMC was established in Taiwan in 1987 to become the world's first dedicated semiconductor foundry. This so-called pure-play foundry business represented a novel business model because, unlike conventional vertically integrated manufacturers, TSMC's customers are fab-less semiconductor design houses such as Qualcomm, Broadcom and NVIDIA.

The cost of building and operating fabrication facilities has become prohibitive for all but the very largest companies, such as Intel and Samsung, especially in the case of complex logic applications. Even AMD (Advanced Micro Devices) separated its design and manufacturing businesses in 2008.

The headquarters and main fabrication plants are located in Hsinchu, Taiwan, but it also operates two wholly owned subsidiaries, WaferTech in the United States and TSMC China Company Limited, and a joint venture fabrication in Singapore, SSMC. Its core business is mask production, wafer manufacturing, assembly and testing, but it also provides design and prototyping services. In 2010, it joined the top-ten semiconductor R&D spenders, to reach $945 million (£580 million), equivalent to 7% of sales (called the R&D-intensity), the highest of any pure foundry business. By comparison, the number-one R&D spender in that industry that year was Intel, at $6.6 billion (£4 billion; 17% of sales), and in second place Samsung, at $2.6 billion (£1.6 billion; 8% of sales).

(continued)

In 2011, the company's production capacity reached 13.2 million eight-inch equivalent wafers, and TSMC had more than 450 customers, manufacturing more than 8300 products for computer, communications and consumer electronics applications. In 2012, a partnership between TSMC and Apple began production of the A5 (dual core) and A6 chip for Apple's next-generation iPads and iPhones. TSMC has benefited from the growth in smart mobile devices, and it is estimated that every tablet sold globally contributes about $7 (£4) to its income. In 2011–2012, it made sales of $14 billion (£8 billion), and by specializing in high-technology, capital-intensive contract manufacture it maintained high gross-profit margins, of around 40%, although profitability is dependent on closely matching capacity and demand.

dynamic capabilities.[10] Despite being one of the most widely used and cited concepts, the central construct of dynamic capabilities is not well or universally defined.

Rather than trying to define such a complex concept, a more useful way of identifying and operationalizing dynamic capabilities is to focus on the *functions* of dynamic capability. In other words, we ask: 'What does dynamic capability do?' instead of 'What is dynamic capability?' For example:

* Sensing opportunities and threats[11]
* Absorptive and adaptive capability[12]
* Enhancing, combining, protecting and, where necessary, reconfiguring tangible and intangible resources.[13]

Assessing Capabilities

One of the most difficult challenges in practice is to identify capabilities. This technique for analysing tangible and intangible resources is based on the identification and development of the strengths in the key product development and delivery system attributes and the intangible resources which produce them. The method consists of three parts:[14]

* Identifying the key attributes of the most successful products and services offered by the organization.
* Mapping these attributes to the resources or competencies of the organization, including tangible and intangible resources.
* Assessing the potential for sustaining, protecting and exploiting these resources, including knowledge management.

Tool to help you to explore the technique of identifying capabilities in detail is available on the Innovation Portal at **www.innovation-portal.info**

Identifying Key Attributes

A pragmatic view on the nature of competitive advantage is advanced by Coyne, whose argument starts with the observation that any company which is making repeat sales in a competitive market must enjoy an advantage in the eyes of the customers who are making the repeat purchases.[15]

He goes on to argue that for a *sustainable* competitive advantage to exist three conditions must apply:

- Customers must perceive a consistent difference in important attributes between the producer's product/service and the attributes offered by competitors.
- This difference is the direct consequence of a capability gap between the producer and its competitors.
- Both the difference in important attributes and the capability gap can be expected to endure over time.

Coyne suggests that there are four, and only four, types of resource capability:

- *Regulatory*: the possession of legal entities (e.g. patents and trademarks)
- *Positional*: the results of previous endeavour (e.g. reputation, trust, value chain configuration)
- *Business systems*: the ability to do things well (e.g. consistent conformance to specification)
- *Organizational* characteristics (e.g. the ability to manage change).

It is now possible to ask: 'What is the nature of the package of product/delivery system attributes which customers value?' and to go on to ask: 'What is responsible for producing the valued attributes?' The product/delivery system attributes will include factors such as price, quality, specification and image.

The Valued Attributes

It may be necessary to identify different rankings for different categories of customers (e.g. new as opposed to long-standing customers, retailers as opposed to end users).

In carrying out this analysis of attributes it is appropriate to seek consensus between the relevant executives with respect to questions such as:

- Can executives agree an importance weighting for each attribute?
- Can executives agree a benchmark score for each attribute compared with the competition?
- Can executives agree the *sustainability* of the advantage represented by each attribute?

The degree of congruence, or dissonance, in executives' perceptions of these issues can in itself be illuminating.

In addition to identifying the current strengths in the marketplace it is also appropriate at this stage to identify known deficiencies in the product offering.

BOX 3.1: TYPICAL PRODUCT/DELIVERY SYSTEM ATTRIBUTES WHICH DEFINE COMPETITIVE ADVANTAGE

Image: What is the image of the product range? Is it important?

Price: Is a low-selling price a key buying criterion?

User friendliness: Is it important for the product to be user friendly?

Availability: Is product range availability crucial?

Rapid response to enquiry: Is it important to produce designs, quotations, etc. very quickly?

Quick response to customer demand: Will sales be lost to the competition if they respond more quickly than you do?

Width of product range: Is it important to offer a wide range of products and/or services to customers?

New product to market time: How important is the product development time?

Quality – the product's fitness for purpose: Does the product, or service, deliver exactly the benefits which the customers want?

Quality – the consistent achievement of defined specification: Is constant conformance to spec. vital?

Safety: Is safety in use a major concern?

Regulatory requirements: Does meeting regulatory requirements earlier/better than the competition give a competitive advantage?

Degree of innovation: Is it important for the product or service to represent 'state of the art'?

Ability to vary product specification: Is it important to produce product or service modifications easily and quickly?

Ability to vary product volume: Is it important to be able to increase, or decrease, production volume easily?

Customer service: Is the quality of the overall service which customers receive a key to winning business?

Pre- and after-sales service: Is the supply of advice, spares, etc. a key aspect of winning business?

Mapping Attributes to Resources and Competencies

The important characteristics of strategic competencies are

- They are responsible for delivering a significant benefit to customers.
- They are idiosyncratic to the firm.
- They take time to acquire.
- They are sustainable because they are difficult and time-consuming to imitate.

- They comprise *configurations* of resources.
- They have a strong tacit content and are socially complex – they are the product of experiential learning.

The resources which produce product/delivery system attributes can now be placed in a framework of capabilities:

Regulatory Capability

Regulatory capability comprises resources which are legal entities.

- tangible, on balance sheet, assets
- intangible, off balance sheet, assets, e.g.:

  - patents
  - licences
  - trademarks
  - contracts
  - protectable data.

Positional Capability

Positional capability comprises resources which are not legal entities and are the result of previous endeavour, that is with a high path dependency:

- reputation of company
- reputation of product
- corporate networks
- personal networks
- unprotectable data
- distribution network
- supply chain network
- formal and informal operating systems
- processes.

Functional Capability

Functional capability comprises resources which are either individual skills and know-how or team skills and know-how, within the company, at suppliers, at distributors, etc.

Case Study of Tesco in which you can see the ways in which competitive advantage can be constructed through building capabilities is available on the Innovation Portal at **www.innovation-portal.info**

- employee know-how and skills in:

  - operations
  - finance
  - marketing
  - R&D, etc.

- supplier know-how

- distributor know-how
- professional advisors' expertise, etc.

Case Study of Corning giving an idea of how capabilities are built and deployed over time is available on the Innovation Portal at **www.innovation-portal.info**

Cultural Capability

Cultural capability comprises resources which are the characteristics of the organization:

- perception of quality standards
- tradition of customer service
- ability to manage change
- ability to innovate

- ability to work in a team
- ability to develop staff, suppliers and distributors

- automatic response mechanisms.

While it is possible for a valued product/delivery system attribute to be the result of a tangible asset such as a building or a specialist manufacturing capability, research and experience suggest intangible resources such as product reputation, employee know-how, etc. are the factors most often responsible for producing the attributes which are valued by customers. The identification of the intangibles which are responsible for each key product attribute results in a summary such as that shown in Table 3.2.

The resources which occur frequently in the body of the matrix are those which, either by themselves or in combination with others, constitute the organization's strategic competencies.

Assessing the Potential for Sustaining, Protecting and Exploiting Competencies

Having identified the key resources, it is appropriate to examine development scenarios in terms of protection, sustenance, enhancement and leverage.

TABLE 3.2   An Example of the Matrix of Attributes and Resources

Key product/ Delivery attributes	The resources which produce, or do not produce, the key attributes:			
	Regulatory Capability	Positional Capability	Functional Capability	Cultural Capability
Strengths				
1. e.g. availability		Value chain Configuration	Forecasting skills	
2. e.g. quality				High perception of quality
3. e.g. specification	Patent 'abc'		Technology 'xyz'	
Etc.				
Weaknesses				
1.				
2.				
Summary of the key resources				

This approach to the analysis of intangible resources is the acquisition of a new perspective and language that enable them to codify the tacit knowledge which they have of their companies. In particular, executives have welcomed the, sometimes new, emphasis placed on issues such as:

- How can the key resource of reputation be protected, enhanced and leveraged?
- How can management ensure that every employee is disposed to be both a promoter and custodian of the reputation which employs him/her?

BOX 3.2: ISSUES WITH RESPECT TO THE DEVELOPMENT OF INTANGIBLE RESOURCES

With Respect to Protection

- Do all concerned recognize the value of this intangible resource to the company?
- Can the resource be protected in law?

With Respect to Sustainability

- How long did it take to acquire this resource?
- Is it unique because of all that has happened in creating it?
- How durable is the resource; will it decline with time?
- How easily may the resource be lost?
- How easily and quickly can others identify and imitate the resource?
- Can others easily 'buy' the resource?
- Can others easily 'grow' the resource?
- How appropriable is the resource? Can it 'walk away'?
- Is the resource vulnerable to substitution?

With Respect to Enhancement

- Is the 'stock' of this resource increasing?
- How can we ensure that the 'stock' of this resource *continues* to increase?

With Respect to Exploitation

- Are we making the best use of this resource?
- How else could it be used?
- Is the scope for *synergy* identified and exploited?
- Are we aware of the key linkages which exist between the resources?

- What are the key areas of employee know-how?
- Can they be codified?
- How long do they take to acquire?
- Is the business organised so that working and learning are the same?

This can help define what an organization needs to do over time to maintain and renew resources and competencies. Effective management is about knowing where to locate knowledge resources and the organizational linkages that integrate them together to create competencies. Managing this process is a purposive activity. It requires resources. The objectives of the framework are

- to enable an organization to map its resources and the key linkages between them
- to act as an elicitation device to facilitate a discussion about the meaning and action required – in terms of core competencies and knowledge resources.

First, position each of the competencies identified in Stage 2 by placing each of them at a point on the codification and diffusion scales. The relevant population for diffusion needs to be defined: rather different data are generated when the diffusion population is the firm as opposed to the industry, for example. For discussions about competence it is often helpful to explore how widely knowledge about technologies and linkages are shared within the firm *and* within the industry. Comparing firm- and industry-level diffusion patterns can help firms to recognize that, while a particular technology may not be widely diffused within the firm, it is widely diffused among other firms in the industry. In this way, participants avoid the trap of believing that because something is new to them it is also new to their competitors.

An example of a codification scale is as follows:

Codified

- Can be totally automated.
- Can be partially automated.
- Can be systematically described.
- Can be described and put down on paper.
- Can be shown and described verbally.
- Can be shown inside someone's head.

Uncodified

An example of a diffusion scale to be used at the industry level is:

Diffused
    Known by all firms in all industries.
    Known by many firms in all industries.
    Known by many firms in many industries.

Known by many firms in a few industries.
Known by a handful of firms in a few industries.
Known by only a handful of firms in one industry.
Known only by one firm in one industry.

Undiffused

Such scales may appear rather inexact but, for this purpose, they are exact enough. We can use these 'maps' of competencies to help to identify the management action needed.

Creating and Capturing Value

Capabilities do not necessarily translate into value or competitive advantage. The capacity of the firm to appropriate the benefits of its investment in capabilities depends on two factors: (i) the firm's capacity to translate its capabilities into commercially viable products or processes; (ii) the firm's capacity to defend its advantage against imitators. Some of the factors that enable a firm to benefit commercially from its capabilities can be strongly shaped by its management, for example the provision of complementary assets to exploit the lead. Other factors can be influenced only slightly by the firm's management, and depend much more on the general nature of the technology, the product market and the regime of intellectual property rights, for example the strength of patent protection. We can identify nine factors which influence the firm's capacity to benefit commercially from its capabilities:

1. Secrecy
2. Accumulated tacit knowledge
3. Lead times and after-sales service
4. The learning curve
5. Complementary assets
6. Product complexity
7. Standards
8. Pioneering radical new products
9. Strength of patent protection.

We begin with those over which management has some degree of discretion for action, and move on to those where its range of choices is more limited.

1. Secrecy is considered an effective form of protection by industrial managers, especially for process innovations. However, it is unlikely to provide absolute protection, because some process characteristics can be identified from an analysis of the final product, and because process engineers make up a professional community and talk to each other and move from one firm to another, so that information and knowledge inevitably leak out.

2. Accumulated tacit knowledge can be long and difficult to imitate, especially when it is closely integrated in specific firms and regions. Examples include product design skills, ranging from those of Zara in clothing design to those of Rolls-Royce in aircraft engines.

3. Lead times and after-sales service are considered by practitioners as major sources of protection against imitation, especially for product innovations. Taken together with a strong commitment to product development, they can establish brand loyalty and credibility, accelerate the feedback from customer use to product improvement, generate learning-curve cost advantages (see below) and therefore increase the costs of entry for imitators.

4. The learning curve in production generates both lower costs and a particular and powerful form of accumulated and largely tacit knowledge that is well recognized by practitioners. In certain industries and technologies (e.g. semiconductors, continuous processes), the first-comer advantages are potentially large, given the major possibilities for reducing unit costs with increasing cumulative production. However, such 'experience curves' are not automatic, and require continuous investment in training and learning.

5. Complementary assets. The effective commercialization of an innovation very often depends on assets (or competencies) in production, marketing and after-sales to complement those in technology. For example, EMI did not invest in them to exploit its advances in electronic scanning. On the other hand, strong complementary assets enabled IBM to catch up in the personal computer market.

6. Product complexity. Product complexity is recognized by managers as an effective barrier to imitation. Contrast the personal computer and commercial aircraft industries. With the advent of the microprocessor and standard software, the technological barriers to imitation in personal computers are low, resulting in strong competition from low-cost economies. In contrast, Boeing and Airbus have faced no such threat to their positions in large civilian aircraft, since the costs and lead times for imitation remain very high.

7. Standards. The widespread acceptance of a company's product standard widens its own market and raises barriers against competitors. The market leader normally has the advantage in a standards war, but this can be overturned through radical technological change, or a superior response to customers' needs. Competing firms can adopt either 'evolutionary' strategies minimizing switching costs for customers (e.g. backwards compatibility with earlier generations of the product) or 'revolutionary' strategies based on greatly superior performance–price characteristics, such that customers are willing to accept higher switching costs.

8. Pioneering radical new products. It is not necessarily a great advantage to be a technological leader in the early stages of the development of radically new products, when the product performance characteristics, and features valued by users, are not always clear, either to the producers or to the users themselves. Especially for consumer products, valued features emerge only gradually through a process of dynamic competition, which involves a considerable amount of trial, error and learning by both producers and users. New features valued by users in one product can easily be recognized by competitors and incorporated in subsequent products. This is why market leadership in the early stages of the development of personal computers was so volatile, and why pioneers are often displaced by new entrants. Pioneers in radical consumer innovations rarely succeed in establishing long-term market positions.

9. Strength of patent protection can be a strong determinant of the relative commercial benefits to innovators and imitators. Patents are judged to be more effective in protecting product innovations than process innovations in all sectors except petroleum refining, probably reflecting the importance of improvements in chemical catalysts for increasing process efficiency. It also shows that patent protection is rated more highly in chemical-related sectors (especially drugs) than in other sectors. This is because it is more difficult in general to 'invent round' a clearly specified chemical formula than round other forms of invention.

Radically new technologies are now posing new problems for the protection of intellectual property, including the patenting system. The number of patents granted to protect software technology is growing in the United States, and so are the numbers of financial institutions getting involved in patenting for the first time. Debate and controversy surround important issues, such as the possible effects of digital technology on copyright protection, the validity of patents to protect living organisms and the appropriate breadth of patent protection in biotechnology.

Finally, we should note that firms can use more than one of the above nine factors to defend their innovative lead. For example, in the pharmaceutical industry secrecy is paramount during the early phases of research, but in the later stages of research patents become critical. Complementary assets such as global sales and distribution become more important at the later stages. Despite all the merger and acquisitions in this sector, these factors, combined with the need for a significant critical mass of R&D, have resulted in relatively stable international positions of countries in pharmaceutical innovation over a period of some 70 years. Firms typically deploy all the useful means available to them to defend their innovations against imitation.

In some cases the advantages of pioneering technology, intellectual property and standards combine to create a sustainable market position.

Beware of Core Rigidities

As Dorothy Leonard-Barton points out, 'core competencies' can also become 'core rigidities' in the firm, when established competencies become too dominant.[16] In addition to sheer habit, this can happen because established competencies are central to today's products, and because large numbers of top managers may be trained in them. As a consequence, important new competencies may be neglected or underestimated (e.g. the threat to mainframes from mini- and microcomputers by management in mainframe companies). In addition, established innovation strengths may overshoot the target. Many examples show that when 'core rigidities' become firmly entrenched their removal often requires changes in top management.

> Case Study of Polaroid illustrating some of these themes in much greater detail is available on the Innovation Portal at **www.innovation-portal.info**

INNOVATION IN ACTION 3.2

Capabilities and Cognition at Polaroid

Polaroid was a pioneer in the development of instant photography. It developed the first instant camera in 1948, the first instant colour camera in 1963, and introduced sonar automatic focusing in 1978. In addition to its competencies in silver halide chemistry, it had technological competencies in optics and electronics, and mass manufacturing, marketing and distribution expertise. The company was technology-driven from its foundation in 1937, and the founder Edwin Land had 500 personal patents. When Kodak entered the instant photography market in 1976, Polaroid sued the company for patent infringement, and was awarded $924.5 million (£566 million) in damages. Polaroid consistently and successfully pursued a strategy of introducing new cameras, but made almost all its profits from the sale of the film (the so-called razor-blade marketing strategy also used by Gillette), and between 1948 and 1978 the average annual sales growth was 23%, and profit growth 17% per year.

Polaroid established an electronic imaging group as early as 1981, as it recognized the potential of the technology. However, digital technology was perceived as a potential technological shift, rather than as a market or business disruption. By 1986 the group had an annual research budget of $10 million (£6 million), and by 1989 42% of the R&D budget was devoted to digital imaging technologies. By 1990 28% of the firm's patents related to digital technologies. Polaroid was therefore well positioned at that time to develop a digital camera business. However, it failed to translate prototypes into a commercial digital camera until 1996, by which time there were 40 other companies in the market, including many strong Japanese camera and electronics firms. Part of the problem was adapting the product development and marketing channels to the new product needs. However, other more fundamental problems related to long-held cognitions: a continued commitment to the razor-blade business model, and pursuit of image quality. Profits from the new market for digital cameras were derived from the cameras rather than the consumables (film). Ironically, Polaroid had rejected the development of ink-jet printers, which rely on consumables for profits, because of the relatively low quality of their (early) outputs. Polaroid had a long tradition of improving its print quality to compete with conventional 35mm film.

Source: Tripsas, M. and G. Gavetti (2000) Capabilities, cognition, and inertia: Evidence from digital imaging. *Strategic Management Journal*, **21**, 1147–61. Reproduced by permission of John Wiley & Sons, Ltd.

Summary

- Resources can be tangible – including assets, plant and equipment and location – or intangible – such as employee skills and intellectual property. However, as these are generally freely available in the market they do not necessarily in isolation confer a sustainable competitive advantage.

- Capabilities are more functional than resources, and by definition are rare combinations of resource which are difficult to imitate and create value for the organization.

- Dynamic capabilities allow organizations to adapt, innovate and renew, and are therefore critical in conditions of uncertainty and for long-term growth.

- Capabilities create value and contribute to competitiveness a number of ways, including the ability to differentiate processes and products which are difficult to imitate.

Further Resources

For recent reviews of the core competence and dynamic capability perspectives, see David Teece's *Dynamic Capabilities and Strategic Management: Organizing for innovation and growth* (Oxford University Press, 2011), Joe Tidd (ed.) *From Knowledge Management to Strategic Competence* (Imperial College Press, 3rd edition, 2012) and Connie Helfat's *Dynamic Capabilities: Understanding strategic change in organizations* (Blackwell, 2006). Lockett, Thompson and Morgenstern (2009) provide a useful review in 'The development of the resource-based view of the firm: A critical appraisal', *International Journal of Management Reviews*, **11** (1), as do Wang and Ahmed (2007), 'Dynamic capabilities: A review and research agenda', *International Journal of Management Reviews*, **9** (1).

References

1. Prahalad, C. and G. Hamel (1990) The core competence of the corporation, *Harvard Business Review*, **68** (3): 79–91.

2. Coyne, K. P., S. J. D. Hall and P. G. Clifford (1997) Is your Core Competence a Mirage?, *The McKinsey Quarterly*, 1: 40–54.

3. Keupp, M. M., M. Palmié and O. Gassmann (2012) The strategic management of innovation: A systematic review and paths for future research, *International Journal of Management Reviews*, **14** (1): 367–390.

4. Barney, J. B. (1991) Firm resources and sustained competitive advantage, *Journal of Management*, **17** (1): 99–120; Barney, J. B. (2001) Is the resource-based 'view' a useful perspective for strategic management research? Yes, *Academy of Management Review*, **26** (1): 41–56; Barney, J. B. (2001) Resource-based theories of competitive advantage: A ten-year retrospective on the resource-based view, *Journal of Management*, **27**: 643–650; Barney, J. B. (2002) *Gaining and Sustaining Competitive Advantage*, 2nd edn. Upper Saddle River, NJ: Prentice Hall.

5. Amit, R. and P. J. H. Schoemaker (1993) Strategic assets and organisational rent, *Strategic Management Journal*, **14**: 33–46; Helfat, C. E., S. Finkelstein, W. Mitchell *et al.* (2007) *Dynamic Capabilities: Understanding strategic change in organisations*, Malden: Blackwell Publishing.

6. Hall, R. (1992) The strategic analysis of intangible resources, *Strategic Management Journal*, **13**: 135–144; Hall, R. (1993) A framework linking intangible resources and capabilities to sustainable competitive advantage, *Strategic Management Journal*, **14**: 607–618.

7. Oskarsson, C. (1993) *Technology Diversification: The phenomenon, its causes and effects*. Gothenburg: Department of Industrial Management and Economics, Chalmers University.

8. Zollo, M. and S. G. Winter (2002) Deliberate learning and the evolution of dynamic capabilities, *Organization Science*, **13** (3): 339–351; Winter, S. G. (2003) Understanding dynamic capabilities, *Strategic Management Journal*, **24**: 991–995.

9. Helfat, C. E. and M. A. Peteraf (2003) The dynamic resource-based view: Capability lifecycles, *Strategic Management Journal*, **24**: 997–1010; Zahra, S. A., H. J. Sapienza and P. Davidsson (2006) Entrepreneurship and dynamic capabilities: A review, model and research agenda, *Journal of Management Studies*, **43** (4): 917–955.

10. Teece, D. J. and G. Pisano (1994) The dynamic capabilities of firms: An introduction, *Industrial and Corporate Change*, **3**: 537–556; Teece, D. J. (2000) Strategies for managing knowledge assets: The role of firm structure and industrial context, *Long Range Planning*, **33** (1): 35–54; Teece, D. J. (2006) *Explicating Dynamic Capabilities: The nature and microfoundations of (long run) enterprise performance*. University of California, Berkeley: WP; Teece, D. J. (2007) Explicating dynamic capabilities: The nature and microfoundations of (sustainable) enterprise performance, *Strategic Management Journal*, **28** (13): 1319–1350.

11. Pavlou, P. A. and O. A. E. Sawy (2011) Understanding the elusive black box of dynamic capabilities. *Decision Sciences*, **42** (1): 239–273.

12. Wang, C. L. and P. K. Ahmed (2007) Dynamic capabilities: A review and research agenda, *International Journal of Management Reviews*, **9** (1): 31–51; Lockett,

A., S. Thompson and U. Morgenstern (2009) The development of the resource-based view of the firm: A critical appraisal, *International Journal of Management Reviews*, **11** (1): 9–28; Ellonen, H. K., A. Jantunen and O. Kuivalainen (2011) The role of dynamic capabilities in developing innovation-related capabilities, *International Journal of Innovation Management*, **15** (3): 459–478.

13. Danneels, E. (2002) The dynamics of product innovation and firm competences, *Strategic Management Journal*, **23**: 1095–1121; Danneels, E. (2007) The process of technological competence leveraging, *Strategic Management Journal*, **28** (5): 511–533; Danneels, E. (2008) Organizational antecedents of second-order competences, *Strategic Management Journal*, **29**: 519–543.

14. This section is based on the method developed by Richard Hall, 'What are competencies?', in J. Tidd (2012) *From Knowledge Management to Strategic Competence*, 3rd edn. London: Imperial College Press.

15. Coyne, K. P. (1986) Sustainable competitive advantage: What it is and what it isn't, *Business Horizons*, **January/February**.

16. Leonard-Barton, D. (1991) Core capabilities and core rigidities: A paradox in managing new product development. *Strategic Management Journal*, **13**: 111–125.

Deeper Dive explanations of innovation concepts and ideas are available on the Innovation Portal at **www.innovation-portal.info**

Quizzes to test yourself further are available online via the Innovation Portal at **www.innovation-portal.info**

Summary of online resources for Chapter 3 –
all material is available via the Innovation Portal at
www.innovation-portal.info

Cases	**Media**	**Tools**	**Activities**	**Deeper Dive**
• Marshalls • Zara • Tesco • Corning • Polaroid	• Tesco • 3M: Breakthrough products and services	• Competitiveness profiling • Functional mapping • Identifying capabilities	• Identifying capabilities	• Blue Ocean strategy • Business model innovation • Innovation capabilities in China

Chapter 4

Leadership and Organization of Innovation

LEARNING OBJECTIVES

After this chapter you should be able to:

- understand how the leadership and organization of innovation is much more than a set of processes, tools and techniques, and the successful practice of innovation demands the interaction and integration of three different levels of management: individual, collective and climate

- at the personal or individual level, understand how different leadership and creative styles influence the ability to identify, assess and develop new ideas and concepts

- at the collective or social level, identify how teams, groups and processes each contribute to successful innovation behaviours and outcomes

- at the context or climate level, assess how different factors can support or hinder innovation and entrepreneurship.

The Innovative Organization

There is no single universal ideal-type of leadership or organization which supports innovation. However, by studying case studies of innovative organizations and comparing these systematically with less-innovative organizations, we can begin to identify consistent patterns of good leadership and organization. Larger-scale academic research confirms that these factors tend to contribute to superior performance (Table 4.1).

TABLE 4.1   Components of the Innovative Organization

Component	Key features
Shared vision, leadership and the will to innovate	Clearly articulated and shared sense of purpose Stretching strategic intent 'Top management commitment'
Appropriate structure	Organization design which enables creativity, learning and interaction. Not always a loose 'skunk works' model; key issue is finding appropriate balance between 'organic and mechanistic' options for particular contingencies
Key individuals	Promoters, champions, gatekeepers and other roles which energize or facilitate innovation
Effective team working	Appropriate use of teams (at local, cross-functional and inter-organizational level) to solve problems Requires investment in team selection and building
High-involvement innovation	Participation in organization-wide continuous improvement activity
Creative climate	Positive approach to creative ideas, supported by relevant motivation systems
External focus	Internal and external customer orientation

Innovation Leadership

The contribution that leaders make to the performance of their organizations can be significant. Upper echelons theory argues that decisions and choices by top management have an influence on the performance of an organization (positive or negative!), through their assessment of the environment, strategic decision-making and support for innovation. The results of different studies vary, but the reviews of research on leadership and performance suggest leadership directly influences around 15% of the differences found in the performance of businesses, and contributes around an additional 35% through the choice of business strategy.[1] So directly and indirectly leadership can account for half of the variance in performance observed across organizations. At higher levels of management the problems to be solved are more likely to be ill defined, demanding leaders to conceptualize more.

Researchers have identified a long list of characteristics that could have something to do with being effective in certain situations, which typically include the following traits:[2]

- bright, alert and intelligent
- seek responsibility and take charge

- skilful in their task domain
- administratively and socially competent
- energetic, active and resilient
- good communicators.

Although these lists may describe some characteristics of some leaders in certain situations, measures of these traits yield highly inconsistent relationships with being a good leader.[3] In short, there is no brief and universal list of enduring traits that all good leaders must possess under all conditions.

Studies in different contexts identify not only the technical expertise of leadership influencing group performance but also broader cognitive ability, such as creative problem-solving and information-processing skills. For example, studies of groups facing novel, ill-defined problems confirm that both expertise and cognitive-processing skills are key components of creative leadership, and both are associated with effective performance of creative groups.[4] Moreover, this combination of expertise and cognitive capacity is critical for the evaluation of others' ideas. A study of scientists found that they most valued their leader's inputs at the early stages of a new project, when they were formulating their ideas, and defining the problems, and later at the stage where they needed feedback and insights to the implications of their work. Therefore, a key role of creative leadership in such environments is to provide feedback and evaluation, rather than to simply generate ideas.[5] This evaluative role is critical, but is typically seen as not being conducive to creativity and innovation, where the conventional advice is to suspend judgement to foster idea generation. Also, it suggests that the conventional linear view that evaluation follows idea generation may be wrong. Evaluation by creative leadership may precede idea generation and conceptual combination.

The quality and nature of the leader–member exchange (LMX) has also been found to influence the creativity of subordinates.[6] A study of 238 knowledge workers from 26 project teams in high-technology firms identified a number of positive aspects of LMX, including monitoring, clarifying and consulting, but also found that the frequency of negative LMX was as high as the positive, around a third of respondents reporting these.[7] Therefore, LMX can either enhance or undermine subordinates' sense of competence and self-determination. However, analysis of exchanges perceived to be negative and positive revealed that it was typically how something was done rather than what was done, which suggests that task and relationship behaviours in leadership support and LMX are intimately intertwined, and that negative behaviours can have a disproportionately negative influence.

Intellectual stimulation by leaders has a stronger effect on organizational performance under conditions of perceived uncertainty. Intellectual stimulation includes behaviours that increase others' awareness of and interest in problems, and develops their propensity and ability to tackle problems in new ways. It is also associated with commitment to an organization.[8] Stratified system theory (SST) focuses on the cognitive aspects of leadership, and argues that conceptual capacity is associated with superior performance in strategic decision-making where there is a need to integrate complex information and think abstractly in order to assess the environment. It also is likely to demand a combination of these problem-solving capabilities and social skills, as leaders will depend upon others to identify and implement solutions.[9]

This suggests that under conditions of environmental uncertainty the contribution of leadership is not simply, or even primarily, to inspire or build confidence, but rather to solve problems and make appropriate strategic decisions.

Rafferty and Griffin propose other sub-dimensions to the concept of transformational leadership that may have a greater influence on creativity and innovation, including articulating a vision and inspirational communication.[10] They define a vision as 'the expression of an idealized picture of the future based around organizational values', and inspirational communication as 'the expression of positive and encouraging messages about the organization, and statements that build motivation and confidence' (p. 337). They found that the expression of a vision has a negative effect on followers' confidence, unless accompanied with inspirational communication. Mission awareness increases the probability of success of R&D projects, but the effects are stronger at the earlier stages: in the planning and conceptual stage mission awareness explained two-thirds of the subsequent project success.[11] Leadership clarity is associated with clear team objectives, high levels of participation, commitment to excellence and support for innovation.[12]

The creative leader needs to do much more than simply provide a passive, supportive role, to encourage creative followers. Perceptual measures of leaders' performance suggest that in a research environment the perception of a leader's technical skill is the single best predictor of research group performance, explaining around half of innovation performance.[13] Keller found that the type of project moderates the relationships between leadership style and project success, and found that transformational leadership was a stronger predictor in research projects than in development projects.[14] This strongly suggests that certain qualities of transformational leadership may be most appropriate under conditions of high complexity, uncertainty or novelty, whereas a transactional style has a positive effect in an administrative context, but a negative effect in a research context.[15]

A review of 27 empirical studies of the relationships between leadership and innovation investigates when and how leadership influences innovation and identifies six factors leaders should focus on:[16]

- Upper management should establish an innovation policy that is promoted throughout the organization. It is necessary that the organization through its leaders communicate to employees that innovative behaviour will be rewarded.

Case Study of Nokia Networks is available on the Innovation Portal at **www.innovation-portal.info**

- When forming teams, some heterogeneity is necessary to promote innovation. However, if the team is too heterogeneous, tensions may arise; when heterogeneity is too low, more directive leadership is required to promote team reflection (e.g. by encouraging discussion and disagreement).

Video Clip interview with Fabian Schlage, innovation manager, which illustrates some of these themes is available on the Innovation Portal at **www.innovation-portal.info**

- Leaders should promote a team climate of emotional safety, respect and joy through emotional support and shared decision-making.
- Individuals and teams have autonomy and space for idea generation and creative problem-solving.

- Time limits for idea creation and problem solutions should be set, particularly in the implementation phases.
- Finally, team leaders, who have the expertise, should engage closely in the evaluation of innovative activities.

Creative Style

Traditionally, people have been assessed and selected for different tasks on the basis of such characteristics, such as using psychometric questionnaires or tests. For example, the Kirton Adaption-Innovation (KAI) scale assesses different dimensions of creativity, including originality, attention to detail and reliance on rules. The scale is a psychometric approach for assessing the creativity of individuals. By posing a series of questions, it seeks to identify an individual's attitudes towards originality, attention to detail and following rules. It seeks to differentiate 'adaptive' from 'innovative' styles:

- Adaptors characteristically produce a sufficiency of ideas based closely on existing agreed definitions of a problem and its likely solutions, but stretching the solutions. These ideas help to improve and 'do better'.
- Innovators are more likely to reconstruct the problem, challenge the assumptions and to emerge with a much less expected solution which very probably is also at first less acceptable. Innovators are less concerned with doing things better than with doing things differently.

Video Clip of Ken Robinson which highlights some of the challenges in building a creative organization is available on the Innovation Portal at **www.innovation-portal.info**

It is important to recognize that creativity is an attribute that we all possess, but the preferred style of expressing it varies widely. Recognizing the need for different kinds of individual creative styles is an important aspect of developing successful innovations and new ventures. Expertise, competence and knowledge base also contribute to creative efforts.

Activity for you to complete the questionnaire in the box, being as honest as possible, then calculate your score using the guide in the answer is available on the Innovation Portal at **www.innovation-portal.info**

Collective and Social

It takes five years to develop a new car in this country. Heck, we won World War 2 in four years...

Ross Perot's critical comment on the state of the US car industry in the late 1980s captured some of the frustration with existing ways of designing and building cars. In the years that followed significant strides were made in reducing the development cycle, with Ford and Chrysler succeeding in dramatically reducing time and improving quality. Much of the advantage was gained through extensive team working; as Lew Varaldi, project manager of Ford's Team Taurus project, put it: 'it's amazing the dedication and commitment you get from people . . . we will never go back to the old ways because we know so much about what they can bring to the party'.[17]

Experiments indicate that teams have more to offer than individuals do in terms of both fluency of idea generation and flexibility of the solutions developed. Focusing this potential on innovation tasks is the prime driver for the trend towards high levels of team working – in project teams, in cross-functional and inter-organizational problem-solving groups and in cells and work groups where the focus is on incremental, adaptive innovation.

Many use the terms 'group' and 'team' interchangeably. In general, the word 'group' refers to an assemblage of people who may just be near to each other. Groups can be a number of people that are regarded as some sort of unity or are classed together on account of any sort of similarity. For us, 'team' means a combination of individuals who come together or who have been brought together for a common purpose or goal in their organization. A team is a group that must collaborate in their professional work in some enterprise or on some assignment and share accountability or responsibility for obtaining results. There are a variety of ways to differentiate working groups from teams. One senior executive with whom we have worked described groups as individuals with nothing in common, except a zip/postal code. Teams, however, were characterized by a common vision.

Considerable work has been done on the characteristics of high-performance project teams for innovative tasks, and the main findings are that such teams rarely happen by accident.[18] They result from a combination of selection and investment in team building, allied to clear guidance on their roles and tasks, and a concentration on managing group process as well as task aspects.[19] For example, research within the Ashridge Business School developed a model for 'superteams', which includes components of building and managing the internal team, and its interfaces with the rest of the organization.[20]

Holti, Neumann and Standing provide a useful summary of the key factors involved in developing team working.[21] Although there is considerable current emphasis on team working, we should remember that teams are not always the answer. In particular, there are dangers in putting nominal teams together where unresolved conflicts, personality clashes, lack of effective group processes and other factors can diminish their effectiveness. Tranfield *et al.* look at the issue of team working in a number of different contexts and highlight the importance of selecting and building the appropriate team for the task and the context.[22]

Teams are increasingly being seen as a mechanism for bridging boundaries within the organization – and, indeed, in dealing with inter-organizational issues. Cross-functional teams can bring together the different knowledge sets needed for tasks like product development or process improvement – but they also represent a forum where often deep-rooted differences in perspectives can be resolved.[23] Successful organizations are those which invest in multiple methods for integrating across groups – and the cross-functional team is one of the most valuable resources.

Self-managed teams working within a defined area of autonomy can be very effective, for example Honeywell's defence avionics factory reports a dramatic improvement in on-time delivery – from below 40% in the 1980s to 99% in 1996 – to the implementation of self-managing teams.[24] In the Netherlands one of the most successful bus companies, Vancom Zuid-Limburg, has used self-managing teams to both reduce costs and improve customer satisfaction ratings, and one manager now supervises over 40 drivers, compared to the industry average ratio of 1:8. Drivers are also encouraged to participate in problem finding and solving in areas like maintenance, customer service and planning.[25]

Key elements in effective high-performance team working include:

* clearly defined tasks and objectives
* effective team leadership
* good balance of team roles and match to individual behavioural style
* effective conflict resolution mechanisms within the group
* continuing liaison with external organization.

Teams typically go through four stages of development, popularly known as 'forming, storming, norming and performing'.[26] That is, they are put together and then go through a phase of resolving internal differences and conflicts around leadership, objectives, etc. Emerging from this process is a commitment to shared values and norms governing the way the team will work, and it is only after this stage that teams can move on to the effective performance of their task. Common approaches to team building can support innovation, but are not sufficient.

Tools to help you with teambuilding are available on the Innovation Portal at **www.innovation-portal.info**

Central to team performance is the make-up of the team itself, with good matching between the role requirements of the group and the behavioural preferences of the individuals involved. Belbin's work has been influential here in providing an approach to team role matching. He classifies people into a number of preferred role types, for example 'the plant' (someone who is a source of new ideas), 'the resource investigator', 'the shaper' and the 'completer/finisher'. Research has shown that the most effective teams are those with diversity in background, ability and behavioural style. In one noted experiment highly talented but similar people in 'Apollo' teams consistently performed less well than mixed, average groups.[27]

With increased emphasis on cross-boundary and dispersed team activity, a series of new challenges are emerging. In the extreme case a product development team could begin work in London, pass on to their US counterparts later in the day who in turn pass on to their Far Eastern colleagues – effectively allowing a 24-hour non-stop development activity. This makes for higher productivity potential, but only if the issues around managing dispersed and virtual teams can be resolved. Similarly, the concept of sharing knowledge across boundaries depends on enabling structures and mechanisms.[28]

Many people who have attempted to use groups for problem-solving find out that using groups is not always easy, pleasurable or effective. Table 4.2 summarizes some of the positive and negative aspects of using groups for innovation.

A survey of 1207 firms aimed to identify how different organizational practices contributed to innovation performance.[29] It examined the influences of 12 common practices, including cross-functional teams, team incentives, quality circles and ISO 9000 quality standards, on successful new product development. The study found significant differences in the effects of different practices, depending upon the novelty of the development project. For instance, both quality circles and ISO 9000 were associated with the successful development of incremental new products, but both practices had a significant negative influence on the success

TABLE 4.2   Potential Assets and Liabilities of Using a Group

Potential assets of using a group	Potential liabilities of using a group
1. Greater availability of knowledge and information	1. Social pressure toward uniform thought limits contributions and increases conformity
2. More opportunities for cross-fertilization; increasing the likelihood of building and improving upon ideas of others	2. Group think: groups converge on options, which seem to have greatest agreement, regardless of quality
3. Wider range of experiences and perspectives upon which to draw	3. Dominant individuals influence and exhibit an unequal amount of impact upon outcomes
4. Participation and involvement in problem-solving increases understanding, acceptance, commitment, and ownership of outcomes	4. Individuals are less accountable in groups allowing groups to make riskier decisions
5. More opportunities for group development; increasing cohesion, communication and companionship	5. Conflicting individual biases may cause unproductive levels of competition; leading to 'winners' and 'losers'

Source: S. Isaksen and J. Tidd (2006) *Meeting the Innovation Challenge*. John Wiley & Sons, Ltd, Chichester. Reproduced by permission of John Wiley & Sons, Ltd.

Case Study of Cerulean, which illustrates how a mature, small to medium-sized company seeks to develop an organizational culture that supports radical innovation, is available on the Innovation Portal at **www.innovation-portal.info**

Video Clip of an interview with Patrick McLaughlin, at Cerulean, discussing some of these issues is available on the Innovation Portal at **www.innovation-portal.info**

of radical new products. However, the use of teams and team incentives was found to have a positive on both incremental and radical new product development. This suggests that great care needs to be taken when applying so-called universal best practices, as their effects often depend on the nature of the project.

Our own work on high-performance teams, consistent with previous research, suggests a number of characteristics that promote effective teamwork:[30]

- **A clear, common and elevating goal:** Having a clear and elevating goal means having understanding, mutual agreement and identification with respect to the primary task a group faces. Active teamwork towards common goals happens when members of a group share a common vision of the desired future state. Creative teams have clear and common goals. The goals were clear and compelling, but also open and challenging. Less creative teams have conflicting agendas, different missions and no agreement on the result. The tasks for the least creative teams were tightly constrained, considered routine and overly structured.

- **Results-driven structure:** Individuals within high-performing teams feel productive when their efforts take place with a minimum of grief. Open communication, clear coordination of tasks, clear roles and accountabilities, monitoring performance, providing feedback, fact-based judgement, efficiency and strong impartial management combine to create a results-driven structure.

- **Competent team members:** Competent teams are composed of capable and conscientious members. Members must possess essential skills and abilities, a strong desire to contribute, be capable of collaborating effectively and have a sense of responsible idealism. They must have knowledge in the domain surrounding the task (or some other domain which may be relevant) as well as with the process of working together. Creative teams recognize the diverse strengths and talents and use them accordingly.

- **Unified commitment:** Having a shared commitment relates to the way the individual members of the group respond. Effective teams have an organizational unity: members display mutual support, dedication and faithfulness to the shared purpose and vision, and a productive degree of self-sacrifice to reach organizational goals. Team members enjoy contributing and celebrating their accomplishments.

- **Collaborative climate:** Productive teamwork does not just happen. It requires a climate that supports cooperation and collaboration. This kind of situation is characterized by mutual trust, in which everyone feels comfortable discussing ideas, offering suggestions and willing to consider multiple approaches.

- **Standards of excellence:** Effective teams establish clear standards of excellence. They embrace individual commitment, motivation, self-esteem, individual performance and constant improvement. Members of teams develop a clear and explicit understanding of the norms upon which they will rely.

- **External support and recognition:** Team members need resources, rewards, recognition, popularity and social success. Being liked and admired as individuals and respected for belonging and contributing to a team is often helpful in maintaining the high level of personal energy required for sustained performance. With the increasing use of cross-functional and interdepartmental teams within larger complex organizations, teams must be able to obtain approval and encouragement.

- **Principled leadership:** Leadership is important for teamwork. Whether it is a formally appointed leader or leadership of the emergent kind, the people who exert influence and encourage the accomplishment of important things usually follow some basic principles. Leaders provide clear guidance, support and encouragement, and keep everyone working together and moving forward. Leaders also work to obtain support and resources from within and outside the group.

- **Appropriate use of the team:** Teamwork is encouraged when the tasks and situations really call for that kind of activity. Sometimes the team itself must set clear boundaries on when and why it should be deployed. One of the easiest ways to destroy a productive team is to overuse it or use it when it is not appropriate to do so.

- **Participation in decision-making:** One of the best ways to encourage teamwork is to engage the members of the team in the process of identifying the challenges and opportunities for improvement, generating ideas and transforming ideas into action. Participation in the processes of problem-solving and decision-making actually builds teamwork and improves the likelihood of acceptance and implementation.

- **Team spirit:** Effective teams know how to have a good time, release tension and relax their need for control. The focus at times is on developing friendship, engaging in tasks for mutual pleasure and recreation. This internal team climate extends beyond the need for a collaborative climate. Creative teams have the ability to work together without major conflicts in personalities. There is a high degree of respect for the contributions of others. Less creative teams are characterized by animosity, jealousy and political posturing.
- **Embracing appropriate change:** Teams often face the challenges of organizing and defining tasks. In order for teams to remain productive, they must learn how to make necessary changes to procedures. When there is a fundamental change in how the team must operate, different values and preferences may need to be accommodated.

There are also many challenges to the effective management of teams. We have all seen teams that have 'gone wrong'. As a team develops, there are certain aspects or guidelines that can be helpful to keep them on track. Hackman identifies a number of themes relevant to those who design, lead and facilitate teams. In examining a variety of organizational work groups, he found some seemingly small factors that if overlooked in the management of teams will have large implications that tend to destroy the capability of a team to function. These small and often hidden 'tripwires' to major problems include:[31]

- **Group versus team:** One of the mistakes that are often made when managing teams is to call the group a team, but to actually treat it as nothing more than a loose collection of individuals. This is similar to making it a team 'because I said so'. It is important to be very clear about the underlying goal and reward structure. People are often asked to perform tasks as a team, but then have all evaluation of performance based on an individual level. This situation sends conflicting messages, and may negatively affect team performance.
- **Ends versus means:** Managing the source of authority for groups is a delicate balance. Just how much authority can you assign to the team to work out its own issues and challenges? Those who convene teams often over-manage them by specifying the results as well as how the team should obtain them. The end, direction or outer limit constraints ought to be specified, but the means to get there ought to be within the authority and responsibility of the group.
- **Structured freedom:** It is a major mistake to assemble a group of people and merely tell them in general and unclear terms what needs to be accomplished and then let them work out their own details. At times, the belief is that if teams are to be creative they ought not to be given any structure. It turns out that most groups would find a little structure quite enabling, if it were the right kind. Teams generally need a well-defined task. They need to be composed of an appropriately small number to be manageable but large enough to be diverse. They need clear limits as to the team's authority and responsibility, and they need sufficient freedom to take initiative and make good use of their diversity. It's about striking the right kind of balance between structure, authority and boundaries – and freedom, autonomy and initiative.
- **Support structures and systems:** Often challenging team objectives are set, but the organization fails to provide adequate support in order to make the objectives a reality. In general, high-performing teams need a reward system that recognizes and reinforces excellent team performance. They also need access to good-quality and adequate information, as well as training in team-relevant tools and skills. Good team performance is also dependent

on having an adequate level of material and financial resources to get the job done. Calling a group a team does not mean that they will automatically obtain all the support needed to accomplish the task.

Case Study of Philips Lighting highlighting some of these issues is available on the Innovation Portal at **www.innovation-portal.info**

- **Assumed competence:** Technical skills, domain-relevant expertise and experience and abilities often explain why someone has been included within a group, but these are rarely the only competencies individuals need for effective team performance. Members will undoubtedly require explicit coaching on skills needed to work well in a team.

INNOVATION IN ACTION 4.1

Organizational Climate for Innovation at Google

Google appears to have learnt a few lessons from other innovative organizations, such as 3M. Technical employees are expected to spend 20% of their time on projects other than their core job, and similarly managers are required to spend 20% of their time on projects outside the core business, and 10% on completely new products and businesses. This effort devoted to new, non-core business is not evenly allocated weekly or monthly, but when possible or necessary. These are contractual obligations, reinforced by performance reviews and peer pressure, and integral to the 25 different measures of and targets for employees. Ideas progress through a formal qualification process, which includes prototyping, pilots and tests with actual users. The assessment of new ideas and projects is highly data-driven and aggressively empirical, reflecting the IT basis of the firm, and is based on rigorous experimentation within 300 employee user panels, segments of Google's 132 million users and trusted third parties. The approach is essentially evolutionary in the sense that many ideas are encouraged, most fail but some are successful, depending on the market response. The generation and market testing of many alternatives, and tolerance of (rapid) failure, are central to the process. In this way the company claims to generate around 100 new products each year, including hits such as Gmail, AdSense and Google News.

However, we need to be careful to untangle cause and effect, and determine how much of this is transferable to other companies and contexts. Google's success to date is predicated on dominating the global demand for search engine services through an unprecedented investment in technology infrastructure – estimated at over a million computers. Its business model is based upon 'ubiquity first, revenues later', and is still reliant on search-based advertising. The revenues generated in this way have allowed it to hire the best, and to provide the space and motivation to innovate. Despite this, it is estimated to have only 120 or so product offerings, and the most recent blockbusters have all been acquisitions: YouTube for video content, DoubleClick for Web advertising and Keyhole for mapping (now Google Earth). In this respect it looks more like Microsoft than 3M.

Source: Derived from Iyer, B. and T. H. Davenport (2008) Reverse engineering Google's innovation machine. *Harvard Business Review*, April, 58–68.

Context and Climate

'Climate' is defined as the recurring patterns of behaviour, attitudes and feelings that characterize life in the organization. These are the objectively shared perceptions that characterize life within a defined work unit or in the larger organization. Climate is distinct from culture in that it is more observable at a surface level within the organization and more amenable to change and improvement efforts. 'Culture' refers to the deeper and more enduring values, norms and beliefs within the organization. Climate and culture are different: traditionally, studies of organizational culture are more qualitative, whereas research on organizational climate is more quantitative, but a multidimensional approach helps to integrate the benefits of each perspective. What is needed is a common-sense set of levers for change that leaders can exert direct and deliberate influence over.

Table 4.3 summarizes some research on how climate influences innovation. Many dimensions of climate have been shown to influence innovation and entrepreneurship, but here we discuss six of the most critical factors.

Trust and Openness

The trust and openness dimension refers to the emotional safety in relationships. These relationships are considered safe when people are seen as both competent and sharing a common set of values. When there is a strong level of trust, everyone in the organization dares to put forward ideas and opinions. Initiatives can be taken without fear of reprisals and ridicule in case of failure. Communication is open and straightforward. Where trust is missing, count on high expenses for any mistakes that may result. People also are afraid of being exploited and robbed of their good ideas.

TABLE 4.3   Climate Factors Influencing Innovation

Climate factor	Most Innovative (score)	Least Innovative (score)	Difference
Trust and Openness	253	88	165
Challenge and Involvement	260	100	160
Support and Space for Innovation	218	70	148
Conflict and Debate	231	83	148
Risk-taking	210	65	145
Freedom	202	110	92

Source: Derived from S. Isaksen and J. Tidd (2006) *Meeting the Innovation Challenge.* Chichester: John Wiley & Sons, Ltd, with permission of John Wiley & Sons, Ltd.

When trust and openness are too low, you may see people hoarding resources (i.e. information, software, materials, etc.). However, trust can bind and blind. If trust and openness are too high, relationships may be so strong that time and resources at work are often spent on personal issues. It may also lead to a lack of questioning each other that, in turn, may lead to mistakes or less productive outcomes. Cliques may form where there are isolated 'pockets' of high trust. In this case it may help to develop forums for interdepartmental and intergroup exchanges of information and ideas.

Challenge and Involvement

Challenge and involvement is the degree to which people are involved in daily operations, long-term goals and visions. High levels of challenge and involvement mean that people are intrinsically motivated and committed to making contributions to the success of the organization. The climate has a dynamic, electric and inspiring quality. However, if the challenge and involvement are too high you may observe that people are showing signs of 'burn out', they are unable to meet project goals and objectives, or they spend 'too many' long hours at work.

If challenge and involvement are too low, you may see that people are apathetic about their work, are not interested in professional development or are frustrated about the future of the organization. One of the ways to improve the situation could be to get people involved in interpreting the vision, mission, purpose and goals of the organization for themselves and their work teams.

Video Clip interview with Emma Taylor of Denso Systems, which highlights some of these issues, is available on the Innovation Portal at **www.innovation-portal.info**

Support and Space for Innovation

Idea time is the amount of time people can (and do) use for exploring innovation. In the high idea-time situation, possibilities exist to discuss and test impulses and fresh suggestions that are not planned or included in the task assignment, and people tend to use these possibilities. When idea time is low, every minute is booked and specified. If there is insufficient time and space for generating new ideas, you may observe that people are only concerned with their current projects and tasks. Conversely, if there is too much time and space for new ideas you may observe that people are showing signs of boredom and that decisions are made through a slow, bureaucratic, processes.

Case Studies exploring organizations that illustrate the building and sustaining of a climate to support high involvement innovation are available on the Innovation Portal at **www.innovation-portal.info**

Tool to help you with high involvement innovation audit, which enables exploration and reflection around this issue, is available on the Innovation Portal at **www.innovation-portal.info**

Conflict and Debate

Conflict in an organization refers to the presence of personal, interpersonal or emotional tensions. Although conflict is a negative dimension, all organizations have some level of personal tension. Conflicts can occur over tasks, processes or relationships. Task conflicts focus on disagreements about the goals and content of work, the 'what?' needs to be done and 'why?' Process conflicts are around 'how?' to achieve a task, means and methods. Relationship or affective conflicts are more emotional, and are characterized by hostility and anger. In general, some task and process conflict is constructive, helping to avoid groupthink, and to consider more diverse opinions and alternative strategies. However, task and process conflicts only have a positive effect on performance in a climate of openness and collaborative communication; otherwise, it can degenerate into relationship conflict or avoidance.

Relationship conflict is generally energy-sapping and destructive, as emotional disagreements create anxiety and hostility. If the level of conflict is too high, groups and individuals dislike or hate each other and the climate can be characterized as 'warfare'. Plots and traps are common in the life of the organization. There is gossip and backbiting going on. You may observe gossiping at water coolers (including character assassination), information hoarding, open aggression or people lying or exaggerating about their real needs. In these cases, you may need to take initiative to engender cooperation among key individuals or departments.

So the goal is not necessarily to minimize conflict and maximize consensus but to maintain a level of constructive debate consistent with the need for diversity and a range of different preferences and styles of creative problem-solving. Group members with similar creative preferences and problem-solving styles are likely to be more harmonious but much less effective than those with mixed preferences and styles. So if the level of conflict is constructive, people behave in a more mature manner. They have psychological insight and exercise more control over their impulses and emotions.

Risk-taking

Tolerance of uncertainty and ambiguity constitutes risk-taking. In a high risk-taking climate, bold new initiatives can be taken even when the outcomes are unknown. People feel that they can take a gamble on some of their ideas. People will often go out on a limb and be first to put an idea forward. In a risk-avoiding climate there is a cautious, hesitant mentality. People try to be on the safe side. They set up committees and cover themselves in many ways before making a decision. If risk-taking is too low, employees offer few new ideas or few ideas that are well outside of what is considered safe or ordinary. In risk-avoiding organizations people complain about boring, low-energy jobs and are frustrated by the long, tedious process used to get ideas to action.

Freedom

Freedom is described as the independence in behaviour exerted by the people in the organization. In a climate with much freedom, people are given autonomy to define much of their own work. They are able to exercise discretion in their day-to-day activities. They take the initiative to acquire and share information and to make plans and decisions about their work. If there is not enough freedom, people demonstrate very little initiative for suggesting new and better ways of doing things. They may spend a great deal of time and energy obtaining permission and gaining support or perform all their work by the book. If there is too much freedom, people may pursue their own independent directions and have an unbalanced concern weighted towards themselves rather than the work group or organization.

INNOVATION IN ACTION 4.2

Increasing Challenge and Involvement in an Electrical Engineering Division

The organization was a division of a large, global electrical power and product supply company headquartered in France. The division was located in the South East of the USA and had 92 employees. Its focus was to help clients automate their processes particularly within the automotive, pharmaceutical, microelectronics and food and beverage industries. For example, this division would make the robots that put cars together in the automotive industry or provide public filtration systems.

When this division was merged with the parent company, it was losing about $8 million a year. A new general manager was brought in to turn the division around and make it profitable quickly.

An assessment of the organization's climate identified that it was strongest on the debate dimension but was very close to the stagnated norms when it came to challenge and involvement, playfulness and humour, and conflict. The quantitative and qualitative assessment results were consistent with their own impressions that the division could be characterized as conflict driven, uncommitted to producing results, and people were generally despondent. The leadership decided, after some debate, that they should target challenge and involvement, which was consistent with their strategic emphasis on a global initiative on employee commitment. It was clear to them that they also needed to soften the climate and drive a warmer, more embracing, communicative and exuberant climate.

The management team re-established training and development and encouraged employees to engage in both personal and business-related skills development. They also provided mandatory safety training for all employees. They committed to increase communication by holding monthly all-employee meetings, sharing quarterly reviews on performance, and using cross-functional strategy review sessions. They implemented mandatory 'skip level' meetings to allow more direct interaction between senior managers and all levels of employees. The general manager held 15-minute meetings will all employees at least once a year. All employee suggestions and recommendations were invited and feedback and recognition was required to be immediate. A new monthly recognition and rewards program was launched across the division for both managers and employees that was based on peer nomination. The management team formed employee review teams to challenge and craft the statements in the hopes of encouraging more ownership and involvement in the overall strategic direction of the business.

In 18 months the division showed a $7 million turnaround, and in 2003 won a worldwide innovation award. The general manager was promoted to a national position.

Source: S. Isaksen and J. Tidd (2006) *Meeting the Innovation Challenge*. Chichester: John Wiley & Sons, Ltd. Reproduced by permission of John Wiley & Sons, Ltd.

Summary

- Leadership and organization of innovation are much more than a set of processes, tools and techniques, and the successful practice of innovation demands the interaction and integration of three different levels of management: individual, collective and climate.

- At the personal or individual level, the key is to match the leadership styles with the task requirement and type of teams. General leadership requirements for innovative projects include expertise and experience relevant to the project, articulating a vision and inspirational communication, intellectual stimulation and quality of leader–member exchange (LMX).

- At the collective or social level, there is no universal best practice but successful teams require clear, common and elevating goals, unified commitment, cross-functional expertise, collaborative climate, external support and recognition, and participation in decision-making.

- At the context or climate level, there is no 'best innovation culture', but innovation is promoted or hindered by a number of factors, including Trust and Openness, Challenge and Involvement, Support and Space for Ideas, Conflict and Debate, Risk-taking and Freedom.

Further Resources

We address the relationships between leadership, innovation and organizational renewal more fully in our book *Meeting the Innovation Challenge: Leadership for transformation and growth*, by Scott Isaksen and Joe Tidd (John Wiley & Sons, Ltd, 2006).

Many books and articles look at specific aspects, for example the development of creative climates, Lynda Gratton, *Hot Spots: Why some companies buzz with energy and innovation, and others don't* (Prentice Hall, 2007); team working by T. DeMarco and T. Lister, *Peopleware: Productive projects and teams* (Dorset House, 1999); or R. Katz, *The Human Side of Managing Technological Innovation* (Oxford University Press, 2003) is an excellent collection of readings, and A. H. Van de Ven, D. Polley, H. L. Angle and M. S. Poole, *The Innovation Journey* (Oxford University Press, 2008) provides a comprehensive review of a seminal study in the field, and includes a discussion of individual, group and organizational issues. John Bessant's *High Involvement Innovation* (John Wiley & Sons, Ltd, 2003) looks in detail at employee involvement and how to enable participation in innovation.

Case studies of innovative organizations focus on many of the issues highlighted in this chapter, and good examples include E. Gundling, *The 3M Way to Innovation: Balancing people and profit* (Kodansha International, 2000) and *Corning and the Craft of Innovation* by M. Graham and A. T. Shuldiner (Oxford University Press, 2001).

References

1. Bowman, E. H. and C. E. Helfat (2001) Does corporate strategy matter? *Strategic Management Journal*, **22**: 1–23.

2. Clark, K. E. and M. B. Clark (1990) *Measures of Leadership*, Greensboro, NC: The Center for Creative Leadership; Clark, K. E., M. B. Clark and D. P. Campbell (1992) *Impact of Leadership*, Greensboro, NC: The Center for Creative Leadership.

3. Mann, R. D. (1959) A review of the relationships between personality and performance in small groups, *Psychological Bulletin*, **56**: 241–270.

4. Connelly, M. S., J. A. Gilbert, S. J. Zaccaro *et al.* (2000) Exploring the relationship of leader skills and knowledge to leader performance, *The Leadership Quarterly*, **11**: 65–86; Zaccaro, S. J., J. A. Gilbert, K. K. Thor and M. D. Mumford (2000) Assessment of leadership problem-solving capabilities, *The Leadership Quarterly*, **11**: 37–64.

5. Farris, G. F. (1972) The effect of individual role on performance in creative groups, *R&D Management*, **3**: 23–8; Ehrhart, M. G. and K. J. Klein (2001) Predicting followers' preferences for charismatic leadership: The influence of follower values and personality, *The Leadership Quarterly*, **12**: 153–180.

6. Scott, S. G. and R. A. Bruce (1994) Determinants of innovative behavior: A path model of individual innovation in the workplace, *Academy of Management Journal*, **37** (3): 580–607.

7. Amabile, T. M., E. A. Schatzel, G. B. Moneta and S. J. Kramer (2004) Leader behaviors and the work environment for creativity: Perceived leader support, *The Leadership Quarterly*, **15** (1): 5–32.

8. Pinto, J. and D. Slevin (1989) Critical success factors in R&D projects, *Research-Technology Management*, **32**: 12–18.

9. Mumford, M. D., S. J. Zaccaro, F. D. Harding *et al.* (2000) Leadership skills for a changing world: Solving complex social problems, *The Leadership Quarterly*, **11**: 11–35.

10. Rafferty, A. E. and M. A. Griffin (2004) Dimensions of transformational leadership: Conceptual and empirical extensions, *The Leadership Quarterly*, **15** (3): 329–354.

11. Podsakoff, P. M., S. B. Mackenzie, J. B. Paine and D. G. Bachrach (2000) Organizational citizenship behaviors: A critical review of the theoretical and empirical literature and suggestions for future research, *Journal of Management*, **26** (3): 513–563.

12. West, M.A., C. S. Borrill, J. F. Dawson *et al.* (2003) Leadership clarity and team innovation in health care, *The Leadership Quarterly*, **14** (4–5): 393–410.

13. Andrews, F. M. and G. F. Farris (1967) Supervisory practices and innovation in scientific teams, *Personnel Psychology*, **20**: 497–515; Barnowe, J. T. (1975) Leadership performance outcomes in research organizations, *Organizational Behavior and Human Performance*, **14**: 264–280; Elkins, T. and R. T. Keller (2003) Leadership in research and development organizations: A literature review and conceptual framework, *The Leadership Quarterly*, **14**: 587–606.

14. Keller, R. T. (1992) Transformational leadership and performance of research and development project groups, *Journal of Management*, **18**: 489–501.

15. Berson, Y. and J. D. Linton (2005) An examination of the relationships between leadership style, quality, and employee satisfaction in R&D versus administrative environments, *R&D Management*, **35** (1): 51–60.

16. Denti, L. and S. Hemlin (2012) Leadership and innovation in organizations: A systematic review of factors that mediate or moderate the relationship, *International Journal of Innovation Management*, **16** (3).

17. Peters, T. (1988) *Thriving on Chaos*. New York: Free Press.

18. Forrester, R. and A. Drexler (1999) A model for team-based organization performance, *Academy of Management Executive*, **13** (3): 36–49; Conway, S. and R. Forrester (1999) *Innovation and Teamworking: Combining perspectives through a focus on team boundaries*, Birmingham: University of Aston Business School.

19. Thamhain, H. and D. Wilemon (1987) Building high performing engineering project teams, *IEEE Transactions on Engineering Management*, **34** (3): 130–137.

20. Bixby, K. (1987) *Superteams*. London: Fontana.

21. Holti, R., J. Neumann and H. Standing (1995) *Change Everything at Once: The Tavistock Institute's guide to developing teamwork in manufacturing*. London: Management Books 2000.

22. Tranfield, D., I. Parry, S. Wilson, S. Smith and M. Foster (1998) Teamworked organisational engineering: Getting the most out of teamworking, *Management Decision*, **36** (6): 378–384.

23. Jassawalla, A. and H. Sashittal (1999) Building collaborative cross-functional new product teams, *Academy of Management Executive*, **13** (3): 50–53.

24. DTI (1996) *UK Software Purchasing Survey*. London: Department of Trade and Industry.

25. Van Beusekom, M. (1996) *Participation Pays! Cases of successful companies with employee participation*. The Hague: Netherlands Participation Institute.

26. Tuckman, B. and N. Jensen (1977) Stages of small group development revisited, *Group and Organizational Studies*, **2**: 419–427.

27. Belbin, M. (2004) *Management Teams: Why they succeed or fail*. London: Butterworth-Heinemann.

28. Smith, P. and E. Blanck (2002) From experience: Leading dispersed teams, *Journal of Product Innovation Management*, **19**: 294–304.

29. Prester, J. and M. G. Bozac (2012) Are innovative organizational concepts enough for fostering innovation? *International Journal of Innovation Management*, **16** (1): 1–23.

30. Isaksen, S. and J. Tidd (2006) *Meeting the Innovation Challenge: Leadership for transformation and growth*. Chichester: John Wiley & Sons, Ltd.

31. Hackman J. R. (ed.) (1990). *Groups That Work (And Those That Don't): Creating conditions for effective teamwork*. San Francisco: Jossey-Bass.

Deeper Dive explanations of innovation concepts and ideas are available on the Innovation Portal at **www.innovation-portal.info**

Quizzes to test yourself further are available online via the Innovation Portal at **www.innovation-portal.info**

Summary of online resources for Chapter 4 –
all material is available via the Innovation Portal at
www.innovation-portal.info

Cases	**Media**	**Tools**	**Activities**	**Deeper Dive**

Cases
- Nokia Networks
- Cerulean
- Philips Lighting
- Kumba Resources
- Working innovation – involving employees
- Forte's Bakery
- Hosiden Besson

Media
- Fabian Schlage, Nokia Siemens Networks
- Patrick McLaughlin, Cerulean
- Ken Robinson
- Emma Taylor, Denso Systems

Tools
- Teambuilding
- High involvement innovation audit
- Creativity toolkit

Activities
- How creative are you? Creativity questionnaire

Deeper Dive
- Creating innovation energy
- Leadership for innovation
- Creative problem-solving styles
- Team diversity
- Team-member roles

Chapter 5

Innovation as a Process

LEARNING OBJECTIVES

By the end of this chapter you will develop an understanding of:

* innovation as a process rather than a single flash of inspiration
* the difficulties in managing what is an uncertain and risky process
* the key themes in thinking about how to manage this process effectively.

Beyond Spengler

If someone asked you 'When did you last use your Spengler?' they may well be greeted by a quizzical look. But if they asked you when you last used your 'Hoover' – the answer would be fairly easy. Yet it was not Mr Hoover who invented the vacuum cleaner in the late nineteenth century but one J. Murray Spengler. Hoover's genius lay in taking that idea and making it into a commercial reality. In similar vein the father of the modern sewing machine was not Mr Singer, whose name jumps to mind and is emblazoned on millions of machines all round the world, who invented the machine but Elias Howe, in 1846. Singer brought it to technical and commercial fruition.

Perhaps the godfather of them all in terms of turning ideas into reality was Thomas Edison, who during his life registered over 1000 patents. Products for which his organization was responsible include the electric telegraph, light bulb, 35mm cinema film and even the electric chair. Many of the inventions for which he is famous weren't in fact invented by him – the electric light bulb, for example – but were developed and polished technically and their markets opened up by Edison and his team. More than anyone else Edison understood

Case Study of Nokia Siemens Networks giving a flavour of innovation as a journey is available on the Innovation Portal at **www.innovation-portal.info**

Video Clip interview with Fabian Schlage, innovation manager, which illustrates some of these themes is available on the Innovation Portal at **www.innovation-portal.info**

that invention is not enough – simply having a good idea is not going to lead to its widespread adoption and use.

Innovation is not like the cartoon image in which a light bulb flashes on above someone's head. That may well be an important staring point but there is a lot more to it if we are to create value from innovation.

One useful way of looking at the challenge is to see innovation as a journey, travelling from a beginning to an end through landscapes of different kinds, with different people getting on and off the train. If we take this view (of course, only one of many) then we can give names to some of the stations on the way: initial stimulus, concept development, convincing others, securing resources, development and implementation, managing wider diffusion, etc.

It's the same journey whether we are talking about a start-up entrepreneur or an established organization running a regular series of projects. The station names may be written in a different language, but the underlying challenge is the same. In order to create value from our initial idea we have to manage a *process* and not an event.

The importance of seeing innovation as a process is that we need to manage it – it won't just happen. And if we understand the nature of the process – the different landscape, the different stations on the way and what we may need to travel well – then we can be better

Activity to explore the idea of innovation as a journey and the key stages involved – mapping the innovation process – is available on the Innovation Portal at **www.innovation-portal.info**

prepared to make the journey and arrive successfully at our value-creating destination. That's the essence of this book – trying to provide a map of the journey and bring to offer a traveller's guide to making it successfully. It isn't just our ideas: the guidebook is the product of a great deal of learning from the hard-won experience of others who have, successfully or otherwise, made the journey!

A Map of the Process

So let's look at the map in a little more detail (Figure 5.1). The main stages are simple: find an idea to trigger the process, develop it and implement it. In terms of what we will need to do as innovation managers and entrepreneurs, this means we need to focus our attention on some key 'stations':

* searching for trigger ideas
* selecting from the possibilities the one we are going to follow through
* acquiring the resources to make it happen

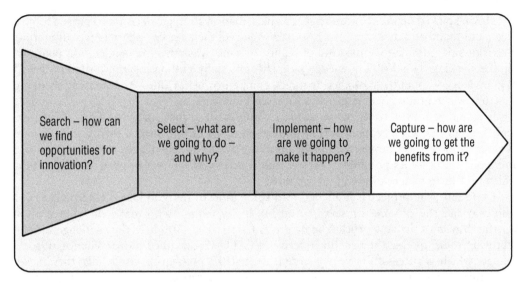

FIGURE 5.1 A model of the innovation process

- developing the idea from initial 'gleam in the eye' to a fully developed reality
- managing its diffusion and take-up in our chosen market
- capturing value from the process.

Each of these stages poses different challenges.

For example, at the search stage we need to recognize that innovation triggers come in all shapes and sizes and from all sorts of directions. They could take the form of new technological opportunities, or changing requirements on the part of markets; they could be the result of legislative pressure or competitor action. They could be a bright idea occurring to someone as they sit in their bathtub. Or they could come as a result of buying in a good idea from someone outside the organization. And they could arise out of dissatisfaction with social conditions or a desire to make the world a better place in some way.

The message here is clear: if we are going to pick up these trigger signals then we need to develop some pretty extensive antennae for searching and scanning around us – and that includes some capability for looking into the future.

But we can't do everything – and so the next stage is very much about *strategic* choices. Does the idea fit a business strategy, does it build on something we know about (or where we can get access to that knowledge easily) and do we have the skills and resources to take it forward?

The trouble with innovation is that it is by its nature a risky business. You don't know at the outset whether what you decide to do is going to work out or even that it will run at all. Yet you have to commit some resources to begin the process – so how do you build a portfolio of projects which balances the risks and the potential rewards?

Having picked up the relevant trigger signals, made a strategic decision to pursue some of them, and found and mobilized the resources we need, the next key phase is actually turning those potential ideas into some kind of reality. In some ways this implementation phase is a bit like weaving a kind of 'knowledge tapestry', gradually pulling together different threads of knowledge – about technologies, markets, competitor behaviour – and weaving them into a picture which gradually emerges as a successful innovation.

It would be foolish to throw good money after bad, so most organizations make use of some kind of risk management as they implement innovation projects. By installing a series of gates as the project moves from a gleam in the eye to an expensive commitment of time and money, it becomes possible to review, and if necessary redirect or even stop, something which may be in danger of going off the rails.

Eventually, the project is launched into some kind of marketplace – externally people who may use the product or service and internally people who make the choice about whether buy in to the new process being presented to them. And here the challenge shifts to capturing value: getting the benefits in terms of financial reward or the satisfaction of social change, which is successfully implemented. Even if the innovation itself fails, there is still the chance to capture some value from the experience in terms of learning about how to do better next time.

In practice this plays out in different ways – but it's the same underlying process. It describes the ways in which an organization renews what it offers the world and the ways it creates and delivers that offering.

- For a start-up entrepreneur the 'search' stage is often called 'opportunity recognition' – but once they have spotted something they think they can exploit the challenge is of making it happen. They have to acquire resources making various pitches to get backing and buy-in. Then they have to develop the venture and finally launch it into their chosen marketplace and capture the rewards and the learning to allow them to do it again.

- For a new product development team in a company it is about searching for ideas (maybe in the R&D lab, maybe via customer survey or maybe some combination of both). Then they have to secure internal resources – pitching for backing against other competing projects from different teams. Then they manage the development process, bringing the product through various stages of prototyping and simultaneously developing the market and launch plans. Finally, launch and, hopefully, widespread adoption – and capturing the gains in commercial terms but also in terms of what has been learnt for next time.

- For a public service team in a hospital the search may be for more efficient ways of delivering the service under resource constraints. Once again, an individual or team has to convince others and secure resources and the permission to explore. They have to develop it and then diffuse it as a new method to an internal market of people in the service who will adopt the new way. And, once again, they capture value, in terms of efficiency improvement but also in terms of learning.

- For the social entrepreneur it is about finding a trigger need, then developing and sharing a vision around how to meet that need better. Securing support and buy-in is followed by development, implementation and, hopefully, widespread adoption – and the value is captured in social improvements as well as in learning.

Hidden Innovation

In 2006, the UK organization NESTA published a report on 'The Innovation Gap' in the United Kingdom, and laid particular emphasis on 'hidden innovation' – innovation activities that are not reflected in traditional indicators such as investments in formal R&D or patents awarded. In research focusing on six widely different sectors which were not perceived to be innovative, the report argued that innovation of this kind was increasingly important, especially in services, and a subsequent study looked in detail at six 'hidden innovation' sectors: oil production, retail banking, construction, legal aid services, education and the rehabilitation of offenders. The study identified four types of hidden innovation:

- **Type I:** Innovation that is identical or similar to activities that are measured by traditional indicators, but which is excluded from measurement (e.g. the development of new technologies in oil exploration).
- **Type II:** Innovation without a major scientific and technological basis, such as innovation in organizational forms or business models (e.g. the development of new contractual relationships between suppliers and clients on major construction projects).
- **Type III:** Innovation created from the novel combination of existing technologies and processes (e.g. the way in which banks have integrated their various back-office IT systems to deliver innovative customer services such as Internet banking).
- **Type IV:** Locally developed, small-scale innovations that take place under the radar, not only of traditional indicators but often also of many of the organizations and individuals working in a sector (e.g. the everyday innovation that occurs in classrooms and multidisciplinary construction teams).

Source: Derived from National Endowment for Science, Technology and the Arts (NESTA), 2006, *The Innovation Gap* and 2007, *Hidden Innovation*, www.nesta.org

Influencing the Process

It's all very well putting a basic process for turning ideas into reality in place. But it doesn't take place in a vacuum; it is subject to a range of internal and external influences which shape what is possible and what actually emerges. In particular, innovation needs:

- Clear strategic leadership and direction, plus the commitment of resources to make this happen. Innovation is about taking risks, about going into new and sometimes completely unexplored spaces. We don't want to gamble – simply changing things for their own sake or because the fancy takes us. No organization has resources to waste in that scattergun fashion: innovation needs a strategy. But, equally, we need to have a degree of courage and leadership, steering the organization away from what everyone else is doing or what we've always done towards new spaces.

In the case of the individual entrepreneur this challenge translates to one in which a clear personal vision can be shared in ways which engage and motivate others to buy in to it and to contribute their time, energy, money, etc. to help make it happen. Without a compelling vision, it is unlikely that the venture will get off the ground.

● An innovative organization in which the structure and climate enable people to deploy their creativity and share their knowledge to bring about change. It's easy to find prescriptions for innovative organizations which highlight the need to eliminate stifling bureaucracy, unhelpful structures, brick walls blocking communication and other factors stopping good ideas getting through. But we must be careful not to fall into the chaos trap – not all innovation works in organic, loose, informal environments or 'skunk works' – and these types of organization can sometimes act against the interests of successful innovation. We need to determine appropriate organization (i.e. the most suitable organization given the operating contingencies). Too little order and structure may be as bad as too much.

This is one area where start-ups often have a major advantage – by definition they are small organizations (often one-person ventures) with a high degree of communication and cohesion. They are bound together by a shared vision and they have high levels of cooperation and trust, giving them enormous flexibility. But the downside of being small is a lack of resources – and so successful start-ups are very often those which can build a network around them through which they can tap into the key resources that they need. Building and managing such networks is a key factor in creating an extended form of organization.

● Proactive links across boundaries inside the organization and to the many external agencies that can play a part in the innovation process – suppliers, customers, sources of finance, skilled resources and of knowledge, etc. These days it's about a global game and one where connections and the ability to find, form and deploy creative relationships is of the essence. Once again, this idea of successful lone entrepreneurs and small-scale start-ups as network builders is critical. It's not necessary to know or have everything to hand, as long as you know where and how to get it.

Figure 5.2 shows the resulting model – what we need to pay attention to if we are going to manage innovation well.

Managing the Process

If we are serious about managing innovation then we should try to ask ourselves questions aimed at improving the way the process operates. For example:

● Do we search as well as we could?
● How well do we manage the selection and resource acquisition process?
● How well do we implement?

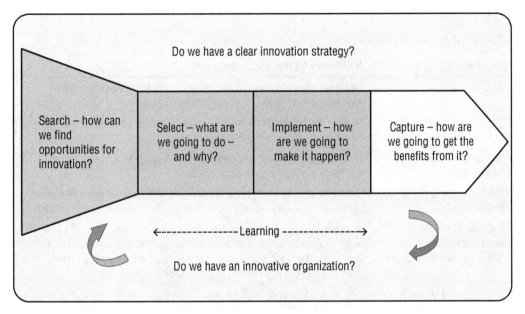

Do we have a clear innovation strategy?

Search – how can we find opportunities for innovation?

Select – what are we going to do – and why?

Implement – how are we going to make it happen?

Capture – how are we going to get the benefits from it?

←-------------- Learning --------------→

Do we have an innovative organization?

FIGURE 5.2   What we need to pay attention to if we are going to manage innovation well

- Do we capture value? Improve our technical and market knowledge for next time? Generate and protect the gains so they are sustainable?
- Do we learn from experience? How do we capture this learning and feed it back into the next time?

Of course, the reality of the journey is never as simple as this map. It's a messy process of stops and starts, dead ends and blocked roads, diversions and hold-ups. And on many occasions we may need to abandon the journey, dust ourselves off and start again in a different direction. But a wide range of studies suggest that there is an underlying journey (= process) and there are consistent lessons about the kinds of thing we can do to improve the ways we make it.

Activity of a basic 'Innovation Fitness Test' which allows you to reflect on some of the key questions about managing this process is available on the Innovation Portal at **www.innovation-portal.info**

Variations on a Theme

It all looks very simple – but the reality is that we have to deal with a complex and uncertain set of events. We can use a process model as a helpful framework but we need to keep reminding ourselves that it is only a model; the reality is much less clear-cut. It's going to vary, for example, by the sector we are working in, the size of our enterprise, the stage in the industry lifecycle and so on. Table 5.1 gives some examples and Table 5.2 looks at the particular case of smaller enterprises in a little more detail.

TABLE 5.1   How Context Affects Innovation Management

Context variable	Modifiers to the basic process
Sector	Different sectors have different priorities and characteristics, e.g. scale-intensive, science-intensive
Size	Small firms differ in terms of access to resources, etc. and so need to develop more linkages
National systems of innovation	Different countries have more or less supportive contexts in terms of institutions, policies, etc.
Lifecycle (of technology, industry, etc.)	Different stages in lifecycle emphasize different aspects of innovation, e.g. new technology industries vs. mature, established firms
Degree of novelty – continuous vs. discontinuous innovation	'More of the same' improvement innovation requires different approaches to organization and management to more radical forms. At the limit firms may deploy 'dual structures' or even split or spin off in order to exploit opportunities
Role played by external agencies such as regulators	Some sectors (e.g. utilities, telecommunications and some public services) are heavily influenced by external regimes which shape the rate and direction of innovative activity. Others (e.g. food or health care) may be highly regulated in certain directions

INNOVATION IN ACTION 5.2

Public Sector Innovation

Minilab is a Danish organization set up to promote and enable public sector innovation in Denmark. 'Owned' by the Ministries of Taxation, Employment and Economic Affairs, it has pioneered a series of initiatives engaging civil servants and members of the public in a wide range of social innovation which have raised productivity, improved service quality and cut costs across the public sector. Case studies of their activities can be found at their website: www.mind-lab.dk/en.

In the United Kingdom, a number of public sector innovation initiatives have resulted in some impressive performance improvements. For example, in the Serious Fraud Office an innovation programme led to reductions of nearly 50% in the time taken to process cases and a direct financial saving of nearly £20 000 per case. In the area of product innovation an initiative called Design Out Crime led to the development of two prototype beer glasses that feature new high-tech ways of using glass, so that they feel the same as conventional glasses but do not break into loose dangerous shards which can be used as weapons to inflict serious injuries.

These and other examples can be found on the Innovation website of the Department of Business, Innovation and Skills (http://www.bis.gov.uk/policies/public-sector-innovation).

TABLE 5.2   Advantages and Disadvantages for Small Firm Innovators

Advantages	Disadvantages
Speed of decision-making	Lack of formal systems for management control, e.g. of project times and costs
Informal culture	Lack of access to key resources, especially finance
High-quality communications – everyone knows what is going on	Lack of key skills and experience
Shared and clear vision	Lack of long-term strategy and direction
Flexibility, agility	Lack of structure and succession planning
Entrepreneurial spirit and risk-taking	Poor risk management
Energy, enthusiasm, passion for innovation	Lack of application to detail, lack of systems
Good at networking internally and externally	Lack of access to resources

Our thinking has also changed over time, for example in the early days of innovation studies the underlying models were pretty simplistic. Innovation happened in a strict linear fashion driven by technological research (knowledge push) or pulled through in response to user demand (need pull). Gradually, we developed a more sophisticated understanding and our present view sees the challenge as being global in terms of the players involved, powerfully shaped by new information and communications technologies and very much about building and working in networks. Table 5.3 presents this

Activity to help you explore different sector patterns of innovation is available on the Innovation Portal at **www.innovation-portal.info**

TABLE 5.3   Rothwell's Five Generations of Innovation Models

Generation	Key features
First/second	Simple linear models – need pull, technology push
Third	Coupling model, recognizing interaction between different elements and feedback loops between them
Fourth	Parallel model, integration within the company, upstream with key suppliers and downstream with demanding and active customers, emphasis on linkages and alliances
Fifth	Systems integration and extensive networking, flexible and customized response, continuous innovation

Source: Rothwell, R., Successful industrial innovation: Critical success factors for the 1990s. *R&D Management*, 1992. 22(3): p. 221-239. Reproduced by permission of John Wiley & Sons, Ltd.

evolution in our thinking about innovation models, based on the work of Roy Rothwell, a pioneering innovation researcher.[1]

As we'll see in later chapters the game is becoming more complex and our models in practice need to reflect this, opening it up to a wide range of stakeholders (users, employees, other organizations) with whom there is interaction on a continuing basis.

Learning to Manage Innovation

It's useful to have a model of the innovation process, but progress along the journey isn't automatic: it involves doing things to make it happen. But which things? There's a lot which can go wrong and plenty of obstacles and unexpected events which can stop us in our tracks. These range from obvious mistakes like not having any kind of plan or having no understanding of the market we are trying to enter right through to problems which arise because of unexpected technical difficulties or shifts in the external environment.

Dealing with these isn't simple; it's a skill which we learn over time. The first time we make the journey will probably involve a lot of mistakes and crises – and we may not even succeed. But repeating the journey gives us the chance to try something else, and gradually we build up a set of behaviours – ways of handling the different stages in the process – which seem to work. It's a learning process but one which builds our innovation management capability.

There are plenty of opportunities for learning – different types of projects teach us different things, for example by working with different technologies or markets. We can learn from and with others as we build networks and partnerships. We can learn through imitating others, watching how they deal with some of the challenges of the process and borrowing and adapting their ideas. And we can learn a great deal from failure – if we take the time to reflect on what went wrong and how we could do things differently next time.

An important idea in innovation management is the concept of what are called 'behavioural routines'. Put simply, they are patterns of behaviour which we learn in order to make something happen. Examples would be how we search for innovation opportunities, how we select, how we implement, and so on. There isn't a right way of doing these; it's a matter of learning what works for us.

Over time the patterns of behaviour (routines) which work get reinforced and we practise and rehearse them.[2] They gradually become embedded in 'the way we do things around here' – and we start putting structures and policies in place to help make sure they keep happening and that we can communicate them to others. The bundle of routines which define how we approach the challenge of innovation is our 'innovation management capability'.

Activity to help you explore the idea of routines and innovation management capability, 'The Way We Do Things Around Here', is available on the Innovation Portal at **www.innovation-portal.info**

No two organizations do things the same way. They each evolve their own specific routines. And this gives rise to a kind of 'personality' where we can see distinctive ways in which organizations approach some of the innovation management challenges. Examples include the 3M company (famous for its 15% rule and for fostering a climate of internal entrepreneurship), Toyota (with its strong emphasis on routines for engaging employees in kaizen – continuous incremental innovation) and Pixar (with its routines around enabling creative interchange and challenge right across the organization).

Case Studies detailing organizations – for example 3M, Marshalls, Corning – in which you can see the emergence of such routines shaping their 'personality' over time are available on the Innovation Portal at **www.innovation-portal.info**

There are plenty of opportunities to learn from the approaches other organizations take. This forms the basis of powerful tools like benchmarking, which enable such learning. But we also need to remember that while these routines may give us a useful template for approaching a challenge in innovation management we still have to learn and embed it for ourselves. This takes time, in configuring the behaviour and in practising and rehearsing it until it becomes part of our own 'way we do things around here'.

The Problem of Partial Models

One of the problems we have in managing anything is that how we think about it shapes what we do about it. So if we have a simplistic model of how innovation works, for example that it's just about invention, then that's what we will organize and manage. We could end up with the best invention department in the world, but there is no guarantee that people would ever actually want any of our wonderful inventions. If we are serious about managing innovation, then we need to check on our mental models and make sure we're working with as complete a picture as possible. Otherwise, we run risks like those in Table 5.4.

Managing innovation is partly about learning to do individual things well through developing appropriate routines. But it's also about learning to link those different things together, to take an overall approach where the whole is greater than the sum of its parts. It's less about being a great solo musician than about conducting an entire orchestra, or to take another metaphor from innovation researchers Keith Goffin and Rick Mitchell, it's like an athlete training for a multiple event like the pentathlon, developing capabilities across a range of challenges.[3]

Dynamic Capability

So far, we have looked at the process and the different stages which have to be managed. And we've looked at the idea of learning to manage this process through developing behaviours which eventually become routines. This is fine: we are building innovation management capability. But there is one more important piece of the puzzle. As we saw in Chapter 1, the problem of innovation is that it involves a moving target: there are always new technologies, new markets, new regulatory conditions, new kinds of competitor behaviour. So we need to make sure that we have a capability which is itself able to change. We call this 'dynamic

TABLE 5.4 The Problem with Partial Models

If innovation is only seen as. . .	. . . the result can be
Strong R&D capability	Technology which fails to meet user needs and may not be accepted – 'the better mousetrap which nobody wants'
The province of specialists in white coats in the R&D laboratory	Lack of involvement of others, and a lack of key knowledge and experience input from other perspectives
Meeting customer needs	Lack of technical progression, leading to inability to gain competitive edge
Technology advances	Producing products which the market does not want or designing processes which do not meet the needs of the user and which are opposed
The province only of large firms	Weak small firms with too high a dependence on large customers
Only about 'breakthrough' changes	Neglect of the potential of incremental innovation. Also an inability to secure and reinforce the gains from radical change because the incremental performance ratchet is not working well
Only associated with key individuals	Failure to utilize the creativity of the remainder of employees, and to secure their inputs and perspectives to improve innovation
Only internally generated	The 'not invented here' effect, where good ideas from outside are resisted or rejected
Only externally generated	Innovation becomes simply a matter of filling a shopping list of needs from outside and there is little internal learning or development of technological competence

capability' – the ability to step back and review the ways we manage innovation, and then adapt or change them.[4]

To take a simple example, the Internet as an interactive space across which an increasing amount of innovation takes place simply wasn't around fifteen years ago. Instead, we had a primitive system reaching relatively few people and largely one-way in the flow of information. But during the intervening years organizations have had to learn a whole new set of tricks to explore the opportunities – and deal with the threats. The failure of businesses like Encyclopædia Britannica to work with the new innovation tools eventually led to its displacement by rivals like Wikipedia with a completely different set of routines linked to co-creation by a wide community of

Case Studies of the changing music industry and Philips Lighting that illustrate the ways in which companies adapt and change their routines – and the problems that arise if they don't – are available on the Innovation Portal at **www.innovation-portal.info**

users. Similarly the music industry's attempts to hold on to old innovation approaches opened up the space for newcomers to reinvent the industry by mobilizing networks of innovation and creating new services with these new approaches.

Key questions in dynamic capability are:

Of the ways we do things round here (our routines) for innovation:

- Which should we do more of?
- Which should we do less of, or even stop?
- Which new things do we need to learn to do to add to our repertoire?

Summary

- Innovation doesn't happen simply because we hope it will. It's a complex process which carries risks and needs careful and systematic *management*. Innovation isn't a single event, like the light bulb going off above a cartoon character's head. It's an extended process of picking up on ideas for change and turning them into effective reality. At its heart it involves stages of searching, selecting, implementing and capturing value. The challenge comes in doing this in an organized fashion and in being able to repeat the trick.

- This core process doesn't take place in a vacuum. We know it is strongly influenced by many factors. In particular, innovation needs:
  - Clear strategic leadership and direction, plus the commitment of resources to make this happen.
  - An innovative organization in which the structure and climate enable people to deploy their creativity and share their knowledge to bring about change.
  - Proactive links across boundaries inside the organization and to the many external agencies who can play a part in the innovation process – suppliers, customers, sources of finance, skilled resources and of knowledge, etc.

- Any organization can get lucky once, but the real skill in innovation management is being able to repeat the trick. So if we want to manage innovation we ought to ask ourselves the following check questions:
  - Do we have effective enabling mechanisms for the core process?
  - Do we have strategic direction and commitment for innovation?
  - Do we have an innovative organization?
  - Do we build rich, proactive links?
  - Do we learn and develop our innovation capability?

- Learning to do this (building innovation management capability) involves finding behaviour patterns which work and then reinforcing and practising them until they become 'routines' (the way we do things around here). They become the structures and procedures through which we make innovation happen.

- In a constantly changing environment it's also important to check and adapt our 'routines', updating, adding and even letting some of them go. This process of regular review and reconfiguration is at the heart of innovation management as a 'dynamic capability'.

Further Resources

A number of writers have looked at innovation from a process perspective; good examples include Keith Goffin and Rick Mitchell's *Innovation Management* (Pearson, 2010), Paul Trott's *Innovation and New Product Development* (Pearson, 2011) and Andrew van de Ven's *Innovation Journey* (Oxford University Press, 1999). Case studies provide a good lens through which this process can be seen and there are several useful collections, including Bettina von Stamm's *Innovation, Design and Creativity* (2nd edition, John Wiley & Sons, Ltd, 2008), Roland Kaye and David Hawkridge *Case Studies of Innovation* (Kogan Page, 2003) and Roger Miller and Marcel Côté's *Innovation Reinvented: Six games that drive growth* (University of Toronto Press, 2012).

Some books cover company histories in detail and give an insight into the particular ways in which firms develop their own bundles of routines, for example David Vise *The Google Story* (Pan, 2008), Graham And Shuldiner' *Corning and the Craft of Innovation* (Oxford University Press, 2001) and Gundling's *The 3M Way to Innovation: Balancing people and profit* (Kodansha International, 2000).

Autobiographies and biographies of key innovation leaders provide a similar, if sometimes personally biased, insight into this. For example, Richard Brandt's *One Click: Jeff Bezos and the rise of Amazon.com'* (Viking, 2011), Walter Issacson *Steve Jobs: The authorised biography* (Little Brown, 2011) and James Dyson *Against the Odds* (Texere, 2003). In addition, several websites – such as the Product Development Management Association's (www.pdma.org) and www.innovationmanagement.se – carry case studies on a regular basis.

Many books and articles focus on particular aspects of the process, for example on technology strategy, Burgelman, Christensen and Wheelwright *Strategic Management of Technology* (McGraw-Hill/Irwin, 5th edition, 2008). On product or service development, Robert Cooper *Winning at New Products* (Kogan Page, 2001), Kahn (ed.) *The PDMA Handbook of New Product Development* (John Wiley & Sons, Ltd, 2012) and Tidd and Hull *Service Innovation: Organizational responses to technological opportunities and market imperatives* (Imperial College Press, 2003). On process innovation, Lager, *Managing Process Innovation* (Imperial College Press, 2011), Zairi and Duggan *Best Practice Process Innovation Management* (Butterworth-Heinemann, 2012) and Gary Pisano *The Development Factory: Unlocking the potential of process innovation* (Harvard Business School Press, 1996). On technology transfer, Mohammed Saad *Development through Technology Transfer* (Intellect, 2000). On implementation Alan Afuah, *Innovation Management: Strategies, implementation and profits* (Oxford University Press, 2003), Osborne and Brown *Managing Change and Innovation in Public Service Organizations* (Psychology Press, 2010) and Bason *Managing Public Sector Innovation*, (Policy Press, 2011). On learning Kim and Nelson *Technology, Learning, and Innovation: Experiences of newly industrializing countries* (Cambridge University Press, 2003), Nooteboom *Learning and Innovation in Organizations and Economies* (Oxford University Press, 2000), Leonard *Wellsprings of Knowledge* (Harvard Business School Press, 1995) and Nonaka *The Knowledge Creating Company* (Harvard Business School Press, 1991).

Websites such as AIM (www.aimresearch.org) and NESTA (www.nesta.org) regularly report academic research around innovation.

References

1. Rothwell, R. (1992) Successful industrial innovation: Critical success factors for the 1990s, *R&D Management* **22** (3): 221–239.

2. Nelson, R. and S. Winter (1982) *An Evolutionary Theory of Economic Change.* Cambridge, MA: Harvard University Press.

3. Goffin, K. and R. Mitchell (2010) *Innovation Management*, 2nd edn. London: Pearson.

4. Teece, D. (2009) *Dynamic Capabilities and Strategic Management.* Oxford: Oxford University Press.

 Deeper Dive explanations of innovation concepts and ideas are available on the Innovation Portal at **www.innovation-portal.info**

 Quizzes to test yourself further are available online via the Innovation Portal at **www.innovation-portal.info**

Summary of online resources for Chapter 5 –
all material is available via the Innovation Portal at
www.innovation-portal.info

Cases	**Media**	**Tools**	**Activities**	**Deeper Dive**
• Nokia Siemens Networks • 3M • Marshalls • Corning • Philips Lighting • The changing music industry	• Fabian Schlage, Nokia Siemens Networks	• Innovation fitness test	• Mapping the innovation process • Innovation fitness test • Sector patterns of innovation • 'The Way We Do Things Around Here'	• The innovation journey • The innovation value chain

Chapter 6

Sources of Innovation

Where Do Innovations Come From?

Where do innovations come from? For many people that question will evoke images like that of Archimedes, jumping up from his bath and running down the street, so enthused by his new idea that he forgot to get dressed. Such 'eureka' moments are certainly a part of innovation folklore – and they underline the importance of flashes of insight which make new connections. They form the basis of the cartoon model of innovation which usually involves thinking bubbles and flashing light bulbs.

But of course there is much more to it than that. Innovation is a process of taking ideas forward, revising and refining them, weaving the different strands of 'knowledge spaghetti' together towards a useful product, process or service. Triggering that process is not just about occasional flashes of inspiration: innovation

Activity to help you explore the theme of sources of innovation – innovation family trees – is available on the Innovation Portal at **www.innovation-portal.info**

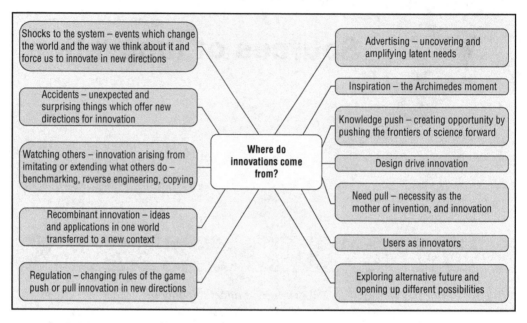

FIGURE 6.1   Where do innovations come from?

comes from many other directions, and if we are to manage it effectively we need to remind ourselves of this diversity. Figure 6.1 indicates the wide range of stimuli which can begin the innovation journey.

Let's look at some of these in more detail.

Knowledge Push

One source of innovation is scientific research. And although there have always been solo researchers, from a very early stage this process of exploring and codifying at the frontiers of knowledge became a systematic activity which involved a wide network of people sharing their ideas. In the twentieth century the rise of the large corporation brought with it the emergence of the research laboratory as a key instrument of progress. Bell Labs, ICI, Bayer, BASF, Philips, Ford, Western Electric, Du Pont – all were founded in the early 1900s as powerhouses of ideas. Their output wasn't simply around product innovation. Many of the key technologies underpinning *process* innovations, especially around

Case Studies of companies – 3M, Philips and Corning – which were founded over one hundred years ago and built their strength on extensive R&D investments are available on the Innovation Portal at **www.innovation-portal.info**

the growing field of automation and information/communications technology, also came from such organized R&D effort.

For example, the rise of the huge global pharmaceutical industry was essentially about big R&D expenditure, much of it spent on development and elaboration punctuated by the occasional breakthrough into 'blockbuster' drug territory. Similarly, the semiconductor and the computer, and other industries which depend on it, have a long-term trajectory of continuous improvement interspersed with occasional breakthroughs.

The same pattern can be seen in products, for example the camera. Originally invented in the late nineteenth century, the dominant design gradually emerged with an architecture which we would recognize: shutter and lens arrangement, focusing principles, back plate for film or plates, etc. But this design was then modified still further, with different lenses, motorized drives, flash technology, etc. – and, in the case of George Eastman's work, to create a simple and relatively idiot-proof model camera (the Box Brownie) which opened up photography to a mass market. More recent development has seen a similar fluid phase around digital imaging devices.

Case Study of Spirit, a key player in the technologies underpinning CISCO and other large corporations, is available on the Innovation Portal at **www.innovation-portal.info**

Need Pull. . .

Of course, simply having a bright idea is no guarantee of adoption. Knowledge push creates a field of possibilities – but not every idea finds successful application and one of the key lessons is that innovation requires some form of demand if it is to take root. Bright ideas are not, in themselves, enough; they may not meet a real or perceived need and people may not feel motivated to change.

In its simplest form this idea of 'need pull' innovation is captured in the saying 'necessity is the Mother of invention'. Innovation is often the response to a real or perceived need for change and so we need to develop a clear understanding of needs and find ways to meet those needs. For example, Henry Ford was able to turn the luxury plaything that was the early automobile into something which became 'a car for Everyman', while Procter & Gamble began a business meeting needs for domestic lighting (via candles) and moved across into an ever-widening range of household needs from soap and nappies to cleaners, toothpaste and beyond. Low-cost airlines have found innovative solutions to the problem of making flying available to a much wider market, while microfinance institutions have developed radical new approaches to help bring banking and credit within the reach of the poor.

Just as the knowledge push model involves a mixture of occasional breakthrough followed by extensive elaboration, so the same is true of need pull. Occasionally, it involves a new to the world idea, but mostly it is extensions, variations and adaptations around those core ideas. Figure 6.2 indicates a typical breakdown, and we could construct a similar picture for process innovations.

INNOVATION IN ACTION 6.1

Maintaining a Stream of Ideas

Two hundred years ago, Churchill Potteries began life in the United Kingdom making a range of crockery and tableware. That it is still able to do so today, despite a turbulent and highly competitive global market, says much for the approach which the company has taken to ensure a steady stream of innovation. Chief executive Andrew Roper highlights the way in which listening to users and understanding their needs has changed the business: 'We have taken on a lot of service disciplines, so you could think of us as less of a pure manufacturer and more as a service company with a manufacturing arm.' Staff spend a significant proportion of their time talking to chefs, hoteliers and others. 'Sales, marketing and technical people spend far more of their time than I could ever have imagined checking out what happens to the product in use and asking the customer, professional or otherwise, what they really want next.'

Source: Derived from 'Ingredients for success on a plate', Peter Marsh, *Financial Times*, 26/3/08, p. 16.

Need pull innovation is particularly important at mature stages in industry or product life cycles when there is more than one offering to choose from – competing depends on differentiating on the basis of needs and attributes, and/or segmenting the offering to suit different adopter types.

It's also important to recognize that innovation is not always about commercial markets or consumer needs. There is also a strong tradition of social need providing the pull for new

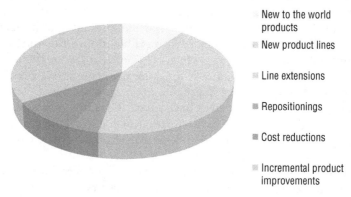

- New to the world products
- New product lines
- Line extensions
- Repositionings
- Cost reductions
- Incremental product improvements

FIGURE 6.2   Types of new product

Source: Based on Griffin, A. (1997) PDMA research on new product development practices. *Journal of Product Innovation Management,* 14: 429. Reproduced by permission of John Wiley & Sons, Ltd.

Understanding User Needs in Hyundai Motor

One of the problems facing global manufacturers is how to tailor their products to suit the needs of local markets. For Hyundai this has meant paying considerable attention to getting deep insights into customer needs and aspirations, an approach which it used to good effect in developing the Santa Fe, reintroduced to the US market in 2007. The headline for its development programme was 'touch the market' and it deployed a number of tools and techniques to enable it. For example, its engineers visited an ice rink and watched an Olympic medallist skate around to help them gain an insight into the ideas of grace and speed which they wanted to embed in the car. This provided a metaphor – 'assertive grace' – which the development teams in Korea and the US were able to use.'

Analysis of existing vehicles suggested some aspects of design were not being covered, for example many sport/utility vehicles (SUVs) were rather 'boxy' so there was scope to enhance the image of the car. Market research suggested a target segment of 'glamour mums' who would find this attractive and the teams then began an intensive study of how this group lived their lives. Ethnographic methods looked at their homes, their activities and their lifestyles, for example team members spent a day shopping with some target women to gain an understanding of their purchases and what motivated them. The list of key motivators which emerged from this shopping study included durability, versatility, uniqueness, child-friendliness and good customer service from knowledgeable staff. Another approach was to make all members of the team experience driving routes around southern California, making journeys similar to those popular with the target segment and in the process getting first-hand experience of comfort, features and fixtures inside the car, etc.[1]

products, processes and services – a theme we'll explore in a later chapter. Whether it is social needs like provision of health care or clean water in developing countries or more effective education or social services in established industrial economies, the need for change is clear and provides an engine for increasing innovation.

Making Processes Better

Of course, needs aren't just about external markets for products and services. We can see the same phenomenon of need pull working inside the business, as a driver of *process* innovation. 'Squeaking wheels' and other sources of frustration provide rich signals for change, and this kind of innovation is often something which can engage a high proportion of the workforce who experiences these needs first hand.

Case Study of continuous improvement is available on the Innovation Portal at **www.innovation-portal.info**

Video Clips about Veeder-Root, a small company exploiting these ideas, and of an interview with Emma Taylor, of the giant Denso Systems, who talks about her experiences in establishing this kind of approach, are available on the Innovation Portal at **www.innovation-portal.info**

Case Studies of innovations in the health care sector where the drive has been to improve the provision of public services through process innovation are available on the Innovation Portal at **www.innovation-portal.info**

This approach provided the basic philosophy behind the 'total quality management' movement in the 1980s, the 'business process re-engineering' ideas of the 1990s and the current widespread application of concepts based on the idea of 'lean thinking' – essentially taking waste out of existing processes.

This kind of process improvement is of particular relevance in the public sector where the issue is not about creating wealth but of providing value for money in service delivery. Many applications of 'lean' and similar concepts can be found which apply this principle, for example in reducing waiting times or improving patient safety in hospitals, in speeding up delivery of services like car taxation and passport issuing and even in improving the collection of taxes!

INNOVATION IN ACTION 6.3

'Pretty in Pink'

Walking through the plant belonging to Ace Trucks (a major producer of forklift trucks) in Japan the first thing which strikes you is the colour scheme. In fact, you would need to be blind not to notice it. Amongst the usual rather dull greys and greens of machine tools and other equipment there are flashes of pink. Not just a quiet pastel tone but a full-blooded, shocking pink which would do credit to even the most image-conscious flamingo. Closer inspection shows these flashes and splashes of pink to be not random but associated with particular sections and parts of machines, and the eye-catching effect comes in part from the sheer number of pink-painted bits, distributed right across the factory floor and all over the different machines.

What is going on here is not a bizarre attempt to redecorate the factory or a failed piece of interior design. The effect of catching the eye is quite deliberate: the colour is there to draw attention to the machines and other equipment which have been modified. Every pink splash is the result of a kaizen project to improve some aspect of the equipment, much of it in support of the drive towards 'total productive maintenance' (TPM), in which every item of plant is available and ready for use 100% of the time. This is a goal like 'zero defects' in total quality – certainly ambitious, possibly an impossibility in the statistical sense, but one which focuses the minds of everyone involved and leads to extensive and impressive problem-finding and -solving. TPM programmes have accounted for year-on-year cost savings of 10–15% in many Japanese firms, and these savings are being ground out of a system which is already renowned for its lean characteristics.

Painting the improvements pink plays an important role in drawing attention to the underlying activity in this factory, in which systematic problem-finding and -solving are part of 'the way we do things around here'. The visual cues remind everyone of the continuing search for new ideas and improvements, and often provide stimulus for other ideas or for places where the displayed pink idea can be transferred to. Closer inspection around the plant shows other forms of display – less visually striking but powerful nonetheless – charts and graphs of all shapes and sizes which focus attention on trends and problems as well as celebrating successful improvements. Photographs and graphics which pose problems or offer suggested improvements in methods or working practices. And flipcharts and whiteboards covered with symbols and shapes of fish bones and other tools being used to drive the improvement process forward.

INNOVATION IN ACTION 6.4

MindLab

MindLab is a Danish organization set up to promote and enable public sector innovation in Denmark. 'Owned' by the Ministries of Taxation, Employment and Economic Affairs, it has pioneered a series of initiatives engaging civil servants and members of the public in a wide range of social innovation which has raised productivity, improved service quality and cut costs across the public sector. Case studies of their activities can be found at their website:

Source: Derived from www.mind-lab.dk/en

Whose Needs? Working at the Edge

One very interesting source of innovation lies at the edges of existing markets. It poses a problem for existing players because the needs of such fringe groups are not seen as relevant to their 'mainstream' activities – and so they tend to ignore them or to dismiss them as not being important. But working with these users and their different needs creates different innovation options, and sometimes what has relevance for the fringe begins to be of interest to the mainstream. US professor Clayton Christensen in his many studies of such 'disruptive innovation' shows this has been the pattern across industries as diverse as computer disk drives, earth-moving equipment, steel making and low-cost air travel.[2]

For much of the time there is stability around markets where innovation of the 'do better' variety takes place and is well managed. Close relationships with existing customers are fostered and the system is configured to deliver a steady stream of what the market wants – and often a great deal more! (What Christensen calls 'technology overshoot' is often a characteristic of this, where markets are offered more and more features which they may not ever use or place much value on but which come as part of the package.)

But somewhere else there is another group of potential users who have very different needs, usually for something much simpler and cheaper, which will help them get something done. Meeting these needs not only creates a new market but can also destabilize the existing one as customers there realize their needs can be met with a different approach. This phenomenon is known as 'disruptive innovation', and we'll explore it in more detail in a later chapter.

Disruptive innovation focuses our attention on the need to look for needs which are not being met, poorly met or sometimes where there is an overshoot. Each of these can provide a trigger for innovation – and often involves disruption because existing players don't see the different patterns of needs.

INNOVATION IN ACTION 6.5

Gaining a Competitive Edge Through Meeting Unserved Needs

The Nintendo Wii opened up radically new competitive space in the computer games industry and for a while enjoyed market leadership. The Wii console is not a particularly sophisticated piece of technology. Compared to the rivals Sony PS3 or the Microsoft Xbox it has less computing power, storage or other features and the games' graphics have a much lower resolution than major sellers like *Grand Theft Auto*. But the key to the phenomenal success of the Wii has been its appeal to an under-served market. Where computer games were traditionally targeted at boys, the Wii extends – by means of a simple interface wand – their interest to all members of the family. There are add-ons to the platform like the Wii board for keep fit and other applications and the market reach extends, for example to include the elderly or patients suffering the after-effects of stroke.

Nintendo has performed a similar act of opening up the marketplace with its DS handheld device, again by targeting unmet needs across a different segment of the population. Many DS users are middle-aged or retired, and the bestselling games are for brain training and puzzles.

One powerful source of ideas at the edge comes from the developing world, where conditions are very different and radically new innovation options are beginning to emerge. Typically, the conditions in these markets are characterized by high volumes of demand – millions of people wanting goods and services – but limited financial resources. So the possibility for a low-cost airline type of approach – offering a simpler, cheaper version of the core product or service – is a very real opportunity. For example, think what a producer in China would do to an industry like pump manufacturing if it began to offer a simple, low-cost 'good enough' household pump for $10 (£6) instead of the high-tech, high-performance variants available from today's industry at prices 10 to 50 times higher?

Importantly, it isn't just the case that fringe markets trigger simpler and cheaper innovations. Sometimes, the novel conditions spawn completely new trajectories. For example, the concept of 'mobile money' emerged from Africa, where the security risks of carrying cash round meant that people began to use the mobile phone system to provide an alternative way of moving money around. Systems like M-PESA have now grown in sophistication and widespread application in emerging markets like Africa and Latin America but are also offering a template for existing markets back in the industrialized world.

Case Study of M-PESA is available on the Innovation Portal at **www.innovation-portal.info**

Video Clip of an interview with Suzana Moreira, whose company, moWoza, is a social innovator using the mobile money platform, is available on the Innovation Portal at **www.innovation-portal.info**

Case Study of the work of the Nokia Institute of Technology is available on the Innovation Portal at **www.innovation-portal.info**

Crisis Driven Innovation

Sometimes the urgency of a need can have a forcing effect on innovation – the example of wartime and other crises supports this view. For example, the demand for iron and iron products increased hugely during the Industrial Revolution and exposed the limitations of

Video Clip of an interview with Ana Sena, innovation manager at INdT, is available on the Innovation Portal at **www.innovation-portal.info**

INNOVATION IN ACTION 6.7

Living Labs

One approach being used by an increasing number of companies involves setting up 'Living Labs' which allow experimentation with and learning from users to generate ideas and perspectives on innovation. These could be amongst particular groups, for example in Denmark a network of such laboratories (http://www.openlivinglabs.eu/ourlabs/Denmark) is particularly concerned with the experience of ageing and the likely products and services which an increasingly elderly population will need. A description of the Lab and its operation can be found at http://www.edengene.co.uk/article/living-labs/.

In Brazil, the Nokia Institute of Technology (INdT) develops user-driven innovation platforms to support mobile products and services and as part of that process tries to enable the large-scale involvement of motivated communities. http://www.indt.org/. Its Mobile Work Spaces Living Lab is working in several technological fields and with communities across rural and urban environments.

---

the old methods of smelting with charcoal. It created the pull which led to developments like the Bessemer converter. In similar fashion the energy crisis has created a significant pull for innovation around alternative energy sources – and an investment boom for such work.

Case Studies of crisis driven innovations in the humanitarian sector are available on the Innovation Portal at **www.innovation-portal.info**

A powerful example of the impact crisis can have on driving innovation can be seen in the context of major humanitarian crises, for example after devastating earthquakes or hurricanes. The need to improvise solutions around logistics, shelter, health care, water and sanitation, and energy force a rapid pace of innovation.

INNOVATION IN ACTION 6.8

Humanitarian Innovation

ALNAP is a learning network of humanitarian agencies including organizations like the Red Cross, Save the Children and Christian Aid. It aims to share and build on experience gained through coping with humanitarian crises – whether natural or man-made – and has spent time reflecting on how many of the innovations developed as a response to urgent needs can be spread to others. Examples include high-energy biscuits which can be quickly distributed or building materials which can be deployed and assembled quickly into makeshift shelters. ALNAP's website gives a wide range of examples of such crisis driven innovations.

Source: Derived from www.alnap.org/resources/innovations.aspx

---

Towards Mass Customization

Another important source of innovation results from our desire for *customization*. Markets are not made up of people wanting the same thing – we all want variety and some degree of personalization. And as we move from a time where products are in short supply to one of mass production so the demand for differentiation increases. We can see this in the case of the motor car as one simple example. Arguably, Henry Ford's plant, based on principles of mass production, represented the most efficient response to the market environment of its time. But that environment changed rapidly during the 1920s, so that what had begun as a winning formula for manufacturing began gradually to represent a major obstacle to change. Production of the Model T began in 1909 and for fifteen years or so it was the market leader. Despite falling margins, the company managed to exploit its blueprint for factory technology and organization to ensure continuing profits. But growing competition (particularly from General Motors, with its strategy of product differentiation) was shifting away from trying to offer the customer low-cost personal transportation towards other design features – such as the closed body – and Ford was increasingly forced to add features to the Model T. Eventually, it was clear that a new model was needed and production of the Model T stopped in 1927.

Case Study of Model T Ford is available on the Innovation Portal at **www.innovation-portal.info**

There has always been a market for personalized custom-made goods (like tailored clothes) and services (e.g. personal shoppers, personal travel agents and personal physicians). But until recently there was an acceptance that this customization carried a high price tag and that mass markets could only be served with relatively standard product and service offerings.

However, a combination of enabling technologies and rising expectations has begun to shift this balance and resolve the trade-off between price and customization. 'Mass customization' (MC) is a widely used term which captures some elements of this. MC is the ability to offer highly configured bundles of non-price factors configured to suit different market segments (with the ideal target of total customization, i.e. a market size of one) but to do this without incurring cost penalties and the setting-up of a trade-off of agility vs. prices.

Of course, there are different levels of customizing – from simply putting a label 'specially made for . . . (insert your name here)' on a standard product right through to sitting down with a designer and co-creating something truly unique. Table 6.1 gives some examples of this range of options.

Understanding what it is that customers value and need is critical in pursuing a customization strategy – and it leads, inevitably, to the next source of innovation in which the users themselves become the source of ideas.

Users as Innovators

It is easy to fall into the trap of thinking about need pull innovation as involving a process in which user needs are identified and then something is created to meet those needs. This assumes that users are passive recipients, but this is often not the case. In many cases users

TABLE 6.1   Options in Customization

Type of customization	Characteristics	Examples
Distribution customization	Customers may customize product/service packaging, delivery schedule and delivery location but the actual product/service is standardized	Sending a book to a friend from Amazon.com. They will receive an individually wrapped gift with a personalized message from you – but it's actually all been done online and in its distribution warehouses. iTunes appears to offer personalization of a music experience but in fact it does so right at the end of the production and distribution chain
Assembly customization	Customers are offered a number of pre-defined options. Products/services are made to order using standardized components	Buying a computer from Dell or another online retailer. Customers choose and configure to suit their exact requirements from a rich menu of options – but Dell only starts to assemble this (from standard modules and components) when the order is finalized. Banks offering tailor-made insurance and financial products are actually configuring these from a relatively standard set of options
Fabrication customization	Customers are offered a number of pre-defined designs. Products/services are manufactured to order	Buying a luxury car like a BMW, where the customer is involved in choosing ('designing') the configuration which best meets their needs and wishes – for engine size, trim levels, colour, fixtures and extras, etc. Only when they are satisfied with the virtual model they have chosen does the manufacturing process begin – and they can even visit the factory to watch their car being built Services allow a much higher level of such customization since there is less of an asset base needed to set up for 'manufacturing' the service – examples here would include made-to-measure tailoring, personal planning for holidays, pensions, etc.
Design customization	Customer input stretches to the start of the production process. Products do not exist until initiated by a customer order	Co-creation, where end-users may not even be sure what it is they want but where – sitting down with a designer – they co-create the concept and elaborate it. It's a little like having some clothes made but rather than choosing from a pattern book they actually have a designer with them and create the concept together. Only when it exists as a firm design idea does it get made. Co-creation of services can be found in fields

(continued)

TABLE 6.1 (*Continued*)

Type of customization	Characteristics	Examples
		like entertainment (where user-led models like YouTube are posing significant challenges to mainstream providers) and in health care, where experiments towards radical alternatives for health care delivery are being explored – see, for example, the Design Council RED project, which is discussed on the Innovation Portal

Source: Derived from Lampel and Mintzberg.[3]

are ahead of the game – their ideas plus their frustrations with existing solutions lead them to experiment and create something new. And sometimes these prototypes eventually become mainstream innovations.

Eric von Hippel of Massachusetts Institute of Technology has made a lifelong study of this phenomenon and gives the example of the pickup truck – a long-time staple of the world automobile industry.[4] This major category did not begin life on the drawing boards of Detroit but rather on the farms and homesteads of a wide range of users who wanted more than a family saloon. They adapted their cars by removing seats, welding new pieces on and cutting off the roof – in the process prototyping and developing the early model of the pickup. Only later did Detroit pick up on the idea and begin the incremental innovation process to refine and mass produce the vehicle. A host of other examples support the view that user-led innovation matters, for example petroleum refining, medical devices, semiconductor equipment, scientific instruments and a wide range of sports goods and the Polaroid camera. Importantly, active and interested users (lead users) are often well ahead of the market in terms of innovation needs.

This phenomenon of user-led innovation is becoming increasingly significant, for example the Linux software which lies at the heart of mobile phones did not originate with a traditional corporation but rather a group of frustrated users who felt there were better ways to write and run operating systems and so built a community to create them. Studies of 'hidden

Video Clips made by Eric von Hippel with the 3M corporation exploring some of these ideas in greater detail are available on the Innovation Portal at **www.innovation-portal.info**

Case Studies of businesses – like Lego, Adidas and Threadless – which have made use of this approach are available on the Innovation Portal at **www.innovation-portal.info**

Video Clips of interviews with people like Catherina van Delden and Helle-Vibeke Carstensen who work actively in this space are available on the Innovation Portal at **www.innovation-portal.info**

innovation' suggest that a significant and growing number of people are involved in such innovation and it accounts for a surprising number of new ideas. And the idea doesn't stop with products: it is very relevant to services and the public sector. For example, the Danish government has had considerable success with engaging users in innovations around the tax system!

We'll explore this important theme in more detail in Chapter 16.

Watching Others – and Learning from Them

Another important source of innovation comes from watching others. Imitation is not only the sincerest form of flattery but also a viable and successful strategy for sourcing innovation. For example, the reverse engineering of products and processes and development of imitations – even around impregnable patents – is a well-known route to find ideas. Much of the rapid progress of Asian economies in the post-war years was based on a strategy of 'copy and develop', taking Western ideas and improving on them.

Tools such as competitiveness profiling, which provide structured ways for learning of this kind, are available on the Innovation Portal at **www.innovation-portal.info**

One powerful variation on this theme is the concept of 'benchmarking'. In this process enterprises make structured comparisons with others to try to identify new ways of carrying out particular processes or to explore new product or service concepts. The learning triggered by benchmarking may arise from comparing between similar organizations (same firm, same sector, etc.), or it may come from looking outside the sector but at similar products or processes.

For example, Southwest Airlines became the most successful carrier in the United States by dramatically reducing the turnaround times at airports – an innovation which it learnt from studying pit stop techniques in the Formula 1 Grand Prix events. Similarly, the Karolinska Hospital in Stockholm made significant improvements to its cost and time performance through studying inventory management techniques in advanced factories.

Benchmarking of this kind is increasingly being used to drive change across the public sector, via 'league tables' linked to performance metrics which aim to encourage the fast transfer of good practice between schools or hospitals and via secondment, visits and other mechanisms designed to facilitate learning from other sectors managing similar process issues such as logistics and distribution. One of the most successful applications of benchmarking has been in the development of the concept of 'lean' thinking, now widely applied to many public and private sector organizations. The origins were in a detailed benchmarking study of car manufacturing plants during the 1980s which identified significant performance differences and triggered a search for the underlying process innovations which were driving those differences.

Case Studies on organizations like Karolinska Hospital and sectors like the global automotive industry which have made use of benchmarking are available on the Innovation Portal at **www.innovation-portal.info**

Recombinant Innovation

Another wrong assumption which we often make about innovation is that it always has to involve something new to the world. The reality is that there is plenty of scope for crossover: ideas and applications which are commonplace in one world may be perceived as new and exciting in another. This is an important principle in sourcing innovation where transferring or combining old ideas in new contexts – a process called 'recombinant innovation' by US researcher Andrew Hargadon – can be a powerful resource.[5] The Reebok pump running shoe, for example, was a significant product innovation in the highly competitive world of sports equipment – yet, although this represented a breakthrough in that field, it drew on core ideas which were widely used in a different world. Design Works, the agency which came up with the design, brought together a team which included people with prior experience in fields like paramedic equipment (from which they took the idea of an inflatable splint providing support and minimizing shock to bones) and operating theatre equipment (from which they took the micro-bladder valve at the heart of the pump mechanisms).

Many businesses – as Hargadon points out – are able to offer rich innovation possibilities primarily because they have deliberately recruited teams with diverse industrial and professional backgrounds and thus bring very different perspectives to the problem in hand. His studies of the design company IDEO show the potential for such recombinant innovation work.

Nor is this a new idea. Thomas Edison's famous 'Invention Factory' in New Jersey was founded in 1876 with the grand promise of 'a minor invention every ten days and a big thing every six month or so'. It was able to deliver on that promise not because of the lone genius of Edison but rather from taking on board the recombinant lesson: Edison hired scientists and engineers from all the emerging new industries of early-twentieth-century USA. In doing so, he brought experience in technologies and applications like mass production and precision machining (gun industry) telegraphy and telecommunications, food processing and canning, automobile manufacture. Some of the early innovations which built the reputation of the business – for example the teleprinter for the New York Stock Exchange – were really simple crossover applications of well-known innovations in other sectors.

> Case Study of the DOME (Designing Out Medical Error) project looking at lessons which could be transferred between a variety of different worlds with the same basic problems of safety is available on the Innovation Portal at **www.innovation-portal.info**

Regulation

Photographs of the industrial towns around the Midlands in the United Kingdom taken in the early part of the twentieth century would not be much use in tracing landmarks or spotting key geographical features. The images, in fact, would reveal very little at all – not because of a limitation in the photographic equipment or processing but because the subject matter itself – the urban landscape – was rendered largely invisible by the thick smog which regularly enveloped the area. Yet sixty years later the same images would show up crystal clear – not because the factories had closed (although there are fewer of them) but because of the continuing effects of the Clean Air Act and other legislation. They provide a clear reminder of another important source of innovation – the stimulus given by changes in the rules and regulations which define the various 'games' for business and society. The Clean Air Act didn't specify how but only what had to change. Achieving the reduction in pollutants emitted to the atmosphere involved extensive innovation in materials, processes and even in product design made by the factories.

Regulation in this way provides a two-edged sword: it both closes off avenues along which innovation had been taking place (and so restricts certain things) and opens up new ones along which change is mandated to happen.

One of the powerful drivers for moving into environmentally sustainable 'clean' technologies is the increasingly tough legislation in areas like carbon emissions and pollution.

And it works the other way: deregulation (the slackening-off of controls) may open up new innovation space. The liberalization and then privatization of telecommunications in many countries led to rapid growth in competition and high rates of innovation, for example.

Given the pervasiveness of legal frameworks in our lives, we shouldn't be surprised to see this source of innovation. From the moment we get up and turn the radio on (regulation of broadcasting shaping the range and availability of the programmes we listen to) to eating our breakfast (food and drink is highly regulated in terms of what can and can't be included in ingredients, how foods are tested before being allowed for sale, etc.) to climbing into our cars and buckling on our seatbelt while switching on our hands-free phone devices (both the result of safety legislation) the role of regulation in shaping innovation can be seen.

Regulation can also trigger counter-innovation – solutions designed to get round existing rules or at least bend them to one's advantage. The rapid growth in speed cameras as a means of enforcing safety legislation on roads throughout Europe has led to the healthy growth of an industry providing products or services for detecting and avoiding them. And at the limit, changes in the regulatory environment can create radical new space and opportunity. Although Enron ended its days as a corporation in disgrace because of financial impropriety, it is worth asking how a small gas pipeline services company rose to become such a powerful beast in the first place. The answer was its rapid and entrepreneurial take-up of the opportunities opened up by the deregulation of markets for utilities like gas and electricity.

Futures and Forecasting

Another way we can identify innovation possibilities is to imagine and explore into the future. What may be the key trends, where may the threats and opportunities lie? For example, Shell has a long history of exploring future options and driving innovations, most recently through its GameChanger programme. Various tools and techniques for forecasting and imagining alternative futures have been developed to help work with these rich sources of innovation and we'll look at them in detail in the next chapter.

Video Clip of a podcast interview with Helen King of Bord Bia, the government body in Ireland responsible for supporting the food industry, exploring the ways in which futures can be used to drive an innovation agenda is available on the Innovation Portal at **www.innovation-portal.info**

Design-driven Innovation

One increasingly significant source of innovation is what researcher Roberto Verganti calls 'design-driven innovation'.[6] Examples include many of the recent successful Apple products where the user experience is one of surprise and pleasure at the look and feel, the intuitive beauty of the product. This emerges not as a result of analysis of user needs but rather through a design process which seeks to give meaning to the shape and form of products – features and characteristics which they didn't know they wanted. But it is also not another version of knowledge or technology push in which powerful new functions are installed. In many ways design-led products are deceptively simple in their usability. Apple's iPod was a comparative latecomer to the mp3 player market yet it created the standard for the others to follow because of the uniqueness of the look and feel – the design attributes. Its subsequent success with its iPad and iPhone owes a great deal to the design ideas of Jonathan Ive, which bring a philosophy to the whole product range and provide one of the key competitiveness factors to the company.

As Verganti points out, people do not buy things only to meet their needs; there are important psychological and cultural factors at work as well. In essence, we need to ask about the 'meaning' of products in people's lives – and then develop ways of bringing this into the innovation process. This is the role of design: to use tools and skills to articulate and create meaning in products – and to increase services as well. He suggests a map in which both knowledge/technology push and market pull can be positioned – and where design-driven innovation represents a third space around creating radical new concepts which have meaning in people's lives (Figure 6.3).

Video Clips of several media interviews looking at the role of design in enhancing services, for example Lynne Maher on patient-centred health care and the RED and Open Door cases, are available on the Innovation Portal at **www.innovation-portal.info**

Design features increasingly in the area of services and design methods and tools are being used to identify and work with user needs in a variety of contexts.

Related to the design idea is that of 'experience innovation', a concept first explored by Joseph Pine.[7] In an increasingly competitive world, differentiation comes increasingly from creating 'experience innovation', especially in services where fulfilling needs takes second place to the meaning and psychological importance of the experience. For example, the restaurant business moves from an emphasis on food as an essential human need towards increasingly significant experience innovation around restaurants as systems of consumption involving the product, its delivery, the physical and cultural context, etc. Increasingly, service providers such as airlines, hotels or entertainment businesses are differentiating themselves along such 'experience innovation' lines.

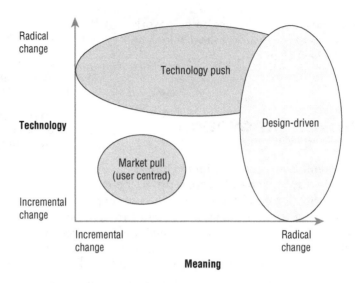

FIGURE 6.3 The role of design-driven innovation

Source: Based on R. Verganti (2009) *Design-Driven Innovation*. Harvard Business School Press.

Accidents

Accidents and unexpected events happen – and in the course of a carefully planned R&D project they could be seen as annoying disruptions. But on occasions accidents can also trigger innovation, opening up surprisingly new lines of attack. The famous example of Fleming's discovery of penicillin is but one of many stories in which mistakes and accidents turned out to trigger important innovation directions. 3M's 'Post-it' notes began when a polymer chemist mixed an experimental batch of what should have been a good adhesive but which turned out to have rather weak properties – sticky but not very sticky. This failure in terms of the original project provided the impetus for what has become a billion-dollar product platform for the company.

In another example from the late 1980s, scientists working for Pfizer began testing what was then known as 'compound UK-92,480' for the treatment of angina. Although promising in the lab and in animal tests, the compound showed little benefit in clinical trials in humans. Despite these initial negative results the team pursued what was an interesting side effect which eventually led to UK-92,480 becoming sildenafil, and sold as the blockbuster drug Viagra.

The secret is not so much recognizing that such stimuli are available but rather creating the conditions under which they can be noticed and acted upon. As Pasteur is reputed to have said, 'Chance favours the prepared mind!' Using mistakes as a source of ideas only happens if the conditions exist to help them emerge. A study by Chesbrough of Xerox highlighted the fact that the company developed many technologies in its laboratories in Palo Alto which did not easily fit its image of itself as 'the document company'. These included Ethernet (later successfully commercialized by 3Com and others and PostScript language and taken forward by Adobe Systems). In fact, 11 of 35 rejected projects from Xerox's labs were later commercialized with the resulting businesses having a market capitalization of twice that of Xerox itself.

In similar fashion shocks to the system which fundamentally change the rules provide not only a threat to the existing status quo but also a powerful stimulus to find and develop something new. The tragedy of the 9/11 bombing of the Twin Towers served to change fundamentally the public's sense of security – but it has also provided a huge stimulus to innovate in areas like security, alternative transportation, fire safety and evacuation, etc.

INNOVATION IN ACTION 6.9

Cleaning up by Accident

Audley Williamson is not a household name of the Thomas Edison variety but he was a successful innovator whose UK business sold for £135 million in 2004. The core product which he invented was called Swarfega and offered a widely used and dermatologically safe cleaner for skin. It is a greenish gel which has achieved widespread use in households as a simple and robust aid with the advertising slogan 'Clean hands in a flash!' But the original product was not designed for this market at all. It was developed in 1941 as a mild detergent to wash silk stockings. Unfortunately, the invention of Nylon and its rapid application in stockings meant that the market quickly disappeared and so Williamson was forced to find an alternative. Watching workers in a factory trying to clean their hands with an abrasive mixture of petrol, paraffin and sand which left their hands cracked and sore led him to rethink the use of his gel as a safer alternative.

Source: Derived from *The Independent*, 28/2/2006, p. 7.

Summary

- Innovations don't just appear perfectly formed – and the process is not simply a spark of imagination giving rise to changing the world. Instead, innovations come from a number of sources and these interact over time.

- Sources of innovation can be resolved into two broad classes: knowledge push and need pull – although they almost always act in tandem. Innovation arises from the interplay between them.

- There are many variations on this theme (e.g. 'need pull' can include social needs, market needs, latent needs 'squeaking wheels', crisis needs).

- While the basic forces pushing and pulling have been a feature of the innovation landscape for a long time, it involves a moving frontier in which new sources of push and pull come into play. Examples include the emerging demand pull from the 'bottom of the pyramid' and the opportunities opened up by an acceleration in knowledge production in R&D systems around the world.

- Regulation is also an important element in shaping and directing innovative activity: by restricting what can and can't be done for legal reasons, new trajectories for change are established which entrepreneurs can take advantage of.

Further Resources

The long-running debate about which sources – demand pull or knowledge push – are most important is well covered in Freeman and Soete's book *The Economics of Industrial Innovation* (MIT Press, 3rd edition, 1997). Particular discussion of fringe markets and unmet or poorly met needs as sources of innovation is covered by Christensen, Anthony and Roth in *Seeing What's Next* (Harvard Business School Press, 2007), Utterback in 'High End Disruption' (*International Journal of Innovation Management*, 2007) and Ulnwick in *What Customers Want: Using outcome-driven innovation to create breakthrough products and services* (McGraw-Hill, 2005), while the 'bottom of the pyramid' and extreme user potential is explored by Prahalad in *The Fortune at the Bottom of the Pyramid* (Wharton School Publishing, 2006). User-led innovation has been researched extensively by Eric von Hippel (http://web.mit.edu/evhippel/www/). Frank Piller, a professor at Aachen University in Germany, has a rich website around the theme of mass customization with extensive case examples and other resources (http://www.mass-customization.de/); the original work on the topic is covered by Pine in *Mass Customisation: The new frontier in business competition* (Harvard University Press, 1993). High involvement innovation is covered by Bessant in *High Involvement Innovation* (John Wiley & Son, Ltd., 2003) and lean thinking ideas and tools by

Jones and Womack in *Lean Solutions* (Free Press, 2005). Andrew Hargadon has done extensive work on 'recombinant innovation' in *How Breakthroughs Happen* (Harvard Business School Press, 2003) and Mohammed Zairi provides a good overview of benchmarking in *Effective Benchmarking: Learning from the best* (Chapman & Hall, 1996).

References

1. Kluter, H. and D. Mottram (2007) Hyundai uses 'Touch the market' to create clarity in product concepts, in *PDMA Visions*, Mount Laurel, NJ: Product Development Management Association, pp. 16–19.

2. Christensen, C. (1997) *The Innovator's Dilemma*. Cambridge, MA: Harvard Business School Press.

3. Lampel, J. and H. Mintzberg (1996) Customizing customization, *Sloan Management Review*, **38** (1): 21–30.

4. Von Hippel, E. (2005) *The Democratization of Innovation*. Cambridge, MA: MIT Press.

5. Hargadon, A. (2003) *How Breakthroughs Happen*. Boston: Harvard Business School Press.

6. Verganti, R. (2009) *Design-driven Innovation*. Boston: Harvard Business School Press.

7. Pine, J. and J. Gilmore (1999) *The Experience Economy*. Boston: Harvard Business School Press.

Deeper Dive explanations of innovation concepts and ideas are available on the Innovation Portal at **www.innovation-portal.info**

Quizzes to test yourself further are available online via the Innovation Portal at **www.innovation-portal.info**

Summary of online resources for Chapter 6 –
all material is available via the Innovation Portal at
www.innovation-portal.info

Cases	**Media**	**Tools**	**Activities**	**Deeper Dive**

Cases
- 3M
- Philips
- Corning
- Spirit
- Torbay Hospital
- Karolinska Hospital
- Aravind Eye Clinics
- Lifespring Hospitals
- NHL hospitals
- M-PESA
- Nokia Institute of Technology
- Crisis driven innovation in humanitarian sector
- Model T Ford
- Lego
- Adidas
- Threadless
- DOME project
- Global automobile industry
- RED/NHS
- Open Door Project
- Continuous improvement

Media
- Veeder-Root
- Emma Taylor, Denso Systems
- Torbay Hospital
- No delays
- Lynne Maher, NHS
- Suzana Moreira, moWoza
- Ana Sena, INdT
- Eric von Hippel
- Frank Piller
- Helle-Vibeke Carstensen, Danish Ministry of Taxation
- Catherina van Delden, Innosabi
- Helen King, Bord Bia

Tools
- Continuous improvement toolkit
- Competitiveness profiling
- Value curves
- Benchmarking

Activities
- Innovation family trees
- Competitiveness profiling

Deeper Dive
- Policy deployment
- Crisis driven innovation

Chapter 7

Search Strategies for Innovation

LEARNING OBJECTIVES

By the end of this chapter you will have explored:

- the need for a strategy to shape search for opportunities
- dimensions of search space: incremental/radical and old/new frame
- strategies for covering the space: exploit and explore
- tools and structures to support these strategies
- the concept of discontinuous and disruptive innovation
- the role of entrepreneurship as a mindset underpinning search, whether in new venture start-ups or in renewing established organizations
- the concept of absorptive capacity and building search capability.

Making Sense of the Sources

It's clear that opportunities for innovation are not in short supply – and they arise from many different directions. The key challenge for innovation management is how to spot the potential in a sea of possibilities, and to do so with often-limited resources. No organization can hope to cover all the bases, so there needs to be some underlying strategy to how the search process is undertaken. So how can we make sense of all the sources out there? In this section we'll begin with some lenses which help us frame the opportunities.

Push or Pull Innovation?

If we take a broad overview, we can see that all of these sources can be looked at as either a 'push' or a 'pull' stimulus for innovation. And this raises the question of which is more important. This has been the subject of many innovation studies over the years, using a variety of different methods to try to establish which is more important (and therefore where organizations could best place their resources). The reality is that innovation is never a simple matter of push or pull but rather their interaction; as Chris Freeman says: 'Necessity may be the mother of invention but procreation needs a partner!'[1] Innovations tend to resolve into vectors – combinations of the two core principles. And these direct our attention in two complementary directions: creating possibilities (or at least keeping track of what others are doing along the R&D frontier) and identifying and working with needs.

In fact, most sources of innovation involve both push and pull components, for example 'applied R&D' involves directing the push search in areas of particular need. Regulation both pushes in key directions and pulls innovations through in response to changed conditions. User-led innovation may be triggered by user needs but it often involves their creating new solutions to old problems, essentially pushing the frontier of possibility in new directions.

There is a risk in focusing on either of the 'pure' forms of push or pull sources. If we put all our eggs in one basket we risk being excellent at invention but without turning our ideas into successful innovations – a fate shared by too many would-be entrepreneurs. But equally too close an ear to the market may limit us in our search. As Henry Ford is reputed to have said, 'If I had asked the market they would have said they wanted faster horses!' The limits of even the best market research lie in the fact that they represent sophisticated ways of asking people's reactions to something which is already there, rather than allowing for something completely outside their experience so far.

Incremental or Radical?

Another key dimension is around incremental or radical innovation. We've seen that there is a pattern of what could be termed 'punctuated equilibrium' with innovation: most of the time innovation is about exploiting and elaborating, creating variations on a theme within an established technical, market or regulatory trajectory. But occasionally there is a breakthrough which creates a new trajectory – and the cycle repeats itself. This suggests that much of our attention in searching for innovation triggers will be around incremental improvement innovation: the different versions of a piece of software, the Mk 2, 3 and 4 of a product or the continuing improvement of a business process to make it closer to lean. But we will need to have some element of our portfolio focused on the longer-range, higher risk, which may lead to the breakthrough and set up a new trajectory.

Timing

A third issue is around timing. At different stages in the product or industry lifecycle the emphasis may be more or less on push or pull. For example, mature industries will tend to focus on pull, responding to different market needs and differentiating by incremental innovation in key directions of user need. By contrast a new industry, for example the emergent

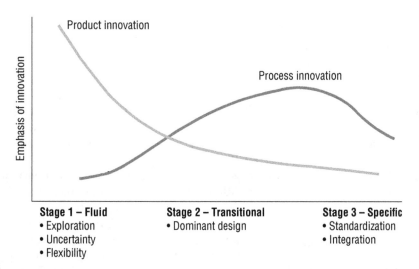

FIGURE 7.1 The innovation lifecycle

Source: Abernathy, W. and J. Utterback (1975) A dynamic model of product and process innovation *Omega* **3**(6): 639-656. Reproduced by permission of Elsevier.

industries based on genetics or nano materials technology, is often about solutions looking for a problem. So we would expect different balances of resources committed to push or pull within these different stages.

Back in the 1970s, two US researchers (William Abernathy and James Utterback) developed a model which has important lessons for how we think about managing innovation (Figure 7.1).[2] In the early stage – the 'fluid' phase – there is a lot of uncertainty and emphasis is placed on product innovation. Typically, entrepreneurs have lots of ideas (most of which fail) about the ways to use new market and technological opportunities. (Think about the rise of the Internet and the continuing proliferation of entrepreneurial ideas as an example of a fluid phase.)

But after a while there is a stabilization around a particular configuration – the 'dominant design' (which may not always be the best in technical terms but is the one which matches the market's needs and aspirations), and then emphasis shifts away from more product variety to process innovation. How can we make this in volume, to a low price, consistent quality, etc.? (Think of Henry Ford: he was a latecomer to the business of car design but his Model T became the dominant design and succeeded principally because of the extensive process innovations around mass production.)

Finally, there is a third, 'mature' phase in which innovation is incremental in both product and process, there is extensive competition and the scene is set for another breakthrough and return to the fluid stage. What this model means is that we could particularly look for radical product innovation ideas in the

Case Study of these patterns of innovation associated with the evolution of the bicycle is available on the Innovation Portal at **www.innovation-portal.info**

fluid phase but in the mature stage we would be better placed concentrating on incremental improvement innovations.

Adoption and Diffusion

A fourth and related issue is around diffusion – the adoption and elaboration of innovation over time. Innovation adoption takes place gradually over time, following some version of an s-curve. At the early stages innovative users with a high tolerance for failure will explore, to be followed by early adopters. This gives way to the majority following their lead until finally the remnant of a potential adopting population – the laggards – adopt or remain stubbornly resistant. Understanding diffusion processes and the influential factors is important because it helps us understand where and when different kinds of triggers are picked up. Lead users and early adopters are likely to be important sources of ideas and variations which can help shape an innovation in its early life, whereas the early and late majority will be more a source of incremental improvement ideas.[3] (We'll explore this in detail in Chapter 12.)

 Activity to help you explore sources of innovation and the role of these models is available on the Innovation Portal at www.innovation-portal.info

The Innovation Treasure Hunt

As we saw in Chapter 2, innovation can take a variety of forms – 'product', 'process', 'position' and 'paradigm'– and comes in incremental or radical flavours. So it would help to have a map of innovation search space (the ground we want to cover) before we start out on our journey. We'll build it with two axes to create a simple view of the search space and then look at how we can cover it (Figure 7.2).

Incremental/Radical Innovation: Do Better/Do Different

The vertical one is all about the novelty involved – from incremental to radical innovation, 'doing what we do but better' to 'do different'. In terms of numbers, most innovation projects are around the incremental area, and the big advantage is that there is a degree of familiarity, the risk is lower and we are moving forward along a path which has already been trodden. The benefits from doing so may be small in themselves but their effect is cumulative.

By contrast, taking a leap forward could bring big gains – but also carries higher risk. Since we are moving into unknown territory, there will be a need to experiment – and a good chance that much of that experimentation will fail. We won't be clear about the directions in which we want to go and so there is a real risk of going up blind alleys or being trapped in one-way streets. Essentially, the kind of searching we do – and the tools we use – will be different.

Established Frame/New Frame

The other axis is linked to how we frame the space in which we look. Just as human beings need to develop mental models to simplify the confusion which the rich stimuli in their

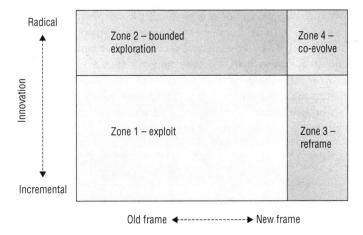

FIGURE 7.2   A map of innovation search space

environment offer them, so individual entrepreneurs and established organizations make use of simplifying frames. They 'look' at the environment and take note of elements which they consider relevant: threats to watch out for, opportunities to take advantage of, competitors and collaborators, etc. Constructing such frames helps give the organization some stability but it also defines the space within which it will search for innovation possibility.

In practice, these models often converge around a core theme, and although organizations may differ, they often share common models about how their world behaves. So most firms in a particular sector will adopt similar ways of framing, assuming certain 'rules of the game', following certain trajectories in common. And this shapes where and how they tend to search for opportunities. It emerges over time but once established becomes the 'box' within which further innovation takes place.

It's difficult to think and work outside this box, because it is reinforced by the structures, processes and tools which the organization uses in its day-to-day work. The problem is also that such ways of working are linked to a complex web of other players in the organization's 'value network' – its key competitors, customers and suppliers – who further reinforce the dominant way of seeing the world.

Powerful though they are, such frames are only models of how individuals and organizations think the world works. It is possible to see things differently, take into account new elements, pay attention to different things and come up with alternative solutions. This is, of course, exactly what entrepreneurs do when they try to find opportunities: they look at the world differently and see opportunity in a different way of framing things. And sometimes their new way of looking at things becomes a widely accepted one, and their innovation changes the game.

Rather like the drunk who has lost his keys on the way home and is desperately searching for them under the nearest lamp post 'because there is more light there', firms have a natural tendency to search in spaces which they already know and understand. But we know that the weak early-warning signals of the emergence of totally new possibilities – radically different technologies, new markets with radically different needs, changing public opinion or political context – won't happen under our particular lamp post. Instead, they are out there in the darkness – so we have to find new ways of searching in space we aren't familiar with.

How can this be done? By luck, sometimes – except that simply being in the right place at the right time doesn't always help. History suggests that even when the new possibility is presented to the firm on a plate its internal capacity to see and act on the possibilities is often lacking. For example, the famous 'not invented here' effect has been observed on many occasions where an otherwise well-established and successful innovative firm rejects a new opportunity which turns out to be of major significance.

INNOVATION IN ACTION 7.1

Technological Excellence may not be Enough. . .

In the 1970s, Xerox was the dominant player in photocopiers, having built the industry from its early days when it was founded on the radical technology pioneered by Chester Carlson and the Battelle Memorial Institute. But despite their prowess in the core technologies and continuing investment in maintaining an edge, it found itself seriously threatened by a new generation of small copiers developed by new entrant Japanese players. Despite the fact that Xerox had enormous experience in the industry and a deep understanding of the core technology, it took the company almost eight years of mishaps and false starts to introduce a competitive product. In that time, Xerox lost around half its market share and suffered severe financial problems.

In similar fashion in the 1950s, the electronics giant RCA developed a prototype portable transistor-based radio using technologies which it had come to understand well. However, it saw little reason to promote such an apparently inferior technology and continued to develop and build its high range devices. By contrast, Sony used it to gain access to the consumer market and to build a whole generation of portable consumer devices – and in the process acquired considerable technological experience, which enabled it to enter and compete successfully in higher-value, more complex markets.

Exploit or Explore?

Having drawn the map, we can begin to look at strategies which individuals and organizations could use to search across it. And that raises an important question: do we exploit or explore? One way we can innovate is by moving forward from what we already know. Individuals and organizations can deploy knowledge resources and other assets to secure returns, and a 'safe' way of doing so is to harvest a steady flow of benefits derived from 'doing what we do better'. This has been termed 'exploitation' by innovation researchers, and it essentially involves using what we already know as the foundation for further incremental innovation. It builds strongly on what is already well established – but in the process leads to a high degree of what is called 'path dependency'. Essentially, what we did in the past will play a strong role in shaping what we do next.

The trouble is that in an uncertain environment the potential to secure and defend a competitive position depends on 'doing something different', that is a radical product or process innovation rather than imitations and variants of what others are also offering. This kind of search had been termed 'exploration' and is the kind which involves big leaps into new knowledge territory – risky, but they enable the organization to do new and very different things.

Whether we are talking about private sector competition or public service reform, we need to recognize that 'exploit' may not always be a sufficient strategy. In the United Kingdom, for example, the National Health Service in 2010 was tasked with finding £20 billion of savings within four years – and while efficiency improvements will certainly contribute a proportion of this through incremental 'do better' innovation, the reality is that some radically different things will be needed. So the challenge is one of exploit *and* explore, with the need to learn some new search approaches and tools to help do that.

A good way to start understanding broad strategies is by looking at what organizations actually do when searching for innovation triggers. Table 7.1 gives an example.

Information of this kind gives us a broad picture, in this case showing that ideas for innovation come from many different sources – suppliers, universities, etc. It reinforces the view that successful innovation is about spreading the net as widely as possible, mobilizing multiple channels. Although surveys of this kind tell us a lot, they also miss important elements, for example:

- Incremental innovation and how it is triggered lies beneath their radar screen, and there is a bias towards product innovation.
- They don't capture much of the organizational change.
- They don't capture 'position' or business model innovation so well, again especially at the incremental end.

INNOVATION IN ACTION 7.2

How We Search for Innovation

We look in the usual places for our industry. We look at our customers. We look at our suppliers. We go to trade bodies. We go to trade fairs. We present technical papers. We have an input coming from our customers. What we also try to do is develop inputs from other areas. We've done that in a number of ways. Where we're recruiting, we try to bring in people who can bring a different perspective. We don't necessarily want people who've worked in the type of instruments we have in the same industry . . . certainly in the past we've brought in people who bring a completely different perspective, almost like introducing greensand into the oyster. We deliberately look outside. We will look in other areas. We will look in areas that are perhaps different technology. We will look in areas that are adjacent to what we do, where we haven't normally looked. And we also do encourage the employees themselves to come forward with ideas.

Source: Patrick McLaughlin, Managing Director, Cerulean.

TABLE 7.1 Sources of Innovation

Approach	How extensively used (% of sample using)	Rank	How effective (scale of 1–10)	Rank
Ethnography	12.9	13	6.8	1
Customer visit teams	30.6	4	6.6	2
Customer focus groups for problem detection	25.5	5	6.4	3
Lead-user methods	24	6	6.4	4
User design	17.4	11	6.0	5
Customer brainstorming	17.4	11	5.9	6
Peripheral vision tools	33.1	2	5.9	7
Customer advisory board	17.6	10	5.8	8
Community of enthusiasts	8	15	5.7	9
Disruptive technologies	22	8	5.7	10
Internal idea capture	38	1	5.5	11
Partners and vendors	22.1	7	5.5	12
Patent mining	33	3	5.5	13
Accessing external technical community	19.5	9	4.9	14
Scanning small businesses and start-ups	13	13	4.9	15
External product design/ crowdsourcing	2	18	4.8	16
External submitted ideas	7.9	16	4.5	17
External idea contest	4.1	17	4.3	18

Source: Based on Cooper, R. and S. Edgett, Ideation for product innovation: What are the best methods?, In *PDMA Visions 2008*, Product Development Management Association. pp.12–16.

Case Studies of Tesco and Cerulean giving you clues about the approaches organizations take and the tools they use are available on the Innovation Portal at **www.innovation-portal.info**

- They tend to focus on the 'obvious' search agents like R&D or market research departments but leave out others who may be involved, e.g. purchasing – and within the business the idea of suggestion schemes and high involvement innovation.
- They deal with established organizations so such surveys tell us very little about where and how new start-ups seek out their opportunities.

- They mainly tells us about the 'exploit' area and gives less detail about the explore side of things.

Video Clip (and transcript) of an interview with Patrick McLaughlin, managing director of Cerulean, is available on the Innovation Portal at **www.innovation-portal.info**

Innovation Search Strategies

Of course, in reality the lines between these 'zones' are not clear-cut, but the idea behind the map is that we are likely to experience very different challenges in each area. Finding opportunities is going to need different strategies – and in the following section we'll look at the challenges in a little more detail.

Strategies for Exploit

Zone 1 is all about 'exploit' search, assuming a stable and shared frame within which adaptive and incremental development takes place. Search 'routines' here are associated with *refining* tools and methods for technological and market research, deepening relationships with established key players. Examples would be working with key suppliers, getting closer to customers and building key strategic alliances to help deliver established innovations more efficiently. Process innovation is enabled by inviting suggestions for incremental improvement across the organization – a high-involvement kaizen model.

Understanding buyer/adopter behaviour has become a key theme in marketing studies since it provides us with frameworks and tools for identifying and understanding user needs. Advertising and branding play a key role in this process – essentially using psychology to tune into, or even stimulate and create – basic human needs. Another strand has focused on detailed studies of what people actually do and how they actually use products and services – using the same approaches which anthropologists use to study new tribes to uncover hidden and latent needs.

Case Studies of Kumba Resources, NPI and Hosiden illustrating how different organizations manage this 'exploit' search task are available on the Innovation Portal at **www.innovation-portal.info**

Video Clip looking at how Veeder-Root approaches the challenge of continuous process innovation is available on the Innovation Portal at **www.innovation-portal.info**

Strategies for Explore

Zone 2 involves searching new territory, pushing the frontiers of what is known and deploying different search techniques for doing so – but still doing so within an established framework. R&D search investments here tend to include big projects with high strategic potential, patenting and intellectual property (IP) strategies aimed at marking out and defending territory,

Tools which highlight the ways of carrying out this kind of search – market research tools and continuous improvement toolkit – are available on the Innovation Portal at **www.innovation-portal.info**

and riding key technological trajectories (such as Moore's law in semiconductors). Market research similarly aims to get close to customers but to push the frontiers via empathic design, latent needs analysis, etc. Although the activity is risky and exploratory, it is still governed strongly by the frame for the sector.

'Explore' strategies are much more about specialist groups and networks inside and outside the organization, for example with university, public and commercial laboratories and other firms. The highly specialized nature of the work makes it difficult for others in the organization to participate. Indeed this gap between worlds can often lead to tensions between the 'operating' and the 'exploring' units, and the boardroom battles between these two camps for resources are often tense. In similar fashion market research is highly specialized and may include external professional agencies in its network with the task of providing sophisticated business intelligence around a focused frontier.

From the standpoint of the entrepreneur, this zone is interesting since there may be significant opportunities. Individuals and start-up businesses with highly specialized knowledge assets, for example hi-tech spinouts from universities, may feature strongly on the radar screens of large established organizations looking to explore. This pattern of 'symbiosis' (mutual dependency and advantage for new and established players) is a common pattern in fields like pharmaceuticals, electronics, software and biotechnology.

Case Studies describing formal R&D and major market research approaches – Philips Lighting and Tesco – are available on the Innovation Portal at **www.innovation-portal.info**

Video Clip of Cerulean exploring the difficulties in bringing a radical innovation culture to bear in an organization with a strong capability in the 'exploit' direction is available on the Innovation Portal at **www.innovation-portal.info**

Tool to help with this kind of search strategy for peripheral vision is available on the Innovation Portal at **www.innovation-portal.info**

Strategies for Reframing

Zone 3 is essentially associated with *reframing*. It involves searching a space where alternative architectures are generated, exploring different permutations and combinations of elements in the environment. Importantly, this often happens by working with elements in the environment not embraced by established business models, for example, working with fringe markets, looking at the 'bottom of the pyramid' or collaborating with 'extreme users'.

This zone often favours entrepreneurs on the outside of established organizations because they can see ways of putting the pieces together differently. Importantly, this may not involve pushing the technological frontiers with radical innovation in the core offering or process. It is often about change in the ways the architecture works.

Table 7.2 describes some of the additional approaches which organizations use to try to extend their peripheral vision and find new innovation opportunities.

Case Study exploring how Fujifilm has entered the world of skin care, reframing its business away from photography and opening up new innovation space is available on the Innovation Portal at **www.innovation-portal.info**

Video Clips describing 3M's experience with lead-user methods are available on the Innovation Portal at **www.innovation-portal.info**

TABLE 7.2 Developing New Ways of Searching

Search Strategy	Mode of operation
Sending out scouts	Dispatch idea hunters to track down new innovation triggers
Exploring multiple futures	Use futures techniques to explore alternative possible futures; and develop innovation options from that
Using the Web	Harness the power of the Web, through online communities and virtual worlds, for example to detect new trends
Working with active users	Team up with product and service users to see the ways in which they change and develop existing offerings
Deep diving	Study what people actually do, rather than what they say they do
Probe and learn	Use prototyping as a mechanism to explore emergent phenomena and act as a boundary object to bring key stakeholders into the innovation process
Mobilize the mainstream	Bring mainstream actors into the product and service development process
Corporate venturing	Create and deploy venture units
Corporate entrepreneurship and intrapreneuring	Stimulate and nurture the entrepreneurial talent inside the organization
Use brokers and bridges	Cast the ideas net far and wide and connect with other industries
Deliberate diversity	Create diverse teams and a diverse workforce
Idea generators	Use creativity tools

INNOVATION IN ACTION 7.3

Scouting for Ideas

The mobile phone company O2 has a trend-scouting group of about 10 people who interpret externally identified trends into their specific business context, while BT has a scouting unit in Silicon Valley which assesses some 3000 technology opportunities a year in California. The four-man operation was established in 1999 to make venture investments in promising telecom start-ups, but after the dotcom bubble burst it shifted its mission towards identifying partners and technologies that BT was interested in. The small team looks at more than 1000 companies per year and then, based on their deep knowledge of the issues facing the R&D operations back in England, they target the small number of cases where there is a direct match between BT's needs and the Silicon Valley company's technology. While the number of successful partnerships that result from this activity is small – typically four or five per year – the unit performs an invaluable service by keeping BT abreast of the latest developments in its technology domain.

INNOVATION IN ACTION 7.4

Online Innovation Markets

Karim Lakhani (Harvard Business School) and Lars Bo Jeppesen (Copenhagen Business School) studied the ways in which businesses are making use of the innovation market platform Innocentive.com. The core model at Innocentive is to host 'challenges' put up by 'seekers' for ideas which 'solvers' offer. They examined 166 challenges and also carried out a Web-based survey of solvers and found that the model offered around a 30% solution rate – of particular value to seekers looking to diversify the perspectives and approaches to solving their problems. The approach was particularly relevant for problems that large and well-known R&D-intensive firms had been unsuccessful in solving internally. Innocentive currently has around 200 000 solvers and as a result considerable diversity; their study suggested that as the number of unique scientific interests in the overall submitter population increased the higher the probability that a challenge was successfully solved. In other words, diversity of potential scientific approaches to a problem was a significant predictor of problem-solving success.

Interestingly, the survey also found that solvers were often bridging knowledge fields – taking solutions and approaches from one area (their own specialty) and applying it to different areas. This study offers systematic evidence for the premise that innovation occurs at the boundary of disciplines.

Strategies for Co-Evolution

Exploring Complexity: Working at the edge of chaos

Zone 4 represents the 'edge of chaos' complex environment where innovation emerges as a product of a process of co-evolution. In this space many different elements are involved and each affects the other so that it becomes impossible to predict the outcome. Think about the emerging future for health care: it's unlikely that the current models (whether publicly or privately funded) will survive long into the future because of the pressures of greater demand, an ageing population, spending cuts, etc. But any new model is going to be hard to predict because so many factors are involved – technology, markets, global distribution, public/private sector split, increasing lobbying by different interest groups, etc. Instead, we should see it as a complex system in which there is extensive interaction and where what happens in one part of the system will affect the others.

Under conditions like these, it is easy to assume that there is nothing we can do – and more importantly for our entrepreneurs, nowhere in which they could find opportunities except by accident or by waiting until the new game has fully emerged. But we do know something about these situations. There is a body of knowledge around 'complexity theory' which specializes in them. And there are some simple principles which can help us work in innovation space of this kind. In particular, there is a pattern of what is called 'co-evolution' in which different interacting elements begin to converge on a particular solution. (An example in nature is the way ice crystals can form into the particular and organized pattern of a snowflake.)

As this pattern begins to emerge, it can be amplified through feedback, making the signal about the pattern clearer than all the other competing background signals. And gradually the system acquires momentum to move in a particular direction – and a dominant pattern emerges. We see this a lot in what is sometimes called the 'fluid phase' in the innovation lifecycle, when new combinations of technologies and markets swirl around and entrepreneurs try out many different ideas. Eventually, out of the turbulent and unpredictable set of possibilities a dominant design emerges which sets the pattern for future innovation – think about the motor car or the bicycle as simple examples.

So for entrepreneurs to work in this complex space there are some simple rules:

* Be in the game early – the signals about the emergence of the dominant design will be weak at first and hard to spot from the outside.
* Be in there actively and prepared to experiment – there is no 'right' answer but a lot of playing with possibilities.
* Be prepared for failure – essentially working in zone 4 is about probe and learn, mostly about what won't work.
* Be aware of others in the system, picking up weak signals and amplifying what seems to work.

To summarize, Table 7.3 shows the different approaches – search strategies – which could be used to explore innovation space.

Strategies for Searching

As we have seen, organizations need to be able to cover all the innovation search space – and to do so with limited resources. So their approaches need to be strategic and in this section we'll briefly look at some of the underlying approaches which successful innovators use. In particular, we'll look at:

* Open innovation
* Networks for innovation
* Knowledge management.

Open Innovation

Building rich and extensive linkages with potential sources of innovation has always been important, for example studies in the United Kingdom in the 1950s identified one key differentiator between successful and less successful innovating firms as the degree to which they were 'cosmopolitan' as opposed to 'parochial' in their approach towards sources of innovation.[4] Entrepreneurs starting up new ventures know the importance of building networks – the essence of what they do in spotting opportunities is to make connections which others may have missed.

TABLE 7.3 Challenges in Navigating Innovation Search Space

Zone	Search challenges
1. 'Business as usual' – innovation but under 'steady state' conditions, little disturbance around core business model	Exploit – extend in incremental fashion boundaries of technology and market. Refine and improve. Build close links/strong ties with key players. Favours established organizations with resources – start-up entrepreneurs are looking to spot niches within the mainstream
2. 'Business model as usual' – bounded exploration within this frame	Exploration – pushing frontiers of technology and market via advanced techniques. Build close links with key strategic knowledge sources, inside and especially outside the organization. Entrepreneurs with key knowledge assets – for example spin-off ventures from a university research lab – can benefit from this search process and link their ideas with the resources which a major organization can bring
3. Alternative frame – taking in new/different elements in environment Variety matching, alternative architectures	Reframing – explore alternative options, introduce new elements. Experimentation and open-ended search Breadth and periphery important. Entrepreneurs have a significant advantage here since they can bring fresh thinking and perspectives to an established game. Mainstream organizations often seek to explore here through setting up internal entrepreneurial groups – corporate venturing, 'intrapreneurs', etc.
4. Radical – new to the world – possibilities. New architecture around as yet unknown and established elements	Emergence – need to co-evolve with stakeholders • Be in there • Be in there early • Be in there actively Entrepreneurs have advantages here since this resembles the 'fluid' state in innovation lifecycle and requires flexibility in thinking, tolerance for failure, willingness to take risks, etc. Big problem is the high rate of failure here which established organizations have some capacity to absorb but which is an issue for start-up entrepreneurs.

There are, of course, arguments for keeping a relatively closed approach – for example there is a value in doing your own R&D and market research because the information collected is then available to be exploited in ways which the business can control. It can choose to push certain lines, hold back on others, keep things essentially within a closed system. But as we've seen the reality is that innovation is triggered in all sorts of ways and a sensible strategy is to cast the net as widely as possible.

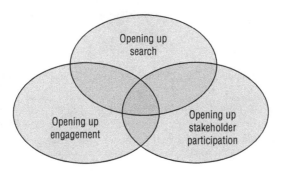

FIGURE 7.3   Convergence around 'open innovation'

This is especially true when we move into our 'explore' spaces on the map. We are going to need different knowledge sets and perspectives, and this requires learning new search strategies. Innovation has always been a multiplayer game, one which involves weaving together many different strands of what could be termed 'knowledge spaghetti' to create something new. What's different about today's context is the sheer volume and distribution of that knowledge – for example it's estimated that nearly $1500 billion ($920 billion) of new knowledge is being created every year in public and private sector R&D around the world. Keeping track of growth on this scale – especially when this R&D is increasingly globalized and coming from an ever-wider range of players – becomes a major headache even for major technology-based firms.

US professor Henry Chesbrough coined the term 'open innovation' to describe the challenge facing even large organizations in keeping track of and accessing external knowledge rather than relying on internally generated ideas.[5] Put simply, open innovation involves the recognition that 'not all the smart guys work for us'.

Of course, it is not simply new R&D knowledge about science and technology which is exploding. There are similar seismic shifts on the market demand side, and on the interests of users in greater customization and even participation in the innovation game.

What this means is a significant acceleration in the opening-up of the innovation search game in a number of converging areas, as indicated by Figure 7.3.

These themes are playing an increasingly important role in shaping our innovation landscape and we will explore them in detail in Chapter 17.

Innovation Networks

One consequence of the increasing openness in innovation is the growing importance of networks as a way of accessing and working with other people's knowledge. There are many ways in which innovation networks can contribute. Box 7.1 gives some examples.

Case Studies of using innovation networks to help accelerate learning around product and process innovation are available on the Innovation Portal at **www.innovation-portal.info**

BOX 7.1: WHY NETWORK?

There are four major arguments pushing for greater levels of networking in innovation:

- Collective efficiency – in a complex environment requiring a high variety of responses it is hard for all but the largest firm to hold these competencies in-house. Networking offers a way of getting access to different resources through a shared exchange process – the kind of theme underlying the cluster model which has proved so successful for small firms in Italy, Spain and many other countries.
- Collective learning – networking offers not only the opportunity to share scarce or expensive resources. It can also facilitate a shared learning process in which partners exchange experiences, challenge models and practices, bring new insights and ideas, and support shared experimentation. 'Learning networks' have proved successful vehicles in industrial development in a variety of cases (see later in the chapter for some examples).
- Collective risk-taking – building on the idea of collective activity, networking also permits higher levels of risk to be considered than any single participant may be prepared to undertake. This is the rationale behind many pre-competitive consortia around high-risk R&D.
- Intersection of different knowledge sets – networking also allows for different relationships to be built across knowledge frontiers and opens up the participating organization to new stimuli and experiences.

Knowledge Management

We've seen throughout the book that knowledge plays a key role in innovation – and so it makes sense to understand how it is created and moved around our organization and in its wider environment. This idea of 'knowledge management' has been studied for many years and there are some useful pointers emerging around helpful strategies. (We'll look in more detail at this question in Chapter 13.)

For example:

- Mobilizing employee ideas and knowledge around incremental product and especially process innovation. This has always been a powerful source of innovation but has been given additional impetus through communication and networking technologies which allow for innovation contests, 'innovation jams' and other approaches, bringing more people into the game.[6]

Video Clips of interviews with organizations which have been working to mobilize high involvement innovation are available on the Innovation Portal at **www.innovation-portal.info**

- Bringing the 'voice of the customer' into all areas of the organization and using that to focus and draw out relevant ideas and knowledge. Amongst recipes for achieving this are to rotate staff so that they spend some time out working with and listening to customers, and the introduction of the concept that 'everybody is someone's customer'.

- Using our understanding of social networks and how ideas flow within and across organizations. Of particular significance in this context is the role played by various forms of 'gatekeeper' in the organization. This concept, which goes back to the pioneering work of Thomas Allen in his studies within the aerospace industry of the 1970s, relates to a model of communication in which ideas flow via key individuals to those who can make use of them in developing innovation.[7]

Activity to help you bring the 'voice of the customer' into the organization – quality function deployment (QFD) – is available on the Innovation Portal at **www.innovation-portal.info**

Tools, such as the quality function deployment (QFD), to help you see how to bring the 'voice of the customer' into the organization are available on the Innovation Portal at **www.innovation-portal.info**

- Using 'communities of practice', for example Procter and Gamble's successes with 'connect and develop' owe much to the company's mobilizing rich linkages between people who know things *within* their giant global operations and increasingly outside it. P&G uses 'communities of practice', where people with different knowledge sets can converge around core themes. Intranet technology links around 10 000

Case Studies of how 3M and Procter and Gamble use these ideas are available on the Innovation Portal at **www.innovation-portal.info**

people in an internal 'ideas market' – and some of the company's significant successes have come from making better internal connections. 3M puts much of its success down to making and managing connections, and Larry Wendling, Vice President for Corporate Research, calls the rich formal and informal networking which links the thousands of R&D and market-facing people across the organization 3M's 'secret weapon'!

- 'Intrapreneurship' – mobilizing internal entrepreneurship. A rich source lies in the entrepreneurial ideas of employees – projects which are not formally sanctioned by the business but build on the energy, enthusiasm and inspiration of people passionate enough to want to try out new ideas. Encouraging this kind of activity is increasingly popular and organizations like 3M and Google make attempts to manage it in a semi-formal fashion, allocating a certain amount of time/space to employees to explore their own ideas. Managing this is a delicate balancing act: on the one hand there is a need to give both permission and resources to enable employee-led ideas to flourish, but on the other there is the risk of these resources being dissipated with nothing to show for them. In many cases there is an attempt to create a culture of what can be termed 'bootlegging' in which there is tacit support for projects which go against the grain.[8]

Learning to Search

As we saw in Chapter 1, managing innovation is something which individuals and organizations learn to do through a mixture of trial and error, imitation and borrowing of good practices, improvisation, etc. Over time, they accumulate experience about what works best for them – and this becomes a highly specific approach, almost like a personality. The idea of 'routines' – repeated, learnt and embedded patterns of behaviour – very much applies here in the area of search tools. Individuals and organizations develop and refine the tools they use to trawl the innovation space, building on tried-and-tested techniques but also experimenting and adding new ones to deal with new challenges in their search space.

For example, much experience has been gained in how R&D units can be structured to enable a balance between applied research (supporting the 'exploit' type of search) and more wide-ranging, 'blue sky' activities (which facilitate the 'explore' side of the equation). These approaches have been refined further along 'open innovation' lines where the R&D work of others is brought into play, and by ways of dealing with the increasingly global production of knowledge, for example the pharmaceutical giant GSK deliberately pursues a policy of R&D competition across several major facilities distributed around the world.

In similar fashion, market research has evolved to produce a rich portfolio of tools for building a deep understanding of user needs – and continues to develop new and further refined techniques, for example empathic design, lead-user methods and increasing use of ethnography.

The choice of techniques and structures depends on a variety of strategic factors like those explored above, balancing their costs and risks against the quality and quantity of knowledge they bring in. Throughout this book, we stress the idea that managing innovation is a *dynamic* capability – something which needs to be updated and extended on a continuing basis to deal with the 'moving frontier' problem. As markets, technologies, competitors, regulations and all sorts of other elements in a complex environment shift, we need to learn new tricks and sometimes let go of older ones which are no longer appropriate.

The label 'absorptive capacity' has been widely used to describe this learning capability and it can be expressed as 'the ability of a firm to recognize the value of new, external information, assimilate it, and apply it'.[9] It's an important concept because it is easy to make the assumption that, because there is a rich environment full of potential sources of innovation, every organization will find and make use of these. The reality is, of course, that they differ widely in their ability to make use of such trigger signals. For various reasons, organizations may find difficulties in growing through acquiring and using new knowledge.

Some may simply be unaware of the need to change never mind having the capability to manage such change. Such firms, a classic problem of small business growth for example, differ from those which recognize in some strategic way the need to change, to acquire and use new knowledge but lack the capability to target their search or to assimilate and make effective use of new knowledge once identified. Others may be clear what they need but lack the capability to find and acquire it. And others may have well-developed routines for dealing with all of these issues and represent resources on which less experienced firms can draw, as is the case with some major supply chains focused around a core player.

The key message from research on absorptive capacity is that acquiring and using new knowledge involves multiple and different activities around search, acquisition, assimilation and implementation.[10] It's essentially about learning to learn – building capabilities for search, acquire, assimilate, etc. which allow organizations to repeat the trick. Developing absorptive capacity involves two complementary kinds of learning. Type 1 (adaptive learning) is about reinforcing and establishing relevant routines for dealing with a particular level of environmental complexity, and type 2 (generative learning) for taking on new levels of complexity.[11]

Tools to help an organization reflect on its level of absorptive capacity and areas which it could consider in developing it further are available on the Innovation Portal at **www.innovation-portal.info**

Summary

- Faced with a rich environment full of potential sources of innovation, individuals and organizations need a strategic approach to searching for opportunities.

- We can imagine a search space for innovation within which we look for opportunities. There are two dimensions: 'incremental/do better vs. Radical/do different innovation', and 'existing frame/new frame'.

- Looking for opportunities can take us into the realms of 'exploit' – innovations built on moving forward form what we already know in mainly incremental fashion. Or it can involve 'explore' innovation, making risky but sometimes valuable leaps into new fields and opening up innovation space.

- Exploit innovation favours established organizations, and start-up entrepreneurs mostly find opportunities within niches in an established framework.

- Bounded exploration involves radical search but within an established frame. This requires extensive resources (e.g. in R&D) but although this again favours established organizations there is also scope for knowledge-rich entrepreneurs (e.g. in high-tech start-up businesses).

- Reframing innovation requires a different mindset, a new way of seeing opportunities – and often favours start-up entrepreneurs. Established organizations find this area difficult to search in because it requires them to let go of the ways they have traditionally worked. In response many set up internal entrepreneurial groups to bring the fresh thinking they need.

- Exploring at the edge of chaos requires skills in trying to 'manage' processes of co-evolution. Again, this favours start-up entrepreneurs with the flexibility, risk-taking and tolerance for failure to create new combinations and the agility to pick up on emerging new trends and ride them.

- Search strategies require a combination of exploit and explore approaches, but these often need different organizational arrangements.

- There are many tools and techniques available to support search in exploit and explore directions; increasingly, the game is being opened up and networks (and networking approaches and technologies) are becoming increasingly important.

- Absorptive capacity (the ability to absorb new knowledge) is a key factor in the development of innovation management capability. It is essentially about learning to learn.

Further Resources

The concept of 'exploit' vs. 'explore' was first discussed by James March and has formed the basis for many studies since then. See March, J. (1991) Exploration and exploitation in organizational learning, *Organization Science*, **2**(1): 71–87; and Benner, M. J. and M. L. Tushman

(2003) Exploitation, exploration, and process management: The productivity dilemma revisited, *Academy of Management. The Academy of Management Review* **28** (2): 238.

Tushman and Anderson explore the challenges for organizations in the midst of major technological upheavals; Tushman, M. and P. Anderson (1987) Technological discontinuities and organizational environments, *Administrative Science Quarterly* **31** (3): 439–465.

The difficulties of reframing are well explored by Day and Shoemaker, who argue the need for 'peripheral vision' amongst entrepreneurs; see Day, G. and P. Schoemaker *Peripheral Vision: Detecting the weak signals that will make or break your company* (Harvard Business School Press, 2006). This theme is also picked up in Foster, R. and S. Kaplan *Creative Destruction* (Harvard University Press, 2002); and Christensen, C., S. Anthony and E. Roth *Seeing What's Next* (Harvard Business School Press, 2007).

Searching at the frontier is one of the questions being addressed by the Discontinuous Innovation Laboratory, a network of around 30 academic institutions and 150 companies; see www.innovation-lab.org for more details. Reports on their work are available for download at www.aim-research.org.

Looking at the edge of familiar markets and finding unexploited space are discussed in Ulnwick, A. *What Customers Cant: Using outcome-driven innovation to create breakthrough products and services* (McGraw-Hill, 2005); and Kim, W. and R. Mauborgne *Blue Ocean Strategy: How to create uncontested market space and make the competition irrelevant* (Harvard Business School Press, 2005).

Open innovation was originated by Henry Chesbrough but has been elaborated on in a number of other studies. Case examples include the Procter and Gamble story, and Alan Lafley's book provides a readable account from the perspective of the CEO: Lafley, A. and R. Charan *The Game Changer* (Profile, 2008).

The concept of absorptive capacity was originated by Cohen and Levinthal and developed by Zahra and George; Zahra, S. A. and G. George (2002) Absorptive capacity: A review, reconceptualization and extension, *Academy of Management Review*, **27**: 185–194.

References

1. Freeman, C. and L. Soete (1997) *The Economics of Industrial Innovation*, 3rd edn. Cambridge: MIT Press.

2. Abernathy, W. and J. Utterback (1975) A dynamic model of product and process innovation, *Omega*, **3** (6): 639–656.

3. Rogers, E. (2003) *Diffusion of Innovations*, 5th edn. New York: Free Press.

4. Carter, C. and B. Williams (1957) *Industry and Technical Progress*. Oxford: Oxford University Press.

5. Chesbrough, H. (2003) *Open Innovation: The new imperative for creating and profiting from technology*. Boston: Harvard Business School Press.

6. Bessant, J. (2003) *High Involvement Innovation*. Chichester: John Wiley & Sons, Ltd.

7. Allen, T. and G. Henn (2007) *The Organization and Architecture of Innovation*. Oxford: Elsevier.

8. Augsdorfer, P. (1996) *Forbidden Fruit*. Aldershot: Avebury.

9. Cohen, W. and D. Levinthal (1990) Absorptive capacity: A new perspective on learning and innovation, *Administrative Science Quarterly*, **35** (1): 128–152.

10. Zahra, S. A. and G. George (2002) Absorptive capacity: A review, reconceptualization and extension, *Academy of Management Review*, **27**: 185–194.

11. Senge, P. (1990) *The Fifth Discipline*. New York: Doubleday.

Deeper Dive explanations of innovation concepts and ideas are available on the Innovation Portal at **www.innovation-portal.info**

Quizzes to test yourself further are available online via the Innovation Portal at **www.innovation-portal.info**

Summary of online resources for Chapter 7 –
all material is available via the Innovation Portal at
www.innovation-portal.info

Cases	**Media**	**Tools**	**Activities**	**Deeper Dive**
• Evolution of the bicycle	• 3M lead-user methods	• Market research toolkit	• Sources of innovation	• Networks for learning
• Tesco	• Tesco goes West	• Continuous improvement toolkit	• Innovation family trees	• Absorptive capacity
• Cerulean	• Patrick McLaughlin, Cerulean	• Futures toolkit	• Quality function deployment (QDF)	
• Kumba Resources	• Veeder-Root	• Search strategies for peripheral vision	• Absorptive capacity audit	
• NPI	• Emma Taylor, Denso Systems	• Learning networks		
• Hosiden	• David Simoes-Brown, 100% Open	• Quality function deployment		
• Philips Lighting	• Catherina Van Delden, Innosabi	• High involvement innovation audit		
• Fujifilm	• Michael Bartl, Hyve			
• Learning networks				
• Procter and Gamble				
• 3M				

Chapter 8

Forecasting Emerging Opportunities for Innovation

LEARNING OBJECTIVES

After this chapter you should be able to:

* understand the uses and limitations of a range of forecasting methods
* apply process and product benchmarking to learn from competitors and best-in-class
* develop scenarios to help identify future opportunities and challenges.

Forecasting

Forecasting the future has a central role in business planning for innovation. In most cases the outputs, that is the predictions made, are less valuable than the process of forecasting itself. If conducted in the right spirit, forecasting should provide a framework for gathering and sharing data, debating interpretations and making assumptions, challenges and risks more explicit.

There are many different methods to support forecasting, each with different benefits and limitations (Table 8.1).

There is no single best method. In practice, there will be a trade-off between the cost, time and robustness of a forecast. The more common methods of forecasting such as trend extrapolation and time series are of limited use for new products, because of the lack of relevant past data. Similarly, product/technology roadmapping is a popular technique for supporting planning in a company, and according to survey of 2000 companies, 89% use it on a regular basis.[1] However, product/technology roadmapping is more suitable for incremental innovation, as it is based on following technological trajectories within a given platform,

TABLE 8.1   Types, Uses and Limitations of Different Methods of Forecasting

Method	Uses	Limitations
Trend extrapolation	Short-term, stable environment	Relies on past data and assumes past patterns
Product and technology roadmapping	Medium-term, stable platform and clear trajectory	Incremental, fails to identify future uncertainties
Regression, econometric models and simulation	Medium-term, where relationship between independent and dependent variables understood	Identification and behaviour of independent variables limited
Customer and marketing methods	Medium-term, product attributes and market segments understood	Sophistication of users, limitation of tools to distinguish noise and information
Benchmarking	Medium-term, product and process improvement	Identifying relevant benchmarking candidates
Delphi and experts	Long-term, consensus-building	Expensive, experts disagree or consensus wrong
Scenarios	Long-term, high uncertainty	Time-consuming, unpalatable outcomes

Video Clip of an interview with Helen King of the Irish Food Board, who talks about her use of forecasting to help shape innovation priorities within the sector, is available on the Innovation Portal at **www.innovation-portal.info**

albeit sometimes over many years. Industry practitioners, research analysts and academics when asked to assess the selection of the forecasting technique identified Delphi method as being the most reliable. However, when also considering the cost of implementation, they rated scenarios higher.[2]

The most appropriate choice of forecasting method will depend on:

- what we are trying to forecast
- rate of technological and market change
- availability and accuracy of information
- the company's planning horizon
- the resources available for forecasting.

Our own research confirms that different forecasting methods are appropriate for routine and novel development projects (Table 8.2). However, there appears to be a poor correlation between frequency of use and effectiveness. For example, market segmentation is one of the most popular techniques overall but is not very effective for more radical projects. In contrast, scenario development is much less popular but more effective for the more radical projects.

TABLE 8.2 Use and Usefulness of Techniques for Product and Service Development

Forecasting Method	High-novelty/ Radical project		Low-novelty/ Incremental projects	
	Usage (%)	Usefulness	Usage (%)	Usefulness
Segmentation*	89	3.42	42	4.50
Delphi/Industry Experts	63	3.83	37	3.71
Surveys/Focus groups*	52	4.50	37	4.00
User-practice Observation	47	3.67	42	3.50
Scenario Development	21	3.75	26	2.80

Usefulness Scale: 1–5, 5 = critical, based on manager assessments of 50 development projects in 25 firms. * denotes difference in usefulness rating is statistically significant at 5% level.

Source: Adapted from Tidd, J. and Bodley, K. (2002) 'The effect of project novelty on the new product development process', *R&D Management*, 32(2), 127–138 with permission from John Wiley & Sons, Ltd.

Industry experts and customer focus groups are also popular, but effective for both low- and high-novelty projects.

Many 'normative' techniques are useful for estimating the future demand for existing products, or perhaps alternative technologies or novel niches, but are of limited utility in the case of more radical systems innovation. Exploratory forecasting, in contrast, attempts to explore the range of future possibilities. The most common methods are:

- customer or market surveys
- internal analysis (e.g. brainstorming)
- external analysis (e.g. benchmarking)
- external analysis (e.g. Delphi or expert opinion)
- scenario development.

Customer or Market Surveys

Most companies conduct customer surveys of some sort. In consumer markets this can be problematic simply because customers are unable to articulate their future needs. For example, Apple's iPod was not the result of extensive market research or customer demand but largely the vision and commitment of Steve Jobs. In industrial markets, customers tend to be better equipped to communicate their future requirements, and consequently, business-to-business innovations often originate from customers. Companies can also consult their direct sales force, but these may not always be the best guide to future customer requirements. Information is often filtered in terms of existing products and services, and biased in terms of current sales performance rather than long-term development potential.

Video Clips featuring Eric von Hippel, pioneer of the lead-user method, which describe the approach and its application within 3M are available on the Innovation Portal at **www.innovation-portal.info**

There is no 'one best way' to identify novel niches but rather a range of alternatives. For example, where new products or services are very novel or complex, potential users may not be aware of, or able to articulate, their needs. In such cases traditional methods of market research are of little use, and there will be a greater burden on developers of radical new products and services to 'educate' potential users.

Internal: Brainstorming

Structured idea generation, or brainstorming, aims to solve specific problems or to identify new products or services. Typically, a small group of experts is gathered together and allowed to interact. A chairman records all suggestions without comment or criticism. The aim is to identify, but not evaluate, as many opportunities or solutions as possible. Finally, members of the group vote on the different suggestions. The best results are obtained when representatives from different functions are present, but this can be difficult to manage. Brainstorming does not produce a forecast as such but can provide useful input to other types of forecasting.

The critical requirement for using brainstorming to support exploratory forecasting is to temporarily suspend any discussion or judgement. This happens latter. The keys to successful brainstorming are:

1. Keep a relaxed atmosphere. Meetings should be disciplined but informal. If possible, choose an informal venue.
2. Get the right size of team. The technique seems to work best with groups of five to seven people.
3. Choose a neutral (ideally external) chairperson. The chair checks that everyone understands what is going on and why. Avoid senior managers, as this can restrict the flow of ideas.
4. Define the problem or objectives clearly.
5. Generate as many ideas as possible.
6. Do not allow any evaluation or discussion.
7. Give everyone an equal opportunity to contribute.
8. Write down every idea – clearly and where everyone can see them.
9. When all the ideas are listed, review them for clarification, making sure everyone understands each item. At this point you can eliminate duplications and remove ideas the group feels are no longer appropriate.

10. Allow ideas to incubate. Brainstorm in sessions with perhaps a few days in between. This gives time for the team members to let the ideas turn over in their mind, which often results in new ideas at a later session.

The evaluation of the ideas happens later, usually with a smaller group and using clear criteria for selection, review or rejection.

Tool to help you with brainstorming is available on the Innovation Portal at **www.innovation-portal.info**

External: Benchmarking

Benchmarking is simply the systematic comparison of something against something else. The 'something' can be a process, product, service or measure of performance.[3]

Benchmarking differs from measurement or process analysis in that there is some point of reference or comparison, that is the 'benchmark'. For example, a comparison of performance can be made against a competitor, an industry standard or regulatory requirement. It consists of the systematic comparison against other organizations on specific dimensions of performance with the purpose of identifying and catching up with best practice.

Managers who have a responsibility to improve continuously their operations frequently cannot do so effectively, because of a simple lack of knowledge: not knowing how much better they could perform. It is human nature, without something to measure up against, to assume that current performance is near enough as good as you can get. Benchmarking leaves no room for such complacency. It is not about aiming to clone the success of other organizations, or indulging in industrial spying. Nor is it measurement for measurement's sake. The real goal is to build on the success of others to improve future performance. By benchmarking on a continuing basis, you are always researching current best practice, not dated ideas. Benchmarking is always carried out with the goal of putting improvements into action.

For example, a factory supervisor was proud at having an unplanned downtime of only two hours a week on his manufacturing line. This was far and away the best performance of any of the three workshops on the site. Then he made an overseas visit and saw a company with a similar operation, which had reduced unplanned downtime to less than 30 minutes. Though not all the practices of the other firm were transferable, once he knew that 30 minutes was achievable, he and his engineers were able to devise their own ways to match and even improve on a standard he had previously thought impossible. In the car industry, benchmarking suggests that the best plants are twice as productive and twice the quality as the worst plants. Such large differences in performance and scope for improvement are not uncommon.

The approach started in the 1980s, when US firms found that their loss of market share to Japanese firms reflected underlying deficiencies in both manufacturing and product development. A pioneer was Xerox, who made systematic comparisons with Japanese competitors and found huge deficiencies in performance, as measured by the frequency of assembly line rejects, defects per machine, and the costs and time required for product development. The improvement resulting from conscious policies to overcome these deficiencies has led to both higher customer satisfaction and higher financial returns on assets.

Benchmarking is now used by organizations around the world – in manufacturing, services, private and public sectors – to help them improve their processes and performance. These include multinational giants, such as Ford, ICI, Nissan and Xerox, government agencies, and small businesses employing a handful of people. They all have one thing in common: a recognition that improvement comes from a clear understanding of how the organization is performing, not just against its own performance last year but also against the best it can measure.

INNOVATION IN ACTION 8.1

Cross-Industry Benchmarking

Rail services and Formula 1 racing do not appear to have much in common, other than wheels. However, train companies in the United Kingdom have begun to benchmark F1 practices and technology.

In an effort to improve train availability and utilization, train maintenance crews have studies how F1 teams conduct rapid pit stops. As a result, turnaround times have been reduced from two days to as little as four hours.

Technology benchmarking is also improving performance. Use of telemetry is advanced in F1 racing to identify emerging problems and to anticipate and correct faults. Train companies are using similar techniques to try to reduce breakdowns and delays. Finally, F1 has pioneered the use of KERS – Kinetic Energy Recovery Systems – to capture wasted energy during braking and to re-use this for acceleration, and train manufacturers are researching how this can be adapted for their use.

Benefits of Benchmarking

Benchmarking is more common in customer-facing areas (customer service, marketing and sales, logistics) than in manufacturing, and is least common in product development and R&D. This balance probably reflects the greater degree of difficulty in obtaining accurate information on competitors' performance in the manufacturing and R&D functions.

Benchmarking helps to provide a disciplined, realistic approach to assessing the performance you should expect in critical areas of your organization. It also helps you learn from the experience of other organizations. The broader benefits of benchmarking include the following:[4]

- Establishes realistic goals. Benchmarking helps to identify the most urgent and important areas for improvement, and reduces the likelihood of a focus on internal needs.
- Improves performance. Benchmarking identifies real problems, rather than pet projects or easy targets.
- Achieves better practice. Benchmarking the processes of other organizations with superior performance provides information on proven good practice, and reduces the risk of following anecdotal management fashion or inappropriate consultancy prescriptions.

- Aids implementation and change. Benchmarking provides detailed and persuasive data on others' superior performance or practice, which helps to motivate and focus managers and staff. It can act as a catalyst. Measuring and studying the way your organization works and comparing it against others often reveals and quantifies unknown weaknesses, which can boost the argument for change.

Benchmarking can help implementation in several ways. In particular, it offers a powerful motivator for change since unfavourable comparisons are hard to ignore. But it can also offer valuable clues about how to manage key processes in different ways. Such learning can come not only from direct comparisons between similar organizations but also from organizations in different sectors carrying out broadly similar processes. For example, Southwest Airlines has achieved an enviable record for its turnaround speed at airport terminals. It drew inspiration from watching how industry carried out a rapid changeover of complex machinery between tasks – and, in turn, those industries learnt from watching activities like pit-stop procedures in the motor racing world. In turn, Ryanair and easyJet benchmarked their operations against those of Southwest.

In this way benchmarking complements conventional strategic management and competitor analysis (Table 8.3). It helps to identify both what to do and how to achieve it. As it is based on primary data, it provides much more detailed and realistic goals for improvement.

How to Benchmark

In most cases, benchmarking should begin with a systematic comparison of appropriate measures of performance against that of competitors, that is what needs to be improved. Unfortunately, this is often as far as most organizations get with benchmarking. We will argue that the most significant benefits are achieved by what in most cases should be the next stage: benchmarking processes, that is how the relevant processes can be changed to improve performance.

In practice, the main requirements are:[5]

- a strong commitment from top management to act on any major opportunities for improvement that are revealed

TABLE 8.3   Benchmarking Complements Competitor Analysis

Competitor analysis	Benchmarking
What to do	How to do it
Competitors	Best-in-class, whatever sector
Products and service	Performance and processes
Distant 'armchair' analysis	Site visits, mutual exchange of knowledge
Secondary data	Primary data

- a small amount of training and guidance for employees who will have to gather the information needed to identify and analyse best practice
- authorizing employees to spend some of their time on benchmarking activities.

Of these, the most critical is top management commitment. To prevent benchmarking becoming an academic snapshot of how you are performing, senior management needs to own the process and be seen to be steering it. Without visible support from the top people, many may resent and oppose being exposed to measurement.

Management support will ensure that after the research there will be action for improved performance in places where performance had not been considered a problem.

Once the commitment of top management has been achieved, the key decisions in planning to benchmark are:

- What to benchmark – performance, products, services or processes?
- What to benchmark against – competitors, standards or best-in-class?
- How to adapt and implement the improvements.

Tool to help you with benchmarking is available on the Innovation Portal at **www.innovation-portal.info**

Activity to help you to explore roadmapping is available on the Innovation Portal at **www.innovation-portal.info**

The importance–performance matrix provides a more systematic way of identifying potential candidates for benchmarking (Figure 8.1). This is simply a graphical means of identifying priorities by combining information on customer requirements against performance relative to competitors. On one axis we plot the customer requirement in order of importance and on the other axis we plot our performance relative to competitors'.

External: Delphi

The opinion of outside experts, or Delphi method, is useful where there is a great deal of uncertainty or for long time horizons.[6] Delphi is used where a consensus of expert opinion is required on the timing, probability and identification of future technological goals or consumer needs and the factors likely to affect their achievement. It is best used in making long-term forecasts and revealing how new technologies and other factors could trigger discontinuities in technological trajectories. The choice of experts and the identification of their level and area of expertise are important; the structuring of the questions is even more important. The relevant experts may include suppliers, dealers, customers, consultants and academics. Experts in non-technological fields can be included to ensure that trends in economic, social and environmental fields are not overlooked.

The Delphi method begins with a postal survey of expert opinion on what the future key issues will be, and the likelihood of the developments. The response is then analysed and the same sample of experts resurveyed with a new, more focused questionnaire. This procedure is repeated until some convergence of opinion is observed, or conversely if no consensus is

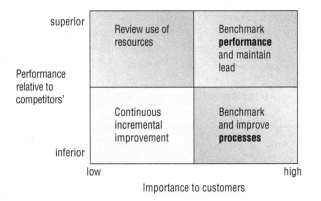

FIGURE 8.1 The importance–performance matrix

reached. The exercise usually consists of an iterative process of questionnaire and feedback among the respondents; this process finally yields a Delphi forecast of the range of experts' opinions on the probabilities of certain events occurring by a quoted time. The method seeks to nullify the disadvantage of face-to-face meetings at which there could be deference to authority or reputation, a reluctance to admit error, a desire to conform or differences in persuasive ability. All of these could lead to an inaccurate consensus of opinion. The quality of the forecast is highly dependent on the expertise and calibre of the experts; how the experts are selected and how many should be consulted are important questions to be answered. If international experts are used, the exercise can take a considerable length of time, or the number of iterations may have to be curtailed. Although seeking a consensus may be important, adequate attention should be paid to views that differ radically from the norm as there may be important underlying reasons to justify such maverick views. With sufficient design, understanding and resources, most of the shortcomings of the Delphi technique can be overcome and it is a popular technique, particularly for national foresight programmes.

In Europe, governments and transnational agencies use Delphi studies to help formulate policy, usually under the guise of 'Foresight' exercises. In Japan, large companies and the government routinely survey expert opinion in order to reach some consensus in those areas with the greatest potential for long-term development. Used in this way, the Delphi method can to a large extent become a self-fulfilling prophecy.

Tools to help you with forecasting – including Delphi – are available on the Innovation Portal at **www.innovation-portal.info**

Scenario Development

Scenarios are internally consistent descriptions of alternative possible futures, based upon different assumptions and interpretations of the driving forces of change.[7] Inputs include quantitative data and analysis, and qualitative assumptions and assessments, such as societal, technological, economic, environmental and political drivers. Scenario development is not, strictly speaking, prediction, as it assumes that the future is uncertain and that the path of current developments can range from the conventional to the revolutionary. It is particularly good at incorporating potential critical events which may result in divergent paths or branches being pursued.

Different definitions of scenarios:

- An internally consistent view of what the future may turn out to be not a forecast, but one possible future outcome.[8]
- A disciplined methodology for imaging possible futures in which organizational decisions may be played out.[9]
- That part of strategic planning which relates to the tools and technologies for managing the uncertainties of the future.[10]

Therefore, a scenario is more than a simple forecast based on projection of past trends, and is not simply a vision of some desired outcome or future. It is an articulation of what is possible under different assumptions and conditions (Table 8.4).

The potential contribution of scenario development to strategy planning is very important, but too often under-utilized. First of all, it helps to understand complex systems by sharing information from horizon scanning, and highlight importance of the changing structure of the industry. Second, a good scenario can also become a dominant vision beyond an organization, promoting a dialogue in the external environment about desirable futures. Finally, scenarios are useful in discovering weaknesses within organizations because they can challenge corporate routine and stakeholders' assumptions.[11] Scenario development is a key part of the long-term planning process in those sectors characterized by high capital investment, long lead times and significant environmental uncertainty, such as energy, aerospace and telecommunications.

Scenario development can be normative or explorative. The normative perspective defines a preferred vision of the future and outlines different pathways from the goal to the present. For example, this is commonly used

Activity to allow you to explore scenarios is available on the Innovation Portal at **www.innovation-portal.info**

TABLE 8.4   Scenario Development versus Strategic Planning

Scenarios	Strategic Planning
Explores potential futures	Focuses on desired futures
Evidence-based	Value-based
Emerging structures and relationships	Known structures and relationships
Incorporates uncertainty	Assumes perfect knowledge
Promotes innovation	Encourages myopia

in energy futures and sustainable futures scenarios. In contrast, the explorative approach identifies the drivers of change, and creates scenarios from these without explicit goals or agenda. Both are used in strategic planning, but the explorative approach is more consistent with developing an innovation strategy.

For scenarios to be effective they need to be inclusive, plausible and compelling (as opposed to being exclusive, implausible or obvious!), as well as challenging to the assumptions of the stakeholders. Scenarios should be transparent and make the assumptions and inputs used explicit. This contributes to their plausibility and persuasiveness. The output is typically two or three contrasting scenarios, but the process of development and discussion of scenarios is much more valuable.

Scenario development may involve many different forecasting techniques, including computer-based simulation. Typically, it begins with the identification of the critical indicators, which may include use of brainstorming and Delphi techniques. Next, the reasons for the behaviour of these indicators is examined, perhaps using regression techniques. The future events which are likely to affect these indicators are identified. These are used to construct the best, worst and most likely future scenarios. Finally, the company assesses the impact of each scenario on its business. The goal is to plan for the outcome with the greatest impact or, better still, retain sufficient flexibility to respond to several different scenarios.

A process for building scenarios:

1. Define the system level, boundaries and time horizon.
2. Develop the focal questions.
3. Identify trends, drivers and uncertainties.
4. Analyse the structures and relationships.
5. Build alternative scenarios and assess the consequences.
6. Develop an action plan and communicate to stakeholders.

Define the System Level and Boundaries

The relevant system may be a specific technology, market, sector or country, or a combination of these, but the exercise must be bounded to provide focus and limit the scope. For example, we could limit the exercise to solar cell technology in Europe.

As we discussed earlier, different forecasting methods work better over different time-frames. Scenario development is able to work over a range of periods, but is best suited to the medium and longer terms, typically multiple years or decades, rather than months. Clearly, the scenarios become less detailed the longer the timeframe. The choice of time horizon will depend on the rate of change of the underlying factors, technological, social, political, etc., as well as the availability of relevant information and data.

Develop the Focal Questions

The type of questions addressed will depend on whether the scenarios are to be normative, with some specific goal, or exploratory, based on current drivers and potential futures. So a normative question could be: 'How can the adoption of solar cells be maximized over the next

Internet Scenarios at Cisco

Cisco develops much of the infrastructure for the Internet, so has a strategic need to explore potential future scenarios. However, almost all organizations rely on the Internet, so these scenarios are relevant to most, including those providing technology, connectivity, devices, software, content and services.

They begin with three focal questions:

- What will the Internet be like in 2025?
- How much bigger will the Internet have grown from today's two billion users and $3 trillion (£1.8 trillion) market?
- Will the Internet have achieved its full potential to connect the world's entire population in ways that advance global prosperity, business productivity, education and social interaction?

Next, they then identify three critical drivers:

- size and scope of broadband network build out
- incremental or breakthrough technological progress
- unbridled or constrained demand from Internet users.

This analysis results in four contrasting scenarios:

- *Fluid Frontiers*: The Internet becomes pervasive, connectivity and devices are ever-more available and affordable, while global entrepreneurship and competition create a wide range of diverse businesses and services.
- *Insecure Growth*: Internet demand stalls because users fear security breaches and cyber-attacks result in increasing regulation.
- *Short of the Promise*: Prolonged economic stagnation in many countries reduces the diffusion of the Internet, with no compensating technological breakthroughs.
- *Bursting at the Seams*: Demand for IP-based services is boundless, but capacity constraints and occasional bottlenecks create a gap between the expectations and reality of Internet use.

If you're interested in the implications and potential strategies which flow from these four scenarios, see the full report on the Cisco website.

Source: Derived from http://www.dummies.com/how-to/content/strategic-planning-case-study-ciscos-internet-scen.html. Erica Olsen (2011) *Strategic Planning Kit for Dummies*, 2nd edn. Chichester: John Wiley & Sons, Ltd.

ten years in Europe?' A more open-ended exploratory question could be: 'What factors will influence the adoption of solar cells over the next ten years in Europe?' The formulation of the questions is central because it will effect which stakeholders are involved and what data and information are collected and assessed.

Identify Trends, Drivers and Uncertainties

History can be a poor guide to the future, whether in politics or finance, but, having bound the scope of the scenarios and by applying specific questions to focus development, past trends and events can be reframed and (re)interpreted to help understand the context and patterns. Two critical requirements at this stage are to challenge assumptions and identify sources of uncertainty.

Case Study of Philips Lighting exploring some of the issues raised here is available on the Innovation Portal at **www.innovation-portal.info**

Risk is usually considered possible to estimate, either qualitatively – high, medium, low – or ideally by probability estimates. Uncertainty is by definition unknowable, but nonetheless the fields and degree of uncertainty should be identified to help to select the most appropriate methods of assessment and plan for contingencies. Traditional approaches to assessing risk focus on the probability of foreseeable risks, rather than true uncertainty, or complete ignorance – what Donald Rumsfeld memorably called the 'unknown unknowns' (12th February, US Department of Defense news briefing).

At the individual, cognitive level, risk assessment is characterized by overconfidence, loss aversion and bias.[12] Overconfidence in our ability to make accurate assessments is a common failing, and results in unrealistic assumptions and uncritical assessment. Loss aversion is well documented in psychology, and essentially means that we tend to prefer to avoid loss rather than to risk gain. Finally, cognitive bias is widespread and has profound implications for the identification and assessment of risk. Cognitive bias results in our seeking and overemphasizing evidence which supports our beliefs and reinforces our bias, but at the same time leads us to avoid and undervalue any information which contradicts our view.[13] Therefore, we need to be aware of and challenge our own biases, and encourage others to debate and critique our data, methods and decisions.

Studies of research and development confirm that measures of cognitive ability are associated with project performance. In particular, differences in reflection, reasoning, interpretation and sense-making all influence the quality of problem formulation, evaluation and solution, and therefore ultimately the performance of research and development. A common weakness is the oversimplification of problems characterized by complexity or uncertainty, and the simplification of problem framing and evaluation of alternatives.[14] This includes adopting a single prior hypothesis, selective use of information that supports this and devaluing alternatives, and illusion of control and predictability. Similarly, marketing managers are likely to share similar cognitive maps and make the same assumptions concerning the relative importance of different factors contributing to new product success, such as the degree of customer orientation versus competitor orientation, and the implications of relationship between these factors, such as the degree of interfunctional coordination.[15]

This suggests that what we need to do is:

● Given uncertainty, explore the implications of a range of possible future trends.

    ● Ensure broad participation and informal channels of communication.

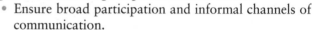

Tools to help you understand the risk assessment matrix are available on the Innovation Portal at **www.innovation-portal.info**

    ● Encourage the use of multiple sources of information, debate and scepticism.

    ● Expect to change strategies in the light of new (and often unexpected) evidence.

Analyse the Structures and Relationships

The next stage is to determine the relationships between the numerous factors, in particular between trends and discrete events. Consideration of conjunctions of trends and events, as opposed to isolated cases, enhances the credibility of a scenario, and presenting scenarios as possibilities, rather than as predictions, improves acceptance. For example, how could the discovery of large reserves of cheap natural gas (e.g. from fracking) influence trends in the reduction of carbon emissions?

Tool to help you explore group creativity to support discussion and debate, and to identify relationships – creativity toolkit – is available on the Innovation Portal at **www.innovation-portal.info**

There are many formal techniques which can help to identify and assess potential linkages, such as cross-impact analysis or causal-loop diagrams. For less complex interactions, it is sufficient to use graphical methods to support group discussion and debate, such as cause-and-effects charts, spider diagrams, mind maps and lotus blossom.

Build Alternative Scenarios and Assess Consequences

There are a number of approaches. For the normative approach, we can begin with the most desired scenario or outcomes, and work backwards through time to see how best to achieve this. This helps to identify sources of uncertainty and potential critical branching events. For the exploratory approach, there are two choices: deductive or inductive. The deductive approach works backwards from critical uncertainties; the inductive works forward from underlying trends and relationships.

For the deductive approach, identify a limited number of critical uncertainties and describe the extremes of each on a map or matrix, then develop narratives for paths into each cell, and descriptions of what would influence a shift between cells. For the inductive approach, we start with a number of different trends and chains of events and construct a plausible storyline for each.

Develop an Action Plan and Communicate to Stakeholders

A strong scenario will be:

● *Consistent*. Each scenario must be internally logical and consistent to be credible.
● *Plausible*. To be persuasive and support action the scenarios and underlying assumptions must be realistic.

- *Transparent*. The assumptions, sources and goals should be made explicit. Without such transparency, emotive or doomsday-style scenarios with catchy titles can be convincing, but highly misleading.
- *Differentiated*. Scenarios should be structurally or qualitatively different, in terms of assumptions and outcomes, not simply degree or magnitude. Any probability assessment of scenarios should be avoided, such as 'most or least probable'. Different subjective assessments of probability will be made by different stakeholders, so probability assessment can close rather than open debate on the range of possible futures.
- *Communicable*. Typically develop between three and five scenarios, each with vivid titles to promote memory and dissemination.
- *Practical, to support action*. Scenarios should be an input to strategic or policy decision-making, and so should have clear implications and recommendations for action.

Organizations using scenario techniques confirm that these are useful to explore future risks in the business environment, to identify trends, understand interdependent forces and to evaluate the implications of different strategic decisions. Building scenarios with broad organizational inputs helps to stretch people's thinking collectively and individually, by about 50%.[16] However, it is difficult to demonstrate the broader contribution of scenario development on performance because of the long timeframes and environmental uncertainties.[17]

Summary

- Forecasting is a valuable input to strategic and policy decision-making and planning, especially under conditions of environmental uncertainty.

- Forecasting methods based on extrapolating past trends or based on feedback from customers or segmentation of markets are useful in the short to medium term, but fail to identify longer-term opportunities and uncertainties.

- Benchmarking is useful to identify product and process improvement and innovation in the medium term, but needs relevant competitor or best-in-class candidates against which to compare systematically.

- Scenario development is a powerful method to explore potential futures based on the interaction of current trends and possible future events. It can be resource-intensive, but is inclusive and transparent and therefore persuasive and supports action.

Further Resources

There are numerous books and papers on forecasting, but only a finite number of methods to master, so be selective. The article by Saffo, P. (2007) Six rules for effective forecasting, *Harvard Business Review*, 85 (7/8): 122–131 is a good place to start. For a strong overview of different methods, try Paul J. H. Schoemaker *Profiting from Uncertainty* (2002, Free Press) or Joseph P. Martino *Technological Forecasting for Decision Making* (1992, McGraw-Hill).

A special issue of the journal *Long Range Planning*, 37 (2): 2004, is devoted to forecasting, and provides a good overview of current thinking. There was a special issue of the journal *Technological Forecasting and Social Change*, 79 (1), January 2012, on 'Scenario method: Current developments in theory and practice', and another special issue of the same journal on 'Delphi technique: Past, present, and future prospects', 78 (9), November 2011. For a comprehensive overview of international research and practice, refer to *The Handbook of Technology Foresight*, edited by Luke Georghiou (Edward Elgar, 2008).

For a practical and applied approach to benchmarking see Karlof, B. *Benchmarking Workbook* (John Wiley & Sons, Ltd, 1996), or Tim Stapenhurst *The Benchmarking Book: A how-to guide to best practice for managers and practitioners* (Butterworth-Heinemann, 2009). For scenario development, see Lindgren, M. and H. Bandhold *Scenario Planning: The link between future and strategy* (Palgrave Macmillan, 2nd edition, 2009) or Gill Ringland *Scenario Planning: Managing for the future* (John Wiley & Sons, Ltd, 1997). Shell also provides a free practical guide to developing scenarios, including detail of its own scenarios for the energy sector: http://s03.static-shell.com/content/dam/shell/static/future-energy/downloads/shell-scenarios/shell-scenarios-explorersguide.pdf.

References

1. Phaal, R., C. Farrukh, R. Mitchell and D. Probert (2003) Starting-up roadmapping fast, *Research: Technology Management*, **46** (2): 52–58.

2. Cheng, A.-C., C.-J. Chen and C.-Y. Chen (2008) A fuzzy multiple criteria comparison of technology forecasting methods for predicting the new materials development, *Technological Forecasting and Social Change*, **75**: 131–141.

3. Zairi, M. (1996) *Benchmarking for Best Practice*, London: Butterworth-Heinemann; Bishop, P., A. Hines and T. Collins (2007) The current state of scenario development: an overview of techniques, *Foresight*, **9** (1): 5–25.

4. Anand, G. and R. Kodali (2008) Benchmarking the benchmarking models, *Benchmarking: An International Journal*, 15 (3): 257–291, a good review of the utility of different approaches; Cox, A. and I. Thomson (1998) On the appropriateness of benchmarking, *Journal of General Management*, 23 (3): 1–20.

5. Karlof, B. (1996) *Benchmarking Workbook*. Chichester: John Wiley & Sons, Ltd.

6. Landeta, J. (2006) Current validity of the Delphi method in social sciences, *Technological Forecasting and Social Change*, **73** (5): 467–482; Fuller, T. and L. Warren (2006) Entrepreneurship as foresight: A complex social network perspective on organisational foresight, *Futures*, **38** (8): 956–971; Gupta, U. G. and R. E. Clarke (1996) Theory and applications of the Delphi technique: A bibliography (1975–1994), *Technological Forecasting and Social Change*, **53** (2): 185–212.

7. Chermack, T. J. (2011) *Scenario Planning in Organizations: How to create, use, and assess scenarios*. San Francisco: Berrett-Koehler Publishers; Lindgren, M. and H. Bandhold (2009) *Scenario Planning: The link between future and strategy*, 2nd edn, Basingstoke: Palgrave Macmillan.

8. Porter, M. E. (1985) *The Competitive Advantage*. New York: Free Press.

9. Schoemaker, P. J. H. (1993) Multiple scenario development: Its conceptual and behavioral foundation, *Strategic Management Journal*, **14** (3): 193–213.

10. Ringland, G. (2010). The role of scenarios in strategic foresight, *Technological Forecasting & Social Change*, 77: 1493–1498.

11. Ringland, G. (2010). The role of scenarios in strategic foresight, *Technological Forecasting & Social Change*, 77: 1493–1498.

12. Westland, J. C. (2008) *Global Innovation Management: A strategic approach*. Basingstoke: Palgrave Macmillan.

13. Gardner, D. (2008) *Risk: The science and politics of fear*. London: Virgin Books.

14. Tenkasi, R. V. (2000) The dynamics of cognitive oversimplification processes in R&D environments: An empirical assessment of some consequences, *International Journal of Technology Management*, 20: 782–798.

15. Tyler, B. B. and D. R. Gnyawali (2002) Mapping managers' market orientations regarding new product success, *Journal of Product Innovation Management*, **19** (4): 259–276; Walsh, J. P. (1995) Managerial and organizational cognition: Notes from a field trip, *Organization Science*, **6** (1): 1–41.

16. Visser, M. P. and T. J. Chermack (2009) Perceptions of the relationship between scenario planning and firm performance: A qualitative study, *Futures*, **41** (9): 581–592.

17. Godet, M. and F. Roubelat (1996) Creating the future: The use and misuse of scenarios, *Long Range Planning*, **29** (2): 164–171.

 Deeper Dive explanations of innovation concepts and ideas are available on the Innovation Portal at **www.innovation-portal.info**

 Quizzes to test yourself further are available online via the Innovation Portal at **www.innovation-portal.info**

Summary of online resources for Chapter 8 –
all material is available via the Innovation Portal at
www.innovation-portal.info

Cases	**Media**	**Tools**	**Activities**	**Deeper Dive**
• Philips Lighting • The dimming of the light bulb • The changing music industry • Search strategies for peripheral vision	• Helen King, Irish Food Board • Eric von Hippel, Lead-user studies • 3M, Identifying lead users	• Brainstorming • Benchmarking • Scenarios • Delphi Method • Futures tools • Risk assessment • Creativity toolkit	• Discontinuous innovation audit • Spot the ball • Roadmapping • Scenarios	• Decision-making under uncertainty

Chapter 9

Selecting Innovation Projects

LEARNING OBJECTIVES

By the end of this chapter you will be able to:

- understand the need for selection decisions in innovation
- recognize the difficulties of decision-making under uncertainty
- appreciate the range of methods to select and the need to balance between speed and detail
- understand the different selection challenges across innovation space.

Why is Selection a Challenge?

Triggers for innovation – as we saw in Chapter 5 – can be found all over the place. The world is full of interesting and challenging possibilities for change. The trouble is that even the wealthiest organization doesn't have deep enough pockets to do them all. Sooner or later it has to confront the issue of 'out of all the things we could do, what are we going to do?' This isn't easy. Making decisions is about resource commitment and so choosing to go in one direction closes off opportunities elsewhere. Organizations cannot afford to innovate at random. They need some kind of framework which helps them allocate scarce resources to a portfolio of innovation projects.

But in a complex and uncertain world we can't make detailed plans ahead of the game and then follow them through in a systematic fashion. Life isn't like that; as John Lennon famously said, it's what happens when you're busy making other plans! By its very nature, innovation is about the unknown, about possibilities and opportunities associated with doing something new and so the process involves dealing with *uncertainty*. The problem is that

Activity to explore some of the problems which may emerge during an innovation project – implementing innovation projects – is available on the Innovation Portal at **www.innovation-portal.info**

we don't know in advance if an innovation will work: will the technology actually do what we hope, will the market still be there and behave as we anticipated, will competitors move in a different and more successful direction, will the government change the rules of the game, and so on?

So our strategic framework for innovation should be flexible enough to help monitor and adapt projects over time as ideas move towards more concrete solutions – and rigid enough to justify continuation or termination as uncertainties and risky guesswork become replaced by actual knowledge.

Meeting the Challenge of Uncertainty

Innovation can be something of a gamble. It's about committing resources to something which has an uncertain outcome. Innovation *management* tries to convert that uncertainty at the outset to something closer to a calculated risk – there is still no guarantee of success but at least there is an attempt to review the options and assign some probabilities as to the chances of a successful outcome.

Some 'bets' are safer than others because they carry lower risk: incremental innovation is about doing what we do, and therefore know about, better. We have some prior knowledge about markets, technologies, regulatory frameworks, etc. and so can make reasonably accurate assessments of risks using this information. But some bets are about radical innovation, doing something completely different and carrying a much higher level of risk because of the lack of information. These could pay off handsomely, but there are also many unforeseen ways in which they could run into trouble.

And we shouldn't forget that under such conditions decision-making is often shaped by emotional forces as well as limited facts and figures. People can be persuaded to take a risk by convincing argument, by expressions of energy or passion, by hooking into powerful emotions like fear (of not moving in the proposed direction) or reward (resulting from the success of the proposed innovation).

The Funnel of Uncertainty

Central to this process is *knowledge* – this is what converts uncertainty to risk. The more we know about something, the more we can take calculated decisions about whether or not to proceed. And in a competitive environment this puts a premium on getting hold of knowledge as early as possible. This explains the value of an insider tip-off in horseracing or stock-market dealings. In innovation management the challenge is to invest in acquiring early knowledge – through technological R&D, through market research, through competitor analysis, trend-spotting and a host of other mechanisms – to get early information to feed decision-making. Robert Cooper uses the powerful metaphor of Russian roulette, suggesting that most people when faced with the uncertainty of pulling the trigger would be happy to 'buy a look' at the gun chamber to improve their knowledge of whether or not there is a bullet in it![1]

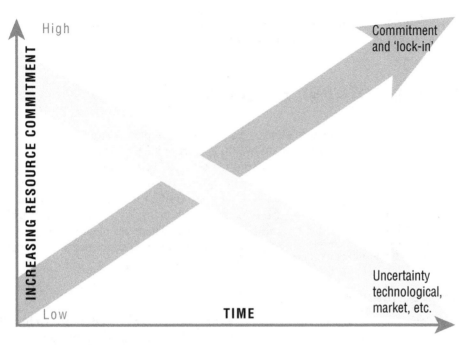

FIGURE 9.1   Uncertainty and resource commitment in innovation projects

Thinking of innovation as a process of reducing uncertainty but increasing resource commitment gives us a classic graph (Figure 9.1). In essence, the further we go into a project the more it costs but the more we know.

In practice, this translates into what we can call the 'innovation funnel' – a roadmap which helps us make (and review) decisions about resource commitment. Figure 9.2 gives an illustration.

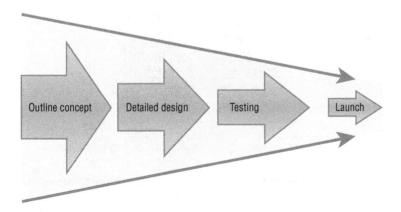

FIGURE 9.2   The innovation funnel

We'll come back to the question of reviewing our selection decisions as we move through the funnel, but for now let's think about how we might make the initial choice.

Choosing between Projects

Research indicates that 30–45% of all projects fail to be completed, and over half of projects overrun their budgets or schedules by up to 200% (Figure 9.3).

Tools to help you map with strategic selection – including financial tools, options, decision matrix, portfolio methods and bubble charts – are available on the Innovation Portal at **www.innovation-portal.info**

So it makes sense to try to improve the chances of success by careful consideration of *which* projects we start. What we're trying to do at this stage is make some assessment of probability – the likelihood of technical and market success. There are plenty of ways of doing this, increasing in cost and time they take to generate (Table 9.1 gives some examples).

Simple Techniques. . .

Checklists are a commonly used example of a simple qualitative technique. A checklist is simply a list of factors which are considered important in making a decision in a specific case. These criteria include technical and commercial details, legal and financial factors, company targets and company strategy. The technique can be strengthened by:

- including some quantitative factors among the whole list of factors
- assigning different weights to different factors
- developing a systematic way of arriving at an overall opinion on the project, such as a score or index.

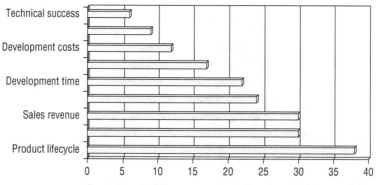

FIGURE 9.3   Uncertainty in project planning

Source: Based on data from Freeman, C. and L. Soete (1997) *The Economics of Innovation*. MIT Press, Cambridge, MA.

TABLE 9.1 Approaches to Project Selection

Selection approach	Advantages	Disadvantages
Simple 'gut feel', intuition	Fast	Lacks evidence and analysis, may be wrong
Simple qualitative techniques, e.g. checklists and decision matrix	Fast and easy to share – provides a useful focus for initial discussions	Lacks factual information and little or no quantitative dimension
Financial measures, e.g. return on investment or payback time	Fast and uses some simple measurement	Doesn't take account of other benefits which may come from the innovation – learning about new technologies, markets, etc.
Complex financial measures, e.g. 'real options' approach	Takes account of learning dimension – the benefits from projects may lie in improved knowledge which we can use elsewhere as well as in direct profits	More complex and time-consuming – difficult to predict the benefits which may arise from taking options in the future
Multidimensional measures, e.g. decision matrix	Compares on several dimensions to build an overall 'score' for attractiveness	Allows consideration of different kinds of benefits but level of analysis may be limited
Portfolio methods and business cases	Compares between projects on several dimensions and provides detailed evidence around core themes	Takes a long time to prepare and present

The value in this technique lies in its simplicity, but by the appropriate choice of factors it is possible to ensure that the questions address, and are answered by, all functional areas. When used effectively, this guarantees a useful discussion, an identification and clarification of areas of disagreement and a stronger commitment, by all involved, to the ultimate outcome.

Table 9.2 shows an example of a checklist, developed by the Industrial Research Institute, which can be adapted to almost any type of project.

. . . And More Detailed Assessments

At the other end of the spectrum, there are detailed assessments of innovation projects which use much more information to shape the decision. One of the most important is the business case, which summarizes the 'story' behind a proposed project. For example, a business case

TABLE 9.2 List of Potential Factors for Project Evaluation

	Score (1–5)	Weight (%)	S × W
Corporate objectives			
Fits into the overall objectives and strategy			
Corporate image			
Marketing and distribution			
Size of potential market			
Capability to market product			
Market trend and growth			
Customer acceptance			
Relationship with existing markets			
Market share			
Market risk during development period			
Pricing trend, proprietary problem, etc.			
Complete product line			
Quality improvement			
Timing of introduction of new product			
Expected product sales life			
Manufacturing			
Cost savings			
Capability of manufacturing product			
Facility and equipment requirements			
Availability of raw material			
Manufacturing safety			
Research and development			
Likelihood of technical success			
Cost			
Development time			
Capability of available skills			
Availability of R&D resources			
Availability of R&D facilities			
Patent status			
Compatibility with other projects			

(continued)

TABLE 9.2 *(Continued)*

	Score (1–5)	Weight (%)	S × W
Regulatory and legal factors			
Potential product liability			
Regulatory clearance			
Financial			
Profitability			
Capital investment required			
Annual (or unit) cost			
Rate of return on investment			
Unit price			
Payout period			
Utilization of assets, cost reduction and cash flow			

for a new product or service should be relatively concise, say, no more than 10–20 pages, and include the following sections:

- details of the product or service
- assessment of the market opportunity
- identification of target customers
- barriers to entry and competitor analysis
- experience, expertise and commitment of the management team
- strategy for pricing, distribution and sales
- identification and planning for key risks
- cash-flow calculation, including breakeven points and sensitivity
- financial and other resource requirements of the business.

The idea is to provide a convincing argument to decision-makers, giving them detailed and relevant information on which to base their choice.

At the heart of our decision-making is some balance between the risks of doing something and the likely rewards. It's a balancing act – and in the end it's a judgement, arguing a case for doing something. (Importantly in the public sector the balancing act is made more difficult by having to consider not only risk and reward but also

Tool to help you map – developing the business case – is available on the Innovation Portal at **www.innovation-portal.info**

reliability – civil servants can't simply risk not providing or maintaining core services like health care or policing.)

We also need to remember that perceptions are important in this process – human beings are not always as rational or effective in assessing risk as they would like to think they are! The Nobel Prize winner Daniel Kahnemann suggests we use two different systems when making judgements: 'system 1' and 'system 2'. System 1 is very fast, having evolved to give human beings the ability to make very quick assessments of complex (and potentially life-threatening) situations. System 2, by contrast, is much slower and involves more evidence and reasoning.[2] Psychologists have identified a large number of ways in which our perception of risk and the choices we make are far from the 'rational' person assumed in many economic models. (For example, we prefer to avoid loss rather than to risk gain, while 'cognitive bias' results in our seeking and overemphasizing evidence which supports our beliefs and leads us to avoid and undervalue any information which contradicts our view.)

Spreading the Risk: Building a Portfolio

In reality even the smallest enterprise is likely to have a number of innovation activities running at any moment. It may concentrate most of its resources on its one major product/service offering or new process, but alongside this there will be a host of incremental improvements and minor change projects which also consume resources and require monitoring. For giant organizations, like Procter and Gamble or 3M, the range of products is somewhat wider – in 3M's case around 60 000. Even project-oriented organizations whose main task could be the construction of a new bridge or office block will have a range of subsidiary innovation projects running at the same time.

As we have seen, the innovation process has a funnel shape with convergence from a wide mouth of possibilities into a much smaller section which represents those projects to which resources will be committed. Which projects should we undertake and how do we get a balance between risk, reward, novelty, experience and many other elements of uncertainty?

The challenge of building a portfolio is as much an issue in non-commercial organizations. For example, should a hospital commit to a new theatre, a new scanner, a new support organization around integrated patient care or a new sterilization method? No organization can do everything, so it must make choices and try to create a broad portfolio which helps with both the 'do what we do better' and the 'do different' agendas.

There are a variety of approaches which have been developed to deal with the question of what is broadly termed 'portfolio management'. These range from simple judgements about risk and reward to complex quantitative tools based on probability theory. But the underlying purpose is the same: to provide a coherent basis on which to judge which projects should be undertaken, and to ensure a good balance across the portfolio of risk and potential reward. Failure to make such judgements can create a number of problems, as Table 9.3 indicates.

Portfolio methods try to deal with the issue of reviewing across a set of projects and look for a balance of economic and non-financial risk/reward factors. A typical example is to construct some form of matrix measuring risk vs. reward, for example on a 'costs of doing the project' vs. expected returns (Figure 9.4).

TABLE 9.3   Problems Arising from Poor Portfolio Management

Without portfolio management there may be. . . .	Impacts
No limit to projects taken on	Resources spread too thinly
Reluctance to kill-off or 'de-select' projects	Resource starvation and impacts on time and cost – overruns
Lack of strategic focus in project mix	High failure rates, or success of unimportant projects and opportunity cost against more important projects
Weak or ambiguous selection criteria	Projects find their way into the mix because of politics or emotion or other factors – downstream failure rates high and resource diversion from other projects
Weak decision criteria	Too many 'average' projects selected, little impact downstream in market

Source: Based on Cooper, R., *Product leadership* 2000, New York: Perseus Books with permission.

Rather than reviewing projects just on these two criteria, it is possible to construct multiple charts to develop an overall picture, for example comparing the relative familiarity of the market or technology – this would highlight the balance between projects that are in unexplored territory as opposed to those in familiar technical or market areas (and thus with a lower risk). Other possible axes include ease of entry vs. market attractiveness (size or growth rate), the competitive position of the

Tool giving you an extended description of different kinds of matrices is available on the Innovation Portal at **www.innovation-portal.info**

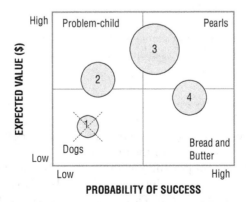

FIGURE 9.4   An example matrix-based portfolio

INNOVATION IN ACTION 9.1

The Arthur D. Little Matrix for Technology Decisions

A number of tools have been developed to help with strategic decision-making around technology investments. Typical of these are those which make some classification of technologies in terms of their open availability and the ease with which they can be protected and deployed to strategic advantage. For example, the consultancy Arthur D. Little uses a matrix which groups technological knowledge into four key groups: base, key, emerging and pacing.

* Base technologies represent those on which product/service innovations are based and which are vital to the business. However, they are also widely known about and deployed by competitors and offer little potential competitive advantage.
* Key technologies represent those which form the core of current products/services or processes and which have a high competitive impact – they are strategically important to the organization and may well be protectable through patent or other form.
* Pacing technologies are those which are at the leading edge of the current competitive game and may be under experimentation by competitors – they have high but as yet unfulfilled competitive potential.
* Emerging technologies are those which are at the technological frontier, still under development and whose impact is promising but not yet clear.

Making this distinction helps identify a strategy for acquisition based on the degree of potential impact plus the importance to the enterprise plus the protectability of the knowledge. For base technologies, it may make sense to source outside, whereas for key technologies an in-house or carefully selected strategic alliance may make more sense in order to preserve the potential competitive advantage. Emerging technologies may be best served by a watching strategy, perhaps through some pilot project links with universities or technological institutes.

Models of this can be refined, for example by adding to the matrix information about different markets and their rate of growth or decline. A fast-growing new market may require extensive investment in the pacing technology in order to be able to build on the opportunities being created, whereas a mature or declining market may be better served by a strategy which uses base technology to help preserve a position but at low cost.

For more detail on this approach see http://www.adlittle.com/.

organization in the project area vs. the attractiveness of the market or the expected time to reach the market vs. the attractiveness of the market.

A useful variant on this set of portfolio methods is the 'bubble chart' in which the different projects are plotted but represented by 'bubbles' – circles whose diameter varies with the size of the project (e.g. in terms of costs). This approach gives a quick visual overview of the balance of different-sized projects against risk and reward criteria.

Bubble Chart for Process Innovation in Fruit of the Loom

The clothing manufacturer Fruit of the Loom reviewed its worldwide process innovation activities using a portfolio framework to help provide a clearer overview and develop focus. It used simple categories:

- 'Incremental' – essentially continuous improvement projects
- 'Radical' – using the same basic technology but with more advanced implementation
- 'Fundamental' – using different technology, for example, laser cutting instead of mechanical

   Plotting on to a simple colour-coded bubble chart enabled a quick and easily communicable overview of their strategic innovation portfolio in this aspect of innovation.

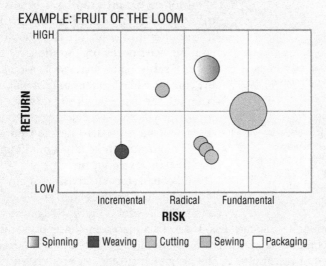

EXAMPLE: FRUIT OF THE LOOM

Source: Oke, private communication, 2003.

Managing Risk over Time

A problem in innovation is that increasing commitment of resources during the life of the project makes it increasingly difficult to change direction. Managing this is a fine balancing act, between the costs of continuing with projects which may not eventually succeed (and which represent opportunity costs in terms of other possibilities) and the danger of closing down too soon and eliminating potentially fruitful options. So it makes sense not to make one big decision to commit everything at the outset when uncertainty is very high but instead to make a series of stepwise decisions.

Each of these involves committing more resources, but this only takes place if the risk/reward assessment justifies it – and the further into the project, the more information about technologies, markets, competitors, etc. we have to help with the assessment. We move from uncertainty, to increasingly well-calculated risk management. Such a staged review process is particularly associated with the work of Robert Cooper, a Canadian researcher who studied thousands of new product development projects.[3]

This model essentially involves putting in a series of gates at key stages and reviewing the project's progress against clearly defined and accepted criteria. Only if it passes will the gate open; otherwise, the project should be killed off or at least returned for further development work before proceeding. Many variations (e.g. 'fuzzy gates') on this approach exist; the important point is to ensure that there is a structure in place which reviews information about both technical and market aspects of the innovation as we move from high uncertainty to high resource commitment but with a clearer picture of progress.

 Tool giving a more detailed description of stage gate approaches is available on the Innovation Portal at **www.innovation-portal.info**

 Case Study detailing the design and implementation of a stage gate system – ABC Electronics – is available on the Innovation Portal at **www.innovation-portal.info**

Models of this kind have been widely applied in different sectors, both in manufacturing and services. It's important to configure the system to the particular contingencies of the organization, for example a highly procedural system which works for a global multiproduct company like Siemens or GM will be far too big and complex for many small organizations. And not every project needs the same degree of scrutiny – for some there will be a need to develop parallel 'fast tracks' where monitoring is kept to a minimum to ensure speed and flow in development.

Of course, the effectiveness of any stage gate system will be limited by the extent to which it is accepted as a fair and helpful framework against which to monitor progress and continue to allocate resources. This places emphasis on some form of shared design of the system; otherwise, there is a risk of lack of commitment to decisions made and/or the development of resentment at the progress of some pet projects and the holding back of others.

The Problem of Radical Innovation

When the innovation decision is about incremental – 'do what we do but better' – innovation there is relatively little difficulty. A business case with relevant information can be assembled, cost-benefits can be argued and the 'fit' with the current portfolio demonstrated. But as the options move towards the more radical end so the degree of resource commitment and risk rises and decision-making resembles more closely a matter of placing bets – and emotional and political influences become significant. At the limit the organization faces real difficulties

Accelerating Ideas to Market: The AIM Process

Coloplast is a Danish company involved in manufacture of a wide range of medical products. Their stage gate process is called AIM and the basic structure is given in the diagram below:

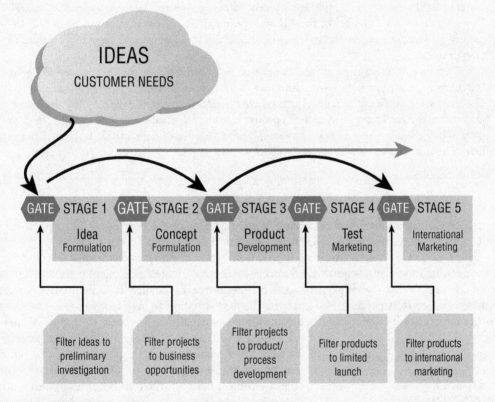

AIM's purpose can be expressed as being:

- To provide common rules of the game for product development within Coloplast.
- To make clear decisions at the right moment.
- To clarify responsibility.

The objective of the AIM process is to ensure a high, uniform level of professionalism in product development yielding high quality products.

It is based on the view that Coloplast must increase the success rate and reduce the development time for new products in order to become a 'world class innovator'.

(*continued*)

The Stage/Gate System

Much of the work in product development is carried out by project teams consisting of selected specialists from marketing (from both product divisions and subsidiaries), R&D, clinical affairs and manufacturing. Each project team will work under the leadership of a skilled and enthusiastic project manager, and the AIM process defines the rules to be followed by the project team.

The AIM process divides the development of new products into five manageable 'stages'. Each stage contains a number of parallel and coordinated activities designed to refine the definitions of customer needs and to develop technological solutions and capacity for efficient manufacturing.

Each stage is followed by a 'gate', a decision point at which the project is reviewed by the 'gatekeepers', senior managers with authority to keep worthy projects moving ahead quickly. The gates serve as the critical quality control checkpoints between the stages. A 'go' decision is made when the gatekeepers decide that a project is likely, technically and economically, to meet the needs of the customers as well as to comply with Coloplast's high standards for Return On Investment, quality and environmental impact.

in making choices about new trajectories, in moving 'outside the box' in which its prior experience and the dominant technological and market trajectories placed it.

The problem with discontinuous innovation is that it presents challenges which do not fit the existing model and require a *reframing* – something which existing players find hard to do. In a process akin to what psychologists call 'cognitive dissonance' in individuals, organizations often selectively perceive and interpret the new situation to match or fit their established worldviews. Since by definition discontinuous shifts usually begin as weak signals of major change, picked up on the edge of the radar screen, it is easy for the continuing interpretation of the signals in the old frame to persist for some time. By the time the disconnect between the two becomes apparent and the need for radical reframing is unavoidable it is often too late. As Dorothy Leonard puts it, core competencies become core rigidities.[4]

 Case Study of Philips Lighting detailing reframing in a major corporation is available on the Innovation Portal at **www.innovation-portal.info**

The problem is not that such firms have weak or ineffective strategic resource allocation mechanisms for taking innovation decisions but rather that these are too good. For as long as the decisions are taken within a framework (their 'box') they are effective, but they break down when the challenge comes from outside that box. It is important to recognize that the justification for rejecting ideas which lie too far outside the framework is expressed in terms which are apparently 'rational', that is the reasons are clear and consistent with the decision rules and criteria associated with the framework. But they are examples of what the Nobel Prize-winning economist Herbert Simon calls 'bounded rationality' – and underpinning them are a number of key psychological effects such as 'groupthink' and 'risky shift'.[5]

Exploring Selection Space

We can use the framework we originally introduced in Chapter 7 to map this selection space and the different challenges posed as we move into areas of higher uncertainty (Figure 9.5).

Once again we can see the familiar challenge of 'exploit' vs. 'explore' innovation – but we also have the challenge of moving to different frames. Essentially, organizations have 'comfort zones' beyond which they are reluctant or unable to consider innovation projects. Their decision-making, even around radical options, is often constrained. This gives rise to the anxiety often expressed about the need for 'out of the box' thinking. Stage gate and portfolio systems depend on using criteria which are 'bought into' by those bringing ideas – a perception that the resource allocation process is 'fair' and appropriate even if the decisions go the 'wrong' way. Under steady-state conditions these systems can and do work well and criteria are clearly established and perceived to be appropriate. But higher levels of uncertainty put pressure on the existing models – and one effect is that they reject ideas which don't fit – and over time build a 'self-censoring' aspect.

When there is a shift to a new mindset, established players may have problems because of the reorganization of their thinking which is required. It is not simply adding new information but changing the structure of the frame through which they see and interpret that information. They need to 'think outside the box' within which their bounded exploration takes place, and this is difficult because it is highly structured and reinforced by organizational structures and processes.

So, for example, the famous 'not invented here' rejection is easier to understand if we see it as a problem of what makes sense within a specific context: the firm has little knowledge or experience in the proposed area, it is not its core business, it has no plans to enter that particular market, etc. Table 9.4 lists some examples of justifications which can be made to rationalize the rejection decision associated with radical innovation options.

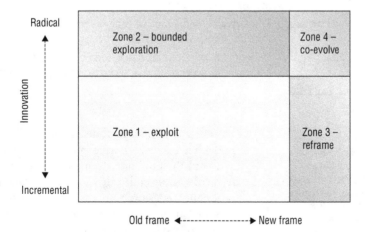

FIGURE 9.5 A map of innovation selection space

TABLE 9.4   Examples of Justifications for Non-adoption of Radical Ideas

Argument	Underlying perceptions from within the established mental model
'It's not our business'	Recognition of an interesting new business idea but rejection because it lies far from the core competence of the firm
'It's not a business'	Evaluation suggests the business plan is flawed along some key dimension – often underestimating potential for market development and growth
'It's not big enough for us'	Emergent market size is too small to meet growth targets of large, established firm
'Not invented here'	Recognition of interesting idea with potential but rejection – often by finding flaws or mismatch to current internal trajectories
'Invented here'	Recognition of interesting idea but rejection because internally generated version is perceived to be superior
'We're not cannibals'	Recognition of potential for impact on current markets and reluctance to adopt potential competing idea
'Nice idea but doesn't fit'	Recognition of interesting idea generated from within but whose application lies outside current business areas – often leads to inventions being shelved or put in a cupboard
'It ain't broke so why fix it?'	No perceived relative advantage in adopting new idea
'Great minds think alike'	'Groupthink' at strategic decision-making level – new idea lies outside the collective frame of reference
'(Existing) customers won't/don't want it'	New idea offers little to interest or attract current customers – essentially a different value proposition
'We've never done it before'	Perception that risks involved are too high along market and technical dimensions
'We're doing OK as we are'	The success trap – lack of motivation or organizational slack to allow exploration outside of current lines
'Let's set up a pilot'	Recognition of potential in new idea but limited and insufficient commitment to exploring and developing it – lukewarm support

Case Study detailing a famous innovation case – gunfire at sea – highlighting the difficulties of introducing radical new ideas to an established institution is available on the Innovation Portal at **www.innovation-portal.info**

These are all ways of defending an established mental model. They may be 'correct' in terms of the criteria associated with the dominant framework but they may also be defensive. Importantly, they can be cloaked in a shroud of 'rationality' – using numbers about market size to reject exploration of a new area, for example. They represent an 'immune system' response which rejects the strange in order to preserve the health of the current body unchanged.

Let's look a little more closely at the selection challenges in each of the zones in Figure 9.5. Zone 1 assumes a stable and shared frame within which adaptive and incremental development takes place. Selection routines, as we saw earlier in this chapter, are those associated with the 'steady state' – portfolio methods, stage gate reviews, clear resource allocation criteria, project management structures, etc. The structures involved in this selection activity are clearly defined with relevant actors, clear decision points, decision rules, criteria, etc.

Zone 2 involves selection from exploration into new territory, pushing the frontiers of what is known and deploying different search techniques for doing so. But this is still taking place within the same basic frame for the business – 'business model as usual'. While the 'bets' may have longer odds, the decision-making is still carried out against an underlying strategic model and sense of core competences. There may be debate and political behaviour at strategic level about choices but there is an underlying framework which defines the arena in which this takes place. Although the activity is risky and exploratory, it is still governed strongly by the frame for the sector, for example Moore's law shaping semiconductor, computer and related industry patterns.

By contrast, Zone 3 is associated with *reframing*. It involves searching and selecting from a space where alternative architectures are generated, exploring different permutations and combinations of elements in the environment. This process, essentially entrepreneurial, is risky and often results in failure but can also lead to emergence of new and powerful alternative business models (BMs). Significantly, this often happens by working with elements in the environment not embraced by established BMs, but this poses problems for existing incumbents, especially when the current BM is successful. Why change an apparently successful formula with relatively clear information about innovation options and well-established routines for managing the process? There is a strong reinforcing inertia about such systems for search and selection. The 'value networks' take on the character of closed systems which operate as virtuous circles and, for as long as they are perceived to create value through innovation, act as inhibitors to reframing.

Selection under these conditions is difficult using existing routines which work well for zones 1 and 2. While the innovations themselves may not be radical, they require consideration through a different lens and the kinds of information (and their perceived significance) which are involved may be unfamiliar or hard to obtain.

For example, in moving into new underserved markets, the challenge is that 'traditional' market research and analysis techniques may be inappropriate for markets which effectively do not yet exist. Many of the 'reasons' advanced for rejecting the innovation proposals outlined in Table 9.4 can be mapped on to difficulties in managing selection in Zone 3 territory, for example 'It's not our business' relates to the lack of perceived competence in analysis of new and unfamiliar variables. 'Not invented here' relates to a similar lack of perceived experience, competence or involvement in a technological field and the inability to analyse and take 'rational' decisions about it. 'It's not a business' relates to apparent market size, which in the initial stages may appear small and unlikely to serve the growth needs of

Case Study detailing a report – Radical innovation: Making the right bets – describing the approaches taken by a number of organizations to deal with the challenges in making decisions around innovation options in zones 3 and 4 is available on the Innovation Portal at **www.innovation-portal.info**

established incumbents. But such markets could grow – the challenge is seeing an alternative trajectory to the current dominant logic of the established business model.

Significantly, radical changes in mindset and subsequent strategic direction often come about as a result of crisis – which has the effect of shattering the mindset – or with the arrival from outside of a new CEO with a different world view.

Zone 4 is a complex environment where innovation emerges as a product of a process of co-evolution. This is not the product of a defined trajectory so much as the result of interactions between independent elements. Processes of amplification and feedback reinforce what begin as small shifts in direction – attractor basins – and gradually define a trajectory. This is the pattern we saw in Chapter 1 in which there is a 'fluid' stage of the innovation lifecycle before a dominant design emerges and sets the standard. It is the state where all bets are potentially options – and high variety experimentation takes place. Selection strategies here are difficult since it is, by definition, impossible to predict what is going to be important or where the initial emergence will start and around which feedback and amplification will happen. Under such conditions the strategy breaks down into three core principles: be in there, be in there early and be in there influentially (i.e. in a position to be part of the feedback and amplification mechanisms).

Once again, this zone poses major challenges to an established set of selection routines – zone 4 is essentially 'unknown unknowns' territory. Analytical tools and evidence-based decision-making (e.g. reviewing business cases) are inappropriate for judging plays in a game where the rules are unclear and even the board on which it is played has yet to be designed!

An example here could be the ways in which the Internet and the products/services which it will carry will emerge as a result of a complex set of interactions amongst users. Or the ways in which chronic diseases like diabetes will be managed in a future where the incidence is likely to rise, where the costs of treatment will rise faster than health budgets can cope and where many different stakeholders are involved – clinicians, drug companies, insurance companies, carers and patients themselves.

Table 9.5 summarizes the selection challenges in the overall innovation space.

TABLE 9.5   Selection Challenges in Innovation

Zone	Selection challenges
1. 'Business as usual' – innovation but under 'steady state' conditions, little disturbance around core business model	Decisions taken based on exploiting existing and understood knowledge and deploying in known fields. Incremental innovation aimed at refining and improving. Requires building strong ties with key players in existing value network and working with them
2. 'Business model as usual' – bounded exploration within this frame	Exploration – pushing frontiers of technology and market via calculated risks – 'buying a look' at new options through strategic investments in further research. Involves risk-taking and high uncertainty

(continued)

TABLE 9.5 *(Continued)*

Zone	Selection challenges
3. Alternative frame – taking in new/different elements in environment	Reframe – explore alternative options, introduce new elements. Challenge involves decision-making under uncertainty but not simply a problem of lack of information and the need to take risky bets to learn more. Here there is also the issue of unfamiliar frames of reference and the difficulty of letting go of a dominant logic. Cognitive dissonance means that incumbents have trouble 'forgetting' enough to see the environment through 'new eyes'
4. Radical – new to the world – possibilities. New architecture around as yet unknown and established elements	Emergence – need to co-evolve with stakeholders • Be in there • Be in there early • Be in there actively

Summary

● In this chapter we have looked at some of the challenges in making the selection decision – moving from considering all the possible trigger signals about what we could do in terms of innovation to committing resources to some particular projects.

● This quickly raises the issue of uncertainty and how we convert it to some kind of manageable risk – and build a portfolio of projects spreading this risk.

● Tools and techniques for doing so for incremental innovation are relatively straightforward (though there is never a guarantee of success), but as we increase the radical nature of the innovation there is a need for different approaches.

● The problem is further compounded because of the simplifying assumptions we make when framing the complex world – and the risk is that in selecting projects which fit our frame we may miss important opportunities or challenges. For this reason we need techniques which help the organization look and make decisions 'outside the box'.

Further Resources

The theme of innovation decision-making, risk management and the use of the stage gate concept is extensively covered in the work of Robert Cooper and colleagues.[1, 5–8] Tools for portfolio management and related approaches are discussed with good examples in Goffin and Mitchell's book[9] and policy deployment approaches in Bessant[10] and Akao.[11] Dodgson, Gann and Salter[12] and Schrage[13] explore the growing range of simulation and prototyping tools which can postpone the commitment decision point, while von Hippel and colleagues expand[14, 15] on the user involvement theme.[16, 17] Peter Koen's work provides useful insights on fuzzy front end tools and methods (a good source is the PDMA ToolBook[18]), and Julian Birkinshaw explores the challenges in developing 'ambidextrous' decision-making structures.[19] A detailed review of the psychological issues and problems around reframing can be found in Hodgkinson and Sparrow,[20] while the work of Karl Weick remains seminal in discussing the ways in which organizations try and make sense of complex worlds.[21, 22]

Useful websites include Innovation Tools (www.innovationtools.com) and InnovationManagement.ee (www.innovationmanagement.se), which provide case examples and links to a wide range of innovation support resources, and the Product Development Management Association (www.pdma.org), which covers many of the decision tools used with practical examples of their application in the online 'Visions' magazine. NESTA (www.nesta.org.uk) and AIM (www.aimresearch.org) provide reports and research papers around core innovation themes, including many of the issues raised in this chapter.

References

1. Cooper, R. (2001) *Winning at New Products*, 3rd edn. London: Kogan Page.

2. Kahnemann, D. (2012) *Thinking, Fast and Slow*. Harmondsworth: Penguin.

3. Cooper, R. (1988) The new product process: A decision guide for management, *Journal of Marketing Management*, **3** (3): 238–255.

4. Leonard, D. (1992) Core capabilities and core rigidities: A paradox in new product development, *Strategic Management Journal*, **13**: 111–125.

5. Simon, H. and J. March (1992) *Organizations*, 2nd edn. Oxford: Basil Blackwell.

6. Cooper, R. (2000) *Product Leadership*. New York: Perseus Press.

7. Cooper, R. (1994) Third-generation new product processes, *Journal of Product Innovation Management*, **11** (1): 3–14.

8. Cooper, R. (1999) The invisible success factors in product innovation, *Journal of Product Innovation Management*, **16** (2): 115–133.

9. Goffin, K. and R. Mitchell (2005) *Innovation Management*. London: Pearson.

10. Bessant, J. (2003) *High Involvement Innovation*. Chichester: John Wiley & Sons, Ltd.

11. Akao, Y. (1991) *Hoshin Kanri: Policy deployment for successful TQM*. Cambridge, MA: Productivity Press.

12. Dodgson, M., D. Gann and A. Salter (2005) *Think, Play, Do: Technology and organization in the emerging innovation process*. Oxford: Oxford University Press.

13. Schrage, M. (2000) *Serious Play: How the world's best companies simulate to innovate*. Boston: Harvard Business School Press.

14. Moser, K. and F. Piller (2006) Special issue on mass customisation case studies: Cases from the international mass customisation case collection, *International Journal of Mass Customisation*, **1** (4).

15. Piller, F. (2006) *Mass Customization: Ein wettbewerbsstrategisches Konzept im Informationszeitalter*, 4th edn. Frankfurt: Gabler Verlag.

16. Von Hippel, E. (2001) User toolkits for innovation, *Journal of Product Innovation Management*, **18**: 247–257.

17. Herstatt, C. and E. von Hippel (1992) Developing new product concepts via the lead user method, *Journal of Product Innovation Management*, **9** (3): 213–221.

18. Belliveau, P., A. Griffin and S. Somermeyer (2002) *The PDMA ToolBook for New Product Development: Expert techniques and effective practices in product development.* New York: John Wiley & Sons, Ltd.

19. Birkinshaw, J. and C. Gibson (2004) Building ambidexterity into an organization, *Sloan Management Review*, **45** (4): 47–55.

20. Hodgkinson, G. and P. Sparrow (2002) *The Competent Organization.* Buckingham: Open University Press.

21. Weick, K. (2001) *Making Sense of the Organization.* Oxford: Blackwell.

22. Weick, K. (1993) The collapse of sensemaking in organizations: The Mann Gulch disaster, *Administrative Science Quarterly*, **38**: 628–652.

 Deeper Dive explanations of innovation concepts and ideas are available on the Innovation Portal at **www.innovation-portal.info**

 Quizzes to test yourself further are available online via the Innovation Portal at **www.innovation-portal.info**

**Summary of online resources for Chapter 9 –
all material is available via the Innovation Portal at
www.innovation-portal.info**

Cases	Media	Tools	Activities	Deeper Dive
• ABC Electronics • Coloplast • Philips Lighting • Gunfire at sea • Radical innovation: Making the right bets	• Dragon's Den	• Portfolio methods • Bubble charts • Financial appraisal tools • Decision matrix • Checklists • Business case development • Business model canvas • Stage gate models	• Implementing innovation projects • Dragon's Den • Bubble charts	• Managing the fuzzy front end of innovation • Sectoral patterns of innovation

Chapter 10

Developing New Products and Services

LEARNING OBJECTIVES

After this chapter you should be able to:

- develop a formal process to support new product development, such as stage gate and the development funnel

- identify the product and organizational factors which influence success and failure

- choose and apply relevant tools to support each stage of product development

- understand the differences between products and services and how these influence development.

The New Product/Service Development Process

The process of new product or service development – moving from idea through to successful products, services or processes – is a gradual one of reducing uncertainty through a series of problem-solving stages, moving through the phases of scanning and selecting and into implementation – linking market- and technology-related streams along the way.

At the outset anything is possible, but increasing commitment of resources during the life of the project makes it increasingly difficult to change direction. Managing new product or service development is a fine balancing act, between the costs of continuing with projects which may not eventually succeed (and which represent opportunity costs in terms of other possibilities) – and the danger of closing down too soon and eliminating potentially fruitful options. With shorter lifecycles and demand for greater product variety, pressure is also placed

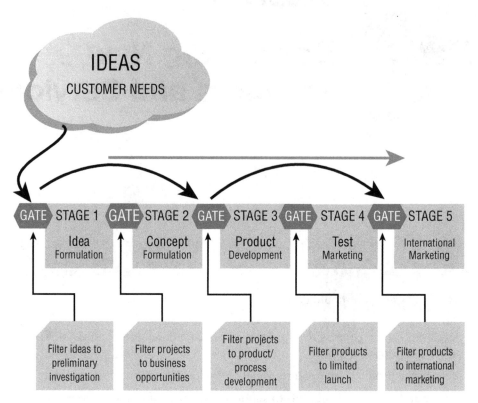

FIGURE 10.1 Stage gate process for new product development

upon the development process to work with a wider portfolio of new product opportunities and to manage the risks associated with progressing these through development to launch.

These decisions can be made on an ad hoc basis, but experience and research suggests some form of structured development system, with clear decision points and agreed rules on which to base go/no-go decisions, is a more effective approach. Attention on internal mechanisms for integrating and optimizing the process is critical, such as concurrent engineering, cross-functional working, advanced tools and early involvement. To deal with this, attention has focused on systematic screening, monitoring and progression frameworks, such as Cooper's 'stage gate' approach (Figure 10.1).[1]

As Cooper suggests, successful product development needs to operate some form of structured, staging process. As projects move through the development process, there are a number of discrete stages, each with different decision criteria, or 'gates', which they must meet. Many variations to this basic idea exist (e.g. 'fuzzy gates'), but the important point is to ensure that there is a structure in place which reviews both technical and marketing data at each stage. A common variation is the 'development funnel', which takes into account the reduction in uncertainty as the process progresses, and the influence of real resource constraints (Figure 10.2).[2]

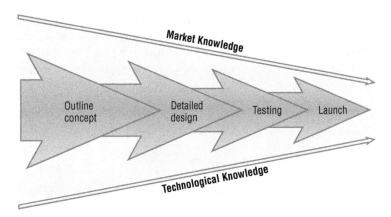

FIGURE 10.2   Development funnel model for new product development

There are numerous other models in the literature, incorporating various stages ranging from three to 13. Such models are essentially linear and unidirectional, beginning with concept development and ending with commercialization. Such models suggest a simple, linear process of development and elimination. However, in practice the development of new products and services is inherently a complex and iterative process, and this makes it difficult to model for practical purposes. For ease of discussion and analysis, we will adopt a simplified four-stage model which we believe is sufficient to discriminate between the various factors that must be managed at different stages:[3]

* *Concept generation* – identifying the opportunities for new products and services.
* *Project assessment and selection* – screening and choosing projects which satisfy certain criteria.
* *Product development* – translating the selected concepts into a physical product (we'll discuss services later).
* *Product commercialization* – testing, launching and marketing the new product.

Concept Generation

Much of the marketing and product development literature concentrates on monitoring market trends and customer needs to identify new product concepts. However, there is a well-established debate in the literature about the relative merits of 'market-pull' versus 'technology-push' strategies for new product development. A review of the relevant research suggests that the best strategy to adopt is dependent on the relative novelty of the new product. For incremental adaptations or product line extensions, 'market pull' is likely to be the preferred route, as customers are familiar with the product type and will be able to express preferences easily. However, there are many 'needs' that the customer may be unaware of, or unable to articulate, and in these cases the balance shifts to a 'technology-push' strategy. Nevertheless, in most cases customers do not buy a technology; they buy products for the benefits that they can receive from them – the 'technology push' must provide a solution for their needs. Thus, some customer or market analysis is also important for more novel technology. This stage is sometimes referred to as the 'fuzzy front end' because it often lacks structure and order, but a number of tools are available to help systematically identify new product concepts, and these are described below.

INNOVATION IN ACTION 10.1

Samsung and the Rise of the Smartphone

Smartphones are a good example of continuous product development and innovation, often with lifecycles measured in months rather than years. Apple's entry into the mobile phone market with its various iPhone generations has received most attention, but Samsung is an equally interesting example of a product development-led success strategy.

There is no accepted definition of a smartphone, or distinction between these and feature-rich phones. However, many accept that Samsung entered the global smartphone market in October 2006 with its BlackJack phone, which at that time was similar in name, appearance and features to the RIM BlackBerry (and, indeed, resulted in a legal challenge from RIM, similar to the legal disputes between Apple and Samsung in 2012). The BlackJack smartphone was launched first in the United States via the operator AT&T, and ran Windows Mobile, and in 2007 won the Best Smart Phone award at CTIA in the United States. Just over a year later, the imaginatively named BlackJack II was launched in December 2008, followed by the third-generation Samsung Jack in May 2009, which became the highest-selling Windows Mobile phone series to date.

Another major milestone was in November 2007, when Samsung became a founding member of the Open Handset Alliance (OHA), which was created to develop, promote and license Google's Android system for smartphones and tablets. Another member company, HTC, launched the first Android smartphone in August 2008, but Samsung followed with its own in May 2009, the I7500, which included the full suite of Google services, 3.2" AMOLED display, GPS and a 5-megapixel camera. However, Samsung has been promiscuous in its choice of operating systems, and, in addition to adopting Windows and Android systems, developed and uses its own. In May 2010, Samsung launched the Wave, its first smartphone based on its own Bada platform, designed for touchscreen interfaces and social networking. Six more Wave phones were launched the following year, with sales in excess of 10 million units.

The real success story is Samsung's Android-based Galaxy S sub-brand, introduced in March 2010, followed by the Galaxy S II in 2011 and S III in 2012, as a direct competitor to Apple's iPhone. In the first quarter of 2012, Samsung sold more than 42 million smartphones worldwide, which represented 29% of global sales, compared to Apple with 35 million (24% market share). By 2012, the OHA had 84 member firms, and the Android system accounted for around 60% of global sales, compared to Apple's OS with 26%. However, estimates of market share differ between analysts, depending on whether they measure share of new sales or existing user-base, and market shares also fluctuate significantly with new product launches. For example, in the month of the launch of the new iPhone, Apple's share of new sales in the United States leaped from 26% to 43%, and Android collapsed from 60% to 47%. This clearly demonstrates the impact of a new product launch.

Moreover, this product-led strategy is not easy to sustain. Nokia and BlackBerry were past leaders in their respective markets for many years, but have recently suffered significant declines in sales and profitability. Despite high levels of research and development and strong brands, they have failed to maintain their lead through new product development. In a single year, 2011–2012, Nokia's market share fell from 24% to just 8%, and RIM, maker of the BlackBerry, from 14% to below 7%. In part, this decline reflects their proprietary operating systems, which have failed to add new features and functions, such as Cloud storage, and both provide access to far fewer apps than Apple's iTunes store or Google's Play for Android.

Project Selection

This stage includes the screening and selection of product concepts prior to subsequent progress through to the development phase. Two costs of failing to select the 'best' project set are: the actual cost of resources spent on poor projects and the opportunity costs of marginal projects which may have succeeded with additional resources.

There are two levels of filtering. The first is the aggregate product plan, in which the new product development portfolio is determined. The aggregate product plan attempts to integrate the various potential projects to ensure that the collective set of development projects meet the goals and objectives of the firm, and help to build the capabilities needed. The first step is to ensure that resources are applied to the appropriate types and mix of projects. The second step is to develop a capacity plan to balance resource and demand. The final step is to analyse the effect of the proposed projects on capabilities, to ensure this is built up to meet future demands.

The second lower-level filters are concerned with specific product concepts. The two most common processes at this level are the development funnel and the stage gate system. The development funnel is a means to identify, screen, review and converge development projects as they move from idea to commercialization. It provides a framework in which to review alternatives based on a series of explicit criteria for decision-making. Similarly, the stage gate system provides a formal framework for filtering projects based on explicit criteria. The main difference is that where the development funnel assumes resource constraints, the stage gate system does not.

Product Development

This stage includes all the activities necessary to take the chosen concept and deliver a product for commercialization. It is at the working level, where the product is actually developed and produced, that the individual R&D staff, designers, engineers and marketing staff must work together to solve specific issues and to make decisions on the details (see research note for the critical role of cross-functional teams in product development). Whenever a problem appears, for example a gap between the current design

Video Clip of an interview with Armin Rau of SICAP exploring some of these issues is available on the Innovation Portal at **www.innovation-portal.info**

and the requirement, the development team must take action to close it. The way in which this is achieved determines the speed and effectiveness of the problem-solving process. In many cases this problem-solving routine involves iterative design–build–test cycles, which make use of a number of tools.

Product Commercialization and Review

In many cases the process of new product development blurs into the process of commercialization. For example, customer co-development, test marketing and use of alpha, beta and gamma test sites yield data on customer requirements and any problems encountered in use but also help to obtain customer buy-in and prime the market. It is not the purpose of this section to examine the relative efficacy of different marketing strategies but rather to identify those factors which influence directly the process of new product development. We are primarily interested in what criteria firms use to evaluate the success of new products, and how these criteria may differ between low- and high-novelty projects. In the former case we expect more formal and narrow financial or market measures, but in the latter case we find a broader range of criteria are used to reflect the potential for organizational learning and future new product options.

Success Factors

There have been numerous studies that have investigated the factors affecting the success of new products. Most have adopted a 'matched-pair' methodology in which similar new products are examined but one is much less successful than the other. This allows us to discriminate between good and poor practice, and helps to control for other background factors.[4]

These studies have differed in emphasis and sometimes contradicted each other, but despite differences in samples and methodologies it is possible to identify some consensus of what the best criteria for success are:

- *Product advantage* – product superiority in the eyes of the customer, real differential advantage, high performance-to-cost ratio, delivering unique benefits to users – appears to be the primary factor separating winners and losers. Customer perception is the key.
- *Market knowledge* – the homework is vital: better development preparation including initial screening, preliminary market assessment, preliminary technical appraisal, detailed market studies and business/financial analysis. Customer and user needs' assessment and understanding is critical. Competitive analysis is also an important part of the market analysis.
- *Clear product definition* – this includes: defining target markets, clear concept definition and benefits to be delivered, clear positioning strategy, a list of product requirements, features and attributes or use of a priority criteria list agreed before development begins.
- *Risk assessment* – market-based, technological, manufacturing and design sources of risk to the development project must be assessed, and plans made to address them. Risk assessments must be built into the business and feasibility studies so they are appropriately addressed with respect to the market and the firms' capabilities.

- *Project organization* – the use of cross-functional, multidisciplinary teams carrying responsibility for the project from beginning to end.
- *Project resources* – sufficient financial and material resources and human skills must be available; the firm must possess the management and technological skills to design and develop the new product.
- *Proficiency of execution* – quality of technological and production activities, and all pre-commercialization business analyses and test marketing; detailed market studies underpin new product success.
- *Top management support* – from concept through to launch. Management must be able to create an atmosphere of trust, coordination and control; key individuals or champions often play a critical role during the innovation process.

These factors have all been found to contribute to new product success, and should therefore form the basis of any formal process for new product development. Note from this list, and the factors illustrated in Figure 10.3 and Figure 10.4, that successful new product

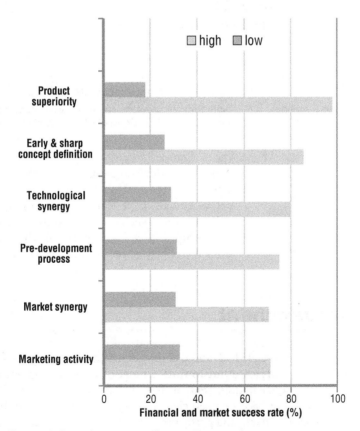

FIGURE 10.3 Factors influencing new product success

Source: Based on Cooper, R. G. (2000) Doing it right: Winning with new product. *Ivey Business Journal,* 64 (6): 1–7.

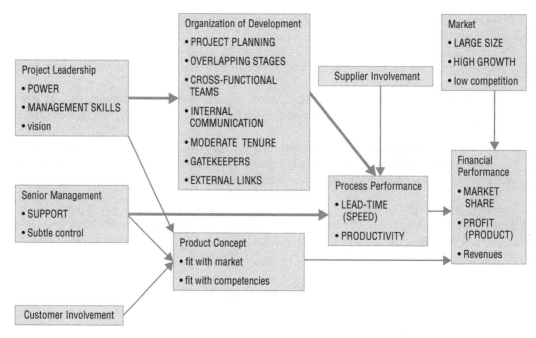

FIGURE 10.4 Key factors influencing the success of new product development

Source: Brown, S.L. and Eisenhardt, K.M. (1995) Product development: Past research, present findings and future directions. *Academy of Management Review* 20: 343–378. Copyright Academy of Management.

Video Clip of a video describing 3M's processes for seeking out breakthrough products and services is available on the Innovation Portal at **www.innovation-portal.info**

and service development requires the management of a blend of product or service characteristics, such as product focus, superiority and advantage, and organizational issues, such as project resources, execution and leadership. Managing only one of these key contributions is unlikely to result in consistent success.

Service Development

Employment trends in all the so-called advanced countries indicate a move away from manufacturing, construction, mining and agriculture towards a range of services, including retail, finance, transportation, communication, entertainment, professional and public services. This trend is in part because manufacturing has become so efficient and highly automated, and therefore generates proportionately less employment, and partly because many services are characterized by high levels of customer contact and are reproduced locally, and are therefore often labour-intensive. In the most advanced service economies such as those of the United States and the United Kingdom, services create up to three-quarters of the wealth and 85% of employment, and yet we know relatively little about managing innovation in this sector. The critical role of services, in the broadest sense, has long been recognized, but service innovation is still not well understood.

Innovation in services in much more than the application of information technology (IT). In fact, the disappointing returns to IT investments in services has resulted in a widespread debate about its causes and potential solutions (the so-called productivity paradox in services). Frequently, service innovations, which make significant differences to the ways customers use and perceive the service delivered, will demand major investments in process innovation and technology by service providers but also demand investment in skills and methods of working to change the business model, as well as major marketing changes. Estimates vary, but returns on investment on IT alone are around 15%, with a typical lag of two to three years, when productivity often falls, but when combined with changes in organization and management these returns increase to around 25%.[5]

In the service sector the impact of innovation on growth is generally positive and consistent, with the possible exception of financial services. The pattern across retail and wholesale distribution, transport and communication services, and the broad range of business services is particularly strong. More recent research has identified the 'hidden innovation' in the creative industries and media, for example film and TV programme development, which is not captured by traditional policy or measures such as R&D or patents, as the case of the BBC shows.

Case Study of the BBC highlighting some of these issues is available on the Innovation Portal at **www.innovation-portal.info**

Most research and management prescriptions have been based on the experience of manufacturing and high-technology sectors. Most simply assume that such practices are equally applicable to managing innovation in services, but some researchers argue that services are fundamentally different. There is a clear need to distinguish what, if any, of what we know about managing innovation in manufacturing is applicable to services, what must be adapted, and what is distinct and different.

We will argue that generic good practices do exist, which apply to the development of both manufactured and service offerings, but that these must be adapted to different contexts, specifically the scale and complexity, degree of customization of the offerings and the uncertainty of the technological and market environments. It is critical to match the configuration of management and organization of development to the specific technology and market environment. For example, service development in retail financial services is very similar to product development for consumer goods.

The service sector includes a very wide range and a great diversity of different activities and businesses, ranging from individual consultants and shopkeepers to huge multinational finance firms and critical non-profit public and third-sector organizations such as government, health and education. Therefore, great care needs to be taken when making any generalization about the service sectors. We will introduce some ways of understanding and analysing the sector later, but it is possible to identify some fundamental differences between manufacturing and service operations:

* *Tangibility*. Goods tend to be tangible, whereas services are mostly intangible, even though you can usually see or feel the results.

- *Perceptions* of performance and quality are more important in services, in particular the difference between expectations and perceived performance. Customers are likely to regard a service as being good if it exceeds their expectations. Perceptions of service quality are affected by:
  - ○ tangible aspects – appearance of facilities, equipment and staff
  - ○ responsiveness – prompt service and willingness to help
  - ○ competence – the ability to perform the service dependably
  - ○ assurance – knowledge and courtesy of staff and ability to convey trust and confidence
  - ○ empathy – provision of caring, individual attention.

- *Simultaneity.* The lag between production and consumption of goods and services is different. Most goods are produced well in advance of consumption, to allow for distribution, storage and sales. In contrast, many services are produced and almost immediately consumed. This creates problems of quality management and capacity planning. It is harder to identify or correct errors in services, and more difficult to match supply and demand.

- *Storage.* Services cannot usually be stored (e.g. a seat on an airline), although some, such as utilities, have some potential for storage. The inability to hold stocks of services can create problems matching supply and demand (i.e. capacity management). These can be dealt with in a number of ways. Pricing can be used to help smooth fluctuations in demand, for example by providing discounts at off-peak times. Where possible, additional capacity can be provided at peak times by employing part-time workers or outsourcing. In the worst cases, customers can simply be forced to wait for the services, by queuing.

- *Customer contact.* Most customers have low or no contact with the operations which produce goods. Many services demand high levels of contact between the operations and ultimate customer, although the level and timing of such contact varies. For example, medical treatment may require constant or frequent contact, but financial services only sporadic contact.

- *Location.* Because of the contact with customers and the near-simultaneous production and consumption of services, the location of service operations is often more important than for operations which produce goods. For example, restaurants, retail operations and entertainment services all favour proximity to customers. Conversely, manufactured goods are often produced and consumed in very different locations. For these reasons the markets for manufactured goods also tend to be more competitive and global, whereas many personal and business services are local and less competitive. For example, only around 10% of services in the advanced economies are traded internationally.

 Case Study of the Bank of Scotland highlighting some of these issues is available on the Innovation Portal at **www.innovation-portal.info**

These service characteristics should be taken into account when designing and managing the organization and processes for new service development, as some of the findings from research on new product development will have to be adapted or may not apply at all. Also, because of the diversity of service operations, we need also to tailor the organization and management to different types of service context (Table 10.1).

TABLE 10.1 Characteristics of Service 'High Innovators'

Business descriptor	Low innovators	High innovators
Innovation outcomes		
• % sales from services introduced <3 years ago	<1%	17%
• % new services versus competitors	>0%	5%
Customer base		
• Focus on key customers	Average	High
• Relative customer base	Similar to competitors	More focused than competitors
Value chain		
• Focus on key suppliers	Average	High/strategic
• Value-added/sales %	72%	60%
• Operating cost added/sales	36%	25%
• Vertical integration versus competitors	Same or more	Same or less
Innovation input		
• 'What' R&D	0.1% sales	0.7% sales
• 'How' R&D	0.1% sales	0.5% sales
• Fixed assets/sales	growing at 10% p.a.	growing at >20% p.a.
• Overheads/sales %	8%	11%
Innovation context		
• Recent technology change	20%	40%
• Time to market	>1 year	<1 year
Competition		
• Competitor entry	10%	40%
• Imports/exports versus market	2%	12%
Quality of offer		
• Relative quality versus competitors	Declining	Improving
• Value for money	Just below competitors	Better than competitors
Output		
• Real sales	9%	15%

Source: Clayton (2003) in Tidd, J. and F.M. Hull, eds, *Service Innovation: Organizational Responses to Technological Opportunities and Market Imperatives*, Imperial College Press, London. Copyright Imperial College Press/World Scientific Publishing Co.

Innovation and quality performance appear to be improved by cross-functional teams, by sharing information and by involvement with customers and suppliers.[6] Service delivery is improved by customer focus and project management, and by knowledge sharing and collaboration in teams. Time to market is reduced by knowledge sharing and collaboration, and customer focus and project organization, but cross-functional teams can prolong the process. Costs are reduced by setting standards for projects and products, and by the involvement of customers and suppliers, but can be increased by using cross-functional teams. Although individual practices can make a significant contribution to performance (Figure 10.5), it is clear that it is the coherent combination of practices and their interaction that creates superior performance in specific contexts. These research findings can be used to help assess the effectiveness of existing strategies, processes, organization, tools, technology and systems (SPOTS), and to identify where and how to improve.

 Tool to help you develop new services – SPOTS – is available on the Innovation Portal at **www.innovation-portal.info**

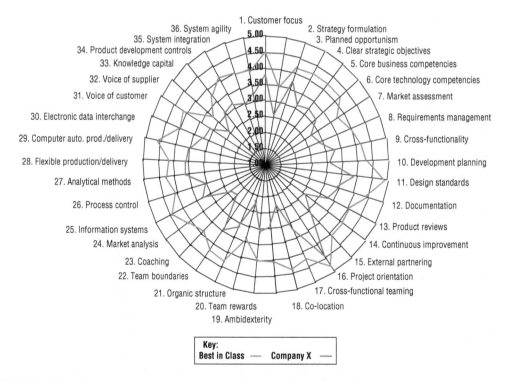

FIGURE 10.5 Factors influencing the effectiveness of new service development

Source: Tidd, J. and Hull, F.M. (2006) Managing service innovation: the need for selectivity rather than 'best practice'. *New Technology, Work and Employment* 21 (2): 139–161. Reproduced by permission of John Wiley & Sons, Ltd.

Tools to Support New Product Development

Concept Generation

Most studies have highlighted the importance of understanding users' needs. Designing a product to satisfy a perceived need has been shown to be an important discriminator of commercial success. Common approaches include:

- *Surveys and focus groups* – where a similar product exists surveys of customers' preferences can be a reliable guide to development. Focus groups allow developers to explore the likely response to more novel products where a clear target segment exists.
- *Latent needs analysis* – are designed to uncover the unarticulated requirements of customers by means of their responses to symbols, concepts and forms.
- *Lead-users* – are representative of the needs of the market, but some time ahead of the majority, and so represent future needs. Lead users are one of the most important sources of market knowledge for product improvements.
- *Customer-developers* – in some cases new products are partly or completely developed by customers. In such cases the issue is how to identify and acquire such products.
- *Competitive analysis* – of competing products, by reverse engineering or benchmarking features of competing products.
- *Industry experts or consultants* – who have a wide range of experience of different users' needs. The danger is that they may have become too immersed in the user's world to have the breadth of vision required to assess and evaluate the potential of the innovation. The use of 'proxy experts' helps to overcome this problem. They suggest selecting a specific group of respondents who have knowledge of the product category or usage context.
- *Extrapolating trends* – in technology, markets and society to guess the short- to medium-term needs.
- *Building scenarios* – alternative visions of the future based on varying assumptions to create robust product strategies. Most relevant to long-term projects and product portfolio development.
- *Market experimentation* – testing market response with real products, but able to adapt or withdraw rapidly. Only practical where development costs are low, lead-times short and customers tolerant of product underperformance or failure. Sometimes referred to as 'expeditionary marketing', or more modestly 'test marketing'.

Project Selection

Different combinations of criteria are used to screen and assess projects prior to development. The most common are based on discounted cash flows, such as net present value/internal rate of return, followed by cost–benefit analysis, and simple calculations of the payback period. In addition to these financial criteria, most organizations also use a range of additional measures:

- *Ranking* – a means of ordering a list of candidate projects in relative value or worthiness of support, broken down into several factors, so both objective and judgemental data can be assessed. These techniques are likely to be of most use in the early stages of the process, since they are fairly 'rough-cut' methods.

- *Profiles* – projects are given scores on each of several characteristics, and are rejected if they fail to meet some pre-determined threshold. The projects which dominate on all or most of the factor scores are selected. These methods can be used at all stages of the development process.
- *Simulated outcomes* – alternative outcomes to which probabilities can be attached, or alternate paths depending on chance outcomes and when the projects have different payoffs for different outcomes. The range of possible outcomes and the likelihood of a specific outcome are found. It is used especially in the analysis of sets of projects which are interdependent (the aggregate project plan).
- *Strategic clusters* – projects not selected solely for maximization of some financial measure, but for the support they give to the strategic position. Groups are clustered according to their support for specific objectives, and then these groups are rated according to strategic importance and funded accordingly (again, this is important at the aggregate project plan level).
- *Interactive* – an iterative process between the R&D director and project managers, where project proposals are improved at each stage to more closely align with the objectives. The aim of this is to develop projects that more nearly fit the strategic and tactical objectives of the firm. These methods are used mainly at the aggregate project plan level, or at the early stages of specific projects.

Product Development

There are a number of tools, or methodologies, which have been developed to help solve the problems, and most require the integration of different functions and disciplines (Table 10.2). The most significant tools and methods used are:

- *Design for Manufacture (DFM)* – 'the full range of policies, techniques, practices and attitudes that cause a product to be designed for the optimum manufacturing cost, the optimum achievement of manufactured quality and the optimum achievement of lifecycle support (serviceability, reliability and maintainability)'. It includes design for assembly (DFA), design for producibility (DFP) and other design rule approaches. Studies from the car industry indicate that up to 80% of the final production costs are determined at the design stage.
- *Rapid Prototyping* – is the core element of the design–build–test cycle, and can increase the rate and amount of learning that occurs in each cycle. The first design is unlikely to be complete, and so designers go through several iterations, learning more about the problem and alternative solutions each time. The number of iterations will depend on the time and cost constraints of the project. One study found that frequent prototyping proved useful for intra-team communication, obtaining customer feedback and manufacturing process development. Having an actual prototype as a visual model enables more reliable assessment of preferences and suggestions.
- *Computer-aided Techniques (CAD/CAM)* – potential benefits include reduction in development lead times, economies in design, ability to design products too complex to do manually and the combination of CAD with production automation computer-aided

TABLE 10.2 Use and Usefulness of Techniques for Product and Service Development

	High Novelty		Low Novelty	
	Usage (%)	Usefulness	Usage (%)	Usefulness
Segmentation*	89	3.42	42	4.50
Market experimentation	63	4.00	53	3.70
Industry experts	63	3.83	37	3.71
Surveys/focus groups*	52	4.50	37	4.00
User-practice observation	47	3.67	42	3.50
Partnering customers*	37	4.43	58	3.67
Lead users*	32	4.33	37	3.57
Probability of technical success	100	4.37	100	4.32
Probability of commercial success	100	4.68	95	4.50
Market share*	100	3.63	84	4.00
Core competencies*	95	3.61	79	3.00
Degree of internal commitment	89	3.82	79	3.67
Market size	89	3.76	84	3.94
Competition	89	3.76	84	3.81
Gap analysis	79	2.73	84	2.81
Strategic clusters*	42	3.63	32	2.67
Prototyping*	79	4.33	63	4.08
Market experimentation	68	4.31	63	4.08
QFD	47	3.33	37	3.43
Cross-functional teams*	63	4.47	37	3.74
Project manager (heavyweight)*	52	3.84	32	3.05

Usefulness Scale: 1–5, 5 = critical, based on manager assessments of 50 development projects in 25 firms. * denotes difference in usefulness rating is statistically significant at 5% level

Source: Derived from Tidd, J. and K. Bodley (2002) The effect of project novelty on the new product development process. *R&D Management, 32* (2): 127–138 with permission from John Wiley & Sons, Ltd.

manufacture (CAM) to achieve the benefits of integration. However, these benefits are not always realized, owing to organizational shortcomings.

● *Quality Function Deployment (QFD)* – is a set of planning and communications routines which are used to identify critical customer attributes and create a specific link between these and design parameters; it focuses on and coordinates the skills within the organization

Case Study describing the development of the Lexus brand highlighting some of these issues is available on the Innovation Portal at **www.innovation-portal.info**

to design, manufacture and then market products that customers value. The aim is to answer three primary questions: What are the critical attributes for customers? What design parameters drive these attributes? What should the design parameter targets be for the new design?

INNOVATION IN ACTION 10.2

Tata's Transformation of Jaguar Land Rover (JLR)

The Indian company Tata is probably best known overseas for its ill-fated Nano micro-car. However, less well documented is its success at the other end of the automotive market. In March 2008, Tata bought Jaguar Land Rover from Ford for $2.3 billion (£1.4 billion), around half of what Ford had paid for the group of companies. Since then, Tata has grown JLR through a sustained investment in new product development. By 2012, JLR's annual sales had risen by 37%, during an economic recession, helped by sales of its new in 2011 Range Rover Evoque and increased demand in Russia and China, which accounted for almost a quarter of its total sales, and contributed to the 57% increase in the profits of JLR. The profit margin of 20% was three times that of parent Tata's domestic business. The two British luxury car brands were valued at over £14 billion in 2012.

Tata acquired JLR cheaply because Ford had failed to develop the company and its products. In 2007, Ford contributed about £400 million into the two brands towards R&D, before they were sold to Tata Motors, and the first of the new product range had been developed and announced under ownership of Ford. The mid-size luxury Jaguar XF was revealed in August 2007, with first customer deliveries in March 2008. The more radical, aluminium full-size luxury Jaguar XJ was launched in late 2009, with the first deliveries in April 2010. By 2011, Tata had tripled this annual R&D spend to £1.2 billion, representing about 10% of the two brands' annual revenue (4% is a more typical R&D intensity in the auto industry). The design-led and segment-spanning SUV Range Rover Evoque was launched in 2011, and quickly had a six-month order book, despite the economic recession and premium pricing. All three cars won numerous industry and consumer awards.

In December 2010, 1500 new jobs were created as the Halewood factory ramped-up its operations to launch the new Range Rover Evoque, which began production in July 2011. By April 2012, the company needed to recruit more than 1000 additional staff for its advanced manufacturing plant in Solihull, to take the workforce to almost 4500 at the Halewood plant, trebling the number employed there compared to three years before. The company has announced an investment of £355 million for new engine plant, which will create 750 new jobs. JLR is now the UK's largest automotive design, engineering and manufacturing employer, accounting for 20% of the UK's total exports to China.

Tata already builds some Land Rover models in India, and in 2012 selected a joint venture partner in China, Chery Automobile. In 2012, Tata's chief financial officer, C. R. Ramakrishnan, committed to further investments in JLR. 'Over the past five to six years, Jaguar Land Rover has spent around £700 million to £800 million annually on capital expenditure and product development. Going forward, we will double that.' And he aimed to develop 40 new products and variants between 2013 and 2018. The new Jaguar F-type sports car was launched in 2013, following a £200 million investment at the Bromwich facility, and another 1000 new staff.

Quality function deployment (QFD) is a useful technique for translating customer requirements into development needs, and encourages communication between engineering, production and marketing. Unlike most other tools of quality management, QFD is used to identify opportunities for product improvement or differentiation, rather than to solve problems. Customer-required characteristics are translated or 'deployed' by means of a matrix into language which engineers can understand. The construction of a relationship matrix (also known as 'the house of quality') requires a significant amount of technical and market research. Great emphasis must be made on gathering market and user data in order to identify potential design trade-offs, and to achieve the most appropriate balance between cost, quality and performance. The construction of a QFD matrix involves the following steps:

1. Identify customer requirements, primary and secondary, and any major dislikes.
2. Rank requirements according to importance.
3. Translate requirements into measurable characteristics.
4. Establish the relationship between the customer requirements and technical product characteristics, and estimate the strength of the relationship.
5. Choose appropriate units of measurement and determine target values based on customer requirements and competitor benchmarks.

Symbols are used to show the relationship between customer requirements and technical specifications, and weights attached to illustrate the strength of the relationship. Horizontal rows with no relationship symbol indicate that the existing design is incomplete. Conversely, vertical columns with no relationship symbol indicate that an existing design feature is redundant as it is not valued by the customer. In addition, comparisons with competing products, or benchmarks, can be included. This is important because relative quality is more relevant than absolute quality: customer expectations are likely to be shaped by what else is available, rather than by some ideal.

QFD (Figure 10.6) was originally developed in Japan, and is claimed to have helped Toyota reduce its development time and costs by 40%. More recently, many leading American firms have adopted QFD, including AT&T, Digital and Ford, but results have been mixed: only around a quarter of projects have resulted in any quantifiable benefit. In contrast, there has

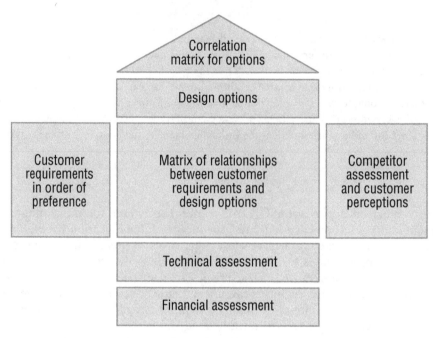

FIGURE 10.6 Quality function development (QFD) matrix

Activity to help you explore the QFD tool in greater detail is available on the Innovation Portal at **www.innovation-portal.info**

Tools to help you with market research – such as conjoint analysis – are available on the Innovation Portal at **www.innovation-portal.info**

been relatively little application of QFD by European firms.[7] This is not the result of ignorance, but rather a recognition of the practical problems of implementing QFD.

Clearly, QFD requires the compilation of a lot of marketing and technical data, and more importantly the close cooperation of the development and marketing functions. Indeed, the process of constructing the relationship matrix provides a structured way of getting people from development and marketing to communicate, and therefore is as valuable as any more quantifiable outputs. It is particularly powerful in identifying and overcoming trade-offs in customer requirements.[8] However, where relations between the technical and marketing groups are a problem, which is too often the case, the use of QFD may be premature.

Summary

There is a vast amount of management research on the subject of new product and service development, and we are now pretty certain what works and what does not. There are no guarantees that following the suggestions in this chapter will produce a blockbuster product, service or business, but if these elements are not managed well, your chances of success will be much lower. This is not supposed to discourage experimentation and calculated risk-taking but rather to provide a foundation for evidence-based practice. Research suggests that a range of factors affect the success of a potential new product or service:

- Some factors are product-specific (e.g. product advantage, clear target market and attention to pre-development activities).

- Other factors are more about the organizational context and process (e.g. senior management support, formal process and use of external knowledge).

- A formal process for new product and service development should consist of distinct stages, such as concept development, business case, product development, pilot and commercialization, separated by distinct decision points, or gates, which have clear criteria, such as product fit and product advantages.

- Different stages of the process demand different criteria and different tools and methods. Useful tools and methods at the concept stage include segmentation, experimentation, focus groups and customer partnering; and at the development stage useful tools include prototyping, design for production and QFD.

- Services and products are different in a number of ways, especially intangibility and perceived benefits, and so will demand the adaptation of the standard models and prescriptions for new product development.

Further Resources

The classic texts on new product development are those by Robert Cooper, for example *Winning at New Products: Accelerating the process from idea to launch* (Perseus Books, 2001) and Cooper, R. G. (2000) Doing it right: Winning with new products, *Ivey Business Journal*, **64** (6): 1–7, or anything by Kim Clark and Steven Wheelwright, such as Wheelwright, S. C. and K. B. Clark (1997) Creating project plans to focus product development, *Harvard Business Review*, September–October, or their book *Revolutionizing Product Development* (Free Press, 1992). Paul Trott provides a good review of research in his text *Innovation Management and New Product Development* (FT Prentice Hall, 5th edition, 2012), but for a more concise review of the research see van der Panne, G., C. Beers and A. van Kleinknecht (2003) Success and failure of innovation: A literature review, *International Journal of Innovation Management*, **7** (3): 309–338. A useful and practical handbook is *The PDMA*

ToolBook of New Product Development, edited by Abbie Griffin (John Wiley & Sons, Ltd, 3rd edition, 2012), which is particularly strong on process and tools. An excellent guide to applying QFD is *Quality Function Deployment and Six Sigma: A QFD handbook* by J. P. Ficalora and L. Cohen (Prentice-Hall, 2012).

References

1. Cooper, R. G. (2000) Doing it right: Winning with new products, *Ivey Business Journal*, **64** (6): 1–7.

2. Wheelwright, S. C. and K. B. Clark (1997) Creating project plans to focus product development, *Harvard Business Review*, **70** (2): 70–82.

3. Tidd, J. and K. Bodley (2002) The effect of project novelty on the new product development process, *R&D Management*, **32** (2): 127–138.

4. van der Panne, G., C. Beers and A. van Kleinknecht (2003) Success and failure of innovation: A literature review, *International Journal of Innovation Management*, **7** (3): 309–338.

5. Crespi, G., C. Criscuolo and J. Haskel (2006) Information technology, organisational change and productivity growth: Evidence from UK firms. *The Future of Science, Technology and Innovation Policy: Linking research and practice.* SPRU 40th Anniversary Conference, Brighton.

6. Tidd, J. and F. M. Hull (2006) Managing service innovation: The need for selectivity rather than 'best-practice', *New Technology, Work and Employment*, **21** (2): 139–161; Tidd, J. and F. M. Hull (eds) (2003) *Service Innovation: Organizational Responses to Technological Opportunities and Market Imperatives*, London: Imperial College Press.

7. Griffin, A. (1992) Evaluating QFD's use in US firms as a process for developing products, *Journal of Product Innovation Management*, **9**: 171–187.

8. Pullman, M. E., W. L. Moore and D. G. Wardell (2002) A comparison of quality function deployment and conjoint analysis in new product design, *Journal of Product Innovation Management*, **19**: 354–364.

 Deeper Dive explanations of innovation concepts and ideas are available on the Innovation Portal at **www.innovation-portal.info**

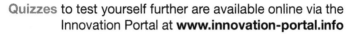

Quizzes to test yourself further are available online via the Innovation Portal at **www.innovation-portal.info**

Summary of online resources for Chapter 10 –
all material is available via the Innovation Portal at
www.innovation-portal.info

Cases	**Media**	**Tools**	**Activities**	**Deeper Dive**
• BBC • Bank of Scotland • Lexus	• Armin Rau, SICAP • 3M, Breakthrough products and services	• Service development • Conjoint analysis • Lead-user methods • SPOTS	• Quality function deployment (QFD)	• Fuzzy front end • Cross-functional team effectiveness and project uncertainty

Chapter 11

Developing Business and Talent through Corporate Venturing

LEARNING OBJECTIVES

After this chapter you should be able to:

* understand the motives and management of corporate ventures
* identify the advantages and drawbacks of different structures for corporate ventures
* assess the likely success of corporate venture outcomes.

Internal Venturing and Entrepreneurship

Samsung began life as a noodle-processing company, Nokia was originally a manufacturer of rubber galoshes and 3M's first business was sandpaper. By a process of strategic diversification, experimentation, innovation and a little luck, each has evolved and continuously created new businesses.

Corporate ventures, broadly defined, are a range of different ways of developing innovations, alternative to conventional internal processes for new product or service development, which often go beyond product development towards the creation of a new business development. We discussed in Chapter 10 the many benefits of using structured approaches to new product and service development, such as stage gate and development funnel processes, but these approaches also have a major disadvantage, because decisions at the different gates are likely to favour those innovations close to existing strategy, markets and products, and are likely to filter out or reject potential innovations further from the organization's comfort zone.

For this reason we need different mechanisms to identify, develop and exploit innovations which do not fit current businesses or markets.

An internal corporate venture attempts to exploit the resources of the large corporation, but to provide an environment more conducive to radical innovation. The key factors that distinguish a potential new venture from the core business are risk, uncertainty, newness and significance. However, it is not sufficient to promote entrepreneurial behaviour within a large organization. Entrepreneurial behaviour is not an end in itself, but must be directed and translated into desired business outcomes. Entrepreneurial behaviour is not associated with superior organizational performance, unless it is combined with an appropriate strategy in a heterogeneous or uncertain environment.[1] This suggests the need for clear strategic objectives for corporate venturing and appropriate organizational structures and processes to achieve those objectives.

Figure 11.1 suggests a range of venture types that can be used in different contexts. Corporate ventures are likely to be most appropriate where the organization needs to exploit some internal competencies and retain a high degree of control over the business. Joint ventures and alliances involve working with external partners, discussed in the previous chapter, will demand some release of control and autonomy but in return introduce the additional competencies of the partners. Spin-out or new venture businesses are the extreme case, often necessary where there is little relatedness between the core competencies and new venture business. Note that these options are not mutually exclusive, for example a spin-out business can become an alliance partner or a corporate venture can spin-out. Also, all types of venture require a venture champion, a strong business case and sufficient resources to be successful.

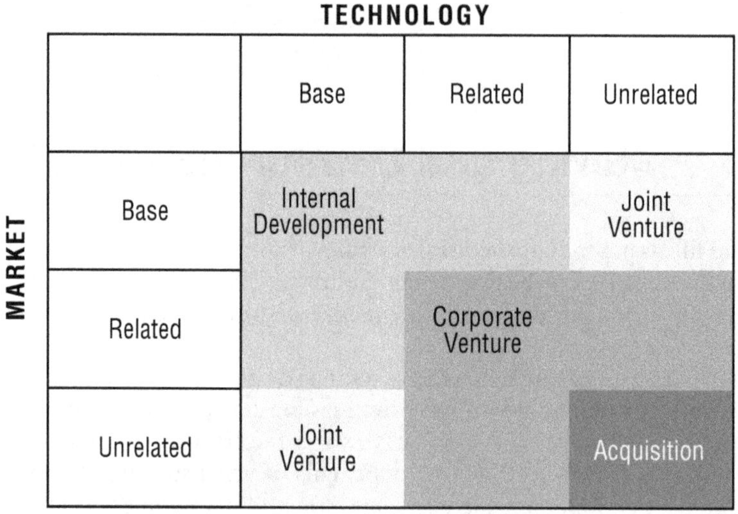

FIGURE 11.1   Role of venturing in the development and commercialization of innovations

Source: Burgelman, R. (1984) Managing the internal corporate venturing process. *Sloan Management Review*, 25(2) 33–48. © 1984 from MIT Sloan Management Review/Massachusetts Institute of Technoplogy. All rights reserved. Distributed by Tribune Media Services.

Why Do It?

There are a wide range of motives for establishing corporate ventures:[2]

- Grow the business.
- Exploit underutilized resources.
- Introduce pressure on internal suppliers.
- Divest non-core activities.
- Satisfy managers' ambitions.
- Spread the risk and cost of product development.
- Combat cyclical demands of mainstream activities.
- Learn about the process of venturing
- Diversify the business.
- Develop new technological or market competencies.

We will discuss each of these motives in turn, and provide examples. The first three are primarily operational; the remainder more strategic.

INNOVATION IN ACTION 11.1

Corporate Venturing at Nortel Networks

Nortel Networks is a leader in a high-growth, high-technology sector, and around a quarter of all its staff are in R&D, but it recognizes that it is extremely difficult to initiate new businesses outside the existing divisions. Therefore, in December 1996, it created the Business Ventures Programme (BVP) to help to overcome some of the structural shortcomings of the existing organization, and identify and nurture new business ventures outside the established lines of business: 'The basic deal we're offering employees is an extremely exciting one. What we're saying is, "Come up with a good business proposal and we'll fund and support it. If we believe your business proposal is viable, we'll provide you with the wherewithal to realize your dreams."' The BVP provides:

- guidance in developing a business proposal
- assistance in obtaining approval from the board
- an incubation environment for start-ups
- transition support for longer-term development.

The BVP selects the most promising venture proposals, which are then presented jointly by the BVP and employee(s) to the advisory board. The advisory board applies business and

(continued)

---

financial criteria in its decision whether to accept, reject or seek further development, and if accepted the most appropriate executive sponsor, structure and level of funding. The BVP then helps to incubate the new venture, including staff and resources, objectives and critical milestones. If successful, the BVP then assists the venture to migrate into an existing business division, if appropriate, or creates a new line, business or spin-off company:

> The programme is designed to be flexible. Among the factors determining whether or not to become a separate company are the availability of key resources within Nortel, and the suitability of Nortel's existing distribution channels . . . Nortel is not in this programme to retain 100% control of all ventures. The key motivators are to grow equity by maximizing return on investment, to pursue business opportunities that would otherwise be missed, and to increase employee satisfaction.

In 1997, the BVP attracted 112 business proposals and, given the staff and financial resources available, aimed to fund up to five new ventures. The main problems experienced have been the reaction of managers in established lines of business to proposals outside their own line:

At the executive council level, which represents all lines of business, there is a lot of support . . . where it breaks down in terms of support is more in the political infrastructure, the middle to low management executive level where they feel threatened by it . . . the first stage of our marketing plan is just titled 'Overcoming internal barriers'. That is the single biggest thing we've had to break through.

Initially, there was also a problem capturing the experience of ventures that failed to be commercialized:

> Failures were typically swept under the rock; nobody really talked about them . . . that is changing now and the focus is on celebrating our failures as well as our successes, knowing that we have learnt a lot more from failure than we do from success. Start-up venture experience is in high demand. Generally, it's the projects that fail, not the people.

To Grow the Business

The desire to achieve and maintain expected rates of growth is probably the most common reason for corporate venturing, particularly when the core businesses are maturing. Very few large, publically-listed firms are able to achieve a rate of growth in excess of general GDP. However, the pressure to achieve this for publically listed firms is significant, as financial markets and investors expect the maintenance or improvement of rates of growth. The need to grow underlies many of the other motives for corporate venturing.

Video Clip entitled 'Tesco Goes West' highlighting these issues is available on the Innovation Portal at **www.innovation-portal.info**

To Exploit Underutilized Resources in New Ways

This includes both technological and human resources. Typically, a company has two choices where existing resources are underutilized: either to divest and outsource the process or to generate additional contribution from external clients. However, if the company wants to retain direct and in-house control of the technology or personnel it can form an internal venture team to offer the service to external clients.

Case Study of Spirit highlighting this theme is available on the Innovation Portal at **www.innovation-portal.info**

To Introduce Pressure on Internal Suppliers

This is a common motive, given the current fashion for outsourcing and market testing internal services. When a business activity is separated to introduce competitive pressure a choice has to be made – whether the business is to be subjected to the reality of commercial competition or just to learn from it. If the corporate clients are able to go so far as to withdraw a contract, which is not conducive to learning, the business should be sold to allow it to compete for other work.

To Divest Non-core Activities

Much has been written of the benefits of strategic focus, 'getting back to basics', and creating the 'lean' organization–rationalization, which prompts the divestment of those activities that can be outsourced. However, this process can threaten the skill diversity required for an ever-changing competitive environment. New ventures can provide a mechanism to release peripheral business activities, but to retain some management control and financial interest.

To Satisfy Managers' Ambitions

As a business activity passes through its lifecycle it will require different management styles to bring out the maximum gain. This may mean that the management team responsible for a business area will need to change, whether between conception to growth, growth to maturity or maturity to decline phases. A paradoxical situation often arises because of the changing requirements of a business area: top managers in place who are ambitious and want to see growth managing businesses which are reaching the limits of that growth. To retain the commitment of such managers the corporation will have to create new opportunities for change or expansion. For example, Intel has long had a venture capital programme that invests in related external new ventures, but in 1998 it established the New Business Initiative to bootstrap new businesses developed by its staff: 'They saw that we were putting a lot of investment into external companies and said that we should be investing in our own ideas . . . our employees kept telling us they wanted to be more entrepreneurial.' The initiative invests only in

Video Clip of an interview with David Hall talking about the challenges of entrepreneurship is available on the Innovation Portal at **www.innovation-portal.info**

ventures unrelated to the core microprocessor business, and in 1999 attracted more than 400 proposals, 24 of which gained funding.

To Spread the Risk and Cost of Product Development

Two situations are possible in this case: (i) where the technology or expertise needs to be developed further before it can be applied to the mainstream business or sold to current external markets; or (ii) where the volume sales on a product awaiting development must sell to a target greater than the existing customer groups to be financially justified. In both cases the challenge is to understand how to venture outside current served markets. Too often, when the existing customer base is not ready for a product, the research unit will just continue its development and refinement process. If intermediary markets were exploited these could contribute to the financial costs of development, and to the maturing of the final product.

To Combat Cyclical Demands of Mainstream Activities

In response to the problem of cyclical demand Boeing set up two groups, Boeing Technology Services (BTS) and Boeing Associated Products (BAP), specifically with the function of keeping engineering and laboratory resources more fully employed when its own requirements waned between major development programmes. The remit for BTS was 'to sell off excess engineering laboratory capacity without a detrimental impact on schedules or commitments to major Boeing product-line activities'; it stuck carefully to this charter, and was careful to turn off such activity when the mainstream business required the expertise. BAP was created to commercially exploit Boeing inventions that were usable beyond their application to products manufactured by Boeing. About 600 invention disclosures are submitted by employees each year, and these are reviewed in terms of their marketability and patentability. Licensing agreements are used to exploit these inventions; 259 agreements were made. Beyond the financial benefits to the company and to the employees of this programme, it is seen to foster the innovation spirit within the organization.

To Learn about the Process of Venturing

Venturing is a high-risk activity because of the level of uncertainty attached, and we cannot expect to understand the management process as we do for the mainstream business. If a learning exercise is to be undertaken, and a particular activity is to be chosen for this process, it is critical that goals and objectives are set, including a review schedule. This is important not just for the maximum benefit to be extracted but also for the individuals who will pioneer that venture. For example, NEES Energy, a subsidiary of New England Electric Systems Inc., was set up to bring financial benefits, but was also expected to provide a laboratory to help the parent company learn about starting new ventures.

To Diversify the Business

While the discussion so far has implied that business development would be on a relatively small scale, this need not be the case. Corporate ventures are often formed in an effort to create new businesses in a corporate context, and therefore represent an attempt to grow via diversification. Such diversification may be vertical, that is downstream or upstream of the current process in order to capture a greater proportion of the value added; or horizontal, that is by exploiting existing competencies across additional product markets.

Case Studies of Kodak and Fujifilm highlighting some of these issues are available on the Innovation Portal at **www.innovation-portal.info**

To Develop New Competencies

Growth and diversification are generally based on the exploitation of existing competencies in new products markets, but a corporate venture can also be used as an opportunity for learning new competencies.[3] An organization can acquire knowledge by experimentation, which is a central feature of formal R&D and market research activities. However, different functions and divisions within a firm will develop particular frames of reference and filters based on their experience and responsibilities, and these will affect how they interpret information. Greater organizational learning occurs when more varied interpretations are made, and a corporate venture can better perform this function as it is not confined to the needs of existing technologies or markets.

In practice, the primary motives for establishing a corporate venture are strategic: to meet strategic goals and long-term growth in the face of maturity in existing markets (Box 11.1). However, personnel issues are also important. Sectorial and national differences exist. In the United States, new ventures are also used to stimulate and develop entrepreneurial management, and in Japan they help provide employment opportunities for managers and staff relocated from the core businesses (Table 11.1). Nonetheless, the primary objectives are strategic and long term, and therefore warrant significant management effort and investment.

BOX 11.1: OBJECTIVES OF CORPORATE VENTURING

1. Long-term growth
2. Diversification
3. Exploit under-utilized resources
4. Promote entrepreneurial behaviour/satisfy mangers' ambitions/retain talent
5. Combat cyclical demands of mainstream business
6. Short-term financial returns
7. Reduce/spread cost of R&D and product development
8. Develop new capabilities
9. Survival

Source: Derived from Tidd, J. and S. Taurins (1999) Learn or leverage? Strategic diversification and organizational learning through corporate ventures. *Creativity and Innovation Management*, 8 (2): 122–129, with permission from John Wiley & Sons, Ltd.

TABLE 11.1 Motives, Structure and Management of Corporate Ventures

Primary motive	Preferred structure	Key management task
Satisfy managers' ambition	Integrated business team	Motivation and reward
Spread cost and risk of development	Integrated business team	Resource allocation
Exploit economies of scope	Micro-venture department	Reintegration of venture
Learn about venturing	New venture division	Develop new skills
Diversify the business	Special business unit	Develop new assets
Divest non-core activities	Independent business unit	Management of intellectual property rights

Source: Derived from Tidd, J. and S. Taurins (1999) Learn or leverage? Strategic diversification and organisational learning through corporate ventures. *Creativity and Innovation Management*, **8** (2): 122–129 with permission from John Wiley & Sons, Ltd.

INNOVATION IN ACTION 11.2

Identifying New Opportunities at QinetiQ

Businesses tend to limit their strategic vision to the conventional boundaries of the existing industry. This they believe is an immutable given. When challenged to think 'out of the box' or to be more creative in their business models, because they do not explicitly acknowledge the boundaries in which they operate, they continue competing in traditional spaces.

Companies that do not permit themselves to be limited by current industry boundaries more often create new profitable spaces. In traditional strategy, pain points would be identified and solutions found. Here we use pain points to find the non-customer.

The boundary busting framework enables the process of exploration into unknown territory of the non-customer. By applying a set of six alternative 'lenses' participants challenge the assumptions underpinning these traditional boundaries.

For each boundary type, we apply the 'Rule of Opposites', which is a set of specific critical questions performed to extract insight into potential new market spaces. Not all boundaries will yield new market opportunities, but may reveal insight which can be exploited across other boundaries.

Critical to identifying new market opportunities will be the ability to visualize and articulate the emergent previously ignored customer, to which a reconstructed value proposition has been offered.

The process undertaken includes:

1. Articulate the current bounds of the industry the product operates in across the dimensions of industry definition – strategic groups, chain of buyers, proposition, appeal, and time and trends.
2. For each existing customer, map out their buyer experience cycle to identify pain points.
3. Explicitly identify the core customer, then remove this customer from any further consideration.
4. Apply 'Rule of Opposites' to each boundary in turn to unearth whether new customer groups exist beyond the current boundary of the industry.
5. Once a new customer is articulated and brought to life undertake field work to find this person and prove the new opportunity.
6. Hypothesize a set of offerings that would meet this person's needs.
7. From the full range of new opportunities, distil down a set of propositions that minimally meet the needs of the largest catchment of non-customers.

Be aware that this process might initially feel strange, more like opening 'Pandora's box' than a structured analysis. The outcome of the market boundary analysis is a set of non-customer spaces. It is important to acknowledge that not all of the six dimensions of alternative marketplaces will yield results, typically two to four of the paths will present significant insight.

Source: Carlos de Pommes, QinetiQ, www.qinetiq.com

Managing Corporate Ventures

There are two critical dimensions to managing ventures: who owns them and who funds them. These two dimensions suggest four different combinations:[4]

1. *Opportunistic* – no dedicated ownership or resources for venturing. This approach relies on a supportive organizational climate to encourage proposals which are developed and evaluated locally on a project-by-project basis. For example, Zimmer Medical Devices responded to a new hip replacement proposed by a trauma surgeon by creating the Zimmer Institute to train more than 6000 surgeons in the new minimally invasive procedure.
2. *Enabling* – no formal corporate ownership, but the provision of dedicated support, processes and resources. This approach works best where new ventures can be owned by existing divisions in the business. For example, Google provides time, funding and rewards for the development of ideas which extend the core business.
3. *Advocacy* – organizational ownership is clearly assigned, but little or no special funding is provided. This works when there are sufficient resources in the business, but insufficient specialist skills or support for venturing. For example, DuPont created the Market Driven

Growth initiative which includes four-day business planning training and workshops and agreed access to and mentoring by senior staff.

4. *Producer* – includes both formal ownership and dedicated funding of ventures. This demands significant corporate resources and commitment to venturing, and therefore a critical mass of potential projects to justify this approach. Examples include IBM's Emerging Business Opportunities programme and Cargill's Emerging Business Accelerator initiative. In such cases the goal is to build new businesses, rather than just new products or services.

A corporate venture is rarely the result of a spontaneous act or serendipity. Corporate venturing is a process that has to be managed. The management challenge is to create an environment that encourages and supports entrepreneurship, and to identify and support potential entrepreneurs. In essence, the venturing process is simple, and consists of identifying an opportunity for a new venture, evaluating that opportunity and subsequently providing adequate resources to support the new venture. There are six distinct stages, divided between definition and development.[5]

Definition Stages

1. Establish an environment that encourages the generation of new ideas and the identification of new opportunities, and establish a process for managing entrepreneurial activity.
2. Select and evaluate opportunities for new ventures, and select managers to implement the venturing programme.
3. Develop a business plan for the new venture, decide the best location and organization of the venture and begin operations.

Development Stages

4. Monitor the development of the venture and venturing process.
5. Champion the new venture as it grows and becomes institutionalized within the corporation.
6. Learn from experience in order to improve the overall venturing process.

Creating an environment which is conducive to entrepreneurial activity is the most important, but most difficult, stage. Superficial approaches to creating an entrepreneurial culture can be counterproductive. Instead, venturing should be the responsibility of the entire corporation, and top management should demonstrate long-term commitment to venturing by making available sufficient resources and implementing the appropriate processes.

The conceptualization stage consists of the generation of new ideas and identification of opportunities that could form the basis of a new business venture. The interface between R&D and marketing is critical during the conceptualization stage, but the scope of new venture conceptualization is much broader than the conventional activities of the R&D or marketing functions, which understandably are constrained by the needs of existing businesses. At this stage three basic options exist:

1. Rely on R&D personnel to identify new business opportunities based on their technological developments (i.e. essentially a 'technology-push' approach).

2. Rely on marketing managers to identify opportunities, and direct the R&D staff into the appropriate development work (i.e. essentially a 'market-pull' approach).
3. Encourage marketing and R&D personnel to work together to identify opportunities.

Video Clip of an interview with Roy Sandbach of Procter and Gamble highlighting some of these issues is available on the Innovation Portal at **www.innovation-portal.info**

Having identified the potential for a new venture, a product champion must convince higher management that the business opportunity is both technically feasible and commercially attractive and therefore justifies development and investment. Potential corporate entrepreneurs face significant political barriers:

- They must establish their legitimacy within the firm by convincing others of the importance and viability of the venture.
- They are likely to be short of resources, but will have to compete internally against established and powerful departments and managers.
- As advocates of change and innovation, they are likely to face at best organizational indifference and at worst hostile attacks.

To overcome these barriers a potential venture manager must have political and social skills, in addition to a viable business plan. In addition, the product champion must be able to work effectively in a non-programmed and unpredictable environment. This contrasts with much of the R&D conducted in the operating divisions, which is likely to be much more sequential and systematic. Therefore, a product champion requires dedication, flexibility and luck to manage the transition from product concept to corporate venture, in addition to sound technical and market knowledge. The product champion is likely to require a complementary organizational champion, who is able to relate the potential venture to the strategy and structure of the corporation. A number of key roles must be filled when a new venture is established:

- *technical innovator* – responsible for the main technological development
- *business innovator* or *venture manager* – responsible for the overall progress of the venture
- *product champion* – promotes the venture through the early critical stages
- *executive champion* or *organizational champion* – acts as a protector and buffer between the corporation and venture
- *high-level executive* – responsible for evaluating, monitoring and authorizing resources for the venture, but not the operation of specific ventures.

A checklist for assessing the proximity of the venture proposal to existing skills and capabilities would include:

- What are the key capabilities required for the venture?
- Where, how and when is the firm going to acquire the capabilities, and at what cost?
- How will these new capabilities affect current capabilities?
- Where else could they be exploited?
- Who else would be able to do this, perhaps better?

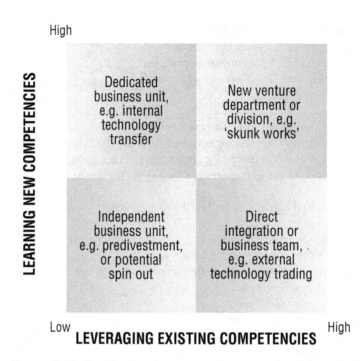

FIGURE 11.2   The most effective structure for a corporate venture depends on the balance between leverage or learning (exploit versus explore)

Source: Tidd J. and Taurins, S. (1999). Learn or leverage? Strategic diversification and organisational learning through corporate ventures. *Creativity and Innovation Management*, **8** (2): 122–129.

In particular, the strategic importance will determine the degree of administrative control required, and the proximity to existing skills and capabilities will determine the degree of operational integration that is desirable. In general, the greater the strategic importance, the stronger the administrative linkages between the corporation and venture (Figure 11.2). Similarly, the closer the skills and capabilities are to the core activities, the greater the degree of operational integration necessary for reasons of efficiency (Table 11.2). Design options for corporate ventures include:

* direct integration with existing business
* integrated business teams
* a dedicated staff function to support efforts company-wide
* a separate corporate venturing unit, department or division
* divestment and spin-off.

Each structure will demand different methods of monitoring and management, that is procedures, reporting mechanisms and accountability. These choices are illustrated by studies of venturing in Europe and the United States.[6]

TABLE 11.2 Type of New Venture and Links with Parent

| Venture type | Relatedness of: | | | Focal activity of venture | Linkages with parent firm |
	Product technology	Process technology	Product market		
Product development	Low	Low	High	Development and production	Marketing
Technological innovation	Low	High	High	R&D	Research, marketing and production
Market diversification	High	High	Low	Branding and marketing	Development and production
Technology commercialization	High	Low	Low	Marketing and production	Development
Blue-sky	Low	Low	Low	Development, production and marketing	Finance

Source: Adapted from Tidd, J. and S. Taurins (1999) Learn or leverage? Strategic diversification and organisational learning through corporate ventures. *Creativity and Innovation Management*, 8 (2), 122–9 with permission from John Wiley & Sons, Ltd.

Direct Integration

Direct integration as an additional business activity is the preferred choice where radical changes in product or process design are likely to impact immediately on the mainstream operations and if the people involved in that activity are inextricably involved in day-to-day operations. For example, many engineering-based companies have introduced consultancy to their business portfolio, and in other technical organizations with large laboratory facilities these too have been sold out for analysis of samples, testing of materials, etc. In such cases it is not possible to outsource such activities, because the same personnel and equipment are required for the core business.

Integrated Business Teams

Integrated business teams are most appropriate where the expertise will have been nurtured within the mainstream operations, and may support or require support from those operations for development. Strategically, the product is sufficiently related to the mainstream business's key technologies or expertise that the centre wishes to retain some control. This control may be either to protect the knowledge that is intrinsic in the activity or to ensure a flow-back of future development knowledge. A business team of secondees is established to coordinate sourcing of both internal and external clients, and is usually treated as a separate accounting entity in order to ease any subsequent transition to a special business unit.

New Ventures Department

A new ventures department is a group separate from normal line management that facilitates external trading. It is most suitable when projects are likely to emerge from the operational business on a fairly frequent basis and when the proposed activities may be beyond current markets or the type of product package sold is different. This is the most natural way for the trading of existing expertise to be developed when it lies fragmented through the organization, and each source is likely to attract a different type of customer. The group has responsibility for marketing, contracting and negotiation, but technical negotiation and supply of services take place at the operational level.

New Venture Division

A new venture division provides a safe haven where a number of projects emerge throughout the organization, and allows separate administrative supervision. Strategically, top management can retain a certain level of control until each venture's strategic importance is clearly understood, but the efficiency of the mainstream business needs to be maintained without distraction, so some autonomy is required. Operational links are loose enough to allow information and know-how to be exchanged with the corporate environment. The origins of such a division vary:

- An effort to bring existing technologies and expertise throughout the company together for adaptation to new or existing markets.
- To combine research from different fields or locations, to accelerate the development of new products.
- To purchase or acquire expertise currently outside of the business for application to internal operations, or to assist new developments.
- To examine new market areas as potential targets for existing or adapted products within the current portfolio.

Where a critical mass of projects exists, a separate new venture division allows greater focus on the external environment, and the separation from the core corporation facilitates a more global and cross-divisional view to be taken. Unfortunately, the division can often become a kind of dustbin for every new opportunity, and therefore it is critical to define the limits of its operation and its mission, in particular the criteria for termination or continued support of specific projects.

Special Business Units

Special dedicated new business units are wholly owned by the corporation. High strategic relevance requires strong administrative control. Businesses like this tend to come about because the activity is felt to have enough potential to stand alone as a profit centre, and can thus be assessed and operated as a separate business entity. The requirement is that key people can be identified and extracted from their mainstream operational role.

For the business to succeed under the total ownership and control of a large corporation, it must be capable of producing significant revenue streams in the medium term. On average, the critical mass appears to be around 12% of total corporate turnover, but in some cases the threshold for a separate unit is much higher. A potential new business must not only be judged on its relative size or profitability but also, more importantly, on its ability to sustain its own development costs. For example, a profitable subsidiary may never achieve the status of a separate new business if it cannot support its own product development.

However, physically separating a business activity does not ensure autonomy. The greatest impediment to such a unit competing effectively in the market is a cosy corporate mentality. If managers of a new business are under the impression that the corporate parent will always assist, provide business and second its expertise and services at non-market rates, that business may never be able to survive commercial pressures. Conversely, if the parent plans to retain total ownership, the parent cannot realistically treat that unit independently.

Independent Business Units

Differing degrees of ownership will determine the administrative control over independent business units, ranging from subsidiary to minority interest. Control would only be exercised through a board presence if that were held. There are two reasons for establishing an independent business as opposed to divisionalizing an activity: to focus on the core business by removing the managerial and technical burden of activities unrelated to the mainstream business or to facilitate learning from external sources in the case of enabling technologies or activities. This structure has benefits for both parent and venture:

- Defrayed risk for parent, greater freedom for venture.
- Less supervisory requirement for parent, less interference for venture.
- Reduced management distraction for parent, and greater focus for venture.
- Continued share of financial returns for parent, greater commitment from managers of the venture.
- Potential for flow-back or process improvements or product developments for parent, and learning for the venture.

The assignment of technical personnel is one of the most difficult problems when establishing an independent business unit. If the individuals necessary to coordinate future product development are unwilling to leave the relative security and comfort of a large corporate facility, which is understandable, the new business may be stopped in its tracks. It is critical to identify the most desirable individuals for such an operation, assessed in terms of their technical ability and personal characteristics. It is also important to assess the effect of these individuals leaving the mainstream development operations, as the capability of the parent's operations could be easily damaged.

Nurtured Divestment

Nurtured divestment is appropriate where an activity is not critical to the mainstream business. The product or service has most likely evolved from the mainstream, and while supporting these operations it is not essential for strategic control. The design option provides a way for the corporate to release responsibility for a particular business area. External markets may be built up prior to separation, giving time to identify which employees should be retained by the corporate and providing a period of acclimatization for the venture. The parent may or may not retain some ownership.

Complete Spin-off

No ownership is retained by the parent corporation in the case of a complete spin-off. This is essentially a divest option, where the corporation wants to pass over total responsibility for an activity, commercially and administratively. This may be due to strategic unrelatedness or strategic redundancy, as a consequence of changing corporate strategic focus. A complete spin-off allows both the parent to realize the hidden value of the venture and senior management of the parent to focus on their main business.

INNOVATION IN ACTION 11.3

Lucent's New Venture Group

Lucent Technologies was created in 1996 from the break-up of the famous Bell Labs of AT&T. Lucent established the New Venture Group (NVG) in 1997 to explore how better to exploit its research talent by exploiting technologies which did not fit any of Lucent's current businesses; its mission was to 'leverage Lucent technology to create new ventures that bring innovations to market more quickly . . . to create a more entrepreneurial environment that nurtures and rewards speed, teamwork and prudent risk-taking'. At the same time, it took measures to protect the mainstream research and innovation processes within Lucent from the potential disruption NVG might cause. To achieve this balance, at the heart of the process were periodic meetings between NVG managers and Lucent researchers, where ideas were 'nominated' for assessment. These nominated ideas were first presented to the existing business groups within Lucent, and this created pressure on the existing business groups to make decisions on promising technologies. As the vice president of the NVG noted: 'I think the biggest practical benefit of the (NVG) group was increasing the clockspeed of the system.'

If the nominated idea was not supported or resourced by any of the businesses, the NVG could develop a business plan for the venture. The business plan would include an exit strategy for the venture, ranging from an acquisition by Lucent, external trade sale, IPO (initial public offering) or licence. The initial evaluation stage typically takes two to three months and costs $50 000–$100 000 (£30 000–£60 000). Subsequent stages of internal funding reached $1 million (£600 000) per venture, and in later stages in many cases external venture capital firms were involved to conduct due diligence assessments, contribute funds and management expertise. By 2001, 26 venture companies had been created by the NVG, and included 30 external venture capitalists who invested more than $160 million (£990 000) in these ventures. Interestingly, Lucent reacquired at market prices three of the new ventures NVG had created, all based on technologies that existing Lucent businesses had earlier turned down. This demonstrates one of the benefits of corporate venturing – capturing false negatives – projects which were initially judged too weak to support and that were rejected by the conventional development processes. However, following the fall in telecom and other technology equity prices, in 2002 Lucent sold its 80% interest in the remaining ventures to an external investor group for under $100 million (£60 million).

Source: Derived from Chesbrough, H. (2003) *Open Innovation*. Boston: Harvard Business School Press.

Strategic Impact of Ventures

It is very difficult in practice to assess the success of corporate venturing. Simple financial assessments are usually based on some comparison of the investments made by the corporate parent and the subsequent revenue streams or market valuation of the ventures. Both of the latter are highly sensitive to the timing of the assessment. For example, at the height of the Internet bubble, financial market valuations suggested corporate venture returns of 70% or more, whereas a few years later these paper returns no longer existed. A study of 35 spin-offs from Xerox over a period of 22 years reveals that the aggregate market value of these spin-offs exceeded those of the parent by a factor of two by 2001, and by a factor of five at the peak of the previous stock market bubble.[7]

A historical analysis of the development and commercialization of superconductor technologies at General Electric between 1960 and 1990 reveals how the technology began in internal research and development but reached a point at which there was deemed to be insufficient market potential to justify any further internal investment. Two GE operating businesses were offered the technology but declined to fund further development. Rather than abandon the technology altogether, in 1971 GE established a 40% owned venture called Intermagnetics General Corp. (IGC) to develop the technology further. GE became a major customer of IGC as demand for the technology grew in its Medical Systems business owing to the growth of MRI (magnetic resonance imaging). However, by 1983, the need for the technology had become so central to GE business that GE had to redevelop its own core competencies in the field.[8]

A longitudinal study of 1527 internal corporate venture projects between 1996 and 2009 suggests that the determinants of survival are highly sensitive to their stage of development.[9] In another study of 48 corporate ventures, the authors conclude that corporate venturing is on the rise but that success depends on 'well-defined strategic objectives for the corporate venture unit' to 'avoid misplaced expectations and disappointing outcomes'.[10]

Summary

- There are a wide range of motives for establishing corporate ventures, including to attract, motivate and retain talent, to grow the business, diversify or to develop and exploit new technological or market capabilities.

- The best structure for a corporate venture depends on a number of factors, such as who owns and funds these, and the proximity of the technological or market capabilities to the core businesses.

- The outcomes and success of corporate venturing should be assessed in broad terms, including the long-term survival, growth and evolution of the organization, rather than only by narrow financial evaluations of specific projects. It represents a process of corporate experimentation and evolution.

Further Resources

For an academic review of the field, start with Narayanan, V. K., Y. Yang and S. A. Zahra (2009) Corporate venturing and value creation: A review and proposed framework, *Research Policy*, **38** (1): 58–76. Burgelman and Sayles's *Inside Corporate Innovation* (Macmillan, 1986) remains the classic combination of theory and case studies, but the more recent book by Block and MacMillan, *Corporate Venturing: Creating new businesses within the firm* (Harvard Business School Press, 1995), provides a better review of research on internal corporate ventures.

More recent books which include some interesting examples of venturing in the information and telecommunications sectors are *Webs of Innovation* by Alexander Loudon (FT.com, 2001), which despite its title has several chapters related to venturing, and Henry Chesbrough's *Open Innovation* (Harvard Business School Press, 2003), which includes case studies of the usual suspects such as IBM, Xerox, Intel and Lucent. The book *Inventuring* by Buckland, Hatche and Birkinshaw (McGraw-Hill, 2003) is also a good review of corporate venture initiatives, including those at GE, Intel and Lucent, which suggest a range of successful venture models and common reasons for failure. The text *Corporate Entrepreneurship* by Paul Burns provides a useful framework and case examples (Palgrave Macmillan, 2008), and for a more practical approach see Hisrich and Kearney *Corporate Entrepreneurship* (McGraw-Hill, 2011).

References

1. Dess, G., G. Lumpkin and J. Covin (1997) Entrepreneurial strategy making and firm performance, *Strategic Management Journal*, **18** (9): 677–695.

2. Tidd, J. and S. Taurins (1999) Learn or leverage? Strategic diversification and organisational learning through corporate ventures, *Creativity and Innovation Management*, **8** (2): 122–129.

3. Tidd, J. (2012) *From Knowledge Management to Strategic Competence*, 3rd edn. London: Imperial College Press.

4. Wolcott, R. C. and M. J. Lippitz (2007) The four models of corporate entrepreneurship, *MIT Sloan Management Review*, **49** (1): 74–82.

5. Block, Z. and I. MacMillan (1993) *Corporate Venturing: Creating new businesses within the firm*. Boston: Harvard Business School Press.

6. Wolcott, R. C. and M. J. Lippitz (2007) The four models of corporate entrepreneurship, *MIT Sloan Management Review*, **49** (1): 74–82; Buckland, W. A., A. Hatcher and J. Birkinshaw (2003) *Inventuring*, New York: McGraw-Hill; Campbell, A., J. Birkinshaw, A. Morrison and R. V. Batenburg (2003) The future of corporate venturing, *MIT Sloan Management Review*, **45** (1): 30–37; Dushnitsky, G. (2011) Riding the next wave of corporate venture capital, *Business Strategy Review*, **22** (3): 44–49.

7. Chesbrough, H. (2002) The governance and performance of Xerox's technology spin-off companies, *Research Policy*, **32**: 403–421.

8. Abetti, P. (2002) From science to technology to products and profits: Superconductivity at General Electric and Intermagnetics General (1960–1990), *Journal of Business Venturing*, **17**: 83–98.

9. Masucci, M. (2013) Uncovering the determinants of initiative survival in corporate venture units: A multistage selection perspective, SPRU Seminar, June 2013.

10. Battistini, B., F. Hacklin and P. Baschera (2013) The state of corporate venturing, *Research Technology Management*, **56** (1): 37.

Deeper Dive explanations of innovation concepts and ideas are available on the Innovation Portal at **www.innovation-portal.info**

Quizzes to test yourself further are available online via the Innovation Portal at **www.innovation-portal.info**

Summary of online resources for Chapter 11 –
all material is available via the Innovation Portal at
www.innovation-portal.info

Cases	**Media**	**Tools**	**Activities**	**Deeper Dive**

Cases	Media	Tools	Activities	Deeper Dive
• Spirit • Kodak • Fujifilm	• Tesco Goes West • David Hall • Roy Sandbach, Procter and Gamble	• Selection approaches for radical innovation • Portfolio methods • Business model innovation	• Discontinuous innovation audit • Competence enhancing and competence destroying innovation	• The role of venture capital in innovation

Chapter 12

Commercialization and Diffusion of Innovations

LEARNING OBJECTIVES

After this chapter you should be able to:

- identify the characteristics of an innovation which influence the adoption and diffusion of an innovation, in particular relative advantage, compatibility, complexity, trialability and observability

- understand the process of adoption and diffusion, and how the nature of adopters, involvement, communication and social context influence the rate and level of diffusion

- choose appropriate models of diffusion to plan for different types of innovation and adopter groups.

Why Adopt Innovations?

A better understanding of why and how innovations are adopted (or not) can help us to develop and implement more realistic business plans and public policies.

Diffusion is the means by which innovations are translated into social and economic benefits. We know that the impact of the *use* of innovations is around four times that of their generation,[1] especially the widespread adoption of process innovations has the most significant benefit:[2] technological innovations are the source of productivity and quality improvements; organizational innovations are the basis of many social, health and educational gains; and commercial innovations create new services and products. However, the benefits of innovations can take 10–15 years to be fully effected,[3] and in practice most innovations fail to be adopted widely, and so have limited social or economic impact.[4]

Conventional marketing approaches are adequate for promoting many products and services, but are not sufficient for the majority of innovations. Marketing texts often refer to 'early adopters' and 'majority adopters', and even go so far as to apply numerical estimates of these, but these simple categories are based on the very early studies of the state-sponsored diffusion of hybrid-seed varieties in farming communities, and are far from universally applicable. To better plan for innovations we need a deeper understanding of what factors promote and constrain adoption, and how these influence the rate and level of diffusion within different markets and populations.

Rogers'[5] definition of diffusion is used widely: 'the process by which an innovation is communicated through certain channels over time among members of a social system. It is a special type of communication, in that the messages are concerned with new ideas' (p. 5). However, there are no generally accepted definitions of associated terms such as 'technology transfer', 'adoption', 'implementation' or 'utilization'. Diffusion usually involves the analysis of the spread of a product or idea in a given social system, whereas technology transfer is usually a point-to-point phenomenon. Technology transfer usually implies putting information to use, or more specifically moving ideas from the laboratory to the market. The distinction between adoption, implementation and utilization is less clear. Adoption is generally considered the decision to do or acquire something, whereas implementation and utilization imply some action and adaptation.

The economist's view of the innovation process begins with the assumption that it is simply the cumulative aggregation of individual, rational calculations. These individual decisions are influenced by an assessment of the costs and benefits, under conditions of limited information and environment uncertainty. However, this perspective ignores the effects of social feedback, learning and externalities. The initial benefits of adoption may be small, but with improvement, reinvention and growing externalities the benefits can increase over time and the costs decrease.

Rogers[6] conceptualizes diffusion as a social process, in which actors create and share information through communication. Reflecting its roots in rural sociology and early interest in the adoption of agricultural innovations; the emphasis of this approach is on the roles of opinion leaders and change agents working within social structures and systems. Therefore, a focus on the relative advantage of an innovation is insufficient, as different social systems will have different values and beliefs, which will influence the costs, benefits and compatibility of an innovation, and different social structures will determine the most appropriate channels of communication and the type and influence of opinion leaders and change agents. Rogers distinguishes between three types of decision-making relevant to adoption of an innovation:

- *Individual*, in which the individual is the main decision-maker, independent of peers. Decisions may still be influenced by social norms and interpersonal relationships, but the individual makes the ultimate choice. For example, the purchase of a consumer durable such as a mobile phone.
- *Collective*, where choices are made jointly with others in the social system, and there is significant peer pressure or formal requirement to conform. For example, the sorting and recycling of domestic waste.
- *Authoritative*, where decisions to adopt are taken by a few individuals within a social system, owing to their power, status or expertise (e.g. adoption of ERP systems by businesses, or MRI systems by hospitals).

There is much evidence that opinion leaders are critical of diffusion, especially of changes in behaviour or attitudes (see Innovation in Action 12.1). Therefore, they tend to be a central feature of social and health change programmes, such as sex education. However, they are also evident in more routine examples of product diffusion, ranging from sports shoes to hybrid cars. Opinion leaders carry information across boundaries between groups, much like knowledge bridges. They operate at the edge of groups, rather than from the top, not leaders within a group but brokers between groups. In the language of networks, they have many weak ties, rather than a few strong ones. They tend to have extended personal networks, be accessible and have high levels of social participation. They are recognized by peers as being both competent and trustworthy. They have access and exposure to mass media.

The time dimension is important, and many studies are particularly interested to understand and influence the rate of adoption. It can take years for a new drug to be prescribed after licence, a decade for a new crop variety or fifty years for educational or social changes. This leads to a focus on the communication channels and decision-making criteria and process. Generally, mass-marketing media channels are more effective for generating awareness and disseminating information and knowledge, whereas interpersonal channels such as social media are more important in the decision-making and action stages.

Cross-country comparisons of diffusion reveal that cultural factors also play an important role, for example, high individuality limits the influence of imitation and contagion mechanisms, whereas a high power-distance, a measure of the hierarchies, promotes diffusion, possibly because innovations may be adopted faster within class strata.[7]

INNOVATION IN ACTION 12.1

The Diffusion of Electric and Hybrid Cars

The car industry is an excellent example of a large complex sociotechnical system which has evolved over many years, such that the current system of firms, products, consumers and infrastructure interact to restrict the degree and direction of innovation. Since the 1930s, the dominant design has been based around a petrol- or diesel-fuelled reciprocating combustion engine/Otto cycle, mass-produced in a wide variety of relatively minimally differentiated designs. This is no industrial conspiracy but rather the almost inevitable industrial trajectory, given the historical and economic contexts. This has resulted in car companies spending more on marketing than on research and development. However, growing social and political concerns over vehicle emissions and their regulation have forced the industry to reconsider this dominant design, and in some cases to develop new capabilities to help to develop new products and systems. For example, zero- and low-emission targets and legislation have encouraged experimentation with alternatives to the combustion engine while retaining the core concept of personal, rather than collective or mass, travel.

For example, the zero-emission law passed in California in 1990 required manufacturers selling more than 35 000 vehicles a year in the state to have 2% of all vehicle sales zero-emission

(continued)

by 1998, 5% by 2001 and 10% by 2003. This most affected GM, Ford, Chrysler, Toyota, Honda and Nissan, and potentially BMW and VW, if their sales increased sufficiently over that period. However, the US automobile industry subsequently appealed, and had the quota reduced to a maximum of 4%. As fuel cells were still very much a longer-term solution, the main focus was on developing electric vehicles. At first sight this would appear to represent a rather 'autonomous' innovation, that is the simple substitution of one technology (combustion engine) for another (electric). However, the shift has implications for related systems such as power storage, drivetrain, controls, weight of materials used and the infrastructure for refuelling/recharging and servicing. Therefore, it is much more of a 'systemic' innovation than it first seems. Moreover, it challenges the core capabilities and technologies of many of the existing car manufacturers. The US manufacturers struggled to adapt, and early vehicles from GM and Ford were not successful. However, the Japanese were rather more successful in developing the new capabilities and technologies, and new products from Toyota and Honda have been particularly successful.

However, zero-emissions legislation was not adopted elsewhere, and more modest emission reduction targets were set. Since then, hybrid petrol-electric cars have been developed to help to reduce emissions. These are clearly not long-term solutions to the problem but do represent valuable technical and social prototypes for future systems, such as fuel cells. In 1993, Eiji Toyoda, Toyota's chairman and his team embarked on the project code named G21. G stands for global and 21 the twenty-first century. The purpose of the project was to develop a small hybrid car that could be sold at a competitive price in order to respond to the growing needs and eco awareness of many consumers worldwide. A year later a concept vehicle was developed called the Prius, taken from the Latin for 'before'. The goal was to reduce fuel consumption by 50%, and emissions by more than that. To find the right hybrid system for the G21, Toyota considered 80 alternatives before narrowing the list to four. Development of the Prius required the integration of different technical capabilities, including, for example, a joint venture with Matsushita Battery.

The prototype was revealed at the Tokyo Motor Show in October 1995. It is estimated that the project cost Toyota $1 billion (£620 million) in R&D. The first commercial version was launched in Japan in December 1997, and after further improvements such as battery performance and power source management, introduced to the US market in August 2000. For urban driving the economy is 60 MPG, and 50 for motorways – the opposite consumption profile of a conventional vehicle, but roughly twice as fuel efficient as an equivalent Corolla. From the materials used in production, through driving, maintenance, and finally its disposal, the Prius reduced CO_2 emissions by more than a third, and has a recyclability potential of approximately 90%. The Prius was launched in the United States at a price of $19 995 (£12 000), and sales in 2001 were 15 556 in the United States, and 20 119 in 2002. However, industry experts estimate that Toyota was losing some $16 000 (£10 000) for every Prius it sold because it costs between $35 000 and $40 000 (£22 000–£25 000) to produce. Toyota did make a profit on its second-generation Prius launched in 2003, and other hybrid cars such as the Lexus range in 2005, because of improved technologies and lower production costs.

The Hollywood celebrities soon discovered the Prius: Leonardo DiCaprio bought one of the first in 2001, followed by Cameron Diaz, Harrison Ford and Calista Flockhart. British politicians took rather longer to jump on the hybrid bandwagon, with the then leader of the opposition

David Cameron driving a hybrid Lexus in 2006. In 2005, 107 897 cars were sold in the United States, about 60% of global Prius sales, and four times more than the sales in 2000, and twice as many in 2004. Toyota plans to sell a million hybrids by 2010.

In addition to the direct income and indirect prestige, the Prius and other hybrid cars have created for Toyota, the company has also licensed some of its 650 patents on hybrid technology to Nissan and Ford, which are expected to develop hybrid vehicles for 2007, and Ford plans to sell 250 000 hybrids by 2010. Mercedes-Benz showed a diesel-electric S-class at the Frankfurt auto show in autumn 2005, and Honda has developed its own technology and range of hybrid cars, and is also probably the world leader in fuel cell technology for vehicles.

Sources: A. Pilkington and R. Dyerson (2004) Incumbency and the disruptive regulator: The case of the electric vehicles in California. *International Journal of Innovation Management*, 8 (4): 339–354; *The Economist* (2004) Why the future is hybrid, 4 December; *Financial Times* (2005) Too soon to write off the dinosaurs, 18 November; *Fortune* (2006) Toyota: The birth of the Prius, 21 February.

Models of Diffusion

Research on diffusion attempts to identify what influences the rate and direction of adoption of an innovation. The diffusion of an innovation is typically described by an S-shaped (logistic) curve (Figure 12.1).

Hundreds of marketing studies have attempted to fit the adoption of specific products to the S-curve, ranging from television sets to new drugs. In most cases mathematical techniques can provide a relatively good fit with historical data, but research has so far failed to identify robust generic models of adoption. In practice the precise pattern of adoption of an innovation will depend on the interaction of demand-side and supply-side factors:

- *Demand-side factors* – direct contact with or imitation of prior adopters, adopters with different perceptions of benefits and risk.
- *Supply-side factors* – relative advantage of an innovation, availability of information, barriers to adoption, feedback between developers and users.

The basic epidemic S-curve model is the earliest and is still the most commonly used. It assumes a homogeneous population of potential adopters, and that innovations spread by information transmitted by personal contact, observation and the geographical proximity of existing and potential adopters. This model suggests that the emphasis should be on communication, and the provision of clear technical and economic information. However, the epidemic model has been criticized because it assumes that all potential adopters are similar and have the same needs, which is unrealistic.

The most influential marketing model of diffusion was developed by Frank Bass in 1969, and has been applied widely to the adoption of consumer durables.[8] The Bass model

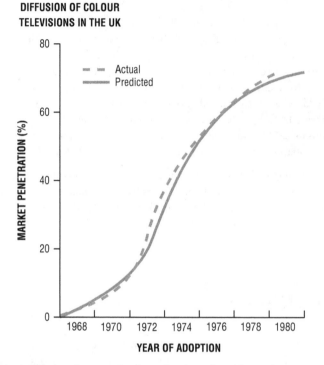

FIGURE 12.1   Typical diffusion S-curve for the adoption of an innovation

Source: Meade, N. and Islam, T. (2006) Modeling and forecasting the diffusion of innovation: A 25-year review. *International Journal of Forecasting*, **22**(3): 519–545.

assumes that potential adopters are influenced by two processes: individual independent adopters, influenced mostly by personal, private assessment and trials; and later adopters, more influenced by interpersonal communication, social media and mass-marketing channels. Combining these two types of adopters produces a skewed S-curve because of the early adoption by innovators, and suggests that different marketing processes are needed for the innovators and subsequent imitators. The Bass model is highly influential in economics and marketing research, and the distinction between the two types of potential adopters is critical in understanding the different mechanisms involved in the two user segments.

Bandwagons may occur where an innovation is adopted because of pressure caused by the sheer number of those who have already adopted an innovation, rather than by individual assessments of the benefits of an innovation (see Innovation in Action 12.2). In general, as soon as the number of adopters has reached a certain threshold level, the greater the level of ambiguity of the innovations benefits, the greater the subsequent number of adopters. This process allows technically inefficient

Tool giving a description of diffusion curves is available on the Innovation Portal at **www.innovation-portal.info**

> ### INNOVATION IN ACTION 12.2
>
> ## Diffusion of Management Fads and Fashions
>
> Over the past 40 years, we have seen many apparent panaceas for the problems of becoming competitive. Organizations are constantly seeking new answers to old problems, and the scale of investment in the new fashions of management thinking have often been considerable. The original evidence for the value of these tools and techniques was strong, with case studies and other reports testifying to their proven value within the context of origin. But there is also extensive evidence to suggest that these changes do not always work, and in many cases lead to considerable dissatisfaction and disillusionment. Examples include:
>
> * total quality management (TQM)
> * business process re-engineering (BPR)
> * benchmarking best practice
> * networking/clustering
> * knowledge management
> * disruptive or open innovation.
>
> These are all examples of innovation bandwagons, which diffuse more through peer-pressure and imitation, than evaluation of the benefits of adoption.
>
> *Source:* Tidd, J. and J. Bessant (2013) *Managing Innovation: Integrating technological, market and organizational change*, 5th edn. John Wiley & Sons, Ltd.

innovations to be widely adopted, or technically efficient innovations to be rejected. Examples include the QWERTY keyboard, originally designed to prevent professional typists from typing too fast and jamming typewriters; and the DOS operating system for personal computers, designed by and for computer enthusiasts.

Bandwagons occur because of a combination of competitive and institutional pressures.[9] Where competitors adopt an innovation, a firm may adopt because of the threat of lost competitiveness, rather than as a result of any rational evaluation of benefits. For example, many firms adopted business process re-engineering (BPR) in the 1980s in response to increased competition, but most failed to achieve significant benefits. The main institutional pressure is the threat of lost legitimacy, for example being considered by peers or customers as being less progressive or competent.

The critical difference between bandwagons and other types of diffusion is that they require only limited information to flow from early to later adopters. Indeed, the more ambiguous the benefits of an innovation, the more significant bandwagons are on rates of adoption. In short, better products do not necessarily result in more sales. Not everybody requires a better mousetrap.

Also, it is unrealistic to assume that adopters will have perfect knowledge of the value of an innovation. Therefore, Bayesian models of diffusion introduce lack of information as a constraint to diffusion. Potential adopters are allowed to hold different beliefs regarding the value of the innovation, which they may revise according to the results of trials to test the innovation. Because these trials are private, imitation cannot take place and other potential adopters cannot learn from them. This suggests that better-informed potential adopters may not necessarily adopt an innovation earlier than the less well informed, which was an assumption of earlier models.[10]

Most studies are concerned only with the rate of adoption or final proportion of a population which adopts an innovation. However, diffusion should be treated as a vector, with both magnitude and direction. The direction of the diffusion of innovations needs more attention: how and why different types of innovations are adopted (or not). This is critical for innovations which have profound social and economic implications, such as development, health and environment.

Factors Influencing Adoption

There are many barriers to the widespread adoption of innovations, including:

* *economic* – personal costs versus social benefits, access to information, insufficient incentives
* *behavioural* – priorities, motivations, rationality, inertia, propensity for change or risk
* *organizational* – goals, routines, power and influence, culture and stakeholders
* *structural* – infrastructure, sunk costs, governance.

Numerous variables have been identified as affecting the diffusion and adoption of innovations, but these can be grouped into three clusters: characteristics of the innovation itself, characteristics of individual or organizational adopters and the characteristics of the environment. Characteristics of an innovation found to influence adoption include relative advantage, compatibility, complexity, observability and trialability. Individual characteristics include age, education, social status and attitude to risk. Environmental and institutional characteristics include economic factors such as the market environment and sociological factors such as communications networks. However, while there is a general agreement regarding the relevant variables, there is very little consensus on the relative importance of the different variables, and in some cases disagreements over the direction of relationships.

In predicting the rate of adoption of an innovation, five factors explain 49–87% of the variance:

* relative advantage
* compatibility
* complexity
* trialability
* observability.

However, the contextual or environmental factors are also important, as demonstrated by the fact that diffusion rates of different innovations are highly variable, and the rates for the same innovation in different contexts also vary significantly.

Activity to help you explore this theme – Adoption and Diffusion Analysis – is available on the Innovation Portal at **www.innovation-portal.info**

Relative Advantage

Relative advantage is the degree to which an innovation is perceived as better than the product it supersedes, or competing products. Relative advantage is typically measured in narrow economic terms, for example cost or financial payback, but non-economic factors such as convenience, satisfaction and social prestige may be equally important. In theory, the greater the perceived advantage, the faster the rate of adoption.

It is useful to distinguish between the primary and secondary attributes of an innovation. Primary attributes, such as size and cost, are invariant and inherent to a specific innovation irrespective of the adopter. Secondary attributes, such as relative advantage and compatibility, may vary from adopter to adopter, being contingent upon the perceptions and context of adopters. In many cases, a so-called attribute gap will exist. An attribute gap is the discrepancy between a potential user's perception of an attribute or characteristic of an item of knowledge and how the potential user would prefer to perceive that attribute. The greater the sum of all attribute gaps, the less likely a user is to adopt the knowledge. This suggests that preliminary testing of an innovation is desirable in order to determine whether significant attribute gaps exist. The idea of pre-testing information for the purposes of enhancing its value and acceptance is not widely practised.

Case Study of Murray Design highlighting some of these issues is available on the Innovation Portal at **www.innovation-portal.info**

Compatibility

Compatibility is the degree to which an innovation is perceived to be consistent with the existing values, experience and needs of potential adopters. There are two distinct aspects of compatibility: existing skills and practices, and values and norms. The extent to which the innovation fits the existing skills, equipment, procedures and performance criteria of the potential adopter is important, and relatively easy to assess.

However, compatibility with existing practices may be less important than the fit with existing values and norms.[11] Significant misalignments between an innovation and an adopting organization will require changes in the innovation or organization, or both. In the most successful cases of implementation, mutual adaptation of the innovation and organization occurs. However, few studies distinguish between compatibility with value and norms, and compatibility with existing practices. The extent to which the innovation fits the existing skills, equipment, procedures and performance criteria of the potential adopter is critical. Few innovations initially fit the user environment into which they are introduced. Significant misalignments between the innovation and the adopting organization will require changes in the innovation or organization, or, in the most successful cases of implementation, mutual adaptation of both. Initial compatibility with existing practices may be less important, as it

Case Study which highlights some of these issues – Gunfire at sea – is available on the Innovation Portal at **www.innovation-portal.info**

may provide limited opportunity for mutual adaptation to occur.

In addition, so-called network externalities can affect the adoption process. For example, the cost of adoption and use, as distinct from the cost of purchase, may be influenced by: the availability of information about the technology from other users, of trained skilled users, technical assistance and maintenance, and of complementary innovations, both technical and organizational.

Complexity

Complexity is the degree to which an innovation is perceived as being difficult to understand or use. In general, innovations which are simpler for potential users to understand will be adopted more rapidly than those which require the adopter to develop new skills and knowledge.

However, complexity can also influence the direction of diffusion, not only the rate of adoption. Evolutionary models of diffusion focus on the effect of 'network externalities', that is the interaction of consumption, pecuniary and technical factors which shape the diffusion

Tool which helps work with these ideas – the Risk Assessment Matrix – is available on the Innovation Portal at **www.innovation-portal.info**

process. For example, within a region the cost of adoption and use, as distinct from the cost of purchase, may be influenced by: the availability of information about the technology from other users, of trained skilled users, technical assistance and maintenance, and of complementary innovations, both technical and organizational.

Trialability

Trialability is the degree to which an innovation can be experimented with on a limited basis. An innovation that is trialable represents less uncertainty to potential adopters, and allows learning by doing. Innovations which can be trialled will generally be adopted more quickly than those which cannot. The exception is where the undesirable consequences of an innovation appear to outweigh the desirable characteristics. In general, adopters wish to benefit from the functional effects of an innovation, but avoid any dysfunctional effects. However, where it is difficult or impossible to separate the desirable from the undesirable consequences, trialability may reduce the rate of adoption.

Developers of an innovation may have two different motives for involving potential users in the development process: first, to acquire knowledge from the users needed in the development process, to ensure usability and to add value and, second, to attain user 'buy-in', that is user acceptance of the innovation and commitment to its use. The second motive is independent of the first, because increasing user acceptance does not necessarily improve the quality of the innovation. Rather, involvement may increase the user's tolerance of any inadequacies. In the case of point-to-point transfer, typically both motives are present.

However, in the case of diffusion it is not possible to involve all potential users, and therefore the primary motive is to improve usability rather than attain user buy-in. But even the representation of user needs must be indirect, using surrogates such as specially selected user groups. These groups can be problematic for a number of reasons. First, because they may possess atypically high levels of technical knowledge, and are therefore not representative. Second, where the group must represent diverse user needs, such as both experienced and novice users, the group may not work well together. Finally, when user representatives work closely with

Audio Clip of an interview with Richard Reed of Innocent Smoothies exploring some of these issues is available on the Innovation Portal at **www.innovation-portal.info**

developers over a long period of time they may cease to represent users, and instead absorb the developer's viewpoint. Thus, there is no simple relationship between user involvement and user satisfaction. Typically, very low levels of user involvement are associated with user dissatisfaction, but extensive user involvement does not necessarily result in user satisfaction.

Observability

Observability is the degree to which the results of an innovation are visible to others. The easier it is for others to see the benefits of an innovation, the more likely it will be adopted. The simple epidemic model of diffusion assumes that innovations spread as potential adopters come into contact with existing users of an innovation.

Peers who have already adopted an innovation will have what communication researchers call 'safety credibility', because potential adopters seeking their advice will believe they know what it is really like to implement and utilize the innovation. Therefore, early adopters are well positioned to disseminate 'vicarious learning' to their colleagues. Vicarious learning is simply learning from the experience of others, rather than direct personal experimental learning. However, the process of vicarious learning is neither inevitable nor efficient because, by definition, it is a decentralized activity.

Video Clip of an interview with Melissa Clark-Reynolds of Minimonos exploring some of these issues is available on the Innovation Portal at **www.innovation-portal.info**

Demonstrations of innovations are highly effective in promoting adoption. Experimental, private demonstrations or pilots can be used to assess attributes of an innovation and the relative advantage for different target groups and to test compatibility. Exemplary, public demonstrations can improve observability, reduce perceived complexity and promote private trials. However, note the different purpose and nature of experimental and exemplary demonstrations. Resources, urgency and uncertainty should determine the appropriate type of demonstration. Public demonstrations for experimental purposes are ill advised and are likely to stall diffusion.

In the case of systemic or network innovations, a wider range of factors have to be managed to promote adoption and diffusion. In such cases a wider set of actors and institutions on the supply and demand side are relevant, in what has been called an 'adoption network'.[12] On the supply side, other organizations may provide the infrastructure, support and complementary products and services which can promote or prevent adoption and diffusion. For example, in 2008 the two-year battle between the new high-definition DVD formats was decided not by price or any technical superiority but rather because the BluRay consortium managed to recruit more film studios to its format than the competing HD-DVD format. As soon as the uncertainty over the future format was resolved, there was a step change increase in the rate of adoption.

INNOVATION IN ACTION 12.3

The Pre-Diffusion Phase

The S-shaped diffusion curve is empirically observed for a broad range of new products such as the telephone, hybrid corn and the microwave oven. However, a critical, but under-researched, issue in diffusion research is what happens *before* this well-known S-shaped diffusion curve. From a managerial perspective it is important to realize that diffusion requires that several conditions be met, for example products have to be developed, produced and distributed and the necessary infrastructural arrangements have to be in place. It is seldom realized, however, that prior to any S-shaped diffusion curve the market introduction of a new product is more typically followed by an erratic pattern of diffusion, referred to as the 'pre-diffusion phase'. The lack of attention to this so-called pre-diffusion phase is one of the main limitations of mainstream research and practice.

The Pre-Diffusion Phase for New Products

We define the pre-diffusion phase to begin after the market introduction of the first new product and to end when the diffusion of this type of product takes off (i.e. when the regular S-shaped diffusion curve begins). After the introduction of the first product, instead of a smooth S-curve, in practice an erratic process of diffusion may occur. In this situation the market is unstable. In the field of telecommunications, for example, the diffusion of new communication products and services often starts with the periodic introduction, decline and reintroduction of product variants in multiple small-scale applications before mainstream applications and product designs appear and the diffusion takes off.

The table shows estimates of the length of the pre-diffusion phase for a sample of products from different industries.

From the table we can see that a significant pre-diffusion phase exists for most types of innovation. The average length of this phase for the sample of products is more than a decade. Moreover, the data show that, even within industries, the variation in the length of the pre-diffusion phase is considerable.

Different Perspectives on, and Main Causes of, the Occurrence of the Pre-Diffusion Phase

The pre-diffusion phase has been described from different scientific perspectives, each of which proposes alternative causes of this phase. Marx, for example, was an economist who more than 150 years ago described why it takes so long to implement new methods of production in companies and why these new methods at first diffuse remarkably slowly among companies in an industry. Marx focused on the supply side of the market when describing the diffusion of these methods of production (so-called capital goods). From this perspective, the pre-diffusion phase is seen as a kind of trial-and-error process that is required to improve the production methods

Length of the pre-diffusion phase of products from different industries

Product	Industry	Market introduction	Diffusion begins	Length of pre-diffusion phase (years)
Jet engine	Aerospace and defence	1941	1943	2
Radar		1934	1939	5
ABS	Automobile and parts	1959	1978	19
Airbag		1972	1988	16
Memory metal	Materials, compound and metals	1968	1972	4
Dyneema		1975	1990	15
Flash memory	IT and telecommunications hardware and software	1988	2001	13
Mobile telephony		1946	1983	37
Transistor	Electronic components and equipment	1949	1953	4
Television		1939	1946	7
Contraceptive pill	Medical equipment and medicines	1928	1962	34
MRI		1980	1983	3
Microwave oven	Personal goods and household equipment	1947	1955	8
Air conditioning		1902	1915	13

Average = 13; standard deviation = 11.

Source: Derived from multiple sources and original work from Ortt. For further details see J. R. Ortt (2010) Understanding the pre-diffusion phases, in J. Tidd (ed.) *Gaining Momentum: Managing the diffusion of innovations.* London: Imperial College Press.

and to adapt these methods to the prevailing way of working in companies (and the other way around) before these methods become profitable.

About a century later, diffusion researchers took a different perspective and focused on the demand side of the market (Rogers, 2003). These researchers, mostly sociologists, tend to see diffusion as a communication process in a population or a segment of customers. The researchers have a bias towards the smooth S-shaped diffusion curve, but upon closer inspection their findings also indicate how demand-side factors may cause a pre-diffusion phase. Characteristics of subsequent groups of customers are often assessed in diffusion research. The very first group of customers, the innovators, are often deviant from the remainder of the potential customers and thereby can hamper the communication process that is required for diffusion.

(continued)

Moore (2002) elaborates on this idea and concludes that a 'chasm' occurs between subsequent groups of customers. Moore focuses on the interaction of the demand and supply side of the market when he explains this chasm. The first types of customers, referred to as 'technology enthusiasts' and 'visionaries', are customers willing to experiment with the product. Mainstream customers, however, hardly communicate with these sub-segments, so the diffusion does not proceed smoothly. Moreover, the mainstream customers want completely different product versions: they want reliable, foolproof and complete packages of products and services. Rather than testing these requirements themselves, they prefer to see how well-known companies or customers have already successfully implemented the product in their process of working. The technology enthusiasts or visionaries cannot fulfil this role and a chasm therefore occurs.

Main Managerial Consequences of the Pre-diffusion Phase

Each of these perspectives has its own way of explaining why this phase is managerially important. Marx's perspective implies that large-scale diffusion of new production methods is often preceded by considerable periods of experimentation. The costs incurred in this pre-diffusion phase can be considerable; the profits for the first company that in an economically viable way masters the application of these methods can be very large as well. Marx's perspective illustrates the importance of managing the innovation process before the implementation of new methods of production. Chasms in the diffusion process, noticed by Rogers and Moore, indicate that market introduction strategies of new products are crucially important as well. Segments of potential customers may be hard to distinguish and subsequent segments of customers may require completely different product variants and business models and thereby hamper the smooth diffusion process.

From a management perspective, the pre-diffusion phase is very risky. It is remarkable how many companies involved in the invention of new products lose out. About half of the pioneers that are first to introduce a *successful* product in the market fail and vanish before their product diffuses on a large scale. One of the main reasons is that the pre-diffusion phase can last a very long time. In general, the pre-diffusion phase requires considerable investment yet does not generate the same amount of income. The existence of the pre-diffusion phase has profound managerial implications: it shows that introducing a new product usually is a matter of deep pockets and long breath.

Sources: Marx, K. (1976) *Capital: A critique of political economy*, Harmondsworth: Penguin; Moore, G. A. (2002) *Crossing the Chasm: Marketing and selling disruptive products to mainstream customers*, New York: HarperCollins; Ortt, J. R. and N. Delgoshaie (2008) Why does it take so long before the diffusion of new high-tech products takes off? In Abu-Hijleh, B., M. Arif, T. Khalil and Y. Hosni (eds) *Proceedings of the 17th International Conference on Management of Technology* (6–10 April), Dubai; Ortt, J. R. and J. P. L. Schoormans (2004) The pattern of development and diffusion of breakthrough communication technologies, *European Journal of Innovation Management*, 7 (4): 292–302; Rogers, E. M. (2003) *Diffusion of Innovations*, 5th edn. New York: Free Press.

On the demand side, the uncertainty of potential adopters, and communication with and between them, needs to be managed. While early adopters may emphasize technical performance and novelty above other factors, the mainstream mass market is more likely to be concerned with factors such as price, quality, convenience and support. This transition from the niche market and needs of early adopters through to the requirements of more mass markets has been referred to as 'crossing the chasm' by Moore.[13] Moore studied the successes and many more failures of Silicon Valley and other high-technology products, and argues that the critical success factors for early adopters and mass markets are fundamentally different, and that most innovations fail to make this transition. Therefore, the successful launch and diffusion of a systemic or network innovation demands attention to traditional marketing issues such as the timing and positioning of the product or service, but also significant effort to demand-side factors such as communication and interactions between potential adopters.[14]

Applying Diffusion to Innovation Strategy

Developing a business plan will not usually be enough to ensure effective and successful commercialization. For example, Everett Rogers identified five factors to increase the effectiveness of your planning and implementation. He suggested that if your plan shows the relative advantage of your solutions over previous approaches and their compatibility or consistency with existing values, experiences or needs, the likelihood of them being implemented increases. Also, as you make the plan easy to understand and use (less complex), observable, and give people a chance to try parts of it, the greater the chance of successful implementation. Therefore, we can use these five categories to develop a checklist to help us develop and assess the effectiveness of a business plan and to identify places where it could be strong or needs improvement or modification.[15]

Relative Advantage

Being better than the previous solution: how well does my plan show how much better off people will be when they adopt the plan?

- Why is this plan better than what has been done before?
- What advantages or benefits may there be to accepting the plan?
- Who will gain from the implementation of the plan?
- How will I (or others) be rewarded by adopting the plan?
- How can I emphasize the plan's benefits to all?

Compatibility

Consistent with values, experiences and needs: how well does my plan demonstrate that it is compatible with current values, past experiences and needs?

- Is the plan consistent with current practice?
- Does the plan meet the needs of a particular group?

Case Study of Plaswood Recycling exploring some of these issues is available on the Innovation Portal at **www.innovation-portal.info**

- Does it offer better ways to reach our common goals?
- Who will naturally support and agree with the plan?
- Can it be favourably named, packaged or presented?

Complexity

Being difficult to understand and use: how well does my plan provide for easy communication, comprehension and use?

- Is the plan easy for others to understand?
- Can it be explained clearly to many different people?
- Will the plan be easily communicated?
- How can the plan be made more simple or easy to understand?
- Is the plan easy to use or follow?

Trialability

May be experimented with on a limited basis: how well does my plan allow for trialability?

- Can the plan be tried out or tested?
- Can uncertainty be reduced?
- Can we begin with a few parts of the plan?
- How can others be encouraged to try out the plan?
- Can the plan be modified by you or others?

Observability

Results are visible to others: how well does my plan provide results that are easily observed and visible to others?

- Is the plan easy for others to find or obtain?
- Can the plan be made more visible to others?
- How can I make the plan easier for others to see?
- Will others be able to see the effects of the plan?
- Are there good reasons for not making the entire plan visible?

Other Questions

The following are some general questions that will help your planning and implementation efforts:

- What other resources will I need; how can I get them?
- What obstacles exist; how can we prevent or overcome them?

- What new challenges will be created; and dealt with?
- How can I encourage commitment to the plan?
- What feedback about the plan is needed?

INNOVATION IN ACTION 12.4

Why Innovations Fail to be Adopted

This research examined the factors which influence the adoption and diffusion of innovations drawing upon case studies of successful and less successful consumer electronics products, such as the Sony PlayStation and MiniDisc, Apple iPod and Newton, TomTom GO, TiVo and RIM BlackBerry.

The study finds that a critical factor influencing successful diffusion is the careful management of acceptance by the early adopters, which in turn influences the adoption by the main market. Strategic issues such as positioning, timing and management of the adoption network are identified as being important. The adoption network is defined as a configuration of users, peers, competitors, and complementary products and services and infrastructure. However, the positioning, timing and adoption networks are different for the early and main market adopters, and failure to recognize these differences is a common cause of the failure of innovations to diffuse widely. Also, innovation contingencies such as the degree of radicalness and discontinuity affect how these factors interact and how these need to be managed to promote acceptance. The relevant assessment of the radicalness and discontinuity of an innovation is not based on the technological aspects, but rather the effects on user behaviour and consumption.

To promote use by early adopters, the research recommends that four enabling factors need to be managed: legitimate the innovation through reference customers and visible performance advantage; trigger word of mouth within specialist communities of practice; stimulate imitation to increase the user base and peer pressure; and collaborate with opinion leaders. Significantly, the study argues that the subsequent successful diffusion of an innovation into the mainstream market has very little to do with the merits of the product itself, and much more to do with the positive acceptance of early adopters and repositioning and targeting for the main market by influencing the relevant adoption network.

Source: Frattini, F. (2010) Achieving adoption network and early adopters acceptance for technological innovations, in Tidd, J. (ed.) *Gaining Momentum: Managing the diffusion of innovations*. London: Imperial College Press.

Summary

- The commercialization and diffusion of an innovation depends on the characteristics of the innovation, the nature of potential adopters and the process of communication.

- The relative advantage, compatibility, complexity, trialability and observability of an innovation all affect the rate of diffusion.

- The skills, psychology, social context and infrastructure of adoption also affect adoption.

- Epidemic models assume that innovations spread by communication and imitation between adopters, but this is not always the dominant mechanism. The Bass model adds the role of individual decision-makers.

- In bandwagons early adopters influence subsequent adopters through competitive and peer pressures.

Further Resources

The challenges of forecasting the future development, adoption and diffusion of innovations are dealt with by many authors in the innovation field. Everett Rogers' classic text, *Diffusion of Innovations*, first published in 1962, remains the best overview of this subject, the most recent and updated edition being published in 2003 (Simon & Schuster). More up-to-date accounts can be found in *Determinants of Innovative Behaviour*, edited by Cees van Beers, Alfred Kleinknecht, Roland Ortt and Robert Verburg (Palgrave, 2008), and our own *Gaining Momentum: Managing the diffusion of innovations*, edited by Joe Tidd (Imperial College Press, 2009). The chapter by Paul Stoneman and Giuliana Battisti in the *Handbook of the Economics of Innovation*, volume 2, on the 'Diffusion of New Technology' provides a solid introduction (edited by Bronwyn H. Hall and Nathan Rosenberg, Elsevier, 2010).

References

1. Geroski, P. A. (2000) Models of technology diffusion, *Research Policy*, **29**: 603–625; (1991) Innovation and the sectoral sources of UK productivity growth, *Economic Journal*, **101**: 1438–1451; (1994) *Market Structure, Corporate Performance and Innovative Activity*. Oxford: Oxford University Press.

2. Griliches, Z. and A. Pakes (1984) *Patents R&D and Productivity*. Chicago: University of Chicago Press; Stoneman, P. (1983) *The Economic Analysis of Technological Change*. Oxford: Oxford University Press.

3. Jaffe, A. B. (1986) Technological opportunity and spillovers of R&D: Evidence from firms' patents, profits and market values, *American Economic Review*, **76**: 948–999.

4. Ortt, J. R. (2009) Understanding the pre-diffusion phases, in Tidd, J. (ed.) *Gaining Momentum: Managing the diffusion of innovations*. London: Imperial College Press.

5. Rogers, E. M. (2003) *Diffusion of Innovations*. New York: Free Press.

6. Rogers, E. M. (2003) *Diffusion of Innovations*. New York: Free Press.

7. Van den Bulte, C. and G. L. Lilien (2001) Medical innovation revisited: Social contagion versus marketing effort, *American Journal of Sociology*, **106** (5): 1409–1435; Van den Bulte, C. and S. Stremersch (2004) Social contagion and income heterogeneity in new product diffusion, *Marketing Science*, **23** (4): 530–544.

8. Bass, F. M. (1980) The relationship between diffusion rates, experience curves, and demand elasticities for consumer durable technological innovations, *Journal of Business*, **53**: 51–67; Bass, F. M. and A. V. Bultez (1982) A note on optimal strategic pricing of technological innovations, *Marketing Science*, **1**: 371–378; Bass, F. M., T. Krishnan and D. Jain (1994) Why the Bass model fits without decision variables, *Marketing Science*, **13** (3): 203–223; Bass, F. M. (1969) A new product growth model for consumer durables, *Management Science*, **15**: 215–227.

9. Abrahamson, E. and L. Plosenkopf (1993) Institutional and competitive bandwagons: Using mathematical modelling as a tool to explore innovation diffusion, *Academy of Management Journal*, **18** (3): 487–517.

10. Griffiths, T. L. and J. B. Tenebaum (2006) Optimal predications in everyday cognition, *Psychological Science*, **45**: 56–63.

11. Leonard-Barton, D. and D. K. Sinha (1993) Developer–user interaction and user satisfaction in internal technology transfer, *Academy of Management Journal*, **36** (5): 1125–1139.

12. Chakravorti, B. (2003) *The Slow Pace of Fast Change: Bringing innovation to market in a connected world*. Boston: Harvard Business School Press; (2004) The new rules for bringing innovations to market, *Harvard Business Review*, **82** (3): 58–67; (2004) The role of adoption networks in the success of innovations, *Technology in Society*, **26**: 469–482.

13. Moore, G. (1991) *Crossing the Chasm: Marketing and selling technology products to mainstream customer*, New York: Harper Business; Moore, G. (1998) *Inside the Tornado: Marketing strategies from Silicon Valley's cutting edge*. Chichester: Wiley: Capstone.

14. Lee, Y. and G. C. O'Connor (2003) New product launch strategy for network effects products, *Journal of the Academy of Marketing Science*, **31** (3): 241–255.

15. Isaksen, S. and J. Tidd (2006) *Meeting the Innovation Challenge: Leadership for transformation and growth.* Chichester: John Wiley & Sons, Ltd; Tidd, J. (2009) *Gaining Momentum: Managing the diffusion of innovations.* London: Imperial College Press.

 Deeper Dive explanations of innovation concepts and ideas are available on the Innovation Portal at **www.innovation-portal.info**

 Quizzes to test yourself further are available online via the Innovation Portal at **www.innovation-portal.info**

Summary of online resources for Chapter 12 –
all material is available via the Innovation Portal at
www.innovation-portal.info

Cases	**Media**	**Tools**	**Activities**	**Deeper Dive**
• Murray Design • Gunfire at sea • Plaswood Recycling	• Richard Reed, Innocent Smoothies • Melissa Clark-Reynolds, Minimonos	• Risk assessment matrix • Soft systems analysis • Diffusion curves	• Adoption and diffusion analysis	• From Models to the Management of Diffusion

Chapter 13

Exploiting Knowledge and Intellectual Property

LEARNING OBJECTIVES

After this chapter you should be able to:

- identify different types of knowledge and intellectual property
- choose and apply appropriate methods of knowledge management
- develop a strategy for licensing intellectual property.

Innovation and Knowledge

In this chapter we discuss how individuals and organizations identify 'what they know' and how best to exploit this. We examine the related fields of knowledge management, organizational learning and intellectual property. Key issues include the nature of knowledge, for example explicit versus tacit knowledge; the locus of knowledge, for example individual versus organizational; and the distribution of knowledge across an organization. More narrowly, knowledge management is concerned with identifying, translating, sharing and exploiting the knowledge within an organization. One of the key issues is the relationship between individual and organizational learning, and how the former is translated into the latter, and ultimately into new processes, products and businesses. Finally, we review different types of formal intellectual property, and how these can be used in the development and commercialization of innovations.

In essence, managing knowledge involves five critical tasks:

- Generating and acquiring new knowledge.
- Identifying and codifying existing knowledge.

- Storing and retrieving knowledge.
- Sharing and distributing knowledge across the organization.
- Exploiting and embedding knowledge in processes, products and services.

Generating and Acquiring Knowledge

Organizations can acquire knowledge by experience, experimentation or acquisition. Of these, learning from experience appears to be the least effective. In practice, organizations do not easily translate experience into knowledge. Moreover, learning may be unintentional or it may not result in improved effectiveness. Organizations can incorrectly learn, and they can learn that which is incorrect or harmful, such as learning faulty or irrelevant skills or self-destructive habits. This can lead an organization to accumulate experience of an inferior technique, and may prevent it from gaining sufficient experience of a superior procedure to make it rewarding to use, sometimes called the 'competency trap'.

Experimentation is a more systematic approach to learning. It is a central feature of formal R&D activities, market research and some organizational alliances and networks. When undertaken with intent, a strategy of learning through incremental trial and error acknowledges the complexities of existing technologies and markets, as well as the uncertainties associated with technology and market change and in forecasting the future. The use of alliances for learning is less common and requires an intent to use them as an opportunity for learning, a receptivity to external know-how and partners of sufficient transparency. Whether the acquisition of know-how results in organizational learning depends on the rationale for the acquisition and the process of acquisition and transfer. For example, the cumulative effect of outsourcing various technologies on the basis of comparative transaction costs may limit future technological options and reduce competitiveness in the long term.

A more active approach to the acquisition of knowledge involves scanning the internal and external environments. As we discussed in Chapter 7, searching consists of searching for, filtering and evaluating potential opportunities from outside the organization, including related and emerging technologies, new market and services, which can be exploited by applying or combining with existing competencies. Opportunity recognition, which is a precursor to entrepreneurial behaviour, is often associated with a flash of genius, but in reality is probably more often the result of a laborious process of environmental scanning. External scanning can be conducted at various levels. It can be an operational initiative with market- or technology-focused managers becoming more conscious of new developments within their own environments, or a top-driven initiative where venture managers or professional capital firms are used to monitor and invest in potential opportunities.

Identifying and Codifying Knowledge

It is useful to begin with a clearer idea of what we mean by 'knowledge'. It has become all things to all people, ranging from corporate IT systems to the skills and experience of individuals. There is no universally accepted typology, but the following hierarchy is helpful:

- *Data* are a set of discrete raw observations, numbers, words, records and so on, which are typically easy to structure, record, store and manipulate electronically.

- *Information* is data that have been organized, grouped or categorized into some pattern. The organization may consist of categorization, calculation or synthesis. This organization of data endows information with relevance and purpose, and in most cases adds value to data.
- *Knowledge* is information that has been contextualized, given meaning and therefore made relevant and easier to operationalize. The transformation of information into knowledge involves making comparisons and contrasts, identifying relationships and inferring consequences. Therefore, knowledge is deeper and richer than information, and includes framed expertise, experience, values and insights.

The concept of disembodied knowledge can become a very abstract idea, but it can be assessed in practice. Here are some types of knowledge identified in a study of the biotechnology and telecommunications industries:[1]

- variety of knowledge
- depth of knowledge
- source of knowledge, internal and external
- evaluation of knowledge and awareness of competencies
- knowledge management practices, the capability to identify, share and acquire knowledge
- use of IT systems to store, share and reuse knowledge
- identification and assimilation of external knowledge
- commercial knowledge of markets and customers
- competitor knowledge, current and potential
- knowledge of supplier networks and value chain
- regulatory knowledge
- financial and funding stakeholder knowledge
- knowledge of intellectual property rights (IPR), own and others'
- knowledge practices, including documentation, intranets, work organization and multidisciplinary teams and projects.

There are essentially two different types of knowledge, each with different characteristics:

- *Explicit knowledge*, which can be codified, that is expressed in numerical, textual or graphical terms, and therefore is more easily communicated (e.g. the design of a product).
- *Tacit or implicit knowledge*, which is personal, experiential, context-specific and hard to formalize and communicate (e.g. how to ride a bicycle).

Note that the distinction between explicit and tacit is not necessarily the result of the difficulty or complexity of the knowledge but rather how easy it is to express that knowledge. Each of these contributes to the intellectual assets and innovative performance of companies, but in different ways. In general, the less tangible and more tacit knowledge of individuals, groups and practices is necessary to exploit the more explicit and tangible types of knowledge, such as R&D and IPR, and these in turn can lead to better use and access to external sources of knowledge, owing to a strengthening of position, reputation and trust.

Video Clip exploring the case of Xerox and its range of knowledge management programmes is available on the Innovation Portal at www.innovation-portal.info

It is also useful to distinguish between learning how and learning why. Learning *how* involves improving or transferring existing skills, whereas learning *why* aims to understand the underlying logic or causal factors with a view to applying the knowledge in new contexts.

As we have seen, knowledge can be embodied in people, organizational culture, routines and tools, technologies, processes and systems. Organizations consist of a variety of individuals, groups and functions with different cultures, goals and frames of reference. Knowledge management consists of identifying and sharing knowledge across these disparate entities. There is a range of integrating mechanisms which can help to do this. Nonaka and Takeuchi argue that the conversion of tacit to explicit knowledge is a critical mechanism underlying the link between individual and organizational knowledge. They state that all new knowledge originates with an individual, but that through a process of dialogue, discussion, experience sharing and observation such knowledge is amplified at the group and organizational levels. This creates an expanding community of interaction, or 'knowledge network', which crosses intra- and inter-organizational levels and boundaries. Such knowledge networks are a means to accumulate knowledge from outside the organization, share it widely within the organization and store it for future use. This transformation of individual knowledge into organizational knowledge involves four cycles:[2]

- *Socialization* – tacit to tacit knowledge, in which the knowledge of an individual or group is shared with others. Culture, socialization and communities of practice are critical for this.
- *Externalization* – tacit to explicit knowledge, through which the knowledge is made explicit and codified in some persistent form. This is the most novel aspect of Nonaka and Takeuchi's model. They argue that tacit knowledge can be transformed into explicit knowledge through a process of conceptualization and crystallization. Boundary objects are critical here.
- *Combination* – explicit to explicit knowledge, where different sources of explicit knowledge are pooled and exchanged. The role of organizational processes and technological systems is central to this.
- *Internalization* – explicit to tacit knowledge, whereby other individuals or groups learn through practice. This is the traditional domain of organizational learning.

Storing and Retrieving Knowledge

Storing knowledge is not a trivial problem, even now that the electronic storage and distribution of data is so cheap and easy. The biggest hurdle is the codification of tacit knowledge. The other common problem is to provide incentives to contribute, retrieve and reuse relevant knowledge. Many organizations have developed excellent knowledge intranet systems, but these are often underutilized in practice.

In practice, there are two common but distinct approaches to knowledge management. The first is based on investments in IT, usually based on groupware and intranet technologies. This is the favoured approach of many management consultants. But introducing knowledge management into an organization consists of much more than technology and training. It can

---

Knowledge Management at Arup

Arup is an international engineering consultancy firm which provides planning, designing, engineering and project management services. The business demands the simultaneous achievement of innovative solutions and significant time compression imposed by client and regulatory requirements.

Since 1999, the organization has established a wide range of knowledge management initiatives to encourage sharing of know-how and experience across projects. These initiatives range from organizational processes and mechanisms, such as cross-functional communications meetings and skills networks, to technology-based approaches, such as the Ovebase database and intranet.

To date, the former has been more successful than the latter. For example, a survey of engineers in the firm indicated that in design and problem-solving discussions with colleagues were rated as being twice as valuable as knowledge databases, and consequently engineers were four times as likely to rely on colleagues. Two primary reasons were cited for this. First, the difficulty of codifying tacit knowledge. Engineering consultancy involves a great deal of tacit knowledge and project experience which is difficult to store and retrieve electronically. Second, the complex engineering and unique environmental context of each project limits the reuse of standardized knowledge and experience.

---

require fundamental changes to organizational structure, processes and culture. The second approach is more people- and process-based, and attempts to encourage staff to identify, store, share and use information throughout the organization. However, the storage, retrieval and reuse of knowledge demands much more than good IT systems. It also requires incentives to contribute to and use knowledge from such systems, whereas many organizations instead encourage and promote the generation and use of new knowledge.

Richard Hall goes some way towards identifying the components of organizational memory. His main purpose is to articulate intangible resources and he distinguishes between intangible assets and intangible competencies. Assets include IPR and reputation. Competencies include the skills and know-how of employees, suppliers and distributors, as well as the collective attributes which constitute organizational culture. His empirical work, based on a survey and case studies, indicates that managers believe that the most significant of these intangible resources are the company's reputation and employees' know-how, both of which may be a function of organizational culture. These include:[3]

- *Intangible*, off balance sheet assets, such as patents, licences, trademarks, contracts and protectable data.
- *Positional*, which are the result of previous endeavour (i.e. with a high path dependency), such as processes and operating systems, and individual and corporate reputation and networks.

- *Functional*, which are either individual skills and know-how or team skills and know-how, within the company, at the suppliers or distributors.
- *Cultural*, including traditions of quality, customer service, human resources or innovation.

The key questions in each case are:

Activity to help you explore these themes – Capabilities Assessment – is available on the Innovation Portal at **www.innovation-portal.info**

- Are we making the best use of this resource?
- How else could it be used?
- Is the scope for synergy identified and exploited?
- Are we aware of the key linkages which exist between the resources?

Sharing and Distributing Knowledge

In practice, large organizations often do not know what they know. Many organizations now have databases and groupware to help store, retrieve and share data and information, but such systems are often confined to 'hard' data and information, rather than more tacit knowledge. As a result functional groups or business units with potentially synergistic information may not be aware of where such information could be applied.

Knowledge sharing and distribution is the process by which information from different sources is shared and, therefore, leads to new knowledge or understanding. Greater organizational learning occurs when more of an organization's components obtain new knowledge and recognize it as being of potential use. Tacit knowledge is not easily imitated by competitors because it is not fully encoded, but for the same reasons it may not be fully visible to all members of an organization. As a result, organizational units with potentially synergistic information may not be aware of where such information could be applied. The speed and extent to which knowledge is shared between members of an organization is likely to be a function of how codified the knowledge is.

This process of connecting different knowledge and people is underpinned by 'communities of practice'. A community of practice is a group of people related by a shared task, process or the need to solve a problem, rather than by formal structural or functional relationships.[4] Through practice, a group within which knowledge is shared becomes a community of practice through a common understanding of what it does, of how to do it and of how it relates to other communities of practice.

Within communities of practice, people share tacit knowledge and learn through experimentation. Therefore, the formation and maintenance of such communities represents an important link between individual and organizational learning. These communities naturally emerge around local work practice and so tend to reinforce functional or professional silos, but also can extend to wider, dispersed networks of similar practitioners.

The existence of communities of practice facilitates the sharing of knowledge within a community, owing to both the sense of collective identity and the existence of a significant common knowledge base. However, the sharing of knowledge between communities is much more problematic, owing to the lack of both these elements. Thus, the dynamics of knowledge sharing within and between communities of practice are likely to be very different, with the sharing of knowledge between communities typically much more complex, difficult and problematic.

Many factors can prevent the sharing of knowledge between communities of practice, such as the distinctiveness of different knowledge bases, and the lack of common knowledge, goals, assumptions and interpretative frameworks. These differences significantly increase the difficulty not just of sharing knowledge between communities but also of appreciating the knowledge of another community.

However, there are some proven mechanisms to help knowledge transfer between different communities of practice:[5]

- An organizational *translator*, who is an individual able to express the interests of one community in terms of another community's perspective. The translator must be sufficiently conversant with both knowledge domains and trusted by both communities. Examples of translators include the 'heavyweight product manager' in new product development who bridges different technical groups and the technical and marketing groups.
- A knowledge *broker*, who differs from a translator in that they participate in different communities rather than simply mediate between them. They represent overlaps between communities, and are typically people loosely linked to several communities through weak ties who are able to facilitate knowledge flows between them. An example would be a quality manager responsible for the quality of a process that crosses several different functional groups.
- A *boundary object or practice*, which is something of interest to two or more communities of practice. Different communities of practice will have a stake in it, but from different perspectives. A boundary object could be a shared document (e.g. a quality manual), an artefact (e.g. a prototype), a technology (e.g. a database) or a practice (e.g. a product design). A boundary object provides an opportunity for discussion, debate (and conflict) and therefore can encourage communication between different communities of practice.

Video Clip of an interview with Francisco Pinheiro of Atos highlighting some of these themes is available on the Innovation Portal at **www.innovation-portal.info**

For example, formally appointed 'knowledge brokers' can be used to systematically scavenge the organization for old or unused ideas, to pass these around the organization and imagine their application in different contexts. For instance, Hewlett-Packard created a SpaM group to help identify and share good practice among its 150 business divisions. Before the new group was formed, divisions were unlikely to share information because they often competed for resources and were measured against each other. Similarly, Skandia, a Swedish insurance company active in overseas markets, attempts to identify, encourage and measure its intellectual capital, and has appointed a 'knowledge manager' who is responsible for this. The company has developed a set of indicators that it uses both to manage knowledge internally and for external financial reporting.

Case Study of Joint Solutions detailing some of the issues introduced here is available on the Innovation Portal at **www.innovation-portal.info**

More generally, cross-functional team working can help to promote this inter-communal exchange. Functional diversity tends to extend the range of knowledge available and increase the number of options considered, but it can also have a negative effect on group cohesiveness and the cost of projects and efficiency of decision-making. However, a major benefit of cross-functional team working is the access it provides to the bodies of knowledge that are external to the team. In general a high frequency of knowledge sharing outside of a group is associated with improved technical and project performance, as gatekeeper individuals pick up and import vital signals and knowledge. In particular, cross-functional composition in teams is argued to permit access to disciplinary knowledge outside. Therefore, cross-functional team working is a critical way of promoting the exchange of knowledge and practice across disciplines and communities.

Tools to help you work with some of these concepts are provided by the Knowledge Management toolkit, which is available on the Innovation Portal at **www.innovation-portal.info**

INNOVATION IN ACTION 13.2

Profiting from Digital Media

The business model for capturing the value from video used to be simple but conservative: own and enforce the copyright, global cinema release, followed by DVD rental and sale, and lastly TV and other broadcast. The DVD stage used to be critical, typically generating income of $23.4 billion (£14 billion) in the United States, compared to $9.6 billion (£6 billion) from cinema release. Note that when DVD was introduced in 1997 three of the major studios initially refused to publish on it, as they feared losing revenue from the existing proven VHS tape format.

However, annual DVD sales have begun to stabilize at around nine billion units worldwide, and in some markets have begun to decline. Therefore, the industry has begun to promote the successor to DVD, the high-definition DVD. After a stupid format war, Blu-ray became the new standard for high-definition disks early in 2008. Initial sales of the new format have been slow, not helped by uncertainty of the format war, with nine million Blu-ray disks shipped in 2007, compared to nine billion conventional DVDs – just 0.1% of the market (in addition some 40 million Blu-ray PS3 games were sold; since its launch in 2006 the Sony PlayStation 3 has sold some 11 million games consoles, which also play Blu-ray disks). Surveys in the United States and Europe suggest that 80% of consumers are happy with the picture and sound quality of DVD and standard definition broadcast. Therefore, formats such as Blu-ray and high-definition satellite and cable broadcasts are aimed at the 20% 'early adopters' who value (i.e. are prepared to pay a premium for) higher-definition pictures and sound, primarily for films and sports coverage.

However, for the majority who favour cost and convenience over quality, the Internet is the current preferred medium, legal or otherwise. Illegal sites lead the way, such as ZML, which offers 1700 movies for (illegal) download, whereas to date the legal services like MovieFlix and FilmOn tend to be restricted to independent or amateur content. Hollywood has been slow to adapt its business model, and still relies on cinema releases, followed by DVD rental and sales, and finally broadcast. Legal download and streaming offer the potential for lower cost (and prices), as this removes much of the cost of creating, distributing and selling physical media, as well as greater convenience for consumers in terms of choice and flexibility. However, DVD sales depend on the major chain stores for distribution, for example in the United States Wal-Mart accounts for around 40% of sales, and this represents a powerful resistance to change. As a result, in 2008 legal online film distribution was only around $58 million (£36 million) in the United States, less than 5% of total film sales. Television broadcasters have been faster to adopt such services, such as the BBC i-Player in the United Kingdom, mainly because their current business model is based on subscription or advertising, without the film studios' legacy of reliance on physical media and retail distributors. Apple iTunes and TV, Netflix and Amazon LOVEFiLM have begun to dominate the growing market for on-demand streaming video. Netflix is one of the leading streaming services, with 40 million subscribers in the United States, but in 2013 its DVD rental service still generated the majority of its profits as the operating margin of DVD rental was nearly 50%, compared to 20% for streaming content.

As a result of the growing importance of Internet sales of video material, in 2007 the Writers' Guild of America went on strike for better payment terms for electronic distribution and sales. The Hollywood studios' offer was for the payments for Internet sales to be based on the precedent set by DVD – 1.2% of gross receipts – whereas the writers wanted something closer to book or film publishing – 2.5% of gross. The final settlement, reached in February 2008, was a compromise, with a royalty on download rentals of 1.2% of gross, and 0.36–0.70% of gross on download sales, and up to 2% where video streaming is part-funded by advertising. A partial victory for the authors, but this compares with 20% of gross receipts claimed by some leading actors of blockbusters. Clearly, there is work to be done on the final business model for the creation, sale and distribution of digital video. Greater clarity of the regime for managing intellectual property is a start, and faster broadband will soon make higher-quality download practical for the mass markets, so all that remains is a little innovation in the business model.

Sources: The Economist, 23 February 2008, Volume 386, Issue 8568; *ALCS News*, Spring 2008.

Exploiting Intellectual Property

In some cases knowledge, in particular in its more explicit or codified forms, can be commercialized by licensing or selling the IPR, rather than the more difficult and uncertain route of developing new processes, products or businesses.

For example, in one year (2009) IBM reported licence income of $1.1 billion (£670 million), and in the United States the total royalty income of industry from licensing was around $100 billion (£62 billion). Much of this is from payments for licences to use software, music or films. For example, in 2005 the global sales of legal music downloads exceeded $1 billion (although illegal downloads are estimated to be worth three to four times this figure), still only around 5% of all music company revenue, with music downloaded to mobile phones accounting for almost a quarter of this. Patterns of use vary by country, for example in Japan 99.8%

of all music downloads are to mobile phones, rather than to dedicated mp3 players. However, despite the growth of legal sites for downloading music and an aggressive programme of pursuing users of illegal file-sharing sites, the level of illegal downloads has not declined.

This clearly demonstrates two of the many problems associated with intellectual property: these may provide some legal rights, but such rights are useless unless they can be effectively enforced; and once in the public domain, imitation or illegal use is very likely. For these reasons, secrecy is often a more effective alternative to seeking IPR. However, IPR can be highly effective in some circumstances and, as we will argue later, can be used in less obvious ways to help to identify innovations and assess competitors. A range of IPR exists, but those most applicable to technology and innovation are patents, copyright and design rights and registration.

Patents

All developed countries have some form of patent legislation, the aim of which is to encourage innovation by allowing a limited monopoly, usually for 20 years, and more recently many developing and emerging economies have been encouraged to sign up to the TRIPS (Trade Related Intellectual Property System). Legal regimes differ in the detail, but in most countries the issue of a patent requires certain legal tests to be satisfied:

- *Novelty* – no part of 'prior art', including publications, written, oral or anticipation. In most countries the first to file the patent is granted the rights, rather than the first to invent.
- *Inventive step* – 'not obvious to a person skilled in the art'. This is a relative test, as the assumed level of skill is higher in some fields than others. For example, Genentech was granted a patent for the plasminogen activator t-PA which helps to reduce blood clots, but despite its novelty a Court of Appeal revoked the patent on the grounds that it did not represent an inventive step because its development was deemed to be obvious to researchers in the field.
- *Industrial application* – utility test requires the invention to be capable of being applied to a machine, product or process. In practice a patent must specify an application for the technology, and additional patents sought for any additional application. For example, Unilever developed Ceramides and patented their use in a wide range of applications. However, it did not apply for a patent for application of the technology to shampoos, which was subsequently granted to a competitor.
- *Patentable subject* – for example, discoveries and formulae cannot be patented, and in Europe neither can software (the subject of copyright) or new organisms, although both these are patentable in the United States. For example, contrast the mapping of the human genome in the United States and Europe: in the States the research is being conducted by a commercial laboratory which is patenting the outcomes, and in Europe by a group of public laboratories which is publishing the outcomes on the Internet.
- *Clear and complete disclosure* – note that a patent provides only certain legal property rights, and in the case of infringement the patent holder needs to take the appropriate legal action. In some cases secrecy may be a preferable strategy. Conversely, national patent databases represent a large and detailed reservoir of technological innovations which can be interrogated for ideas.

Patents can also be used to identify and assess innovation, at the firm, sector or national level. However, great care needs to be taken when making such assessments, because patents are only a partial indicator of innovation.

The main advantages of patent data are that they reflect the corporate capacity to generate innovation, are available at a detailed level of technology over long periods of time, are comprehensive in the sense that they cover small as well as large firms and are used by practitioners themselves. However, patenting tends to occur early in the development process, and therefore can be a poor measure of the output of development activities, and tells us nothing about the economic or commercial potential of the innovation.

Crude counts of the number of patents filed by a firm, sector or country reveal little, but the quality of patents can be assessed by a count of how often a given patent is cited in later patents. This provides a good indicator of its technical quality, albeit after the event, although not necessarily commercial potential. Highly cited patents are generally of much greater importance than patents which are never cited, or are cited only a few times. The reason for this is that a patent which contains an important new invention – or major advance – can set off a stream of follow-on inventions, all of which may cite the original, important invention upon which they are building.

The most useful indicators of innovation based on patents are (Table 13.1):

- *Number of patents* – indicates the level of technology activity, but crude patent counts reflect little more than the propensity to patent of a firm, sector or country.
- *Cites per patent* – indicates the impact of a company's patents.

TABLE 13.1 Patent Indicators for Different Sectors

	Current impact index (expected value 1.0)	Technology life cycle (years)	Science linkage (science references/patents)
Oil and gas	0.84	11.9	0.8
Chemicals	0.79	9.0	2.7
Pharmaceuticals	0.79	8.1	7.3
Biotechnology	0.68	7.7	14.4
Medical equipment	2.38	8.3	1.1
Computers	1.88	5.8	1.0
Telecommunications	1.65	5.7	0.8
Semiconductors	1.35	6.0	1.3
Aerospace	0.68	13.2	0.3

Source: Narin, F. (2012) Assessing technological competencies, in Tidd, J. (ed.) *From Knowledge Management to Strategic Competence*, 3rd edn. London: Imperial College Press, pp. 179–219.

- *Current impact index (CII)* – this is a fundamental indicator of patent portfolio quality; it is the number of times the company's previous five years of patents, in a technology area, were cited from the current year, divided by the average citations received.
- *Technology strength (TS)* – indicates the strength of the patent portfolio, and is the number of patents multiplied by the current impact index (i.e. patent portfolio size inflated or deflated by patent quality).
- *Technology cycle time (TCT)* – indicates the speed of invention, and is the median age, in years, of the patent references cited on the front page of the patent.
- *Science linkage (SL)* – indicates how leading edge the technology is, and is the average number of science papers referenced on the front page of the patent.
- *Science strength (SS)* – indicates how much the patent applies basic science, and is the number of patents multiplied by science linkage (i.e. patent portfolio size inflated or deflated by the extent of science linkage).

Companies whose patents have above-average current impact indices (CII) and science linkage (SL) indicators tend to have significantly higher market-to-book ratios and stock-market returns. However, having a strong intellectual property portfolio does not, of course, guarantee a company's success. Many additional factors influence the ability of a company to move from quality patents to innovation and financial and market performance. The decade of troubles at IBM, for example, is certainly illustrative of this, since IBM has always had very high-quality and highly cited research in its laboratories.

There are major inter-sectoral differences in the relative importance of patenting in achieving its prime objective, namely to act as a barrier to imitation. For example, patenting is relatively unimportant in automobiles, but critical in pharmaceuticals. Moreover, patents do not yet fully measure technological activities in software since copyright laws are often used as the main means of protection against imitation, outside the United States.

Examples of the strategic value of patents include recent acquisitions and battles for IPR. Alleged infringements include:

- Apple aggressively defends its patents against alleged infringements, including HTC & Samsung in 2011, seeking to ban sales of competing mobile devices.
- Nokia won patent dispute regarding touch-screen technology with Apple in 2011, now receives 2% iPhone revenues, in excess of $30 billion (£19 billion) annually.
- Oracle launched a case against Google, alleging Android infringes Java patents, claiming $6.1 billion (£4 billion) in damages.
- Nortel sold its entire patent portfolio in 2011 for $4.5 billion (£2.8 billion) to a consortium of firms: Apple, Microsoft, Sony, Ericsson & RIM (BlackBerry).
- In response, Google acquired Motorola's mobile telephony patents in 2011 for $12.5 billion (£7.7 billion), because of the vulnerability of its Android platform.

Using 'international patents', where a single patent filing can include up to 144 countries, in 2009 the United States filed 487 000 patents, Euro 6 group, 387 000 and Japan, 218 000. Compare this to emerging economies such as China, 48 000 and India, 32 000 and this suggests that at current relative growth rates China will catch up in 20–30 years.[6]

The Goldilocks Patent Strategy: Exploiting (Nearly) New Technologies

A study of the relationships between the age of patents and financial performance appears to provide some additional support for a 'fast-follower' strategy, rather than a 'first-mover' approach. It found that the median age of the patents of a firm is correlated with its stock-market value, but not in a linear way. For firms utilizing very recent patents or older patents, the relationship is negative, resulting in below-average performance over time, whereas firms using patents close to the median age outperform the average over time.

The study examined 288 firms over 20 years, and 204 000 patents. When patents are filed they must list the other patents which they cite, by patent number and year of filing. This data allows the median age of the patent to be calculated – the median difference between the patent application date and the dates of the prior patents cited. This provides an indication of the age of the technological inputs used, but needs to be compared to the average within different technology patents classes, as the technology life cycle varies significantly between the 400 patent classes, from months to decades. This comparison reveals a variation in the median ages of technologies used by different firms operating in the same technical fields, indicating different technology strategies. Finally, this data is compared with the financial performance, in this case share performance, of the firms over time. The results show that firms at the technological frontier, defined as one or more standard deviations ahead of their industry, or for those using mature technologies, that is 1.3 or more standard deviations behind the industry average, the stock returns underperform. However, the stock-market returns outperform for firms exploiting median-age technologies.

One interpretation of this observed relationship is that the firms with the very new patents face the very high costs and uncertainty associated with emerging technology, including development and commercialization. Conversely, the firms using mature patent portfolios face more limited opportunity to exploit these commercially. However, the firms with patents closer to the median age (in the relevant patent classes) have reduced much of the very high cost and uncertainty associated with the newer patents, but retain significant scope for further development and commercialization. Therefore one lesson may be for firms to more carefully manage the age profile of their patents, and to focus exploitation on a specific time window. This is not simply about being a fast follower, which implies some degree of imitation, but another argument for closer integration between technological and market strategies.

Source: Heeley, M. B. and R. Jacobson (2008) The recency of technological inputs and financial performance. *Strategic Management Journal*, **29**: 723–744. Reproduced by permission of John Wiley & Sons, Ltd.

Copyright

Copyright is concerned with the expression of ideas, and not the ideas themselves. Therefore, the copyright exists only if the idea is made concrete, for example in a book or recording. There is no requirement for registration, and the test of originality is low compared to patent law, requiring only that 'the author of the work must have used his own skill and effort to create the work'. Like patents, copyright provides limited legal rights for certain types of material for a specific term. For literary, dramatic, musical and artistic works copyright is normally for 70 years after the death of the author, 50 in the United States, and for recordings, film, broadcast and cable programmes 50 years from their creation. Typographical works have 25 years' copyright. The type of materials covered by copyright include:

- 'original' literary, dramatic, musical and artistic works, including software and in some cases databases
- recordings, films, broadcasts and cable programmes
- typographical arrangement or layout of a published edition.

Design Rights

Design rights are similar to copyright protection but mainly apply to three-dimensional articles, covering any aspect of the 'shape' or 'configuration', internal or external, whole or part, but specifically exclude integral and functional features, such as spare parts. Design rights exist for 15 years, or 10 years if commercially exploited. Design registration is a cross between patent and copyright protection, is cheaper and easier than patent protection but more limited in scope. It provides protection for up to 25 years, but covers only visual appearance – shape, configuration, pattern and ornament. It is used for designs that have aesthetic appeal, for example consumer electronics and toys. For example, the knobs on top of Lego bricks are functional, and would therefore not qualify for design registration but were also considered to have 'eye appeal' and therefore granted design rights.

Licensing IPR

Once you have acquired some form of formal legal IPR, you can allow others to use it in some way in return for some payment (a licence), or you can sell the IPR outright (or assign it). Licensing IPR can have a number of benefits:

- reduce or eliminate production and distribution costs and risks
- reach a larger market
- exploit in other applications
- establish standards
- gain access to complementary technology
- block competing developments
- convert competitor into defender.

Considerations when drafting a licensing agreement include degree of exclusivity, territory and type of end use, period of licence and type and level of payments – royalty, lump sum or

---

INNOVATION IN ACTION 13.4

Using Patents Strategically

Each year, some 400 000 patents are filed around the world. However, only a small proportion of these are ever exploited by the owners, and many are not renewed. Based on a review of the research and case studies of 14 firms from different sectors, the study identified a range of different patent strategies:

- *Offensive* – multiple patents in related fields to limit or prevent competition.
- *Defensive* – specific patents for key technologies which are intended to be developed and commercialized, to minimize imitation.
- *Financial* – primary role of patents are to optimize income through sale or licence.
- *Bargaining* – patents designed to promote strategic alliances, adoption of standards or cross-licensing.
- *Reputation* – to improve the image or position of a company (e.g. to attract partners, talent or funding, or to build brands or enhance market position).

In practice, firms may combine different strategies, or more likely have no explicit strategy for patenting (which is our experience outside the pharmaceutical and biotechnology sectors). The European Patent Office (EPO) suggest only two alternatives: patenting as a cost centre (i.e. to provide the necessary legal support) or as a profit centre (to generate income). However, this ignores the more strategic positioning possibilities patents can provide if they are viewed as more than just a legal or income issue.

Source: Derived from Gilardoni, E. (2007) Basic approaches to patent strategy. *International Journal of Innovation Management*, **11** (3): 417–440.

---

cross-licence. Pricing a licence is as much an art as a science, and depends on a number of factors such as the balance of power and negotiating skills. Common methods of pricing licences are:

- *Going market rate* – based on industry norms (e.g. 6% of sales in electronics and mechanical engineering).
- *25% rule* – based on licensee's gross profit earned through use of the technology.
- *Return on investment* – based on licensor's costs.
- *Profit sharing* – based on relative investment and risk. First, estimate total lifecycle profit. Next, calculate relative investment and weight according to share of risk. Finally, compare results to alternatives (e.g. return to licensee, imitation and litigation).

There is no 'best' licensing strategy, as it depends on the strategy of the organization and the nature of the technology and market. For example, Celltech licensed its asthma treatment to Merck for a single payment of $50 million (£30 million), based on sales projections. This isolated Celltech from the risk of clinical trials and commercialization, and provided a much-needed cash injection. Toshiba, Sony and Matsushita license DVD technology for royalties of only 1.5% to encourage its adoption as the industry standard. Until the recent legal proceedings, Microsoft applied a 'per processor' royalty to its OEM (original equipment manufacturer) customers for Windows to discourage them from using competing operating systems.

INNOVATION IN ACTION 13.5

ARM Holdings

ARM Holdings designs and licenses high-performance, low-energy-consumption 16- and 32-bit RISC (reduced instruction set computing) chips, which are used extensively in mobile devices such as mobile phones, cameras, electronic organizers and smart cards. ARM was established in 1990 as a joint venture between Acorn Computers in the United Kingdom and Apple Computer. Acorn did not pioneer the RISC architecture, but it was the first to market a commercial RISC processor in the mid-1980s. Perhaps ironically, the first application of ARM technology was in the relatively unsuccessful Apple Newton PDA (personal digital assistant). One of the most recent successful applications has been in the Apple iPod. ARM designs but does not manufacture chips, and receives royalties of between 5 cents (3p) and $2.50 (£1.50) for every chip produced under licence. Licensees include Apple, Ericsson, Fujitsu, HP, NEC, Nintendo, Sega, Sharp, Sony, Toshiba and 3Com. In 1999, it announced joint ventures with leading chip manufacturers such as Intel and Texas Instruments to design and build chips for the next generation of hand-held devices. It is estimated that ARM-designed processors were used in 10 million devices in 1996, 50 million in 1998, 120 million devices sold in 1999 and a billion sold in 2004, and more than two billion in 2006, and 20 billion by 2012, representing around 80% of all mobile devices. In 1998, the company was floated in London and on the NASDAQ in New York, and it achieved a market capitalization of £3 billion in December 1999, with an annual revenue growth of 40% to £15.7 million. The company now employs around 2000 people, headquartered in Cambridge, UK, with design centres in Taiwan, India and the United States. It has sold 800 processor licences to more than 250 companies, and has created 30 millionaires amongst its staff.

The main strategic motives for licensing are:[7]

- strategic freedom to operate
- access to knowledge
- entry to new markets
- establish technological leadership
- enhance reputation.

The benefits of licensing depend very much on the absorptive capacity of an organization and its complementary assets.[8] Absorptive capacity, such as internal R&D and know-how, allows an organization to more easily identify, evaluate and adapt external knowledge, whereas complementary assets allow an organization to create additional value by combining internal and external knowledge, for example applying technology to a new market segment.

However, the successful exploitation of IPR also incurs costs and risks, for example:

- cost of search, registration and renewal
- need to register in various national markets
- full and public disclosure of your idea
- need to be able to enforce.

In most countries the basic registration fee for a patent is relatively modest, but in addition applying for a patent includes the cost of professional agents, such as patent agents, translation for foreign patents, official registration fees in all relevant countries and renewal fees. Pharmaceutical patents are much more expensive, up to five times more, owing to the complexity and length of the documentation. In addition to these costs, firms must consider the competitive risk of public disclosure, and the potential cost of legal action should the patent be infringed. Costs vary by country, because of the size and attractiveness of different national markets, and because of differences in government policy. For example, in many Asian countries the policy is to encourage patenting by domestic firms, so the process is cheaper.

Summary

- The generation, acquisition, sharing and exploitation of knowledge are central to successful innovation, but there is a wide range of different types of knowledge, and each plays a different role.

- One of the key challenges is to identify and exchange knowledge across different groups and organizations, and a number of mechanisms can help, mostly social in nature but supported by technology.

- Tacit knowledge is critical but is difficult to capture, and draws upon individual expertise and experience. Therefore, where possible, tacit knowledge needs to be made more explicit and codified to allow it to be more readily shared and applied to different contexts.

- Codified knowledge can form the basis of legal IPR, and these can form a basis for the commercialization of knowledge. However, care needs to be taken when using IPR, as these can divert scarce management and financial resources and can expose an organization to the imitation and illegal use of its IPR.

Further Resources

Knowledge management and intellectual property are both very large and complex subjects. For knowledge management, we would recommend the books by Friso den Hertog, *The Knowledge Enterprise* (Imperial College Press, 2000), for applications and examples, and for theory Nonaka's *The Knowledge Creating Company* (Oxford University Press, 1995). We provide a good combination of theory, research and practice of knowledge management in *From Knowledge Management to Strategic Competence*, edited by Joe Tidd (Imperial College Press, 3rd edition, 2012), which examines the links between knowledge, innovation and performance. More critical accounts of the concept and practice of knowledge management can be found in the editorial by J. Swan and H. Scarborough (2001) Knowledge management: Concepts and controversies, *Journal of Management Studies*, 38 (7): 913–921; J. Storey and E. Barnett (2000) Knowledge management initiatives: Learning from failure, *Journal of Knowledge Management*, 4 (2): 145–156; and Pritchard, C., R. Hull, M. Chumer and H. Willmott *Managing Knowledge: Critical Investigations of Work and Learning* (Macmillan, 2000). Harry Scarborough also edits *The Evolution of Business Knowledge* (Oxford University Press, 2008), which reports the findings of the UK national research programme on the relationships between business and knowledge (including one of our research projects).

For a comprehensive technical legal overview of intellectual property, see David Bainbridge's *Intellectual Property* (Pearson, 9th edition, 2012) or for a much more concise summary try John Palfrey's *Intellectual Property Strategy* (MIT Press, 2011). For understanding the strategic role and limitations of intellectual property, we like the theoretical approach adopted by David Teece, for example, in his book *The Transfer and Licensing of Know-how and Intellectual Property* (World Scientific, 2006), or for a more applied treatment of the topic see *Licensing Best Practices: Strategic, territorial and technology issues*, edited by Robert Goldscheider and Alan Gordon (John Wiley & Sons, Ltd, 2006), which includes practical case studies of licensing from many different countries and sectors.

References

1. Marques, D. P., F. J. G. Simon and C. D. Caranana (2006) The effect of innovation on intellectual capital: An empirical evaluation in the biotechnology and telecommunications industries, *International Journal of Innovation Management*, **10** (1): 89–112.

2. Nonaka, I. and H. Takeuchi (1995) *The Knowledge Creating Company*. Oxford: Oxford University Press.

3. Hall, R. (2012) What are strategic competencies? in J. Tidd (ed.) *From Knowledge Management to Strategic Competence*, 3rd edn. London: Imperial College Press.

4. Brown, J. S. and P. Duguid (2001) Knowledge and organization: A social practice perspective, *Organization Science*, **12** (2): 198–213; (1991) Organizational learning and communities of practice: Towards a unified view of working, learning and organization, *Organizational Science*, **2** (1): 40–57; Hildreth, P., C. Kimble and P. Wright (2000) Communities of practice in the distributed international environment, *Journal of Knowledge Management*, **4** (1): 27–38.

5. Star, S. L. and J. R. Griesemer (1989) Institutional ecology, translations and boundary objects, *Social Studies of Science*, **19**: 387–420; Carlile, P. R. (2002) A pragmatic view of knowledge and boundaries: Boundary objects in new product development, *Organization Science*, **13** (4): 442–455.

6. Godinhoa, M. M. and V. Ferreirac (2012) Analyzing the evidence of an IPR take-off in China and India, *Research Policy*, **41**: 499–511.

7. Lichtenthaler, U. (2007) The drivers of technology licensing: An industry comparison, *California Management Review*, **49** (4): 67–89.

8. Mazzola, E., M. Bruccoleri and G. Perrone (2012) The effect on inbound, outbound and coupled innovation on performance, *International Journal of Innovation Management*, **16** (6): DOI 1240008; Walter, J. (2012) The influence of firm and industry characteristics on returns from technology licensing deals: Evidence from the US computer and pharmaceutical sectors, *R&D Management*, **42** (5): 435–454.

Deeper Dive explanations of innovation concepts and ideas are available on the Innovation Portal at **www.innovation-portal.info**

 Quizzes to test yourself further are available online via the Innovation Portal at **www.innovation-portal.info**

Summary of online resources for Chapter 13 –
all material is available via the Innovation Portal at
www.innovation-portal.info

Cases	**Media**	**Tools**	**Activities**	**Deeper Dive**
• Joint Solutions • Novo Nordisk • Apple versus Android • Managing internal knowledge connections	• Xerox • Francisco Pinheiro, Atos	• Identifying innovative capabilities • TRIZ • Knowledge Management toolkit	• Acquiring technological knowledge • Knowledge mapping • Identifying innovative capabilities	• Linking knowledge and innovation management

Chapter 14

Business Models and Capturing Value

LEARNING OBJECTIVES

By the end of this chapter you will:

- understand the concept of business models
- appreciate their role as a framework for describing how value is created and captured
- develop the skills to map and build business models and to use these to explore value capture.

What's a Business Model?

A helpful approach to the question of capturing value is the concept of business models. Put simply, a business model is an explanation of how value is created for customers, and making it explicit can help us focus on how we can capture this in innovation. For example:

- A theatre uses scripts, actors, scenery, lighting and music to create a theatrical experience which the audience values.
- A car company mobilizes an extensive supply network to bring together components and services, and assembles them into a car which the customer values.
- A supermarket procures various food and non-food products and makes them available on its shelves to customers to collect them conveniently – they value this and are prepared to pay more than the supermarket paid for the items because they value the service this collection, storage and display offers them.

- An insurance company provides a guarantee of payment to offset the cost of losses from accidental damage, theft or other incident, and customers value the peace of mind which this brings and are prepared to pay for it.
- A smart phone retailer provides a platform across which communications, entertainment and personalized application traffic can flow, and customers are prepared to pay to own or rent the device because of the functions it offers them.

Every organization, public or private sector, offers some kind of 'value proposition' – a product or service or some combination which end users value. In commercial markets this is something they are prepared to pay for, but in other contexts, such as public sector, services like education, welfare and health care are similarly 'valued' by those who consume them.

Innovation, as we have seen, is all about creating new or better ways of delivering such value and so if we are concerned to capture value it makes sense to begin by making explicit the model we are using to create it and to check whether it does the job well. And importantly, whether it is sustainable in the long term or whether it is vulnerable to replacement or challenge by someone else – the idea of competition which we talked about in Chapter 1.

Value creation doesn't just happen: it is the result of a structured process which involves:

- a value proposition – what is valued?
- a target market – by whom?
- a supplier – who?
- a set of activities – how?
- a representation of the value – how much?

Figure 14.1 illustrates this simple model and Table 14.1 gives some examples.

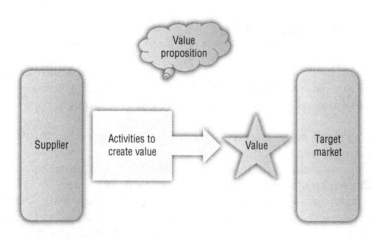

FIGURE 14.1 Outline framework for a business model

TABLE 14.1   Examples of Business Models

Example	Value proposition?	For whom?	By whom – key players on supply side?	Core activities to deliver that value
Razor blades	Shaving with a fresh sharp blade every time instead of having to sharpen a razor	Men (and later women)	Manufacturers like Gillette	Design and development Manufacture and distribution of blades, advertising and marketing, etc.
National Health Service (UK)	Health care for all free at the point of delivery	All population (as opposed to health care for those who can afford it)	Mobilizes entire medical system of primary and secondary care	Health care services
Online banking	24/7 bank opening and ability to operate independent of physical banking offices	Customers unable or unwilling to use 'normal' banking hours but who appreciate the convenience Eventually all customers – becomes the dominant model	IT platforms, call centre staff, other customer interfaces Back-office systems and providers	Customer service and relationship management
Streaming music services, e.g. Spotify	Rent a huge collection of music and have it available on many mobile devices	Customers keen to access large volume and variety of music and have it available whenever they want it	IT platforms, IP relationship with music providers	Access control IT distribution and streaming Rights management Rental processing

Business model 'innovation' is about creating new models or changing existing ones to maximize the value created and return it to the organization which created it – capturing value. So we need to make explicit in our model two more elements – the costs of our creating the value and the ways in which we can return that value (the 'revenue') which we can then use for other activities.

So, for example, a pharmaceutical company spends around 20% of its sales on R&D, funding extensive laboratories and facilities to create new drugs. It pays for testing and approvals, for manufacture and packaging and for marketing across a global network.

> **Activity** choose a product or service which you have consumed recently. Try to set out the underlying business model. What value is created, for whom, by whom and how?

Activity pick an example organization and try to map out the business model including how value is created and captured – the 'revenue stream'

People value the health benefits which a drug gives them – and they or the agencies (insurance companies, governments, etc. which represent them) pay for this. The flow of revenue funds the direct costs and generates a surplus, which can be reinvested.

This may sound simplistic but understanding how business models create value is a core part of our innovation discussion. If we can't make explicit how value is created and how we will capture it, then the best idea in the world may not have an impact. Equally, if we understand how this process works we can improve it – streamline it and reduce the waste and friction in it. We can extend its application to new markets and we can adapt and shape the innovation for them. If we go back to our idea of innovation strategy then these three concepts – changing what we offer, how we create and deliver that and to whom – are three of the core dimensions of the '4Ps' model (Figure 14.2), which we saw in Chapter 2.

Crucially, we can also change the business model itself – replacing, for example, a simple grocer's shop with a supermarket or replacing that with an online service. Or shifting between making and selling a product and renting out the functions which it performs – Rolls-Royce

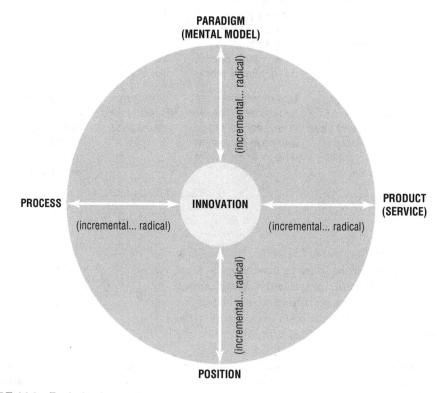

FIGURE 14.2 Exploring innovation space

no longer sells jet engines but charges customers for the number of useful hours of power which they provide over a thirty-year life. This kind of innovation is our fourth part of the '4Ps' innovation space: 'paradigm innovation'.

Activity think of an example organization and try to explore how innovation in the 4Ps space create value

Generic and Specific Business Models

In reality there are some generic business models which operate, for example:

- *Product or service provider* – offers an end-product or service
- *Ownership of key assets and renting them out* – examples would be car parks, luggage and goods storage businesses
- *Finance provider* – offers access to money and services around that
- *Systems integrator* – pulls together components on behalf of an end customer. Examples would be building contractors, software service providers or computer builders like Dell
- *Platform provider* – offers a platform across which others can add value. Examples would be of smart phones and the various apps which run across them, but another could be Intel, whose chipsets enable others to offer computing functions
- *Network provider* – offers access to various kinds of network service. Examples would be a mobile phone or broadband company
- *Skills provider* – sells or rents access to human resources and knowledge. Examples would be recruitment agencies, professional consultancies and contract services
- *Outsourcer* – offers to take over responsibility for management and delivery of key activities. Examples would be payroll management, IT services or financial transaction processing

And then there is competition about finding new and modified ways of deploying these – playing with the 4Ps in terms of streamlining or changing processes, modifying the product/service offering or changing the positioning in new markets or in the story we tell about our offer.

For example, the basic airline business model is that people pay for the service of transportation. Over the years we have seen competition amongst airlines based on incremental innovations in the service offered – different destinations, different catering, different aircraft, different seating and sleeping options, provisions of lounge accommodation, transportation to/from the terminal, etc. Process innovations have reduced the costs and improved the flow in areas like check-in, reservations, fuel efficiency, terminal turnaround times, etc. Position innovation has segmented the market, first into different classes and experiences and, in recent times, radically opening up the market through low-cost short-haul flying. And this has led to a paradigm innovation: from being seen as a luxury service for the few, flying has now become the possible mode of travel for the many, rather as Henry Ford changed the earlier transport paradigm with his Model T.

Activity try to identify generic and specific business models in manufacturing or services

Case Studies detailing the changing face of the music, lighting and imaging industries are available on the Innovation Portal at **www.innovation-portal.info**

Activity what business models could you use to identify and exploit new sources of value in these industries?

The generic pattern of innovation is played out by many different players, each of whom is trying to compete by modifying some aspect of the business model through innovation. So transatlantic carriers offer flat-beds or different customer lounges. Low-cost carriers compete on price, translating their savings through process innovations into lower ticket prices. Niche airlines offer services to remote locations or serving specialist segments, for example helicopters serving oil platforms.

Over time we can see a pattern of occasional breakthroughs in the underlying business model followed by long periods of elaboration – do better innovation – around that. For example, the music industry emerged during the early twentieth century when the radio and gramophone made it possible to listen to and own recordings. This dominant model lasted until the late part of the century, when growth in consumer electronics led to the Walkman and other forms of personal music ownership and portability, on a platform of different storage media – cassettes, CDs, etc. The digital revolution, and particularly the invention of compression technology around mp3, led to the move into virtual space – and the business model challenge became one of delivering value while staying within the bounds of intellectual property rights law. After a period in which various illegal but widely used models proliferated – Napster and beyond – the dominant model became iTunes, which orchestrated a very different value network. But that too is being challenged by an alternative business model associated with renting rather than owning music, via online streaming and temporary on-device storage.

Why Use Business Models?

The purpose of a business model is to provide a clear representation of where and how value is created and can be captured. That's useful for a number of reasons:

- It provides a roadmap for how an innovation can create value – it won't just happen, it needs a framework.
- It provides a way of sharing the idea with others – makes the business vision explicit. That can be useful for entrepreneurs trying to pitch their ideas to venture capitalists or to innovation teams trying to win resources and support for an internal innovation project.
- It offers a helpful checklist of areas to consider in making sure the idea and the route to creating value with it is well thought out.

A close relation of the business model is the 'business case', which we have already seen in Chapter 9. The idea of a business case is essentially constructing a story with enough detail about what we are trying to achieve, how we will do it, for whom, when, what the costs and rewards will be, etc. In other words, it is the story about the underlying business model and how we are going to implement it. A business case without a clear and robust underlying business model is likely to be limited in its impact.

Activity to help you explore the process of constructing a case story – Business case development – is available on the Innovation Portal at **www.innovation-portal.info**

Building a Business Model

Let's look at how we would construct a business model as a representation of how value is created – and how we could best capture it. There are plenty of models for how to do this, but they have the same underlying architecture, which can be expressed in a small number of key questions:

- What? – the value proposition.
- By whom? – the supply side.
- For whom? – the demand side.
- How? – the key activities by the supply side to create value for the demand side.

If it is going to be robust then the 'revenue' from the demand side needs to be greater than the costs on the supply side of doing it.

Beyond that there are important questions about timing (can we ensure the flow of resources out is supported by the flow of revenue in?) and long-term sustainability – how can we protect our model so that others can't instantly copy it, and how can we develop our idea in the long term to counter other competitors coming in to try?

We can build the model in a simple fashion; first, what is the core value proposition?

Here we need to think about the features of the innovation and how it represents something new which people will value over what they currently have. What differentiates it – what is our USP? Why hasn't someone already done this is often a useful question to ask at this stage: we may be reinventing the wheel or we may be trying to do something which others have found to their cost is impossible. But we may also find that things have changed and we are now able to do something which was previously impossible, for example the opportunities offered by having GPS positioning in smart phones open up a whole set of possibilities for location-based services which couldn't have been offered even ten years ago.

Value proposition

Next, we need to think about the demand side – who is going to value this? It's important here to think about targeting as precisely as we can, for example not just saying we will offer a bicycle for rent in a big city but specifying for whom – tourists who want to explore, business people who want to avoid congestion of public transport or taxis, etc. And we need to think about how we would reach those people – which channels would we use to find them and make our offer clear to them? Online advertising? Point of sale – little advertising stations where the bikes can be found? Newspaper or TV advertising? Then we need to think about how we will interact with them – do we have someone in a stall renting the bikes out personally like a shop or do we go for an online booking and self-service unlocking model?

In other words, we need to think hard about the specifics of the demand side and how best to make sure the value we are offering in our proposition reaches and is appreciated by the target market.

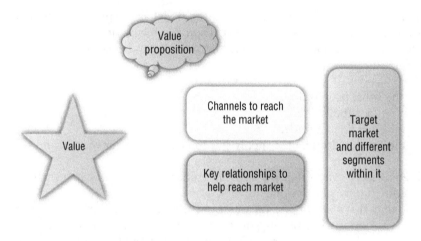

But the offering which we hope they value isn't going to magically appear – we need to create and deliver it. So we also need to think hard about the supply side – what are the key activities we'd need to do to be able to offer our value proposition? For example, we'd need to purchase or build a fleet of bikes, we'd need to distribute them around cities and we'd need to track them so we know where they are. We'd need to provide for maintaining them and making sure they were available and fit to use – and we'd probably need some kind of emergency response service in case of accidents or breakdowns. We'd certainly need a way of taking money for the bikes! We might not choose to do this all ourselves – we could partner with others – for example local shops who might offer the bikes and take the money on our behalf or a local bicycle repair shop that would undertake the maintenance side of things for us. But we'd need to build this network and manage the key relationships in that.

In other words we need to think equally hard about the specifics of the supply side and how we are going to deliver the best version of our value proposition.

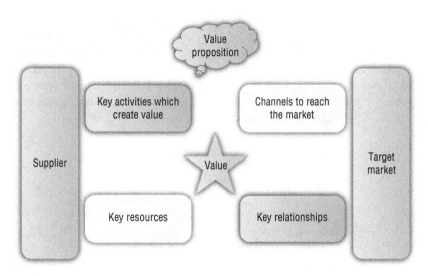

Next, we need to think about how we will capture the value from this – what are the different sources of 'revenue' or reward which flow to us from people in our target segment who value what we offer them? This is certainly the money they are prepared to pay but it may also be information – useful feedback about how to improve our offering. We can also build up information about the kind of people who are using our offering and use that to help design other products and services for them. (For example, Amazon and Google not only provide a service but also gain huge understanding of the people consuming it, which can be recycled into a variety of other innovations.)

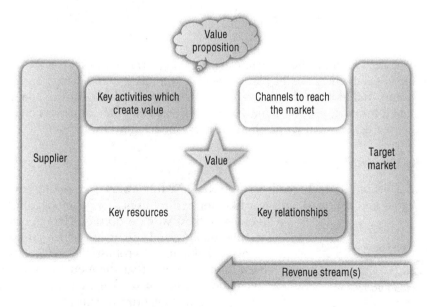

The other side of this equation is, of course, the resources we need to spend – time, energy, money – in creating and delivering our offering. What are these and how do they break down? How much of them is fixed and how much varies with the volume of demand? When do these costs kick in – at the start-up stage or through the operation of our model? We also have to think about the timing of these flows, and make sure the balance between what we spend and what we get back is positive and that we don't spend all our resources before we get something back to help refill the tanks.

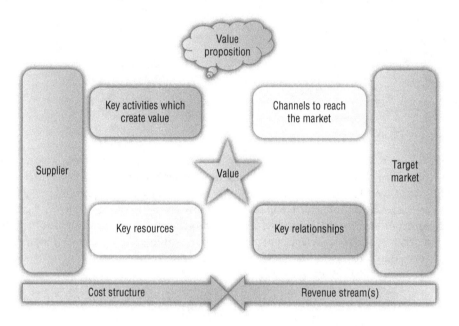

Finally, we need to think about the model in the long term. How easy is it for someone to copy right now – and where are the places where we can protect and defend ourselves from the competition? And looking ahead, how can we develop the idea further to add new kinds of value, or do it for more people on the demand side, or with different players on the supply side? In other words, how can we go about business model innovation?

Mapping Business Models

The core idea behind business models is to provide a framework for making explicit how value is created and captured, and just like our earlier discussion of innovation strategy, there is no 'best way' to do this. The important parts are the thinking and discussion which go around the model to make sure it is robust, that key questions have been thought about, that the model makes sense and has a good chance of working. It's a helpful structure for thinking about capturing value.

Tool for exploring business models – the business model canvas – is available on the Innovation Portal at **www.innovation-portal.info**

In practice, there are many ways of doing this, and there is a growing service industry providing support for it.

Activity to help you explore and map the idea of business models – building business models – is available on the Innovation Portal at **www.innovation-portal.info**

Business Model Innovation

We have seen the importance of having a clear and well-thought-out business model as a means of ensuring we can capture value from innovation. But we also need to recognize that business models themselves are susceptible to innovation – and in many ways this is the most

INNOVATION IN ACTION 14.1

Business Model Innovation

For many years, Costas Markides at London Business School has been researching the links between strategy, innovation and firm performance. In recent work he argues for the need to make a clearer distinction between the technological and market aspects of disruptive innovations, and to pay greater attention to business model innovation.

By definition, business model innovation enlarges the existing value of a market, either by attracting new customers or by encouraging existing customers to consume more. Business model innovation does not require the discovery of new products or services, or new technology, but rather the redefinition of existing products and services and how these are used to create value.

For example, Amazon did not invent book selling, and low-cost airlines such as Southwest and easyJet are not pioneers of air travel. Such innovators tend to offer different product or service attributes to existing firms, which emphasize different value propositions. As a result, business model innovation typically requires different and often conflicting systems, structures, processes and value chains to existing offerings.

However, unlike the claims made for disruptive innovations, new business models can coexist with more mainstream approaches. For example, Internet banking and low-cost airlines have not displaced the more mainstream approaches, but have captured around 20% of the total demand for these services. Also, while many business model innovations are introduced by new entrants, which have none of the legacy systems and products of incumbent firms, the more mainstream firms may simply choose not to adopt the new business models as they make little sense for them. Alternatively, they may make other innovations to create or recapture customers.

Sources: C. Based on Markides (2006) disruptive innovation: in need of a better theory. *Journal of Product Innovation Management*, **23**, 19–25; (2004) *Fast Second: How Smart Companies Bypass Radical Innovation to Enter and Dominate New Markets*, Jossey Bass, San Francisco, CA.

Activity to help you explore this challenge – business model innovation – is available on the Innovation Portal at **www.innovation-portal.info**

powerful challenge to established players in an industry. As we will see in Chapter 18, it is precisely because they have developed such strong and clear models that they are vulnerable when an entrepreneur sees an alternative way of delivering value.

Part of this challenge arises because entrepreneurs look to bring in new elements; they are skilled in reframing innovation opportunities. But it is also common that new business models are associated with system changes which don't simply impact on the component level but pick up new architectures and change the rules of the game.

Table 14.2 provides examples of alternative business models which have been enabled by the Internet and have disrupted the game for many established players.

As we saw earlier, business models can be broken down into generic and specific. Similarly, there are core trends in business model innovation, for example:

- User-driven instead of supplier led, in which the role of active and informed users is reshaping the trajectory of innovation. (We'll look at this in more detail in Chapter 16.)
- 'Servitization' in which manufacturing operations are increasingly being reframed as service offerings. For example, as mentioned earlier, the aircraft engine maker Rolls-Royce redefined its business model as 'power by the hour', recognizing that what its customers actually valued was the provision of power, not the engines themselves. It now charges users for usable hours of power. Chemical companies are increasingly looking to provide rental models in which they offer services to support the effective use of their products rather than simply delivering bulk chemicals.
- Rent not own, in which the value proposition moves to making available the functionality rather than the asset. For example, people are beginning to move to renting music via streaming services like Spotify rather than needing to buy record collections, while in city centres the idea of bicycle and even car rental is displacing the need for ownership.

TABLE 14.2   Examples of Internet as a Route to Business Model Innovation

Old model	Internet-enabled alternative
Airline and travel booking	Disintermediation – DIY or else via online aggregators
Encyclopaedia – expert driven	Wikipedia and open-source options
Printing and publishing – physical networks and specialist	Online coordination, self-publishing, long tail, print-on-demand
Retailing – physical presence via shops, distribution centres, etc.	Amazon and online, long-tail effect, database mining

Summary

* Innovation is about using change to create value, and business models provide a way of articulating and mapping the ways in which this process happens.

* A robust business model should set out the value proposition, the target market, the supply side and the cost and revenue aspects. Building the model will be the focus of much discussion but this helps ensure that innovation proposals are robust and well thought through.

* Business cases represent the stories which can be told based on a clear business model about the need for and likely benefits of innovation.

* We can map the benefits from changes in products/service offerings, process changes or position innovations on a business model framework. But changing the business model itself is also a powerful source of innovation, especially since it often involves changing the underlying system/architecture rather than just the components.

Further Resources

Business models are increasingly being discussed in the innovation literature – for example, Henry Chesbrough,[1] Costas Markides,[2] Robert Galavan,[3] Alan Lafley[4] and Gary Hamel.[5] A good review of the field is given by Sabine Schneider and Patrick Spieth.[6] Examples of business model change as a source of strategic advantage include Procter and Gamble[7,8] and Google.[9] Tools for developing and working with business models include the business model canvas[10] and Blue Ocean strategy.[11]

References

1. Chesbrough, H. (2011) *Open Services Innovation*. San Francisco: Jossey-Bass.

2. Markides, C. and P. Geroski (2004) *Fast Second: How smart companies bypass radical innovation to enter and dominate new markets*. San Francisco: Jossey-Bass.

3. Bessant, J. (2008) Opening up strategic space through discontinuous innovation, in Galavan, R. (ed.) *Strategy, Innovation and Change*. Oxford University Press: Oxford.

4. Lafley, A. and M. Johnson (2010) *Seizing the White Space*. Boston: Harvard Press.

5. Hamel, G. (2007) *The Future of Management*. Boston: Harvard Business School Press.

6. Schneider, S. and P. Spieth (2013) Business model innovation: Towards an integrated future research agenda, *International Journal of Innovation Management*, **17** (1): 1–34.

7. Huston, L. and N. Sakkab (2006) Connect and Develop: Inside Procter & Gamble's new model for innovation, *Harvard Business Review*, **84** (3): 58–66.

8. Lafley, A. and R. Charan (2008) *The Game Changer*. New York: Profile.

9. Iyer, B. and R. Davenport (2008) Reverse engineering Google's innovation machine, *Harvard Business Review*, **83** (3): 102–111.

10. Osterwalder, A. and Y. Pigneur (2010) *Business Model Generation: A handbook for visionaries, game changers, and challengers*. New York: John Wiley & Sons, Inc.

11. Kim, W. and R. Mauborgne (2005) *Blue Ocean Strategy: How to create uncontested market space and make the competition irrelevant*. Boston: Harvard Business School Press.

Deeper Dive explanations of innovation concepts and ideas are available on the Innovation Portal at **www.innovation-portal.info**

Quizzes to test yourself further are available online via the Innovation Portal at **www.innovation-portal.info**

**Summary of online resources for Chapter 14 –
all material is available via the Innovation Portal at
www.innovation-portal.info**

Cases	Media	Tools	Activities	Deeper Dive
• Music industry • Lighting industry • Imaging industry	• Business model innovation	• Business case development • Business model canvas	• Value creation • Revenue stream mapping • 4Ps and value creation • Business model examples • Changing business models • Business case development • Building business models • Business model innovation	• Servitization • Business model options

Chapter 15

Capture Value: Learning to Manage Innovation

LEARNING OBJECTIVES

By the end of this chapter you will have:

* reviewed and consolidated the key themes in this book
* explored key influences on how to manage the innovation process effectively
* developed the ability to review how well individuals and organizations manage the process
* practised taking an audit approach to improving innovation and entrepreneurship.

The Story So Far. . .

Let's take stock of where we've been going in this book and the key themes we've tried to introduce. In Part 1, we introduced the idea of innovation not as some luxury to be thought about occasionally but as a business and social imperative. Unless established organizations change what they offer the world and the ways they create and deliver that offering, they are likely to fall behind their competitors and even disappear. On a more positive side creating new business through coming up with and deploying ideas is well established as a powerful source of economic growth – not to mention a great way to make the successful entrepreneurs behind those ideas very wealthy.

This process works right across the economy – whether we are talking about cars, clothes or silicon chips. It isn't confined to manufacturing. It works just as powerfully for the services which make up the majority of most economies – banks, insurance companies, shops and airlines all have to look hard and often at the innovation challenge if they are to stay ahead.

For public services the same is true, but here we begin to see that it isn't always money which drives the entrepreneurial wheels. Innovation here is targeted at improving education, saving lives, making people more secure and addressing other basic needs. And while some innovation is about taking costs and waste out of established service delivery processes, much is about coming up with new and better ways of improving the quality of human life. Whether in a start-up or across a large public sector department, there is a strong thread of social entrepreneurship running through driven less by a desire for profits than literally wanting to change the world.

But whatever drives innovation and wherever it happens – big firm, small firm, start-up business, public sector department – one thing is clear: successful innovation won't happen simply by wishing for it. This complex and risky process of transforming ideas into things which make a mark needs organizing and managing in strategic fashion. Passion and energy aren't enough. If we are to do more than just gamble enthusiastically then we need to organize and focus the process. And we need to be able to repeat the trick; anyone may get lucky once but being able to deliver a steady stream of innovations requires something a bit more structured and robust.

Activity to help you explore this theme – success and failure in innovation – is available on the Innovation Portal at **www.innovation-portal.info**

Making Innovation Happen

Rather than the cartoon image of a light bulb flashing on above someone's head, we need to think about innovation as an extended sequence of activities – a *process* (Figure 15.1). Innovation is a generic set of activities, running from finding ideas through to their implementation. And we know that this process is influenced along the way by several things which can help or hinder it, for example having a clear sense of direction (an innovation strategy) or working within a creative network of players. We looked particularly at some of the levers we could use as architects and managers of the process. For example, how can we construct innovative organizations which allow creative ideas to come through, let people build on and share knowledge and feel motivated and rewarded for doing so? How can we harness the power of networks, making rich and extensive connections to deliver a stream of innovations?

Activity to help you explore these themes – patterns of innovation – is available on the Innovation Portal at **www.innovation-portal.info**

We've also been looking at the idea of 'routines': patterns of behaviour which an organization learns and practises, reinforces and embeds into 'the way we do things around here'. These can involve structures, policies and procedures, but underneath they describe the ways organizations manage innovation – and the key thing about routines is that they are *learnt*.

Activity to help you explore this theme – the way we do things around here – is available on the Innovation Portal at **www.innovation-portal.info**

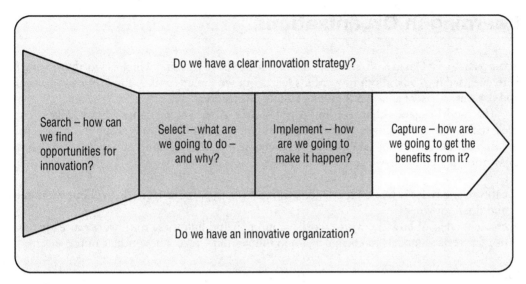

FIGURE 15.1 Simplified model of the innovation process

It's interesting to look at success stories whether we are talking about individual entrepreneurs or giant transnational corporations; a common theme is that success isn't a lucky accident. Rather, they reflect on what worked when things succeed – and crucially also on why they failed. Learning how to manage innovation and entrepreneurship is a key theme, and it doesn't happen automatically. It requires time, space and courage to reflect and recognize mistakes, structure to help focus the reflection, etc.

INNOVATION IN ACTION 15.1

Dynamic Capability at 3M

The costs of not managing learning – of lacking the dynamic capability – can be high. At the least it implies a blunting of one's competitive edge, a slipping against previously strong performance. (For example, 3M was for many years in the top three of *Business Week*'s list of innovative companies. But following a change in CEO and a shift in emphasis away from breakthrough innovation and towards incremental improvement linked to a 'Six Sigma' programme, its position fell to seventh in 2006 and 22nd in 2007. This prompted significant debate both within the company and in its wider stakeholder community and a refocusing of efforts around developing its core innovation capabilities further.) In some cases the fall accelerates and eventually leads to terminal decline – as the fate of companies like Digital, Polaroid or Swissair, once feted for their innovative prowess, indicates.

Learning in Organizations

The psychologist David Kolb developed a simple model of learning which is worth bringing in here. He used it to talk about how adults learn, but we can adapt it to think of entrepreneurs and organizations.[1] Figure 15.2 gives a simple illustration.

The model suggests that learning is not simply about acquiring new knowledge: it is a cycle with a number of stages. It doesn't matter where we enter but only when the whole cycle is complete does learning take place. So to enable effective learning about how to manage innovation better, we need to:

* capture and reflect on our experiences, trying to distil patterns from them about what does and does not work
* create models of how the world works (concepts) and link these to those we already have
* use our revised models to engage again in innovation – trying new things out.

There are many ways we can help this process, for example:

* Rather than simply stepping back for a reflective pause we could employ some structured question frameworks. And we could ask others to help us in the process, acting as critical and challenging partners to help us learn.
* We can develop our own concepts, but we can also use, adapt and try out new ideas developed elsewhere. The 'theory' of innovation has emerged from many experiences codified into a rich body of knowledge and this is available to draw upon. We don't have to reinvent the wheel.
* Similarly, we don't have to make all the mistakes ourselves. We can learn from others' experiences

In the book we have tried to distil some of the accumulated learning about innovation and entrepreneurship, and in the following sections we'll look at some simple aids to structured and critical reflection to help think about how it could be managed better. We'll develop a

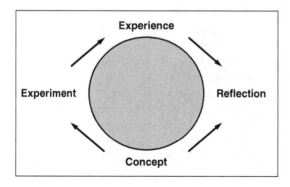

FIGURE 15.2   Simple model of the learning cycle

simple set of reflective questions for each part of the model around how well we are doing – and could we do it better?

Innovation Auditing

Searching for Innovation Opportunities

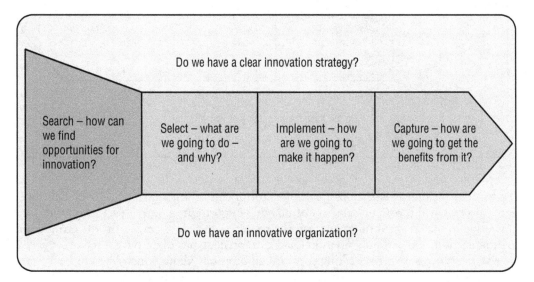

Do we have a clear innovation strategy?

Search – how can we find opportunities for innovation?

Select – what are we going to do – and why?

Implement – how are we going to make it happen?

Capture – how are we going to get the benefits from it?

Do we have an innovative organization?

Ideas, as we've seen, can come from anywhere. Some boffin in a lab may have a 'Eureka!' moment. Or someone talking with a customer may see a need which hasn't been met. A competitor may start offering a service we haven't got in our repertoire. A civil servant may change the rules of the particular game our business is playing

Activity based on this process – innovation fitness test – is available on the Innovation Portal at **www.innovation-portal.info**

and force us to rethink what we do. Or a newcomer from a different industry may spot a way to reframe the game and bring in a completely new way of looking at it – as we see every day on the Internet. And social entrepreneurship often arises from individuals looking at the world and seeing ways in which public services could be delivered better, disadvantaged groups could be enabled or resources more equitably distributed.

Wherever the ideas come from, the challenge for us is to make sure we pick them up and harness them to provide the fuel of the innovation process. Entrepreneurship may give us the drive, but without ideas the engine will be running on empty. So how could we organize and manage this search process? Needless to say, there isn't a standard recipe but, as we saw in Chapter 7, we need to spread the net widely and make sure we cover the spectrum from 'exploit – do what we do better' through to 'explore – do something different'.

Strategic Selection

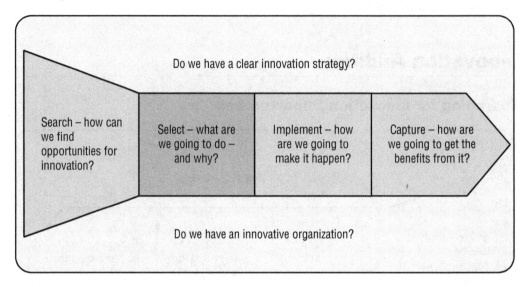

The trouble with ideas is that you can have too much of a good thing. A well-developed search process will throw up all sorts of possible opportunities, interesting ideas which are all waiting to take flight if only they had the resources to help them get off the ground. But no organization, and certainly no individual entrepreneur, has infinite resources, so the next stage in the process involves making some tough decisions about which ideas to back – and why. Inevitably, this is a risky process. We have to take decisions about ideas which are in their earliest stages and which could become the best thing since sliced bread, but which could equally crash into oblivion and take us down with them.

How do those responsible for judging ideas and selecting the best for further investment actually think? What are their concerns and how do they go about building an effective and balanced portfolio of ideas? The judges may be venture capitalists specializing in examining and taking risks with innovative ideas. But they could also be the management board reviewing the company's portfolio of new products or services or a department manager considering a new process to implement across his or her group. Or a hospital administrator looking for new ways to reduce costs or increase the quality of a service being delivered.

As with the previous stage, we have learnt quite a bit about the ways in which this task of selection can be organized and managed – a 'good practice' model which we can learn from and adapt. Smart organizations don't simply gamble. They make choices on the basis of some clear ground rules: does the idea have promise? Is it a good fit with where we are trying to go in our wider business strategy? Does it build on things that we know and can take advantage of – or if not, can we get hold of this knowledge to make it work? They make use of techniques and structures to help them in the selection process – and make sure these are flexible enough to help monitor and adapt projects over time as ideas move towards more concrete innovations. And if they aren't going as well as expected, because of unexpected developments on the technological or market front, they have mechanisms in place to stop the process and either go back to the drawing board or kill it altogether. (Chapter 10 described many of these approaches in more detail and there are a variety of tools to help on the Portal.)

Implementation: Making it Happen

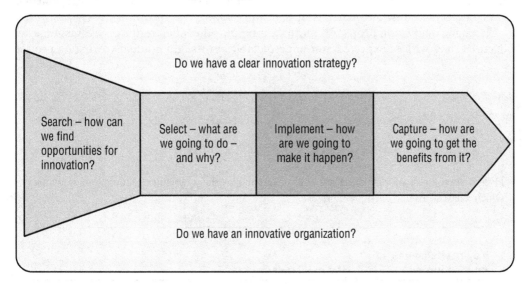

Having decided on which ideas to back, the organization has one small problem left: how to actually make them happen. Moving from a gleam in some entrepreneur's eye to a product or service people use and value, or a business process which employees buy into and work with, can be a somewhat difficult journey. It isn't usually a simple matter of project management, balancing resources against a budget of time and money – the big difference with innovation is that we don't know whether or not things will work until we start doing them. So it's a case of developing something against a background of uncertainty. The only way we reduce the uncertainty is by trying things out and learning, even if what we learn is that it isn't going to work after all.

We're also weaving together different strands of knowledge about the innovation – the 'technological' (will it work as an idea?) and the 'market' (is there a need for this idea and do we understand and meet that need?). So a key aspect of implementation is making sure the threads come together and intertwine successfully, which in practice means making sure the right people get to talk with each other at the right time and for long enough to make something happen.

Innovation is often described in terms of the metaphor of a journey – and this helps us particularly think about the implementation phase. What stages does our idea need to go through before it becomes a successful innovation as a product/service in the marketplace or a process in everyday use within the business? And what structures and techniques do smart entrepreneurs and firms use to help their innovation along this journey, and to check its progress? Chapter 10 explored this theme in detail and highlighted the kind of learning which experienced entrepreneurs and organizations bring into play when dealing with this challenge.

For example, it would be foolish to throw good money after bad, so most organizations make use of some kind of risk management as they implement innovation projects. By installing a series of 'gates' as the project moves from an initial outline idea to an expensive commitment of time and money it becomes possible to review, and if necessary redirect or even stop something which is going off the rails. And they employ a variety of project management structures to help balance flexibility, spread of different knowledge inputs and engagement of key stakeholders against the demands of time and budget.

Managing innovation projects is more than simply scheduling resources against time and budget. Dealing with unexpected and unpredictable events and gradually bringing projects

INNOVATION IN ACTION 15.2

What Makes for Success in Product/Service Innovation?

PDMA survey and source: these are some examples of the mechanisms, tools and structures which smart firms and entrepreneurs use.

Key needs/issues on the journey	Key mechanisms
Systematic process for progressing new products/services	Stage gate model Close monitoring and evaluation at each stage
Early involvement of all relevant functions	Bringing key perspectives into the process early enough to influence design and prepare for downstream problems Early detection of problems leads to less rework
Overlapping/parallel working	Concurrent or simultaneous engineering to aid faster development whilst retaining cross-functional involvement
Appropriate project management structures	Choice of structure (e.g. matrix/line/project/heavyweight project management) to suit conditions and task
Cross-functional team working	Involvement of different perspectives, use of team-building approaches to ensure effective team working and develop capabilities in flexible problem-solving
Advanced support tools	Use of tools (e.g. CAD, rapid prototyping, computer-supported cooperative work aids) to assist with quality and speed of development
Learning and continuous improvement	Carrying forward lessons learnt – via post-project audits, etc. Development of continuous improvement culture

into being requires high levels of flexibility and creativity, and in particular it involves integrating knowledge sets from across organization, functional and disciplinary boundaries. And we've learnt a lot about how to do this, for example through using cross-boundary teams, through various forms of parallel or concurrent working and through the use of simulation and other exploration technologies to anticipate downstream problems and reduce time and resource costs while enhancing innovation quality.

Capturing Value

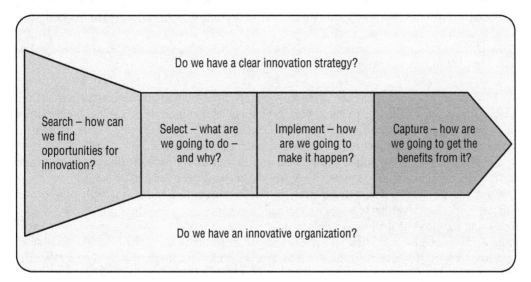

As we've seen in previous chapters, innovation is about creating value – and finding ways to capture that value. In particular, the discussion of business models in the last chapter gives us a framework for thinking hard about what value is being created for whom, and what has to be done to ensure that happens and that the benefits (money, learning, social change) are realized.

Innovation Strategy: Having a Clear Sense of Direction

Innovation doesn't take place in a vacuum. It's subject to a range of internal and external influences which shape what is possible and what actually emerges. In particular, it needs clear strategic leadership and direction, plus the commitment of resources to make this happen. Innovation is about taking risks, about going into new and sometimes completely unexplored spaces. We don't want to gamble or change things simply for their own sake or because the fancy takes us. And passion, drive and energy are critical entrepreneurial characteristics but they carry the risk that we may point them in the wrong direction. No organization has resources to waste in that scattergun fashion. Innovation needs a strategy. But equally, we need to have a degree of courage and leadership, steering the organization away from what everyone else is doing or what we've always done and into new spaces.

Again, we've learnt that successful entrepreneurs and innovating organizations use a range of structures, tools and techniques to help them create, articulate, communicate and deploy a clear strategy. For example, many organizations take time, often off-site and away from the day-to-day pressures of their 'normal' operations, to reflect and develop a shared strategic framework for innovation. Start-up entrepreneurs may not have this luxury, but they certainly need to 'look before they leap' and be sure that they have a coherent and clear strategic plan for their venture. Two key questions underpin this:

• Does the innovation we are considering help us reach the strategic goals (for growth, market share, profit margin – or changing the world in some way through creating social value, etc.) which we have set ourselves?
• Do we know enough about this to pull it off or, if not, do we have a clear idea of how we would get hold of and integrate such knowledge?

Much can be gained through taking a systematic approach to answering these questions. A typical approach could be to carry out some form of competitive analysis which looks at the positioning of the organization in terms of its environment and the key forces acting upon competition. Within this picture questions can then be asked about how a proposed innovation may help shift the competitive positioning favourably – by lowering or raising entry barriers, by introducing substitutes to rewrite the rules of the game, etc.

In carrying out such a systematic analysis, it is important to build on multiple perspectives. This can be done in a variety of ways, for example using tools for competitor and market analysis or looking for ways of deploying competencies – things the individual or organization knows about and is good at. It can build on explorations of the future or use techniques like 'technology road mapping' to help identify courses of action. It's important in all of this to remember that strategy is not an exact science: it's the process of building a shared framework which matters.

For the start-up entrepreneur the challenge will be to share his/her vision with others and get them excited and engaged with it. And unless people within an established organization understand and commit to the strategy it has developed, it will be hard for them to use it to frame their actions. The issue of strategy *deployment* – communicating and enabling people to use the framework – is essential if the organization is to avoid the risk of having 'know-how' but not 'know-why' in its innovation process.

Building an Innovative Organization

The key to innovation and entrepreneurship is, of course, people. And the simple challenge is how to enable them to deploy their creativity and share their knowledge to bring about change. For small start-ups the structures may be very loose and informal, and the sense of trust and cooperation high. But, as we saw earlier, being small has limits in terms of resources and so entrepreneurs here need to work hard at building and maintaining rich creative networks.

It's easy to find prescriptions for innovative organizations which highlight the need to eliminate stifling bureaucracy, unhelpful structures, brick walls blocking communication and other factors stopping good ideas getting through. But we must be careful not to fall into the chaos trap – not all innovation works in organic, loose, informal environments or 'skunk works' – and

TABLE 15.1 Components of the Innovative Organization

Component	Key features
Shared vision, leadership and the will to innovate	Clearly articulated and shared sense of purpose Stretching strategic intent 'Top management commitment'
Appropriate structure	Organization design which enables creativity, learning and interaction. Not always a loose 'skunk works' model; key issue is finding appropriate balance between 'organic' and 'mechanistic' options for particular contingencies
Key individuals	Promoters, champions, gatekeepers and other roles which energize or facilitate innovation
Effective team working	Appropriate use of teams (at local, cross-functional and inter-organizational level) to solve problems. Requires investment in team selection and building
Continuing and stretching individual development	Long-term commitment to education and training to ensure high levels of competence and the skills to learn effectively
Extensive communication	Within and between the organization and outside. Internally in three directions: up, down and sideways
High involvement in innovation	Participation in organization-wide continuous improvement activity
External focus	Internal and external customer orientation. Extensive networking
Creative climate	Positive approach to creative ideas, supported by relevant motivation systems
Learning organization	High levels of involvement within and outside the firm in proactive experimentation, finding and solving problems, communication and sharing of experiences and knowledge capture and dissemination

these types of organization can sometimes act against the interests of successful innovation. We need to determine *appropriate* organization, that is the most suitable organization given the operating contingencies. Too little order and structure may be as bad as too much.

Successful entrepreneurs and innovative organizations recognize this – and make use of a range of structures, tools and techniques to help them achieve this balance. Table 15.1 gives a list of key components in building an innovative organization.

Networking for Innovation

We've always known that innovation is not a solo act. Successful players work hard to build links across boundaries inside the organization and to the many external agencies who can play a part in the innovation process – suppliers, customers, sources of finance, skilled resources and of knowledge, etc. – twenty-first-century innovation is increasingly about 'open innovation', a multiplayer game where connections and the ability to find, form and deploy creative relationships is of the essence.

Making this happen requires skills in finding network partners, building relationships with them and finally linking their contributions with others so that the whole becomes greater than the sum of the parts.

The challenges include:

- how to manage something we don't own or control
- how to see system level effects, not narrow self-interests
- how to build trust and shared risk-taking without tying the process up in contractual red tape
- how to avoid 'free riders' and information 'spillovers'.

Learning to Manage Innovation

No individual or organization is born with the perfect set of capabilities to make innovation happen. Instead, they learn and develop these over time and through trial and error. In this chapter we've looked at a range of 'good practices' which are commonly found across very different entrepreneurial organizations, and some reflection questions to help us think about how well we are doing. But one last set of questions we should ask refers to whether we are good at learning itself – whether we take the time out, use challenging reflection, bring in new concepts and develop our own models for how we will manage innovation in the future. So we should finish with some reflection questions around this theme, and remember that a common characteristic shared by successful serial entrepreneurs and long-running businesses is that they do have an awareness of what it is they do and how they can use their insight to continue to succeed.

Tools to provide structured ways to enable learning – including post-project reviews and benchmarking – are available on the Innovation Portal at **www.innovation-portal.info**

Innovation Auditing in Practice

Learning isn't easy. Individuals and organizations are usually too busy getting on with building and running their ventures to find time to stop and think about how they could do things better. But assuming they did manage to get offline and reflect on how they could improve their innovation management, they would probably find some structured framework for thinking about the process helpful. We can use the idea of comparing against what we've learnt about good practice to develop simple audit frameworks which could be used for diagnosis. How well do we do things compared to what the 'good practice' is? How far would we agree with the kinds of statements we've listed in the chapter associated with good innovators? Where are our strengths? And where would we want to focus our efforts to improve the organization? This kind of audit and review process doesn't carry any prizes but it can help with making the organization more effective in the ways it deals with the innovation challenge. And that could lead to some pretty important outcomes: like survival or growth!

Case Studies of organizations viewed through the lens of this audit framework – 3M, Corning, Electroco, Kao – are available on the Innovation Portal at **www.innovation-portal.info**

INNOVATION IN ACTION 15.3

Measuring Innovation Performance

In reviewing innovative performance we can look at a number of possible measures and indicators:

- Measures of specific outputs of various kinds, e.g. patents and scientific papers as indicators of knowledge produced, or number of new products introduced (and percentage of sales and/ or profits derived from them) as indicators of product innovation success.
- Output measures of operational or process elements, such as customer satisfaction surveys to measure and track improvements in quality or flexibility.
- Output measures which can be compared across sectors or enterprises, e.g. cost of product, market share, quality performance, etc.
- Output measures of strategic success, where the overall business performance is improved in some way and where at least some of the benefit can be attributed directly or indirectly to innovation, e.g. growth in revenue or market share, improved profitability, higher value added.

We could also consider a number of more specific measures of the internal workings of the innovation process or particular elements within it. For example:

- number of new ideas (product/service/process) generated at start of innovation system
- failure rates – in the development process, in the marketplace
- number or percentage of overruns on development time and cost budgets
- customer satisfaction measures – was it what the customer wanted?
- time to market (average, compared with industry norms)
- development man-hours per completed innovation
- process innovation average lead time for introduction
- measures of continuous improvement – suggestions/employee, number of problem-solving teams, savings accruing per worker, cumulative savings, etc.

There is also scope for measuring some of the influential conditions supporting or inhibiting the process, for example the 'creative climate' of the organization or the extent to which strategy is clearly deployed and communicated. And there is value in considering inputs to the process, for example percentage of sales committed to R&D, investments in training and recruitment of skilled staff, etc.

There is no single framework for doing an innovation audit – and no 'right' answer at the end of the process. But using such frameworks can be helpful and we have included some in the website accompanying this book. There are audits which look in general terms, those which focus on capabilities to manage the more radical end of innovation and those which deal with sector differences like how to manage innovation in services. And there are those which focus on aspects of the organization, like how well it is able to engage its whole workforce in the innovation process. Audits can be targeted at the individual, for example on the Portal there is a framework for reflecting on 'how creative are you?'

There are also an increasing number of online audit resources available, and a growing consultancy industry built around providing this kind of 'mirror' on how well an organization is doing at innovation together with some advice on how it could do it better. But it's not the audits so much as using them in the *process* of questioning and developing innovation capability which matters. As the quality guru W. Edwards Deming pointed out, 'If you don't measure it you can't improve it!'

Tools allowing you to explore various aspects of innovation – e.g. discontinuous innovation, absorptive capacity, high involvement innovation and service innovation – are available on the Innovation Portal at **www.innovation-portal.info**

(Table 15.2 lists some of the options available)

Activities based around innovation auditing – including the innovation management project – are available on the Innovation Portal at **www.innovation-portal.info**

TABLE 15.2　Frameworks to Support Reflection on Key Areas of Innovation Management

Key questions and issues in managing innovation	Reflection and development aids available on website
How well do we manage innovation?	Innovation audit
How well do we manage service innovation?	Service innovation (SPOTS) framework
Start-up phase for new ventures	Entrepreneurs checklist
Do we engage our employees fully in innovation?	High involvement innovation audit
How well do we manage discontinuous innovation?	Discontinuous innovation audit
How widely do we search in an open innovation world?	Search strategies audit
Do we have a creative climate for innovation?	Creative climate review
Can we make the most of external knowledge for innovation?	Absorptive capacity review

Dynamic Capability and Changing Our Routines

As we've seen throughout this book the challenge of managing innovation is not simply one of building capability to carry out key tasks like searching, selecting or implementing. It is also about coping with a constantly changing environment where new routines will be needed – new ways of managing the innovation process. This concept of 'dynamic capability' becomes increasingly important as we move to some of the key frontier challenges in innovation, and in the next part of the book we'll look at the implications this has for the ways we operate and the new tricks we need to learn.

In particular, we'll look at:

- open innovation and the changing landscape for searching
- user innovation and the growing importance of active stakeholder involvement in innovation
- discontinuous innovation – learning to cope when the underlying rules of the game are changing
- developing and emerging economies and the way the innovation game is changing as these places become the central focus for economic and social growth
- social innovation – where the core motivation for change becomes improving well-being
- sustainability-led innovation – where the question of how we deal with the resource, energy and environmental challenges of living on the planet takes centre stage.

Case Study detailing an extensive innovation audit process that resulted in the identification of key new areas around which Coloplast intended to build its already-strong innovation capability is available on the Innovation Portal at **www.innovation-portal.info**

Summary

- Wherever innovation happens – big firm, small firm, start-up business, social enterprise – one thing is clear: successful innovation won't happen simply by wishing for it. This complex and risky process of transforming ideas into things which make a mark needs organizing and managing in strategic fashion.

- We know that this process is influenced along the way by several things which can help or hinder it. Is there clear strategic leadership and direction? How can we construct innovative organizations which allow creative ideas to come through, let people build on and share knowledge and feel motivated and rewarded for doing so? How can we harness the power of networks, making rich and extensive connections to deliver a stream of innovations?

- A wide range of structures, tools and techniques exist for helping us think about and manage these elements of the innovation process. The challenge is to adapt and use them in a particular context, essentially a learning process.

- Developing innovative capability needs to begin with an audit of where we are now – and there are many ways of asking and exploring the core questions:

  ○ Do we have a clear process for making innovation happen and effective enabling mechanisms to support it?
  ○ Do we have a clear sense of shared strategic purpose and do we use this to guide our innovative activities?
  ○ Do we have a supportive organization whose structures and systems enable people to be creative and share and build on each other's creative ideas?
  ○ Do we build and extend our networks for innovation into a rich open innovation system?

Further Resources

A wide range of books and online reviews of innovation now offer some form of audit framework, including the Pentathlon model from Cranfield University[2] and Bettina von Stamm's 'Innovation wave' model – see Dodgson, Salter and Gann,[3] Trott[4] and Von Stamm[5, 6] for other examples. Websites include www.innovationforgrowth.co.uk, www.stage-gate.eu/innovation-audit.asp, www.innovationexcellence.com and www.cambridgeaudits.com. AIM Practice (www.aimpractice.com) also has a variety of audit tools around innovation, and NESTA (www.nesta.org) has a number of reports linked to its major Innovation Index project.

References

1. Kolb, D. (1984) *Experiential Learning*. Englewood Cliffs, NJ: Prentice-Hall.

2. Goffin, K. and R. Mitchell (2010) *Innovation Management*, 2nd edn. London: Pearson.

3. Dodgson, M., A. Salter and D. Gann (2008) *The Management of Technological Innovation*, 2nd edn. Oxford: Oxford University Press.

4. Trott, P. (2011) *Innovation Management and New Product Development*, 5th edn. London: Prentice-Hall.

5. Von Stamm, B. (2003) *The Innovation Wave*. Chichester: John Wiley & Sons, Ltd.

6. Von Stamm, B. (2008) *Managing Innovation, Design and Creativity*, 2nd edn. Chichester: John Wiley & Sons, Ltd.

Deeper Dive explanations of innovation concepts and ideas are available on the Innovation Portal at **www.innovation-portal.info**

Quizzes to test yourself further are available online via the Innovation Portal at **www.innovation-portal.info**

Summary of online resources for Chapter 15 –
all material is available via the Innovation Portal at
www.innovation-portal.info

Cases

Media

Tools

Activities

Deeper Dive

Cases	Media	Tools	Activities	Deeper Dive
• 3M • Corning • Electroco • Kao • Coloplast	• Fabian Schlage	• Innovation fitness test • Post-project reviews • Benchmarking • Discontinuous innovation audit • Service innovation audit • High involvement innovation audit • Business model canvas • Start-up audit • Absorptive capacity audit	• Success and failure in innovation • Patterns of innovation • The way we do things around here • Innovation fitness test • Innovation management project	• Measuring innovation

PART II

THE INNOVATION FRONTIER

Chapter 16

Users as Innovators

LEARNING OBJECTIVES

After this chapter you should be able to:

* understand the role of users in the innovation process
* distinguish between different types of user and their contributions, including lead users, extreme users, co-development and crowdsourcing
* identify lead users through their defining characteristics.

Users Aren't Passive

Although 'need pull' represents a powerful trigger for innovation, it is easy to fall into the trap of thinking about the process as a serial one in which user needs are identified and then something is created to meet those needs. The assumption underpinning this is that users are passive recipients, but this is often not the case. Indeed, history suggests that users are sometimes ahead of the game: their ideas plus their frustrations with existing solutions lead to experiment and prototyping and create early versions of what eventually become mainstream innovations.

Eric von Hippel of Massachusetts Institute of Technology has made a lifelong study of this phenomenon and gives the example of the pickup truck – a long-time staple of the world automobile industry. This major category did not begin life on the drawing boards of Detroit but rather on the farms and homesteads of a wide range of users who wanted more than a family saloon. They adapted their cars by removing seats, welding new pieces on and cutting off the roof – in the process prototyping and developing the early model of the pickup. Only later did Detroit pick up on the idea and then begin the incremental innovation process to

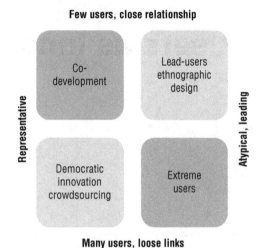

FIGURE 16.1 Types of user-innovation

refine and mass produce the vehicle.[1] A host of other examples support the view that user-led innovation matters, for example petroleum refining, medical devices, semiconductor equipment, scientific instruments and a wide range of sports goods and the Polaroid camera.

Importantly, active and interested users – 'lead users' – are often well ahead of the market in terms of innovation needs (Figure 16.1). In Mansfield's detailed studies of diffusion of a range of capital goods into major firms in the bituminous coal, iron, steel, brewing and railroad industries, he found that in 75% of the cases it took over 20 years for complete diffusion of these innovations to major firms.[2] As von Hippel points out, some users of these innovations could be found far in advance of the general market.[3]

Audio Clip of Tim Craft describing the birth of his company, Anaesthetic Medical Systems, and its underlying philosophy is available on the Innovation Portal at **www.innovation-portal.info**.

Video Clip of an interview with Eric von Hippel in which he describes lead-user methods and their application in the 3M company is available on the Innovation Portal at **www.innovation-portal.info**

One of the fields where this has played a major role is in medical devices where active users amongst medical professionals have provided a rich source of innovations for decades. Central to their role in the innovation process is that they are very early on the adoption curve for new ideas. They are concerned with getting solutions to particular needs and prepared to experiment and tolerate failure in their search for a better solution. One strategy, which we will explore later, around managing innovation is thus to identify and engage with such lead users to co-create innovative solutions. Tim Craft, a practising anaesthetist, developed a range of connectors and other equipment as a response to frustrations and concerns about the safety aspects of the equipment he was using in operating theatres.

User Involvement in Innovation – The Coloplast Example

One of the key lessons about successful innovation is the need to get close to the customer. At the limit (and as Eric Von Hippel and other innovation scholars have noted), the user can become a key part of the innovation process, feeding in ideas and improvements to help define and shape the innovation. The Danish medical devices company Coloplast was founded in 1954 on these principles when nurse Elise Sorensen developed the first self-adhering ostomy bag as a way of helping her sister, a stomach cancer patient. She took her idea to various plastics manufacturers, but none showed any interest at first. Eventually, one, Aage Louis-Hansen, discussed the concept with his wife, also a nurse, who saw the potential of such a device and persuaded her husband to give the product a chance. Hansen's company, Dansk Plastic Emballage, produced the world's first disposable ostomy bag in 1955. Sales exceeded expectations and in 1957, after having taken out a patent for the bag in several countries, the Coloplast company was established. Today, the company has subsidiaries in 20 countries and factories in five countries around the world, with specialist divisions dealing with incontinence care, wound care, skin care, mastectomy care, consumer products (specialist clothing etc.) as well as the original ostomy care division.

Keeping close to users in a field like this is crucial and Coloplast has developed novel ways of building in such insights by making use of panels of users, specialist nurses and other health care professionals located in different countries. This has the advantage of getting an informed perspective from those involved in post-operative care and treatment, who can articulate needs which may for the individual patient be difficult or embarrassing to express. By setting up panels in different countries the varying cultural attitudes and concerns could also be built into product design and development.

An example is the Coloplast Ostomy Forum (COF) board approach. The core objective within COF boards is to try to create a sense of partnership with key players, either as key customers or as key influencers. Selection is based on an assessment of their technical experience and competence but also on the degree to which they will act as opinion leaders and gatekeepers, for example by influencing colleagues, authorities, hospitals and patients. They are also a key link in the clinical trials process. Over the years Coloplast has become quite skilled in identifying relevant people who would be good COF board members, for example by tracking people who author clinical articles or who have a wide range of experience across different operation types. Their specific role is particularly to help with two elements in innovation:

- Identify, discuss and prioritize user needs.
- Evaluate product development projects from idea generation right through to international marketing.

Importantly, COF boards are seen as integrated with the company's product development system. They provide valuable market and technical information into the stage gate decision process.

(continued)

> This input is mainly associated with early stages around concept formulation (where the input is helpful in testing and refining perceptions about real user needs and fit with new concepts). There is also significant involvement around project development, where involvement is concerned with evaluating and responding to prototypes, suggesting detailed design improvements, design for usability, etc.

Case Study of Coloplast is available on the Innovation Portal at **www.innovation-portal.info**

Video Clips of interviews with Michael Bartl of Hyve and Catherina van Delden of Innosabi exploring crowdsourcing are available on the Innovation Portal at **www.innovation-portal.info**

Audio Clips of interviews with David Overton of the Ordnance Survey and David Simoes-Brown of 100% Open exploring issues of co-creating development ideas and 'open innovation' space are available on the Innovation Portal at **www.innovation-portal.info**

Such engagement may provide a powerful new resource for the 'front end' of innovation. One example is Goldcorp, a struggling mining company which threw open its geological data and asked for ideas about where it should prospect. Tapping into the combined insights of 1200 people from 50 countries helped it find 110 new sites, 80% of which produced gold. The business has grown from $100 million (£60 million) in 1999 to over $9 billion (£5.5 billion) today. Companies like Swarowski have recruited an army of new designers using 'crowdsourcing' approaches – and in the process have massively increased their design capacity. Organizations like the BBC, Lego and the Ordnance Survey are increasingly engaging communities of software developers, sharing source code and inviting them to 'use our stuff to build your stuff'.

The approach also opens up significant options in the area of social innovation, for example the crisis response tool 'Ushahidi' emerged out of the Kenyan post-election unrest and involves using crowdsourcing to create and update rich maps which can help direct resources and avoid problem areas. It has subsequently been used in the Brisbane floods in 2013, the Washington snow emergency in 2011 and the aftermath of the tsunami in Japan in the same year.

Lead Users

Lead users are critical to the development and adoption of complex products. As the name 'lead user' suggests, they demand new requirements ahead of the general market of other users, but are also positioned in the market to significantly benefit from the meeting of those requirements. Where potential users have high levels of sophistication, for example in business-to-business markets such as scientific instruments, capital equipment and IT systems, lead users

INNOVATION IN ACTION 16.2

Collective User Innovation

An increasingly important element in the innovation equation is 'co-creation': using the ideas, experience and insights of many people across a community to generate innovation. For example, *Encyclopædia Britannica* was founded in 1768 and currently has around 65 000 articles. Until 1999, it was available only in print version but, in response to a growing number of CD and online-based competitors (such as Microsoft's Encarta) it now has an online version. Encarta was launched in 1993 and offered many new additions to the *Britannica* model, through multimedia illustrations carried on a CD/DVD; like *Britannica*, it was available in a limited number of different languages.

In contrast, Wikipedia is a newcomer, launched in 2004 and available free on the Internet. It has become the dominant player in terms of online searches for information and is currently the sixth-most-visited site in the world. Its business model is fundamentally different: it is available free and is constructed through the shared contributions and updates offered by members of the public.

A criticism of Wikipedia is that this model means that inaccuracies are likely to appear, but although the risk remains there are self-correcting systems in place, which mean that if it is wrong it will be updated and corrected quickly. A study by the journal *Nature* in 2005 (December 15th) found it to be as accurate as *Encyclopaedia Britannica* yet the latter employs around 4000 expert reviewers and a rewrite (including corrections) takes around five years to complete.

Encarta closed at the end of 2009 but *Encyclopaedia Britannica* continues to compete in this knowledge market. After three hundred years of an expert-driven model it moved, in January 2009, to extend its model and invited users to edit content using a variant on the Wikipedia approach. Shortly after that (February 2010), it discovered an error in its coverage of a key event in Irish history which had gone uncorrected in all its previous editions and only emerged when users pointed it out!

can help to co-develop innovations, and are therefore often early adopters of such innovations. The initial research by Von Hippel suggests that lead users adopt an average of seven years before typical users, but the precise lead time will depend on a number of factors, including the technology's lifecycle. One empirical study identified a number of characteristics of lead users:[4]

- Recognize requirements early – are ahead of the market in identifying and planning for new requirements.
- Expect high level of benefits – owing to their market position and complementary assets.
- Develop their own innovations and applications – have sufficient sophistication to identify and capabilities to contribute to development of the innovation.
- Perceived to be pioneering and innovative – by themselves and their peer group.

This has two important implications. First, those seeking to develop innovative complex products and services should identify potential lead users with such characteristics to contribute to the co-development and early adoption of the innovation. Second, that lead users, as early adopters, can provide insights to forecasting the diffusion of innovations. For example, a study of 55 development projects in telecommunications computer infrastructure found that the importance of customer inputs increased with technological newness and, moreover, the relationship shifted from customer surveys and focus groups to co-development because 'conventional marketing techniques proved to be of limited utility were often ignored, and in hindsight were sometimes strikingly inaccurate'.[5]

For example, IDEO, a global design and development consultancy, finds conventional market research methods insufficient and sometimes misleading for new products and services, and instead favours the use of direct observation and prototyping.

INNOVATION IN ACTION 16.3

Learning from Users at IDEO

IDEO is one of the most successful design consultancies in the world; based in Palo Alto, California and London, it helps large consumer and industrial companies worldwide design and develop innovative new products and services. Behind its rather typical Californian wackiness lies a tried-and-tested process for successful design and development:

- Understand the market, client and technology.
- Observe users and potential users in real-life situations.
- Visualize new concepts and the customers who may use them, using prototyping, models and simulations.
- Evaluate and refine the prototypes in a series of quick iterations.
- Implement the new concept for commercialization.

The first critical step is achieved through close observation of potential users in context. As Tom Kelly of IDEO argues, 'We're not big fans of focus groups. We don't much care for traditional market research either. We go to the source. Not the "experts" inside a (client) company, but the actual people who use the product or something similar to what we're hoping to create . . . we believe you have to go beyond putting yourself in your customers' shoes. Indeed we believe it's not even enough to ask people what they think about a product or idea . . . customers may lack the vocabulary or the palate to explain what's wrong, and especially what's missing.'

The next step is to develop prototypes to help evaluate and refine the ideas captured from users. 'An iterative approach to problems is one of the foundations of our culture of prototyping . . . you can prototype just about anything – a new product or service, or a special promotion. What counts is moving the ball forward, achieving some part of your goal.'

Source: Derived from Kelly, T. (2002) *The Art of Innovation: Lessons in Creativity from IDEO,* New York: HarperCollinsBusiness.

Extreme Users

An important variant which picks up on both the lead user and the fringe needs concepts lies in the idea of extreme environments as sources of innovation. The argument here is that the users in the toughest environments may have needs which by definition are at the edge – so any innovative solution which meets those needs has possible applications back into the mainstream. An example would be antilock braking systems (ABS) which are now a commonplace feature of cars but which began life as a special add-on for premium high-performance cars. The origins of this innovation came from a more extreme case, though – the need to stop aircraft safely under difficult conditions where traditional braking could lead to skidding or other loss of control. ABS was developed for this extreme environment and then migrated across to the (comparatively) easier world of automobiles.[6]

Looking for extreme environments or users can be a powerful source of stretch in terms of innovation – meeting challenges which can then provide new opportunity space. As Roy Rothwell puts it in the title of a famous paper, 'tough customers mean good designs'.[7] For example, stealth technology arose out of a very specific and extreme need for creating an invisible aeroplane – essentially something which did not have a radar signature. It provided a powerful pull for some radical innovation which challenged fundamental assumptions about aircraft design, materials, power sources, etc. and opened up a wide frontier for changes in aerospace and related fields.[8] The 'bottom of the pyramid' concept mentioned earlier also offers some powerful extreme environments in which very different patterns of innovation are emerging.

For example, in the Philippines there is little in the way of a formal banking system for the majority of people – and this has led to users creating very different applications for their mobile phones where pay-as-you-go credits are transferred between people and used as currency for various goods and services. In Kenya it is used to increase security: if a traveller wishes to move between cities he or she will not take money but instead forward it via mobile phone in the form of credits which can then be collected from the phone recipient at the other end. This is only one of hundreds of new applications being developed in extreme conditions and by under-served users – and represents a powerful laboratory for new concepts which companies, like Nokia and Vodafone, are working closely to explore.[9] The potential exists to use this kind of extreme environment as a laboratory to test and develop concepts for wider application, for example Citicorp has been experimenting with a design of ATM based on biometrics for use with the illiterate population in rural India. The pilot involves some 50 000 people, but as a spokesman for the company explained, 'We see this as having the potential for global application.'

Video Clips of interviews with Girish Prabhu of Shristi Labs, a company specializing in such solutions, and Suzana Moreira of Mowoza, a social enterprise working in this space in southern Africa, are available on the Innovation Portal at **www.innovation-portal.info**

Case Study of Jugaad Innovation in the area of health care is available on the Innovation Portal at **www.innovation-portal.info**

INNOVATION IN ACTION 16.4

Jugaad Innovation

In a recent book Navi Radjou, Jaideep Prabhu and Simone Ahuja explore an approach to innovation which is rooted in emerging economies like India, China and Latin America – but which draws on some long-established principles. Through a variety of case studies they suggest that crisis conditions often trigger new approaches to innovation, and that the pressure to be frugal and flexible often leads to novel and sometimes breakthrough solutions. The phrase 'scarcity is the mother of invention' might be applied to examples such as the low technology design for a fridge which keeps food and liquid cool yet is based on a simple ceramic pot – the 'mitticool'. Whilst this may seem a low-tech solution the problem in India is that around 500m people have to live with an unreliable electricity supply which means that conventional refrigerators are unusable. The simple device has been so successful it is now mass produced and sold worldwide providing employment for the village in which the idea originated.

'Jugaad' is a Hindi word which roughly translates as 'an innovative fix, an improvised solution born from ingenuity and cleverness'. Such an approach characterizes entrepreneurship – and examples of such innovation can be found throughout history. But the authors argue that the very different conditions across much of the emerging world are creating opportunities for jugaad innovators finding solutions to meet the needs of a large population for an increasingly wide range of good and services. In the process they are marrying very different needs with an increasingly wide range of networked technological options – for example, evolving new forms of banking based on mobile phones or deploying telemedicine to help deal with the problems of distance and skills shortage in healthcare.

Of particular significance is the potential for such solutions to then find their way back to the industrialized world as simpler, ingenious solutions which challenge existing high technology approaches. The potential for such reverse innovation to act as a disruptive force is significant.

Source: Radjou, N., J. Prabhu, and S. Ahuja (2012) *Jugaad innovation: Think frugal, be flexible, generate breathrough innovation.* San Francisco: Jossey Bass. Reproduced by permission of John Wiley & Sons, Inc.

Co-development

The potential for users, either as individuals or as groups, to become involved in the design and production of products has clearly been recognized for some time. However, these conceptions of user–supplier innovation all tend to depict a relationship in which suppliers are able, in some way or another, to harness the experience or ideas of users and apply them to their own product development efforts. Many argue that we are seeing a dramatic shift towards more open, democratized, forms of innovation that are driven by networks of individual users, not firms.[10] Users are now visibly active within all stages of the innovation process, from concept generation through development to diffusion. Users may now be actively engaged with firms in the co-development of products and services and the innovation agenda may no longer be entirely controlled by firms.

In innovation studies the term 'user' generally takes a supplier-centric perspective and in this context the 'user' (e.g. lead user, final user, user innovation, learning by using) tends to be at the level of the firm. Users tend to be characterized as consumers whose needs must be understood, as 'tough customers' who make exacting demands, or as 'lead users' who may modify or develop existing products in response to their exacting and non-standard needs, potentially foreshadowing future demand. It is also understood that users may be drawn into firms' product development processes by developing and distributing supplier-designed 'toolkits'.[11]

Users may be drawn into the linear model of innovation in this way, but some forms of user activity represent the emergence of a parallel system of innovation that does not share the same goals, drivers and boundaries of mainstream commercial activity. Users are seen as having an active role in seeking to shape or reshape their relationship with innovation, beyond the prescribed application or use, or developing an agenda that may conflict with the producer. In this way the boundary between producers and users becomes less distinct, with some users able to develop and extend technologies or use them in entirely novel and unexpected ways. Innovation can become far more open and democratized. Such lack of compliance by users with producers and promoters of innovations need not be viewed as a deviant activity, but can become more central to the processes of innovation and diffusion. This has potentially significant implications for market relationships, business models and intellectual property.

> Case Study of Nokia INdT, which has set up a 'Living Lab' to identify and meet the needs of rural populations in the Amazonas region, is available on the Innovation Portal at **www.innovation-portal.info**

Democratic Innovation and Crowdsourcing

In 2006, journalist Jeff Howe coined the term 'crowdsourcing' in his book *The Power of Crowds*. Crowdsourcing is where an organization makes an open call to a large network to provide some voluntary input or perform some function. The core requirements are that the call is open and that the network is sufficiently large, the 'crowd'. However, the potential inputs and functions of crowdsourcing are diverse, ranging from competitions for individual ideas through to collaborative peer-production of innovation.

Crowdsourcing can be implemented in many ways, but is typically enabled by ICT. Two common, but contrasting, approaches are peer communities and competitions and events.

Peer or User Communities

Within some communities, users will freely share innovations with peers, termed 'free revealing', for example online communities for open-source software, music hobbyists, sports equipment and professional networks. Participation is driven mostly by intrinsic motivations, such as the pleasure of being able to help others or to improve or develop better products, but also by peer recognition and community status. The elements valued are social ties and opportunities to learn new things rather than concrete awards or esteem.[12] Such knowledge sharing and innovation tends to be more collective and collaborative than idea competitions.

Sometimes, user-led innovation involves a community which creates and uses innovative solutions on a continuing basis. Good examples of this include the Linux community around operating systems or the Apache server community around Web server development applications, where communities have grown up and the resulting range of applications is constantly growing – a state which has been called 'perpetual beta', referring to the old idea of testing new software modules across a community to get feedback and development ideas.[13] A growing range of Internet-based applications makes use of communities, for example Mozilla and its Firefox and other products, Propellerhead and other music software communities and the emergent group around Apple's i-platform devices like the iPhone.[14]

Increasing interest is being shown in such crowdsourcing approaches to co-creating innovations – and to finding new ways of creating and working with such communities. The principle extends beyond software and virtual applications, for example Lego makes extensive use of communities of developers in its Lego Factory and other online activities linked to its manufactured products.[15] Adidas has taken the model and developed its 'mi Adidas' concept, where users are encouraged to co-create their own shoes using a combination of website (where designs can be explored and uploaded) and in-store mini-factories where user-created and customized ideas can then be produced.

Case Studies of Adidas and Lego exploring these ideas are available on the Innovation Portal at **www.innovation-portal.info**

Competitions

In a competition, a problem or challenge is set, and potential solutions or ideas are invited. Rewards range from peer or public recognition and community status, but more commonly feature some extrinsic motivation such as free products or cash prizes, for example Dell's crowdsourcing platform Idea Storm, which received more than 15 000 ideas, of which over 400 have been implemented. Contributions and rewards tend to be more individual and competitive than in peer or user communities.

Case Study detailing some of Threadless's work in this area is available on the Innovation Portal at **www.innovation-portal.info**

In similar fashion Facebook chose to engage its users in helping to translate the site into multiple languages rather than commission an expert translation service. Its motive was to try to compete with MySpace, which in 2007 was the market leader, available in five languages. The Facebook 'crowdsource' project began in December 2007 and invited users to help translate around 30 000 key phrases from the site. Eight thousand volunteer developers registered within two months and within three weeks the site was available in Spanish, with pilot versions in French and German also online. Within one year Facebook was available in over 100 languages and dialects – and like Wikipedia it continues to benefit from continuous updating and correction via its user community.

Another important feature of crowdsourcing across user communities is the potential for dealing with the 'long tail' problem, that is how to meet the needs of a small number of people for a particular innovation? By mobilizing user communities around these needs it is possible to share experience and co-create innovation.

Case Study exploring the use of crowdsourcing to improve health innovation – opening up health care innovation – is available on the Innovation Portal at **www.innovation-portal.info**

Summary

- User-innovation is much more than simply good market research or listening to customers.

- Users can contribute to all phases of the innovation process, acting as sources, designers, developers, testers and even the main beneficiaries of innovation.

- Lead users are by definition atypical, but anticipate the needs of the majority, and recognize requirements early, expect high level of benefits and have sufficient sophistication to identify and capabilities to contribute to development of the innovation.

- Crowdsourcing and democratic approaches to innovation began in Internet applications but have spread to other fields such as mass-customization of products, peer-to-peer banking and innovation for developing economies.

Further Resources

For user-innovation, the classic text is Eric von Hippel's *The Sources of Innovation* (Oxford University Press, 1995) and his website (http://web.mit.edu/evhippel/). For more recent and broader reviews see Steve Flowers and Flis Henwood *Perspectives on User Innovation* (Imperial College Press, 2010) and the 2008 special issue on user innovation (*International Journal of Innovation Management*, **12** (3)). Frank Piller, Professor at Aachen University in Germany, has a rich website around the theme of mass customization with extensive case examples and other resources (www.mass-customization.de/); the original work on the topic is covered in Joseph Pine's book *Mass Customisation: The new frontier in business competition* (Harvard University Press, 1993). For crowdsourcing, a good place to begin is the pioneer piece by James Surowiecki, *The Wisdom of Crowds: Why the many are smarter than the few* (Abacus, 2005), and for a more recent overview, see *Crowdsourcing*, by Daren C. Brabham (MIT Press, 2013).

Particular discussion of fringe markets and unmet or poorly met needs as a source of innovation is covered by Clay Christensen *Seeing What's Next* (Harvard Business School Press, 2007) and Ulnwick *What Customers Want: Using outcome-driven innovation to create breakthrough products and services* (McGraw-Hill, 2005). The 'bottom of the pyramid' and extreme user potential is explored in Prahalad's work *The Fortune at the Bottom of the Pyramid* (Wharton School Publishing, 2006), and the idea of 'jugaad innovation' in *Jugaad Innovation: Think frugal, be flexible, generate breakthrough innovation*, by Kevin Roberts, Navi Radjou, Jaideep Prabhu and Simone Ahuja (Jossey-Bass, 2012). The website Next Billion (www.nextbillion.net) provides a wide range of resources and information about 'bottom of the pyramid' and extreme user activity including videos and case studies.

References

1. Von Hippel, E. (1988) *The Sources of Innovation*. Cambridge, MA: MIT Press.

2. Mansfield, E. (1968) *Industrial Research and Technological Innovation: An econometric analysis*. New York: Norton.

3. Von Hippel, E. (1986) Lead users: A source of novel product concepts, *Management Science*, **32** (7): 791–805.

4. Morrison, P., J. Roberts and D. Midgley (2004) The nature of lead users and measurement of leading edge status, *Research Policy*, **33**: 351–362.

5. Callahan, J. and E. Lasry (2004) The importance of customer input in the development of very new products, *R&D Management*, **34** (2): 107–117.

6. Von Hippel, E. (2005) *The Democratization of Innovation*. Cambridge, MA: MIT Press.

7. Rothwell, R. and P. Gardiner (1983) Tough customers, good design, *Design Studies*, **4** (3): 161–169.

8. Rich, B. and L. Janos (1994) *Skunk Works*. London: Warner Books.

9. Corbett, S. (2008) Can the cellphone help end global poverty? *New York Times*, 13 April, http://www.nytimes.com/2008/04/13/magazine/13anthropology-t.html?pagewanted=all&_r=0.

10. Flowers, S. and F. Henwood (2010) *Perspectives on User Innovation*, Imperial College Press; (2008) Special issue on user innovation, *International Journal of Innovation Management*, **12** (3): v–x.

11. Flowers, S. and F. Henwood (2010) *Perspectives on User Innovation*, Imperial College Press; (2008) Special issue on user innovation, *International Journal of Innovation Management*, **12** (3): v–x.

12. Kosonen, M., C. Gan, H. Olander and K. Blomqvist (2013) My idea is our idea! Supporting user-driven innovation activities in crowdsourcing communities, *International Journal of Innovation Management*, **17** (3), DOI 1340010; Afuah, A. and C. L. Tucci (2012) Crowdsourcing as a solution to distant search, *Academy of Management Review*, **37** (3): 355–375.

13. Von Hippel, E. (2005) *The Democratization of Innovation*. Cambridge, MA: MIT Press.

14. Piller, F. (2006) *Mass Customization: Ein wettbewerbsstrategisches Konzept im Informationszeitalter*, 4th edn. Frankfurt: Gabler Verlag.

15. Moser, K. and F. Piller (2006) Special issue on mass customisation case studies: Cases from the international mass customisation case collection. *International Journal of Mass Customisation*, **1** (4): 403–409.

Deeper Dive explanations of innovation concepts and ideas are available on the Innovation Portal at **www.innovation-portal.info**

Quizzes to test yourself further are available online via the Innovation Portal at **www.innovation-portal.info**

Summary of online resources for Chapter 16 –
all material is available via the Innovation Portal at
www.innovation-portal.info

Cases	**Media**	**Tools**	**Activities**	**Deeper Dive**
• Coloplast • Jugaad innovation • Instituto Nokia de Tecnologia (INdT) • 3M: Lead User Methods • Adidas • Lego • Threadless • Opening up health care innovation	• Tim Craft, Anaesthetic Medical Systems • Michael Bartl, Hyve • Catherina van Delden, Innosabi • Girish Prabhu, Shristi Labs • David Overton, Ordnance Survey • Suzana Moreira, moWoza • David Simoes-Brown, 100% Open • Eric von Hippel	• Conjoint analysis • Guide to building and running learning networks • Kano Method	• Partner Search • Acquiring Technological Knowledge	• Innovation Competitions • Crowd-sourcing

Chapter 17

Exploiting Open Innovation and Strategic Alliances

LEARNING OBJECTIVES

After this chapter you should be able to:

- understand what open innovation is, and the range of strategies and mechanisms available to apply it in practice

- assess the advantages and limitations of different strategies, such as outsourcing, licensing, joint ventures and strategic alliances

- identify the factors which influence the motives, outcomes and success of open innovation and strategic alliances.

Open Innovation

Creating and combining different knowledge sets has always been the name of the game both inside and outside the firm. But there has been a dramatic acceleration in recent years led by major firms like Procter and Gamble, GSK, 3M, Siemens and GE towards what has been termed 'open innovation'. The idea behind this is that even large-scale R&D in a closed system like an individual firm isn't going to be enough in the twenty-first-century environment.[1]

Knowledge production is taking place at an exponential rate. The OECD countries' annual spend approached \$1 trillion (£600 billion) on R&D in the public and private sectors by the end of the first decade of this century – a figure which is probably an underestimate, since it ignores the considerable amount of 'research' which is not captured in official statistics.[2] How can any single organization keep up with, or even keep tabs on, such a sea

---

INNOVATION IN ACTION 17.1

Chesbrough's Principles of Open Innovation

- Not all the smart people work for you
- External ideas can help create value, but it takes internal R&D to claim a portion of that value for you
- It is better to build a better business model than to get to market first
- If you make the best use of internal and external ideas, you will win
- Not only should you profit from others' use of your intellectual property, you should also buy others' IP whenever it advances your own business model
- You should expand R&D's role to include not only knowledge generation, but knowledge brokering as well

Source: H. Chesbrough (2003) *Open innovation.* Boston: Harvard Business School Press.

---

of knowledge? And this is happening in widely distributed fashion: R&D is no longer the province of the advanced industrial nations like the United States, Germany or Japan but is increasing most rapidly in the newly growing economies like India and China. In this kind of context, it's going to be impossible to pick up on every development, and even smart firms are going to miss a trick or two.

The case of Procter and Gamble provides a good example of this shift in approach. In the late 1990s, there were concerns about its traditional inward-focused approach to innovation. While it worked, there were worries – not least concerning the rapidly rising costs of carrying out R&D. Additionally, there were many instances of innovations which it may have made but which it passed on – only to find someone else doing so and succeeding. As CEO Alan Lafley explained: 'Our R&D productivity had levelled off, and our innovation success rate—the percentage of new products that met financial objectives—had stagnated at about 35 percent. Squeezed by nimble competitors, flattening sales, lacklustre new launches, and a quarterly earnings miss, we lost more than half our market cap when our stock slid from $118 to $52 (£72–£32) a share. Talk about a wake-up call.'[3]

P&G recognized that much important innovation was being carried out in small entrepreneurial firms, or by individuals, or in university labs and that other major players like IBM, Cisco, Eli Lilly and Microsoft were beginning to open up their innovation systems.

Video Clip of an interview with Roy Sandbach, a Research Fellow within Procter and Gamble, exploring how networking on the inside of a large corporation can enable innovation is available on the Innovation Portal at **www.innovation-portal.info**

As a result it moved to what it has called 'connect and develop' – an innovation process based on the principles of 'open innovation'.

Lafley's original stretch goal was to get 50% of innovations coming from outside the company; by 2006, more than 35% of new products had elements

Connect and Develop at Procter and Gamble

P&G's successes with 'connect and develop' owe much to its mobilizing rich linkages between people who know things within their giant global operations. Amongst its successes in internal networking was the Crest Whitestrips product – essentially linking oral care experts with researchers working on film technology and others in the bleach and household cleaning groups. Another is Olay Daily Facials, which linked the surface active agents expertise in skin care with people from the tissue and towel areas and from the fabric property enhancing skills developed in 'Bounce', a fabric-softening product.

Making it happen as part of daily life rather than as a special initiative is a big challenge. P&G uses multiple methods, including extensive networking via an intranet site called 'Ask me', which links 10 000 technical people across the globe. It acts as a signposting and Web market for ideas and problems across the company. It also operates 21 'communities of practice' built around key areas of expertise such as polymer chemists, biological scientists, people involved with fragrances. And it operates a global-technology council, which is made up of representatives of all of P&G's business units.

which originated from outside, compared with 15% in 2000. Over 100 new products in the next two years came from outside the firm, meaning that, by 2008, 45% of innovations in the new product pipeline had key elements which were discovered or developed externally. The company estimates that R&D productivity has increased by nearly 60% and its innovation success rate has more than doubled. One consequence is that it increased innovation while *reducing* its R&D spend, from 4.8% of turnover in 2000 to 3.4% in 2008. In 2012, R&D spend had been reduced to 2.4% of sales.

Case Studies of Procter and Gamble and other examples of open innovation – open collective innovation – are available on the Innovation Portal at **www.innovation-portal.info**

Central to the model is the concept of mobilizing innovation networks. As chief technology officer Gilbert Cloyd explained: 'It has changed how we define the organization . . . We have 9,000 people on our R&D staff and up to 1.5 million researchers working through our external networks. The line between the two is hard to draw . . . We're . . . putting a lot more attention on what we call 360-degree innovation.' But this is not simply a matter of outsourcing what used to happen internally. As Vice President Larry Huston commented: 'People mistake this for outsourcing, which it most definitely is not . . . Outsourcing is when I hire someone to perform a service and they do it and that's the end of the relationship. That's not much different from the way employment has worked throughout the ages. We're talking about bringing people in from outside and involving them in this broadly creative, collaborative process. That's a whole new paradigm.'

Enabling external networking involves a number of mechanisms. One is a group of 80 'technology entrepreneurs' whose task is to roam the globe and find and make interesting connections. They visit conferences and exhibitions, talk with suppliers and visit universities – essentially a no-holds-barred approach to searching for new possible connections.

They also make extensive use of the Internet. An example is their involvement as founder members of a site called InnoCentive (www.innocentive.com) originally set up by the pharmaceutical giant Eli Lilly in 2001. This is essentially a Web-based marketplace where problem owners can link up with problem solvers – and it currently has around 90 000 solvers available around the world. The business model is simple: companies like P&G, Boeing and DuPont post their problems on the site and if any of the solvers can help they pay for the idea. Importantly, the solvers are a very wide mix, from corporate and university lab staff through to lone inventors, retired scientists and engineers and professional design houses. Jill Panetta, InnoCentive's chief scientific officer, says more than 30% of the problems posted on the site have been cracked, 'which is 30 percent more than would have been solved using a traditional, in-house approach'.

Other mechanisms include a website called YourEncore, which allows companies to find and hire retired scientists for one-off assignments. NineSigma is an online marketplace for innovations, matching seeker companies with solvers in a marketplace similar to InnoCentive. As Gilbert Cloyd commented: 'NineSigma can link us to solutions that are more cost efficient, give us early access to potentially disruptive technologies, and facilitate valuable collaborations much faster than we imagined.' And yet2.com looks for new technologies and markets across a broad frontier, involving around 40% of the world's major R&D players in its network.

The challenge in open innovation is less about understanding the concept than in developing mechanisms which can enable its operation in practice. Approaches like Procter and Gamble's 'Connect and develop' provide powerful templates, but these are only relevant for certain kinds of organization. In other areas new models are being experimented with. For many this involves the construction of different kinds of shared platforms on which different partners can collaborate to create new products and services. The United Kingdom's public sector mapping organization, the Ordnance Survey, has begun opening up its approach to sharing geographical information to a wide variety of partners and has extended an invitation to co-create, similar to the BBC's – in part as it recognizes the huge changes in its sector with the entry of players like Google.

Video Clip of an interview with David Overton describing the approach of the Ordnance Survey is available on the Innovation Portal at www.innovation-portal.info

Others have gone further down the road towards creating open-source communities in which co-creation amongst different stakeholders takes place. Google's support for the Android platform is a good example: the expectation is that the collective innovation across such a space allows for the rapid acceleration and diffusion of innovation.

The logic of open innovation is that organizations need to open up their innovation processes, searching widely outside their boundaries and working towards managing a rich set of network connections and relationships right across the board.[4] Their challenge becomes one of improving the knowledge *flows* in and out of the organization, trading in knowledge as much as goods and services. To assist in this process a new service sector of organizations offering various kinds of brokering and bridging activity has begun to emerge. Examples include mainstream design houses like IDEO and ?Whatif!, which help to link clients with new ideas and connections on the technology and market side, technology brokers aiming at match-making between different needs and means (both Web-enabled and on a face-to-face basis) and intellectual property transfer agents, like the Innovation Exchange, which seek to identify, value and exploit internal IP which may be underutilized.

Video Clips of interviews with Michael Bartl of Hyve, David Simoes-Brown of 100% Open and Richard Philpott of The Innovation Exchange, all of whom are working in this new space, are available on the Innovation Portal at **www.innovation-portal.info**

Benefits and Limits of Open Innovation

Open innovation in often seen only as a way of searching and identifying external sources of innovation. However, open innovation can also be applied to the later stages of the innovation process, including development and commercialization. The open innovation model emphasizes that firms should acquire valuable resources from external firms and share internal resources for new product/service development, but the question of when and how a firm sources external knowledge and shares internal knowledge is less clear. The concept of open innovation is currently very popular in innovation management research and practice, but can be criticized for being too vague and prescriptive.

The original idea of open innovation was that firms should (also) exploit external sources and resources to innovate, a notion that is difficult to contest, but this is not a new idea, simply a repackaging of existing research and practice. However, wider dissemination of the concept shows that it is difficult to research and implement, to the point it has now become all things to all people, lacking explanatory or predictive power. There have been numerous studies of open innovation, but still the empirical evidence on the utility of open innovation is limited and practical prescriptions overly general. Research ranges from individual case studies, which are difficult to generalize, to simple survey-based counts of external sources and partners, which reveal little about the conditions, mechanisms or limitations of open innovation.

However, despite the large volume of empirical work, many of the prescriptions being proposed are fairly general, rather than specific to particular contexts and contingencies. But research shows that the open or closed nature of innovation is historically contingent and does not entail a simple shift from closed to open, as is often suggested in the literature. Patterns of innovation differ fundamentally – by sector, firm and strategy – and so we need to examine the mechanisms that help to generate successful open innovation.

Different Models of Open Innovation

There are many approaches to open innovation, depending on the number and type of sources and partners with which the company collaborates, and phases of the innovation process that the company opens to external contributions. Having a totally open strategy for innovation is rarely the best option, rather different degrees and ways of openness can be pursued successfully, including adopting a totally closed approach.[5] For example, some firms will passively respond to external opportunities when these occur, whereas others will proactively seek out such opportunities, a so-called prospector strategy.[6]

INNOVATION IN ACTION 17.3

Models for Open Innovation

A number of models are emerging around enabling open innovation, for example Nambisan and Sawhney identify four.[7] The 'orchestra' model is typified by a firm like Boeing, which has created an active global network around the 787 Dreamliner with suppliers as both partners and investors and moving from 'build to print' to 'design and build to performance'. In this mode they retain considerable autonomy around their specialist tasks while Boeing retains the final integrating and decision-making – analogous to professional musicians in an orchestra working under a conductor.

By contrast the 'creative bazaar' model involves more of a crowdsourcing approach in which a major firm goes shopping for innovation inputs – and then integrates and develops them further. Examples here would include aspects of the 'Innocentive.com' approach being used by P&G, Eli Lilly and others, or the Dial Corporation in the United States which launched a 'Partners in innovation' website where inventors could submit ideas. BMW's Virtual Innovation Agency operates a similar model.

A third model is what they term 'Jam central', which involves creating a central vision and then mobilizing a wide variety of players to contribute towards reaching it. It is the kind of approach found in many pre-competitive alliances and consortia where difficult technological or market challenges are used – such as the 5th Generation Computer project in Japan – to focus efforts of many different organizations. Once the challenges are met, the process shifts to an exploitation mode, for example in the 5th Generation programme the pre-competitive efforts by researchers from all the major electronics and IT firms led to generation of over 1000 patents, which were then shared out amongst the players and exploited in 'traditional' competitive fashion. Philips deploys a similar model via its InnoHub, which selects a team from internal and external businesses and staff and covering technology, marketing and other elements. It deliberately encourages fusion of people with varied expertise in the hope that this will enhance the chances of 'breakthrough' thinking.

Their fourth model is called 'Mod Station', drawing on a term from the personal computer industry which allows users to make modifications to games and other soft- and hardware. This is typified by many open-source projects, such as Sun Microsystems' OpenSPARC, Google's Android developer platform (and before that Nokia's release of the Symbian operating system), which open up to the developer community in an attempt to establish an open platform for creating mobile applications. It reflects models used by the BBC, by Lego and many other organizations trying to mobilize external communities and amplify their own research efforts while retaining an ability to exploit the new and growing space.

Other models which may be added include NASA's 'infusion' approach in which a major public agency uses its Innovative Partnerships Programme (IPP) to co-develop key technologies, such as robotics. The model is essentially one of drawing in partners who work alongside NASA scientists – a process of 'infusion' in which ideas developed by NASA or by one or more of the partners are worked on. There is particular emphasis on spreading the net widely and seeking partnerships with 'unusual suspects': companies, university departments and others which may not immediately recognize that they have something of value to offer.[8]

Context and Contingencies

Open innovation strategies assist companies in navigating through turbulent times as they facilitate the acquisition of new and relevant information on technologies and markets and facilitate the integration of this knowledge into the innovation process. A closer look at the different contributions from various types of external sources reveals that customers are central when market dynamics are high, suppliers are important in technologically challenging environments and the inclusion from companies of other industries is effective – irrespective of the setting.[9]

Strategy is not limited to the decision of whether to open up a project to a wide range of different types of external partners (the breadth dimension), but it is equally important to consider the depth of the relations with different types of external partners (the depth dimension) and the balance between the development of new and long-standing relations with these external partners (the ambidexterity dimension).[10] For example, higher levels of project novelty are associated with a higher intensity of interaction between actors and the use of more rich mechanisms for knowledge sharing.[11] This suggests that open innovation is not a universal prescription, but may be more relevant to more novel or complex development projects under conditions of uncertainty.

Moreover, in most cases open innovation and internal innovation capabilities are complementary, rather than substitutes. Innovation management practices play an important moderating role as they are likely to enhance firms' capacity to identify, assimilate and utilize external knowledge inputs. Returns from open innovation are greatest when firms maintain their internal research capacity, employ a dedicated incentive system for innovation and advocate strong cross-functional collaboration. Decision-makers are thus well advised not to take positive returns from open innovation for granted. Rather, they need to achieve excellence in key innovation management practices if they are to fully harness the value of openness.[12]

Therefore, the simple dichotomy between open and closed approaches is unhelpful and not realistic, so instead we need to explore the different degrees and types of openness and the extent to which a firm can benefit from external and internal resources and knowledge in the innovation process. This provides an opportunity to investigate the use of various collaboration strategies and the types and contexts of sources of innovation, so managing different types and degrees of inter-firm relationships with external companies in order to create value will involve different degrees of openness for innovation. Many of the challenges of applying open innovation are common to innovation networks, but in addition there are other issues to manage (Table 17.1):

- conditions and context, e.g. environmental uncertainty and project complexity
- control and ownership of resources
- coordination of knowledge flows
- creation and capture of value.

Figure 17.1 highlights a number of different strategies which could be adopted, and we'll explore some of the issues raised in each of these areas.

Outsource

The subcontracting or 'outsourcing' of non-core activities has become popular in recent times. Typically, arguments for subcontracting are framed in terms of strategic focus, or 'sticking to

TABLE 17.1 Potential Benefits and Challenges of Applying Open Innovation

Six principles of open innovation	Potential benefits	Challenges to apply
Tap into external knowledge	Increase the pool of knowledge	How to search for and identify relevant knowledge sources
	Reduce reliance on limited internal knowledge	How to share or transfer such knowledge, especially tacit and systemic
External R&D has significant value	Can reduce the cost and uncertainty associated with internal R&D, and increase depth and breadth of R&D	Less likely to lead to distinctive capabilities and more difficult to differentiate
		External R&D also available to competitors
Do not have to originate research in order to profit from it	Reduce costs of internal R&D, more resources on external search strategies and relationships	Need sufficient R&D capability in order to identify, evaluate and adapt external R&D
Building a better business model is superior to being first to market	Greater emphasis on capturing rather than creating value	First-mover advantages depend on technology and market context
		Developing a business model demands time-consuming negotiation with other actors
Best *use* of internal and external ideas, not *generation* of ideas	Better balance of resources to search and identify ideas, rather than generate	Generating ideas is only a small part of the innovation process
		Most ideas unproven or no value, so cost of evaluation and development high
Profit from others' intellectual property (inbound open innovation), and others' use of our intellectual property (outbound open innovation)	Value of IP very sensitive to complementary capabilities such as brand, sales network, production, logistics, and complementary products and services	Conflicts of commercial interest or strategic direction
		Negotiation of acceptable forms and terms of IP licences

the knitting', but in practice most subcontracting or outsourcing arrangements are based on the potential to save costs: suppliers are likely to have lower overheads and variable costs, and may benefit from economies of scale if serving other firms.

Resource dependence and agency theory are more commonly used to explain vertical relationships, and are concerned with the need to control key technologies in the value chain.

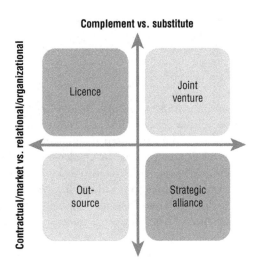

FIGURE 17.1 Strategies to support open innovation

The perceptions of the practices of Japanese manufacturers have led many firms to form closer relationships with suppliers, and indeed, closer links between firms, their suppliers and customers may help to reduce the cost of components, through specialization and sharing information on costs. However, factors such as the selection of suppliers and users, timing and mode of their involvement, and the novelty and complexity of the system being developed may reduce or negate the benefit of close supplier–user links.[13]

The quality of the relationship with suppliers and the timing of their involvement in development are critical factors. Traditionally, such relationships have been short-term, contractual arm's-length agreements focusing on the issue of the cost, with little supplier input into design or engineering. In contrast the 'Japanese', or 'partnership', model is based on long-term relationships, and suppliers make a significant contribution to the development of new products. The latter approach increases the visibility of cost–performance trade-offs, reduces the time to market and improves the integration of component technologies (see the case of TSMC in Innovation in Action 17.4). In certain sectors, particularly machine tools and scientific equipment, there is a long tradition of collaboration between manufacturers and lead users in the development of new products.

In this case some form of 'partnership' or 'lean' relationship is often advocated, based on the quality and development lead-time benefits experienced by Japanese manufacturers of consumer durables, specifically cars and electronics. Lamming identifies a number of defining characteristics of such partnership or 'lean' supply relations:[14]

- Fewer suppliers, longer-term relations
- Greater equity – real 'cost transparency'
- Focus on value flows – the relationship, not the contract

Taiwan Semiconductor Manufacturing Company (TSMC)

TSMC was established in Taiwan in 1987 to become the world's first dedicated semiconductor foundry. This so-called pure-play foundry business represented a novel business model because, unlike conventional vertically integrated manufacturers, TSMC's customers are fabrication-less semiconductor design houses such as Qualcomm, Broadcom and NVIDIA, as well as some outsourcing production from more conventional fabrication companies like Intel. The cost of building and operating fabrication facilities has become prohibitive for all but the very largest companies, such as Intel and Samsung, especially in the case of complex logic applications. Even AMD (Advanced Micro Devices) separated its design and manufacturing businesses in 2008.

The headquarters and main fabrication plants are located in Hsinchu, Taiwan, but it also operates two wholly owned subsidiaries, WaferTech in the United States and TSMC China Company Limited, and a joint venture fabrication in Singapore, SSMC. Its core business is mask production, wafer manufacturing, assembly and testing, but it also provides design and prototyping services. In 2010, it joined the top ten of semiconductor R&D spenders, to reach $945 million (£580 million), equivalent to 7% of sales (called the R&D-intensity), the highest of any pure foundry business. By comparison, the number-one R&D spender in that industry that year was Intel, at $6.6 billion (£3.96 billion; 17% of sales), and in second place Samsung, at $2.6 billion (£3.2 billion; 8% of sales).

In 2011, the company's production capacity reached 13.2 million eight-inch equivalent wafers, and TSMC had more than 450 customers, manufacturing more than 8300 products for computer, communications and consumer electronics applications. In 2012, a partnership between TSMC and Apple began production of the A5 (dual core) and A6 chip for Apple's next-generation iPads and iPhones. TSMC has benefited from the growth in smart mobile devices, and it is estimated that every tablet sold globally contributes about $7 (£4.20) to its income. In 2011–2012, it made sales of $14 billion (£8.4 billion), and by specializing in high-technology, capital-intensive contract manufacture it maintained high gross profit margins, of around 40%, although profitability is dependent on closely matching capacity and demand.

- Vendor assessment, plus development
- Two-way or third-party assessment
- Mutual learning – share experience, expertise, knowledge and investment.

These principles are based on a distillation of the features of the best Japanese manufacturers in the automobile and electronics sectors, and more recent experiments in other contexts, such as aerospace in the United Kingdom and the United States.

Licence

Once you have acquired some form of formal legal intellectual property right (IPR), you can allow others to use it in some way in return for some payment (a licence), or sell the IPR outright (or assign it). Licensing IPR can have a number of benefits, including:

* reducing or eliminating production and distribution costs and risks
* reaching a larger market
* exploiting other applications
* establishing standards
* gaining access to complementary technology
* blocking competing developments
* converting competitors to defenders.

Considerations when drafting a licensing agreement include degree of exclusivity, territory and type of end use, period of licence and type and level of payments – royalty, lump sum or cross-licence. Next, calculate relative investment and weight according to share of risk. Finally, compare results to alternatives (e.g. return to licensee, imitation and litigation). There is no 'best' licensing strategy, as it depends on the strategy of the organization and the nature of the technology and markets. This is discussed in detail in the chapter on exploiting knowledge and intellectual property.

INNOVATION IN ACTION 17.5

Airbus Industrie

Airbus Industrie was formed in France in 1969 as a joint venture between the German firm MBB (now DASA) and French firm Aérospatiale, to be joined by CASA of Spain in 1970 and British Aerospace (now BAE Systems) in 1979. Airbus is not a company but a *groupement d'intérêt economique* (GIE), which is a French legal entity that is not required to publish its own accounts. Instead, all costs and any profits or losses are absorbed by the member companies. The partners make components in proportion to their share of Airbus Industrie: Aérospatiale and DASA each have 37.9%, BAE 20% and CASA 4.2%.

At that time the international market for civil aircraft was dominated by the US firm Boeing, which in 1984 accounted for 40% of the airframe market in the non-communist world. The growing cost and commercial risk of airframe development had resulted in consolidation of the industry and a number of joint ventures. In addition, product lifecycles had shortened owing to more rapid improvements in engine technology. The partners identified an unfilled market niche for a high-capacity, short- to medium-range passenger

(continued)

aircraft, as more than 70% of the traffic was then on routes of less than 4600 km, thus the Airbus A300 was conceived in 1969. The A300 was essentially the result of the French and German partners, the former insisting on final assembly in France and the latter gaining access to French technology. The first A300 flew in 1974, followed by a series of successful derivatives, such as the A310 and the A320. The British partner played a leading role in the subsequent projects, bringing both capital and technological expertise to the venture. Airbus has since proved to be highly innovative with the introduction of fly-by-wire technology, and common platforms and control systems for all its aircraft to reduce the cost of crew training and aircraft maintenance. In 2000, the group announced plans to develop a double-decker 'super' jumbo, the A380, with seats for 555 passengers, costing an estimated $12 billion (£7.2 billion) to develop. Airbus estimated a global market of 1163 very large passenger aircraft and an additional 372 freighters, but needed to sell only 250 A380s to achieve breakeven. This would challenge Boeing in the only market it continued to dominate. (However, Boeing predicted a market of just 320 very large aircraft, as it assumed a future dominance of point-to-point air travel by smaller aircraft, whereas Airbus assumed a growth in the hub-and-spoke model, which demands large aircraft for travel between hubs.) The first commercial service of the A380 began in 2007 with Singapore Airlines, followed by Emirates. By 2011, Airbus had 188 orders for A380s, from 14 countries. In 1998, Airbus outsold Boeing for the first time in history, and in 2011 Airbus delivered more aircraft to customers than Boeing for the ninth successive year, some 500, valued at $140 billion (£84 billion) before discounts.

In 1999, Daimler-Chrysler (DASA), Aérospatiale and CASA merged to form the European Aeronautic Defence and Space Company (EADS), making BAE Systems, formerly British Aerospace, the only non-EADS member of Airbus. The group planned to move from the unwieldy GIE structure to become a company. This would allow streamlining of its manufacturing operations, which were then geographically dispersed across the United Kingdom, France, Germany and Spain, and more importantly help create financial transparency to identify and implement cost savings. Also, some customers had reported poor service and support as Airbus had to refer such work to the relevant member company.

Airbus demonstrated the complexity of joint ventures. The primary motive was to share the high cost and commercial risk of development. On the one hand, the French and German participation was underwritten by their respective governments. This fact has not escaped the attention of Boeing and the US government, which provided subsidies indirectly via defence contracts. On the other hand, all partners had to some extent captive markets in the form of national airlines, although almost three-quarters of all Airbus sales were ultimately outside the member countries. Finally, there were also technology motives for the joint venture. For example, BAE specialized in development of the wings, Aérospatiale the avionics, DASA the fuselages and CASA the tails. However, as suggested above, there were now strong financial, manufacturing and marketing reasons for combining the operations within a single company.

Joint Ventures and Strategic Alliances

Joint ventures, whether formal or informal, typically take the form of an agreement between two or more organizations to co-develop a new technology or product. There are two basic types of formal joint venture: a new company formed by two or more separate organizations, which typically allocate ownership based on shares of stock controlled, or a simpler contractual basis for collaboration. The critical distinction between the two types of joint venture is that an equity arrangement requires the formation of a separate legal entity. In such cases management is delegated to the joint venture, which is not the case for other forms of collaboration.

Unlike more formal joint ventures, a strategic alliance typically has a specific goal and timetable, and does not normally take the form of a separate company. Doz and Hamel identify a range of motives for strategic alliances and suggest strategies to exploit each:[15]

- To build critical mass through co-option.
- To reach new markets by leveraging co-specialized resources.
- To gain new competencies through organizational learning.

In a co-option alliance, critical mass is achieved through temporary alliances with competitors, customers or companies with complementary technology, products or services. Through co-option, a company seeks to group together other relatively weak companies to challenge a dominant competitor. Co-option is common where scale or network size is important, such as mobile telephony and aerospace. For example, Airbus was originally created in response to the dominance of Boeing; Symbian and Linux, in response to Microsoft's dominance; and the Open Handset Alliance and Android, in response to Apple's success. Greater international reach is a common related motive for co-option alliances. Fujitsu initially used its alliance with ICL to develop a market presence in Europe, as did Honda with Rover. However, co-option alliances may be inherently unstable and transitory. Once the market position has been achieved, one partner may seek to take control through acquisition, as in the case of Fujitsu and ICL, or to go unilateral, as in the case of Honda and Rover.[16]

In a co-option alliance, partners are normally drawn from the same industry, whereas in a co-specialized alliance partners are usually from different sectors. In a co-specialized alliance, partners bring together unique competencies to create the opportunity to enter new markets, develop new products or build new businesses. Such co-specialization is common in systems or complex products and services. However, there is a risk associated with co-specialization. Partners are required to commit to their partners' technology and standards. Where technologies are emerging and uncertain and standards are yet to be established, there is a high risk that a partner's technology may become redundant. This has a number of implications for co-specialization alliances. First, that at the early stages of an emerging market where the dominant technologies are still uncertain, flexible forms of collaboration such as alliances are preferable, and at later stages when market needs are clearer and the relevant technological configuration better defined more formal joint ventures become appropriate.[17] Second, to restrict the use of alliances to instances where the technology is tacit, expensive and time consuming to develop.

If the technology is not tacit, a licence is likely to be cheaper and less risky, and if the technology is not expensive or time consuming to develop, in-house development is preferable.[18]

There has been a spectacular growth in strategic alliances, and at the same time more formal joint ventures have declined as a means of collaboration. In the mid-1980s, fewer than 1000 new alliances were announced each year, but by the year 2000 this had grown to almost 10 000 per year (based on data from Thomson Financial). There are a number of reasons for the increase in alliances overall, and more specifically the switch from formal joint ventures to more transitory alliances:[19]

- *Speed*: transitory alliances versus careful planning. Under turbulent environmental conditions, speed of response, learning and lead time are more critical than careful planning, selection and development of partnerships.
- *Partner fit*: network versus dyadic fit. Owing to the need for speed, partners are often selected from existing members of a network, or alternatively reputation in the broader market.
- *Partner type*: complementarity versus familiarity. Transitory alliances increasingly occur across traditional sectors, markets and technologies, rather than from within. Microsoft and Lego to develop an Internet-based computer game; Deutsche Bank and Nokia to create mobile financial services.
- *Commitment*: aligned objectives versus trust. The transitory nature of relationships makes the development of commitment and trust more difficult, and alliances rely more on aligned objectives and mutual goals.
- *Focus*: few, specific tasks versus multiple roles. To reduce the complexity of managing the relationships, the scope of the interaction is more narrowly defined, and focused more on the task than the relationship.

Case Study of Lego exploring some of these themes is available on the Innovation Portal at **www.innovation-portal.info**

But alliances don't always work – as Table 17.2 shows – there are plenty of reasons why what looks good on paper fails to work out in practice!

INNOVATION IN ACTION 17.6

Generative Collaboration for App Development – Apple versus Android

In a comparative case study of the mobile phone platforms iPhone and Android, the effects of different types of supplier relationship were assessed, focussing on the influence of innovation and value creation and capture.

The notion of generative capacity is introduced to the research on open innovation, suggesting that it is generativity rather than openness that drives value-creation through such collaboration. The two contrasting cases illustrate that generativity and innovation can be achieved in different ways: Apple is often characterized (by competitors) as being a proprietary closed system, or 'walled-garden', but with the benefit of a more integrated user experience; Google's Android platform is more open and distributed, but is also criticized (by Apple and its followers) for being too fragmented and uncoordinated.

The study found that the issue is not only the degree of openness that matters, but both openness and control are important to facilitate generative supplier contributions. In the two cases of collaborative innovation it is generativity, not openness, that creates the aggregate value of the innovation. To some extent, control hinders generativity, as when external suppliers of application software must seek permission to be accepted as content, but in other cases control can facilitate generativity, through toolkits, standards and guidelines for suppliers. Similarly, openness can be both generative and hindering. It opens up for new ideas and possibilities, but in some cases a lack of common strategy and coordination can hinder exploration and exploitation, and partners must create their own paths for innovation.

However, they find that the suppliers in the more open innovation networks such as Android and the Open Handset Alliance tend to adopt a more active role as creative peer producers, rather than merely as contractual deliverers in the case of Apple's standard relationship.

Source: Remneland-Wikhamn, B., J. Ljungberg, M. Bergquist and J. Kusschel (2011) Open innovation, generativity and the supplier as peer: The case of iPhone and Android. *International Journal of Innovation Management,* **15** (1): 205–230.

TABLE 17.2   Common Reasons for the Failure of Alliances (review of 16 studies)

Reason for failure	Percentage studies reporting factor (n = 16)
Strategic/goal divergence	50
Partner problems	38
Strong–weak relation	38
Cultural mismatch	25
Insufficient trust	25
Operational/geographical overlap	25
Personnel clashes	25
Lack of commitment	25
Unrealistic expectations/time	25
Asymmetric incentives	13

Source: Derived from Duysters, G., G. Kok and M. Vaandrager (1999) Crafting successful strategic technology partnerships. *R&D Management,* **29** (4), 343–51 by permission of John Wiley & Sons, Ltd.

Summary

- Organizations collaborate for many reasons, to reduce the cost, time or risk of access to unfamiliar technologies or markets.

- The precise form of collaboration will be determined by the motives and preferences of the partners, but their choice will be constrained by the nature of the technologies and markets, specifically the degree of knowledge complexity and tacitness.

- The success of an alliance depends on a number of factors, but organizational issues dominate, such as the degree of mutual trust and level of communication.

- Open innovation is a very broad and therefore popular concept, but needs to be applied with care as its relevance is sensitive to the context. The appropriate choice of partner and specific mechanisms will depend on the type of innovation project and environmental uncertainty.

- In most cases open innovation and internal innovation capabilities are complementary, rather than substitutes.

Further Resources

The open innovation movement includes a lot of relevant work on collaboration and networks, and Henry Chesbrough, Wim Vanhaverbeke and Joel West have edited a good overview of the main research themes in *Open Innovation: Researching a new paradigm* (Oxford University Press, 2008). Recently, there has been a lot of work on open innovation, much of it not very original or insightful, but a good place to start is two journal special issues: *R&D Management*, 2010, **40** (3) and *Technovation*, 2011, **31** (1). For more critical accounts of open innovation, see: Trott, P. and D. Hartmann (2009) Why open innovation is old wine in new bottles, *International Journal of Innovation Management*, **13** (4): 715–736; and Mowery, D. C. (2009) Plus ça change: Industrial R&D in the third industrial revolution, *Industrial and Corporate Change*, **18** (1): 1–50, and our own review Tidd, J. (2014) *Open Innovation Research, Management and Practice*. London: Imperial College Press.

References

1. Chesbrough, H. W. (2003) *Open Innovation: The new imperative for creating and profiting from technology*. Boston: Harvard Business School Publishing; Chesbrough, H. W. and A. K. Crowther (2006) Beyond high tech: Early adopters of open innovation in other industries, *R&D Management*, **36** (3): 229–236; Chesbrough, H. W.,

W. Vanhaverbeke and J. West (2006) *Open Innovation: Researching a new paradigm*, Oxford: Oxford University Press; Gassmann, O., E. Enkel and H. Chesbrough (2010) The future of open innovation, *R &D Management*, **40**: 213–221; Enkel, E., O. Gassmann and H. Chesbrough (2009) Open innovation: Exploring the phenomenon, *R&D Management*, **39** (4): 311–316.

2. Bessant, J. and T. Venables (2008) *Creating Wealth from Knowledge: Meeting the innovation challenge*. Cheltenham: Edward Elgar.

3. Lafley, A. and R. Charan (2008) *The Game Changer*. New York: Profile.

4. Snow, C. and D. Strauss (2009) Community of firms: A new collaborative paradigm of open innovation, *International Journal of Strategic Business Alliances*, **1** (1): 53.

5. Lazzarotti, V. and R. Manzini (2009) Different modes of open innovation: A theoretical framework and an empirical study, *International Journal of Innovation Management*, **13**: 615–636; Lichtenthaler, U. (2008) Open innovation in practice: An analysis of strategic approaches to technology transactions, *IEEE Transactions of Engineering Management*, **55**: 148–157.

6. Enkel, E. and K. Bader (2014) How to balance open and closed innovation: Strategy and culture as influencing factors, in Tidd, J. (2014) *Open Innovation Research, Management and Practice*. London: Imperial College Press.

7. Nambisan, S. and M. Sawhney (2007) *The Global Brain: Your roadmap for innovating smarter and faster in a networked world*. Philadelphia: Wharton School Publishing.

8. Cheeks, N. (2007) How NASA uses 'Infusion Partnerships', in *PDMA Visions*. Mount Laurel, NJ: Product Development Management Association: pp. 9–12.

9. Schweitzer, F. M., O. Gassmann and K. Gaubinger (2011) Open innovation and its ability to embrace turbulent environments, *International Journal of Innovation Management*, **15** (6): 1191–1208.

10. Bahemia, H. and B. Squire (2010) A contingent perspective of open innovation in new product development projects, *International Journal of Innovation Management*, **14** (4): 603–627; Huizingh, E. K. R. E. (2011) Open innovation: State of the art and future perspectives, *Technovation*, **13** (1): 2–9.

11. Hsieh, K.-N. and J. Tidd (2012) Open versus closed new service development: The influences of project novelty, *Technovation*, **32** (11): 600–608.

12. Salge, T. O., T. M. Bohné, T. Farchi and E. P. Piening (2014) Not for everybody: Why some organisations benefit more from open innovation than others, in Tidd, J. *Open Innovation Research, Management and Practice*. London: Imperial College Press.

13. Leonard-Barton, D. and D. Sinha (1993) Developer–user interaction and user satisfaction in internal technology transfer, *Academy of Management Journal*, **36** (5): 1125–1139; Spencer, J. (2003) Firms' knowledge-sharing strategies in the global innovation system: Evidence from the flat panel display industry, *Strategic Management Journal*, **24**: 217–233.

14. Lamming, R. (1993) *Beyond Partnership*. Hemel Hempstead: Prentice-Hall; Nishiguchi, T. (1994) *Strategic Industrial Sourcing: The Japanese advantage*. Oxford: Oxford University Press; Brem, A. and J. Tidd (2012) *Perspectives on Supplier Innovation: Theories, concepts and empirical insights on open innovation and the integration of suppliers*. London: Imperial College Press.

15. Doz, Y. and G. Hamel (1998) *Alliance Advantage: The art of creating value through partnering*. Boston: Harvard Business School Press.

16. Carr, C. (1999) Globalisation, strategic alliances, acquisitions and technology transfer: Lessons from ICL/Fujitsu and Rover/Honda and BMW, *R&D Management*, **29** (4): 405–421.

17. Mauri, A. and G. McMillan (1999) The influence of technology on strategic alliances, *International Journal of Innovation Management*, **3** (4): 367–378.

18. Jay Lambe, C. and R. Spekman (1997) Alliances, external technology acquisition, and discontinuous technological change, *Journal of Product Innovation Management*, **14**: 102–116.

19. Duysters, G. and A. de Man (2003) Transitionary alliances: An instrument for surviving turbulent industries? *R&D Management*, **33**: 49–58; Berg, S., J. Duncan and P. Friedman (1982) *Joint Venture Strategies and Corporate Innovation*. Cambridge, MA: Gunn & Ham.

Deeper Dive explanations of innovation concepts and ideas are available on the Innovation Portal at **www.innovation-portal.info**

Quizzes to test yourself further are available online via the Innovation Portal at **www.innovation-portal.info**

Summary of online resources for Chapter 17 –
all material is available via the Innovation Portal at
www.innovation-portal.info

Cases	**Media**	**Tools**	**Activities**	**Deeper Dive**

- Procter and
  Gamble
- Open collective
  innovation
- Lego
- Apple versus
  Android
- Search strategies
  for peripheral
  vision
- Opening up
  healthcare
  innovation
- Open door

- Roy Sandbach,
  Procter and
  Gamble
- David Overton,
  Ordnance Survey
- Michael Bartl,
  Hyve
- David Simoes-
  Brown, 100%
  Open
- Richard Philpott,
  The Innovation
  Exchange

- Lead user
  methods
- Market
  research tools
- Partnerships
  with people
- Scenarios

- Acquiring
  technological
  knowledge
- Partner
  search

- Beyond
  lead users:
  Co-development
  of innovations
- Supplier
  innovation

Chapter 18

Exploiting Discontinuous Innovation

LEARNING OBJECTIVES

By the end of this chapter you will develop an understanding of:

- what discontinuous innovation is and how it represents a key strategic challenge
- the different ways in which disruption can occur to established markets
- the challenges in managing discontinuous innovation – in spotting emerging changes early and in organizing and acting to deal with them
- triggers of disruptive innovation
- the difficulties in managing what is an uncertain and risky process
- the key themes in thinking about how to manage this process effectively.

INNOVATION IN ACTION 18.1

Innovation in the Glass Industry

It's particularly important to understand that change doesn't come in standard sized jumps. For much of the time it is essentially incremental, a process of gradual improvement over time on dimensions like price, quality, choice, etc. For long periods of time nothing much shifts in either product offering or the way in which this is delivered (product and process innovation is incremental). But sooner or later someone somewhere will come up with a radical change which upsets the apple cart.

(continued)

For example, the glass window business has been around for at least six hundred years and is – since most houses, offices, hotels and shops have plenty of windows – a very profitable business to be in. But for most of those six hundred years the basic process for making window glass hasn't changed. Glass is made in approximately flat sheets which are then ground down to a state where they are flat enough for people to see through them. The ways in which the grinding takes place have improved – what used to be a labour-intensive process became increasingly mechanized and even automated, and the tools and abrasives became progressively more sophisticated and effective. But, underneath, the same core process of grinding down to flatness was going on.

Then in 1952, Alastair Pilkington working in the UK firm of the same name began working on a process which revolutionized glass making for the next 50 years. He got the idea while washing up when he noticed that the fat and grease from the plates floated on the top of the water – and he began thinking about producing glass in such a way that it could be cast to float on the surface of some other liquid and then allowed to set. If this could be accomplished it could be possible to create a perfectly flat surface without the need for grinding and polishing.

Five years, millions of pounds and over 100 000 tonnes of scrapped glass later, the company achieved a working pilot plant and a further two years on began selling glass made by the float glass process. The process produced 80% labour and 50% energy savings and removed the need for, and therefore the cost of, abrasives, grinding equipment, etc. Factories could be made smaller and the overall time to produce glass dramatically cut. So successful was the process that it became – and still is – the dominant method for making flat glass around the world.

Beyond the Steady State

As we've already seen, unless organizations change what they offer the world and the ways in which they create and deliver those offerings, they risk falling behind in today's turbulent and complex environment. Smart firms know this and they invest time and trouble to create systems, structures and processes to ensure a sustained flow of innovation.

But while they are highly competent at what we could call 'steady-state innovation' (essentially doing what they do but better) problems can occur when they confront the need for *discontinuous* innovation. History tells us that when technologies shift, new markets emerge, the regulatory rules of the game change or someone introduces a new business model then established players can suddenly become vulnerable. When confronted with the need to explore doing something radically different, many fail the test.

A key part of the problem is that dealing with discontinuity requires a very different set of capabilities for organizing and managing innovation. Searching in unlikely places, building links to strange partners, allocating resources to high-risk ventures, exploring new ways of looking at the business – all of these challenge the normal way we approach the innovation problem. And while we know a lot about how to manage the steady-state kind of innovation we're much less clear about where and how to start building discontinuous innovation capability.

So what do we know? Let's go back to basics and remind ourselves of two types of innovation – one is about 'doing what we do, but better', and the other involves something completely different. The former tends to be about building on what we already know, incrementally improving along product or process trajectories. That kind of innovation tends, not surprisingly, to favour the established players – they're the ones with the experiences, the resources and the wherewithal to manage technical and market research to push the boundaries. Small and new entrant firms have a hard time breaking into this.

But when something shocks the cosy set-up it can shatter – and in the process open up opportunities for new players to enter what becomes a new game. In fact, it often favours them because they don't have the prior commitments to the old market or technology framework; they're not scared of cannibalizing their established businesses with the new one, since they don't have one to cannibalize! In short, they have nothing to lose and much to gain.

History suggests that when such shocks happen – be they technological shifts, the emergence of totally new markets or the bringing-in of a new business model which reframes the rules of the game – they favour the new entrant over the established incumbent. But this is not a hard-and-fast rule: there are plenty of examples of established players who take on the new and use it to enhance their competitive position.

Think of firms like 3M, Philips, Siemens or General Electric, which have been in business for over a century. Their track record is one of managing both continuous (do what we do, better) and discontinuous innovation, often pioneering or riding on the crest of the waves of change. Equally, we hear about the successful new entrants when a wave of change breaks, but we don't know about the many others who tried and failed to build something out of the new opportunity. What is clear is that standing still in the face of discontinuous change is not an option. Firms need to rediscover and use entrepreneurial flair to find and exploit high-risk new opportunities – and they need some very different approaches to managing the conversion of those weak signals into successful and groundbreaking innovations.

This chapter looks at the challenge of managing discontinuous innovation and what individual entrepreneurs and established organizations can do to take advantage of the opportunities it throws up.

> Activity to help you explore issues raised in this chapter – patterns of discontinuous change – is available on the Innovation Portal at **www.innovation-portal.info**

The Problem – and the Opportunity – in Discontinuous Innovation

Back in the 1880s, there was a thriving industry in the north-eastern United States in the lucrative business of selling ice. The business model was deceptively simple: work hard to cut chunks of ice out of the frozen northern wastes, wrap the harvest and ship it as quickly as possible to the warmer southern states – and increasingly overseas – where it could be used to preserve food. In its heyday, this was a big industry. In 1886, the record harvest ran to 25 million tons, and it employed thousands of people in cutting, storing and shipping the product. And it was an industry with a strong commitment to innovation: developments in ice cutting, snow ploughs, insulation techniques and logistics underpinned the industry's strong growth.

Meanwhile, in another part of the universe – or at least in laboratories around the globe – researchers like the young Carl von Linde were working on the emerging problems of refrigeration. It wasn't long before artificial ice-making became a reality and by 1873 a patented commercial refrigeration system was on the market. In the years which followed, the industry grew. In 1879, there were 35 plants and 10 years later 222 making artificial ice. Effectively, this development signposted the end of the road for the ice-harvesting industry – although for a while both industries grew alongside each other, learning and innovating and together expanding the overall market for ice. Eventually, the ice-harvesting industry was replaced by the new refrigeration industry dominated by new-entrant firms.[1]

From Freezers to Servers: The Same Pattern

This pattern of long periods of innovation under relatively steady conditions punctuated by dramatic shifts is a common one. Let's wind the film forwards to the last part of the twentieth century and a very different industry: the computer disk drive business. Just like the ice industry, it was a thriving sector in which the voracious demands of the growing mini-computer industry for powerful machines for engineering, banking and others meant there was a booming market for disk drive storage units. Firms in the industry worked closely with their customers, understanding the particular needs and demands for more storage capacity, faster access times, smaller footprints, etc. All fine – until a discontinuous change rocked the happily sailing boat of the industry.

In this case the dramatic shift wasn't due to technology but triggered by the emergence of a new market with very different expectations. While the emphasis in the mini-computer world was on high performance and the requirement for storage units correspondingly technologically sophisticated, the emerging market for personal computers had a very different shape. These were much less clever machines, capable of running much simpler software and with massively inferior performance – but at a price which a very different set of people could afford. Importantly, although simpler, they were capable of doing most of the basic tasks which a much wider market was interested in – simple arithmetical calculations, word processing and basic graphics. As the market for these grew so the learning effects meant that these capabilities improved – but from a much lower cost base. This shift affected not only the makers of the new personal computers but also the new firms who supplied them with simpler and cheaper disk drives. In the end, there was the same pattern as we saw in the ice industry– but from a different direction. Of the major manufacturers in the disk drive industry in the 1990s only a handful survived – and leadership in the new industry shifted to new-entrant firms working with a very different model.[2]

These are not isolated examples but typical of a pattern in innovation. Think about the revolution in flying which the low-cost carriers have brought about. Here the challenge came via a new business model rather than technology – based on the premise that if prices could be kept low a large new market could be opened up. In order to make low prices pay, a number of problems needed solving – keeping load factors high, cutting administration costs, enabling rapid turnaround times at terminals – but once the model began to work it attracted not only new customers but also increasingly established flyers who saw the advantages of lower prices.

What these, and many other, examples have in common is that they represent the challenge of *discontinuous* innovation. None of the industries was lacking in innovation or a commitment to further change. But the ice harvesters, mini-computer disk companies or the established airlines all carried on their innovation on a stage covered with a relatively predictable carpet. But shifts in technology, in new market emergence or in new business models pulled this carpet out from under the firms – and created a new set of conditions on which a new game would be played out. The trouble is that, under such conditions, it is the new players who tend to do better because they don't have to wrestle with learning new tricks and letting go of their old ones. This is why discontinuous changes can often be *disruptive* to established players.

Innovation Lifecycles: From Discontinuity to Steady State

We saw in Chapter 2 that innovation patterns change over time and in particular two US researchers (William Abernathy and James Utterback) developed a model describing the pattern in terms of three distinct phases.[3] Initially, under discontinuous conditions, there is what they term a 'fluid phase' during which there is high uncertainty along two dimensions:

- The target: What will the new configuration be and who will want it?
- The technical: How will we harness new technological knowledge to create and deliver this?

No one knows what the 'right' configuration of technological means and market needs will be and so there is extensive experimentation (accompanied by many failures) and fast learning by a range of players, including many new entrepreneurial businesses.

Gradually, these experiments begin to converge around what they call a 'dominant design' – something which begins to set up the rules of the game. This represents a convergence around the most popular (importantly not necessarily the most technologically sophisticated or elegant) solution to the emerging configuration. At this point a 'bandwagon' begins to roll and innovation options become increasingly channelled around a core set of possibilities. It becomes increasingly difficult to explore outside this space because entrepreneurial interest and the resources which that brings increasingly focus on possibilities within the dominant design corridor.

This can apply to products or processes; in both cases, the key characteristics become stabilized and experimentation moves to getting the bugs out and refining the dominant design. For example, the nineteenth-century chemical industry moved from making soda ash (an essential ingredient in making soap, glass and a host of other products) from the earliest days where it was produced by burning vegetable matter through to a sophisticated chemical reaction which was carried out on a batch process (the Leblanc process) which was one of the drivers of the Industrial Revolution. This process dominated for nearly a century but was in turn replaced by a new generation of continuous processes which used electrolytic techniques and originated in Belgium, where they were developed by the Solvay brothers. Moving to the Leblanc process or the Solvay process did not happen overnight; it took decades of work to refine and improve the process, and to fully understand the chemistry and engineering required to get consistent high quality and output.

The period in which the dominant design emerges and emphasis shifts to imitation and development around it is termed the 'transitional phase' in the Abernathy and Utterback model. Activities move from radical concept development to more focused efforts geared around product differentiation and to delivering it reliably, cheaply, with higher quality, extended functionality, etc.

As the concept matures still further so incremental innovation becomes more significant and emphasis shifts to factors like cost, which means efforts within the industries that grow up around these product areas tend to focus increasingly on rationalization, on scale economies and on process innovation to drive out cost and improve productivity. Product innovation is increasingly about differentiation through customization to meet the particular needs of specific users. Abernathy and Utterback term this the 'specific phase'.

Finally, the stage is set for change. The scope for innovation becomes smaller and smaller while outside, for example in the laboratories and imaginations of research scientists, new possibilities are emerging. Eventually, a new technology emerges which has the potential to challenge all the, by now, well-established rules – and the game is disrupted. In the camera case, for example, this is happening with the advent of digital photography, which is having an impact on cameras and the overall service package around how we get, keep and share our photographs. In our chemical case this is happening with biotechnology and the emergence of the possibility of no longer needing giant chemical plants but instead moving to small-scale operations using live organisms genetically engineered to produce what we need.

Although originally developed for manufactured products, the model also works for services. For example, the early days of Internet banking were characterized by a typically fluid phase with many options and models being offered. This gradually moved to a transitional phase building a dominant design consensus on the package of services offered, the levels and nature of security and privacy support, the interactivity of websites, etc. The field has now become mature with much of the competition shifting to marginal issues like relative interest rates.

Table 18.1 sets out the main elements of this model.

TABLE 18.1 Stages in the Innovation Lifecycle

Innovation characteristic	Fluid pattern	Transitional phase	Specific phase
Competitive emphasis placed on. . .	Functional product performance	Product variation	Cost reduction
Innovation stimulated by. . .	Information on user needs, technical inputs	Opportunities created by expanding internal technical capability	Pressure to reduce cost, improve quality, etc.
Predominant type of innovation	Frequent major changes in products	Major process innovations required by rising volume	Incremental product and process innovation
Product line	Diverse, often including custom designs	Includes at least one stable or dominant design	Mostly undifferentiated standard products
Production processes	Flexible and inefficient – aim is to experiment and make frequent changes	Becoming more rigid and defined	Efficient, often capital-intensive and relatively rigid

Discontinuous Can Be *Disruptive*

The term 'disruptive innovation' is particularly associated with the work of Clayton Christensen, a US scholar who looked at the patterns of change in a number of industries including computer disk drives (outlined above), earthmoving equipment, and steelmaking.[2] He noticed a pattern which seemed to run through all of these cases – and one which he has subsequently applied to over 50 industries. For much of the time there is a stability around markets where innovation of the 'do better' variety takes place and is well managed. Close relationships with existing customers are fostered and the system is configured to deliver a steady stream of what the market wants – and usually a great deal more! What he terms 'technology overshoot' is often a characteristic of this, where markets are offered more and more features which they may not ever use or place much value on but which come as part of the package. (Think about software like Microsoft Word and ask yourself whether you really do make use of all the features or just a small but very useful subset? What some programmers call 'bloatware' is another way of thinking about technology overshoot.)

But somewhere else there is another group of potential users who have very different needs – usually for something much simpler and cheaper – which will help them get something done. For example, the emergent home computer industry began amongst a small group of hobbyists who wanted simple computing capabilities at a much lower price than was available from the mini-computer suppliers. In turn the builders of those early PCs wanted disk drives which were much simpler technologically but, importantly, much cheaper and so were not really interested in what the existing disk drive industry had to offer. It was too high tech, massively over-engineered for their needs and, most importantly, much too expensive.

Although they approached the existing drive makers, none of them was interested in making such a device – not surprisingly since they were doing very comfortably supplying expensive high-performance equipment to an established mini-computer industry. Why should they worry about a fringe group of hobbyists as a market? Consequently, the early PC makers had to look elsewhere – and found entrepreneurs willing to take the risks and experiment with trying to come up with a product that did meet their needs. It didn't happen overnight and there were plenty of failures on the way – and certainly the early drives were very poor performers in comparison with what was on offer in the mainstream industry. But gradually the PC market grew, moving from hobbyists to widespread home use and from there – helped by the emergence and standardization of the IBM PC – to the office and business environment. And as it grew and matured so it learnt and the performance of the machines became much more impressive and reliable – but coming from a much lower cost base than mini-computers. The same thing happened to the disk drives within them: the small entrepreneurial firms who began in the game grew and learnt and became large suppliers of reliable products which did the job – but at a massively lower price.

Eventually, the fringe market which the original disk drive makers had ignored because it didn't seem relevant or important enough to worry about grew to dominate – and by the time they realized this it was too late for many of them. The best they could hope for would be to be late-entrant imitators, coming from behind and hoping to catch up.

This pattern is essentially one of *disruption*: the rules of the game changed dramatically in the marketplace with some new winners and losers. Figure 18.1 shows the transition where the new market and suppliers gradually take over from the existing players.

This pattern can be seen in many industries. Think about the low-cost airlines, for example. Here the original low-cost players didn't go head to head with the national flag carriers who offered the best routes, high levels of service and prime airport slots – all for a high price.

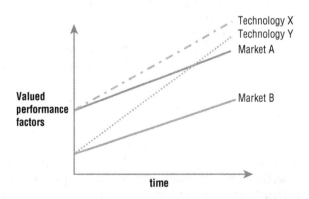

FIGURE 18.1   Disruption patterns

Instead, they sought new markets at the fringe – users who would accept a much lower level of service (no food, no seat allocation, no lounges, no frills at all) but for a basic safe flight would pay a much lower price. As these new users began to use the service and talk about it, so the industry grew and came to the attention of existing private and business travellers who were interested in lower-cost flights, at least for short-haul, because it met their needs for a 'good enough' solution to their travel problem. Eventually, the challenge hit the major airlines, who found it difficult to respond because of their inherently much higher cost structure.

Importantly, this is only one way to upset the market apple cart. Low-end market disruption is a potent threat. Think what a producer in China could do to an industry like pump manufacturing if it began to offer a simple, low-cost 'good enough' household pump for £10 instead of the high-tech high performance variants available from today's industry at prices 10 to 50 times as high? Or medical devices like asthma inhalers once they have come off-patent?

But disruption can also come when technology shifts – like in the ice industry – and opens up new possibilities. It can come through shifts in thinking around the dominant business model. It can come when external agencies like government change the regulatory rules of the game. The result is the same: the carpet is pulled out from beneath the market and a new set of rules comes into play. How new and established players handle the disruption is the challenge, but they should begin by recognizing that there is an increasing likelihood of disruption happening. Table 18.2 gives some examples.

TABLE 18.2   Sources of Discontinuity

Triggers/ sources of discontinuity	Explanation	Problems posed	Examples (of good and bad experiences)
New market emerges	Most markets evolve through a process of growth, segmentation, etc. But at certain times completely new markets emerge which cannot be analysed or predicted in advance or explored through using conventional market research/ analytical techniques	There is a risk that established firms see the new market as being too small or not representing their preferred target group of customers, and they may dismiss the people in this emerging market group as cranks or fringe players. Originators of new products may not see potential in new markets and may ignore them (e.g. text messaging)	Disk drives, excavators, mini-mills Mobile phone/SMS where market which actually emerged was not the one expected or predicted by originator

(continued)

TABLE 18.2 *(Continued)*

Triggers/ sources of discontinuity	Explanation	Problems posed	Examples (of good and bad experiences)
New technology emerges	Step change takes place in product or process technology – may result from convergence and maturing of several streams (e.g. industrial automation, mobile phones) or as a result of a single breakthrough (e.g. LED as new white light source)	Don't see it because beyond the periphery of technology search environment Not an extension of current areas but completely new field or approach Tipping point may not be a single breakthrough but convergence and maturing of established technological streams, whose combined effect is underestimated 'Not invented here' effect – new technology represents a different basis for delivering value (e.g. telephone vs. telegraphy)	Ice harvesting to cold storage Valves to solid-state electronics Photos to digital images Voice-over Internet protocol telephony Filament light bulbs to LED sources
New political rules emerge	Political conditions which shape the economic and social rules may shift dramatically (e.g. the collapse of Communism meant an alternative model – capitalist, competition – as opposed to central planning – and many ex-state firms couldn't adapt their ways of thinking)	Old mindset about how business is done, rules of the game, etc. are challenged and established firms fail to understand or learn new rules	Centrally planned to market economy (e.g. former Soviet Union) Apartheid to post-apartheid South Africa Free trade/globalization results in dismantling protective tariff and other barriers and new competition basis emerges
Running out of road	Firms in mature industries may need to escape the constraints of diminishing space for	Current system is built around a particular trajectory and embedded in a	*Encyclopædia Britannica* finally running out of road as it is displaced by first CD-based then *(continued)*

TABLE 18.2 *(Continued)*

Triggers/ sources of discontinuity	Explanation	Problems posed	Examples (of good and bad experiences)
	product and process innovation and the increasing competition of industry structures by either exit or by radical reorientation of their business	steady-state set of innovation routines which militate against widespread search or risk-taking experiments	online and now open-source encyclopaedias like Wikipedia Sometimes, firms manage to break out and establish a new trajectory (e.g. Nokia, from timber products to mobile phones, or Preussag, from metals and commodities to tourism)
Sea change in market sentiment or behaviour	Public opinion or behaviour shifts slowly and then tips over into a new model (e.g. the music industry is in the midst of a technology-enabled revolution in delivery systems from buying records, tapes and CDs to direct download of tracks in mp3 and related formats) Long-standing issues of concern to a minority accumulate momentum (sometimes through the action of pressure groups) and suddenly the system switches/tips over (e.g. social attitudes to smoking or health concerns about obesity levels and fast foods)	Don't pick up on it or persist in alternative explanations (cognitive dissonance) until it may be too late Rules of the game suddenly shift and then new pattern gathers rapid momentum wrong-footing existing players working with old assumptions	Apple, Napster, Dell, Microsoft vs. traditional music industry McDonald's, Burger King and obesity concerns Tobacco companies and smoking bans Oil/energy and others and global warming Opportunity for new energy sources like wind-power where Danish firms have come to dominate
Deregulation/ shifts in regulatory regime	Political and market pressures lead to shifts in the regulatory	New rules of the game but old mindsets persist and existing	Old monopoly positions in fields like telecommunications

(continued)

TABLE 18.2 *(Continued)*

Triggers/ sources of discontinuity	Explanation	Problems posed	Examples (of good and bad experiences)
	framework and enable the emergence of a new set of rules (e.g. liberalization, privatization or deregulation)	players unable to move fast enough or see new opportunities opened up	and energy were dismantled and new players/combinations of enterprises emerged In particular, energy and bandwidth become increasingly viewed as commodities
			Innovations include skills in trading and distribution, a factor behind the considerable success of Enron in the late 1990s as it emerged from a small gas pipeline business to becoming a major energy trade
Business model innovation	Established business models are challenged by a reframing, usually by a new entrant who redefines/reframes the problem and the consequent rules of the game	New entrants see opportunity to deliver product/service via new business model and rewrite rules – existing players have at best to be fast followers	Amazon.com in retailing Charles Schwab in share trading Southwest and other low cost airlines Direct Line insurance
Unthinkable events	Unimagined and therefore not prepared for events which, sometimes literally, change the world and set up new rules of the game	New rules may disempower existing players or render competencies unnecessary	9/11
Shifts in 'techno-economic paradigm' – systemic changes which impact whole sectors or even whole societies	Change takes place at system level, involving technology and market shifts. This involves the convergence of a number of trends which result in a 'paradigm shift' where the old order is replaced	Hard to see where new paradigm begins until rules become established Existing players tend to reinforce their commitment to old model, reinforced by 'sailing ship' effects	Industrial Revolution Mass production

Managing Discontinuous Innovation

Discontinuous innovation offers threats and opportunities for both new and established players. By changing the rules of the game it puts a premium on entrepreneurial behaviour – being able to spot an emerging opportunity and exploit it. For new entrants it is the 'classic' entrepreneur's challenge of being able to manage the growth of a business from a bright but often high-risk idea – and doing it from a weak asset base. For established players the challenge is one of reinventing themselves to allow at least a part of the business to behave as if it were an entrepreneurial start-up – and of holding back the conservative forces of the mainstream organization to let this happen.

The problem is not that discontinuity happens – it is a near-certainty that disruption will come from somewhere at some time – but what companies do about it, and whether they can do it early enough to exploit the opportunities rather than be threatened by the disruptive changes. And existing players must answer the question of whether what they have already learnt to do about managing innovation is still the right thing to do under these new circumstances.

For example, the problem for the firms in the disk drive industry wasn't that they didn't listen to customers but rather that they listened too well. They built a virtuous circle of demanding customers in their existing marketplace with whom they developed a stream of improvement innovations, continuously stretching their products and processes to do what they were doing better and better. The trouble was that they were getting very close to the wrong customers – the discontinuity which got them into trouble was the emergence of a completely different set of users with very different needs and values.

Not all technological revolutions upset the established players. If they see the new developments early enough and pick up on their significance, they can often strengthen their position. Studies of discontinuous technological shifts across a wide range of industries over an extended time period show that under some conditions major technological shifts could be 'competence destroying' – at which point new entrants would dominate the new industries enabled by radical technology.[4] But under other conditions the radical technologies were 'competence enhancing' and strengthened the hand of existing incumbents. This suggests that disruption is not always a changing of the guard between existing incumbents and new entrants.

We used a model of 'framing' (where organizations put a frame around the world to make sense of it, which they sometimes must modify, hence 'reframing) in Chapters 7 and 9 on search and selection. It's worth reminding ourselves of that model (Figure 18.2) here since it helps focus on the problem of discontinuity – which is all about being able to reframe and work on the right-hand side of the picture.

Table 18.3 contrasts the innovation management challenges posed by these two very different environments. Type 1 organizations are, not surprisingly, something which established players are good at creating and operating – geared to 'doing what we do better' and to repeating the innovation trick, structures and procedures to enable a steady stream of product, process and service innovations. But Type 2 organizations are much more like new entrants: agile and flexible, able to switch directions, to experiment around the emergent new rules of the game.

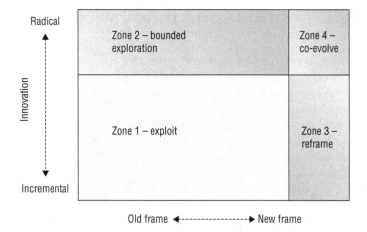

FIGURE 18.2 A map of innovation selection space

TABLE 18.3 Different Archetypes for Steady-State and Discontinuous Innovation

Type 1 Innovation organization	Type 2
Operates within mental framework based on clear and accepted set of rules of the game	No clear rules – these emerge over time. High tolerance for ambiguity
Strategies path dependent	Path independent, emergent, probe and learn
Clear selection environment	Fuzzy, emergent selection environment
Selection and resource allocation linked to clear trajectories and criteria for fit	Risk-taking, multiple parallel bets, tolerance of (fast) failure
Operating routines refined and stable	Operating patterns emergent and fuzzy
Strong ties and knowledge flows along clear channels	Weak ties and peripheral vision important

Dealing with Discontinuity

Working in Type 2 mode means a new set of approaches to organizing and managing innovation, for example how the firm searches for weak signals about potential discontinuities, how it makes strategic choices in the face of high uncertainty, how it resources projects which lie far outside the mainstream of its innovation operations, etc. And it's a problem which extends beyond the firm – discontinuous innovation is often problematic because it may involve building and working with a significantly different set of partners. 'Strong ties' – close and consistent relationships with regular partners in a network – may be important in enabling a steady stream of continuous improvement innovations, but where firms are seeking to do something different they may need links across a very different population in order to gain access to new ideas and different sources of knowledge and expertise.

For new entrants this isn't an issue. They can set their organization and networks up from scratch. But what does an established player do? One option is to set up their own version of new entrant firms, simply spinning off entities which they hope will be able to colonize and settle the new world of a Type 2 environment. This is a low-risk option but also means that there may be little synergy or leverage across to and from the core business. Another option is to try to develop a parallel innovation management capability within the mainstream business, but in order to do this a number of new approaches will be needed.

In practice there are many options between these two poles, including setting up special units within an established business or managing more 'open innovation' operations which leverage the entrepreneurial strengths of smaller players. A number of large firms – for example Microsoft, Intel, Cisco, Siemens and GSK – have developed sophisticated fishing strategies that look around for smaller smart players to buy or at least link up with to help them keep an edge.

The challenge is essentially around building 'dynamic capability' – as we've seen throughout this book. What does discontinuity mean for the 'routines' which organizations learn around innovation management, and in particular:

- What do we need to do more of, and extend?
- What do we need to do less of, or stop?
- What new approaches do we need to add?

Case Study highlighting the experience of various companies in trying to search in this discontinuous space is available on the Innovation Portal at **www.innovation-portal.info**

Figure 18.3 reminds us of our core innovation process model but suggests that we may need to run a parallel model to ensure we can deal with the questions raised by discontinuous conditions.

Table 18.4 maps some answers to these questions against these stages.

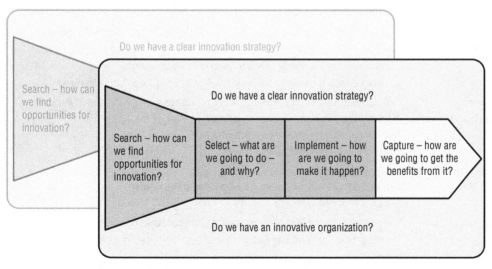

FIGURE 18.3   Managing 'steady-state' and discontinuous innovation

TABLE 18.4   An Emergent 'Good Practice' Model Outline for Discontinuous Innovation

Element in innovation model	Routines for managing discontinuity
Search	Search at the periphery – pick up and amplify weak signals
	Use multiple and alternative perspectives
	Manage the idea generation process inside the firm – enable systematic and high involvement in innovation
	Develop an external scanning capability – scouts and hunters
	Use technological antennae to seek out potential new technologies
	Tune in to weak market signals (e.g. working with fringe users, early trend locations, such as chatrooms on the Internet)
	Develop future exploring capability – scenario and alternatives
	Explore at periphery of firm – subsidiaries, joint ventures, distributors as sources of innovation
	Bring in outside perspectives
Strategic selection	Build pluralism into decision-making processes
	Create 'markets for judgement'
	Decentralize seed funding for new ideas (e.g. via internal venture funds or development budgets)
	Build dual structures for innovation development and decision-making
	Develop 'fuzzy front end' approaches
Implementation	Build flexible project development organizations – emphasize 'probe and learn' rather than 'predictive' project planning
	Work actively with users on co-evolution of innovation
	Build parallel resource networks
Innovation strategy	Explore alternative future scenarios and consider parallel possibilities
	Identify strategic domains within which targeted hunting can take place
	Build capacity for ambiguity/multiple parallel strategies
	Actively explore 'how to destroy the business' to enable reframing
Innovative organization	Build a culture which supports and encourages diversity and curiosity-driven behaviour
	Set up appropriate incentive structures
	Enable complex knowledge flows
Proactive linkages	Develop non-committal exploratory supply relationships in addition to longer-term strategic alliances – 'strategic dalliances'
	Explore and develop parallel 'weak ties'
Capture value	Explore alternative business models better suited to the emergent conditions
	Develop fast learning approaches – entrepreneurial 'probe and learn' experiments

Summary

- While organizations may be highly competent at what we could call 'steady-state innovation' (essentially doing what they do but better) problems can occur when they confront the need for *discontinuous* innovation.

- A key part of the problem is that dealing with discontinuity requires a very different set of capabilities for organizing and managing innovation. Searching in unlikely places, building links to strange partners, allocating resources to high-risk ventures, exploring new ways of looking at the business – all of these challenge the 'normal' way we approach the innovation problem.

- History suggests that when such shocks happen – be they technological shifts, the emergence of totally new markets or the bringing-in of a new business model which reframes the rules of the game – it favours the new entrant over the established incumbent. But this is not a hard-and-fast rule. There are plenty of examples of established players who take on the new and use it to enhance their competitive position.

- Triggers for discontinuous shifts – where the rules of the game are changed – can be radical technological developments, the emergence of new markets, changes in the political or regulatory framework, shifts in public opinion or simply unexpected and sometimes catastrophic events.

- Changing the rules of the game puts a premium on entrepreneurial behaviour – being able to spot an emerging opportunity and exploit it. For new entrants it is the 'classic' entrepreneur's challenge of being able to manage the growth of a business from a bright but often high-risk idea – and doing it from a weak asset base. For established players the challenge is one of reinventing themselves to allow at least a part of the business to behave as if it were an entrepreneurial start-up – and of holding back the conservative forces of the mainstream organization to let this happen.

Further Resources

A number of researchers are actively exploring questions raised by discontinuous innovation – what it is and how it can be anticipated and dealt with. A good compilation of core issues and company experiences in dealing with them can be found in the work of Peter Augsdorfer.[5] Other studies include the work of Richard Leifer and colleagues on radical innovation[6, 7] and Day and Schoemaker on the theme of peripheral vision.[8] The core questions were originally posed by Clayton Christensen, and he has continued to write extensively about disruptive innovation.[2, 9–12]

There are a number of case studies of firms or sectors which have faced these challenges.[13–15]

References

1. Utterback, J. (1994) *Mastering the Dynamics of Innovation*. Boston: Harvard Business School Press.

2. Christensen, C. (1997) *The Innovator's Dilemma*. Cambridge: Harvard Business School Press.

3. Abernathy, W. and J. Utterback (1975) A dynamic model of product and process innovation, *Omega*, **3** (6): 639–656.

4. Tushman, M. and P. Anderson (1987) Technological discontinuities and organizational environments, *Administrative Science Quarterly*, **31** (3): 439–465.

5. Augsdorfer, P., J. Bessant, K. Möslein, F. Piller, and B. von Stamm (2013) *Discontinuous Innovation: Learning to manage the unexpected*. London: Imperial College Press.

6. Leifer, R., C. McDermott, G. O'Conner *et al.* (2000) *Radical Innovation*. Boston: Harvard Business School Press.

7. O'Connor, G. C., R. Leifer, A. Paulson and L. S. Peters (2008) *Grabbing Lightning*. San Francisco: Jossey-Bass.

8. Day, G. and P. Schoemaker (2006) *Peripheral Vision: Detecting the weak signals that will make or break your company*. Boston: Harvard Business School Press.

9. Christensen, C., S. Anthony and E. Roth (2007) *Seeing What's Next*. Boston: Harvard Business School Press.

10. Christensen, C., J. Grossman and M. Hwang (2009) *The Innovator's Prescription: A disruptive solution for health care*. New York: McGraw-Hill.

11. Christensen, C., C. Johnson and M. Horn (2010) *Disrupting Class: How disruptive innovation will change the way the world learns*. New York: McGraw-Hill.

12. Christensen, C. and M. Raynor (2003) *The Innovator's Solution: Creating and sustaining successful growth*. Boston: Harvard Business School Press.

13. Evans, P. and T. Wurster (2000) *Blown to Bits: How the new economics of information transforms strategy*. Cambridge, MA: Harvard Business School Press.

14. Foster, R. and S. Kaplan (2002) *Creative Destruction*. Cambridge, MA: Harvard University Press.

15. Birkinshaw, J., J. Bessant and R. Delbridge (2007) Finding, forming, and performing: Creating networks for discontinuous innovation, *California Management Review*, **49** (3): 67–83.

Deeper Dive explanations of innovation concepts and ideas are available on the Innovation Portal at **www.innovation-portal.info**

Quizzes to test yourself further are available online via the Innovation Portal at **www.innovation-portal.info**

Summary of online resources for Chapter 18 –
all material is available via the Innovation Portal at
www.innovation-portal.info

Cases	**Media**	**Tools**	**Activities**	**Deeper Dive**
• Dealing with discontinuity • Coloplast • Twelve search strategies	• Clayton Christensen	• Discontinuous innovation audit • Innovation life cycle • Twelve search strategies (for peripheral vision)	• Patterns of discontinuous change • Peripheral vision • Developing discontinuous innovation capability • Discontinuous innovation audit	• Disruptive innovation theory

Chapter 19

Social Innovation

LEARNING OBJECTIVES

By the end of this chapter you will develop an understanding of:

- social entrepreneurship and social innovation
- social entrepreneurship as an organized and disciplined process rather than as a well-meaning but unfocused intervention
- the difficulties in managing what is just as much an uncertain and risky process as 'conventional' economically motivated innovation
- the key themes necessary to manage this process effectively.

INNOVATION IN ACTION 19.1

Grameen Bank and the Development of 'Microfinance'

One of the biggest problems facing people living below the poverty line is the difficulty of getting access to banking and financial services. As a result they are often dependent on moneylenders and other unofficial sources – and are often charged at exorbitant rates if they do borrow. This makes it hard to save and invest, and puts a major barrier in the way of breaking out of this spiral through starting new entrepreneurial ventures. Awareness of this problem led Muhammad Yunus, Head of the Rural Economics Program at the University of Chittagong, to launch a project to examine the possibility of designing a credit delivery system to provide banking services

(continued)

targeted at the rural poor. In 1976, the Grameen Bank Project (*grameen* means 'rural' or 'village' in Bengali) was established, aiming to:

- extend banking facilities to the poor
- eliminate the exploitation of the poor by money lenders
- create opportunities for self-employment for unemployed people in rural Bangladesh
- offer the disadvantaged an organizational format which they can understand and manage by themselves
- reverse the age-old vicious circle of 'low income, low saving and low investment' into a virtuous circle of 'low income, injection of credit, investment, more income, more savings, more investment, more income'.

The original project was set up in Jobra (a village adjacent to Chittagong University) and some neighbouring villages and ran from 1976 to 1979. The core concept was of 'microfinance': enabling people (and a major success was with women) to take tiny loans to start and grow tiny businesses. With the sponsorship of the central bank of the country and support of the nationalized commercial banks, the project was extended to Tangail district (a district north of Dhaka, the capital city of Bangladesh) in 1979. Its further success there led to the model being extended to several other districts in the country. In 1983, it became an independent bank as a result of government legislation. Today, Grameen Bank is owned by the rural poor, whom it serves. Borrowers of the Bank own 90% of its shares, while the remaining 10% is owned by the government. It now serves over five million clients, and enables 10 000 families to escape the poverty trap every month.

Grameen Bank has moved into other areas where the same model applies. For example, Grameen Phone is one of the largest mobile telephone operators in Asia but bases its model on providing communication access to the poorest members of society through innovative pricing models.

What Is 'Social Innovation'?

In this book we're looking at the challenge of *change* – and how individuals and groups of entrepreneurs, working alone or inside organizations, try to bring this about. We've seen that innovation is not a simple flash of inspiration but an extended and organized process of turning bright ideas into successful realities – changing the offering (product/service), the ways in which it is created and delivered (process innovation), the context and the ways in which it is introduced to that context (position innovation) and the overall mental models for thinking about what we are doing (business model or 'paradigm' innovation).

Above all, we've seen that getting innovation to happen depends on a focused and determined drive – a passion to change things which we call 'entrepreneurship'. Essentially, this is about being prepared to challenge and change, to take (calculated) risks and put energy and enthusiasm into the venture, picking up and enthusing other supporters along the way. But that rich mixture isn't motivated only by the desire to create wealth; the same focused energy can be applied to solving social problems, creating social value.

INNOVATION IN ACTION 19.2

Social Innovation in Health Care

Veronica Khosa was frustrated with the system of health care in South Africa. A nurse by trade, she saw sick people getting sicker, elderly people unable to get to a doctor and hospitals with empty beds that would not admit patients with HIV. So Veronica started Tateni Home Care Nursing Services and instituted the concept of 'home care' in her country. Beginning with practically nothing, her team took to the streets providing care to people in a way they had never received it – in the comfort and security of their own home. In only a few years, the government had adopted her plan and through the recognition of leading health organizations the idea is spreading beyond South Africa.

Source: Derived from the Ashoka Foundation, https://www.ashoka.org/fellow/veronica-khosa.

Social innovation – innovation for the greater good – has a long tradition, with examples dating back to some of the great social reformers. For example, in the nineteenth century in the United Kingdom the strong Quaker values held by key entrepreneurial figures like George Cadbury led to innovations in social housing, community development and education as well as in the factories which they organized and managed. As Geoff Mulgan and colleagues point out, 'The great wave of industrialization and urbanization in the nineteenth century was accompanied by an extraordinary upsurge of social enterprise and innovation: mutual self-help, microcredit, building societies, cooperatives, trade unions.'[1]

That tradition continues with a growing recognition of the underlying business models which can support the generation of sufficient returns to make a social enterprise sustainable in the long term.[2] In particular:

- Social innovations are usually new combinations or hybrids of existing elements, rather than being wholly new in themselves.
- Implementing them involves cutting across organizational, sectoral or disciplinary boundaries. They create new social relationships between previously separate individuals and groups, contributing to the diffusion and embedding of the innovation, and increasing potential for further innovations.
- Social innovation is also seen as building on the inherent capacities of individuals and communities, which makes the notion of open innovation especially relevant.

The growth in social innovation has also been accelerated through the core trends of open and user-led innovation which we looked at in earlier chapters. These days it becomes easier to reach many different players and to combine their innovative efforts into rich and new types of solution, for example mobilizing patients and carers in an online community concerned with rare diseases or using mobile communications to help deal with the aftermath of humanitarian crises – reuniting families, establishing communications, providing financial aid quickly via mobile money transfers, etc.

Case Studies detailing social innovations are available on the Innovation Portal at **www.innovation-portal.info**

INNOVATION IN ACTION 19.3

Applying Innovation in New Contexts

An innovative application of mobile communications has been to create employment opportunities for disadvantaged groups using 'micro work' principles. 'Impact sourcing' is the term increasingly used to describe the use of advanced communication technologies to permit participation in global labour markets by disadvantaged groups. Increasingly, many tasks – such as translation, proof-reading, optical character recognition (OCR), clean-up or data entry – can be carried out using crowdsourcing approaches; Amazon's Mechanical Turk is extensively used in this fashion. Social entrepreneurs like Leila Janah saw the potential for applying this approach. Her Samasource organization now provides employment for around 2000 people on very low incomes in rural areas. The increasing availability of mobile communications allows for mobilizing and empowering this group and an increasing number of high-tech US companies are sourcing work through her organization.

The model is not simply low-cost outsourcing; through a network of local agencies, Samasource provides not only direct employment opportunities but also training and development such that workers become better able to participate in the growing network of online knowledge work. Organizations like Samasource recognize the risk that the model could simply be used to exploit very low-wage workers; their business model requires that partners employ people earning less than $3 (£1.80) a day and reinvest 40% of revenues in training, salaries and community programmes.

There are similarities to microfinance. The underlying business model is essentially extending a well-known principle (business process outsourcing) to a new context: educated but marginalized people on low incomes who could play a role as knowledge workers. Samasource mobilizes people in a variety of countries and contexts, including rural villages, urban slums and even refugee camps. The model is diffusing widely. Other organizations, such as Digital Divide Data (originally established in South-East Asia in 2001 and now employing nearly 1000 people in Cambodia, Laos and Kenya) and CrowdFlower, perform similar integrating roles, bringing disadvantaged groups into the online workforce.

Definitions and Exploration of the Core Idea

Social innovation is not just about having a concern for the greater good but about mobilizing the core principles we have looked at in this book to directly contribute to it. The core process remains one of finding opportunities, choosing amongst them, implementing and capturing value, but it plays out in a number of different ways, which we'll explore briefly.

Individual Start-ups. . .

In many cases social innovation is an individual-driven thing, where a passion for change leads to remarkable and sustainable results. They include people like:

- Amitabha Sadangi of International Development Enterprises India, who develops low-cost irrigation technologies to help subsistence farmers survive dry seasons
- Anshu Gupta, who has formed a channel for recycling clothes and fabric to meet the needs of rural poor in India. He initiated GOONJ in 1998 with just 67 items of clothing; today, his organization sends out over 40 000 kg of material every month, in 21 states
- Mitch Besser, who founded and is the medical director of the Cape Town-based programme mothers2mothers (m2m), which aims to reduce mother-to-child transmission of HIV and provide care to women living with HIV. He founded mothers2mothers with one site in South Africa in 2001. It has grown to more than 645 sites in South Africa, Kenya, Lesotho, Malawi, Rwanda, Swaziland and Zambia
- Tri Mumpuni, executive director of Indonesian NGO IBEKA (People Centred Economic and Business Institute), who strives to bring light and energy into the lives of rural populations through the introduction of micro-hydropower plants into more than 50 villages.

(These and other examples can be found on the www.ashoka.org website which links a global community of social entrepreneurs.)

> Video Clips of an interview with Melissa Clark-Reynolds, who set up a social innovation project, is available on the Innovation Portal at **www.innovation-portal.info**

Not Just Passionate Individuals

But social entrepreneurship of this kind is also an increasingly important component of 'big business', as large organizations realize that they only secure a licence to operate if they can demonstrate some concern for the wider communities in which they are located. 'Corporate social responsibility' (CSR) is becoming a major function in many businesses and many make use of formal measures – such as the 'triple bottom line' – to monitor and communicate their focus on more than simple profit-making.

By engaging stakeholders directly, companies are also better able to avoid conflicts, or to resolve them when they arise. In some cases, this involves directly engaging with activists who are leading campaigns or protests against a company.

INNOVATION IN ACTION 19.4

Innovation and Assisted Living

BT, the UK telecommunications firm, has – under strong pressure from the regulator – a responsibility to provide services for all elements of society, but it has used the connections in this 'stakeholder network' to move early into creating services for what will be a major expansion in the future with an ageing population. By 2026, 30% of the UK population will be more than 60 years old. The pilot innovation is based on placing sensors in the home to monitor movement and the use of power and water – if something goes wrong it triggers an alarm. It has already begun to generate significant revenues for BT but has also opened up the possibility of relieving pressure on the NHS for beds and services (estimates suggest savings of around £700 million of this kind if fully deployed). Most significantly, the initial project can be seen as a stepping stone, a transitional object to help BT learn about what will be a huge and very different market in the future.

INNOVATION IN ACTION 19.5

Opening up Markets Through Social Innovation

The UK do-it-yourself home and garden retailer B&Q has been honoured for its work on disability where it has used CSR to drive improvements in customer services. What in retrospect looks like a successful business strategy has in fact evolved through real-time learning from partnerships between individual stores and local disability organizations. Following on from its pioneering experiments in having stores entirely staffed by older people, B&Q wanted to ensure that disabled people were able to shop in confidence and that they would be able to access goods and services easily. In the United Kingdom alone there are eight million disabled people; it is estimated that the 'disabled pound' is worth £30 billion and is growing. However, B&Q also saw this initiative as a way of improving wider customer care competencies: 'If we can get it right for disabled people we can get it right for most people.' To begin the process of understanding what it was like to shop and work in B&Q as a disabled person, the company started by talking to disabled people in a single store. It has now established 300 partnerships between store 'disability champions' and local disability groups to understand local needs and develop training on disability awareness and service provision. It sees these partnerships as a way of accessing 'the incredible amount of knowledge, commitment and enthusiasm which exists in this wide variety of organizations'. As a result all B&Q staff take part in disability awareness training and the company has improved store design and now provides printed material in Braille, audio type, large print and CD-Rom. It is also developing its 'Daily Living Made Easier' range of products from grab rails and bath chairs through to visual smoke alarms and lightweight garden tools.

Sometimes there is scope for social entrepreneurship to spin out of mainstream innovative activity. Procter and Gamble's PUR water purification system offers radical improvements to point-of-use drinking water delivery. Estimates are that it has reduced intestinal infections by 30–50%. The product grew out of research in the mainstream detergents business but the initial conclusion was that the market potential of the product was not high enough to justify investment; by reframing it as a development aid, the company has improved its image but also opened up a radical new area for working.

In some cases the process begins with an individual but gradually a trend is established which other players see as relevant to follow, in the process bringing their resources and experience to the game. Examples here would include Fair Trade products, which were originally a minority idea but have now become a mainstream item in every supermarket.

Case Studies detailing several examples of the potential of innovations triggered in response to social needs but which have application potential in other areas – Aravind Eye Clinics, NHL and Lifespring Hospitals – are available on the Innovation Portal at **www.innovation-portal.info**

Public Sector Innovation

Providing basic services like education, health care and a safe society are all hallmarks of a 'civilized' society. But they are produced by an army of people working in what is loosely called 'the public sector' – and as we saw at the start of this book, there is huge scope for innovation in this space. In many ways this sector represents a major application field for social innovation, whilst there may be concerns about costs and using resources wisely, the fundamental driver is around social change.[3]

Occasionally, there is a radical innovation, for example the setting-up of a National Health Service to provide healthcare for all, free at the point of delivery, in the United Kingdom. Or the establishment of the Open University which brought higher education within reach of everyone. But most of the time social innovation in the public sector consists of thousands of small incremental improvements to core services.

Video Clips of interviews with hospital staff and Helle-Vibeke Carstensen of the Danish Ministry of Taxation exploring various issues surrounding improving patient/public services are available on the Innovation Portal at **www.innovation-portal.info**

Audio Clip of a podcast interview with Lynne Maher exploring work to involve patients as 'user innovators' is available on the Innovation Portal at **www.innovation-portal.info**

Innovation in the 'Third Sector'

There is also a long tradition of innovation in the so-called third sector – the voluntary and charitable organ-

Case Studies of RED and Open Door providing other examples of innovation in health care are available on the Innovation Portal at **www.innovation-portal.info**

izations which operate to provide various forms of social welfare and service. Some of these, for example Cancer Research UK and Macmillan Cancer Relief, have created innovation management groups which work to use the kind of approaches that we have been exploring in the book to help improve their operations.

Supporting and Enabling Social Innovation

Social innovation is seen as having a major role in improving living standards – and so it has attracted growing attention from a variety of agencies aiming to support and stimulate it. For example, there are infrastructure investments – like the newly announced Big Society Capital fund in the United Kingdom and specialist venture funds like Acumen in the United States – provide an alternative source of capital, and coordinating agencies, like the Young Foundation, provide further support for the mobilization and institutionalization of social innovation.

Another increasingly significant development is the setting-up by established organizations and successful business entrepreneurs of charitable foundations whose aim is explicitly to enable social entrepreneurship and the scaling of ideas with potential benefits. Examples include the Nike Foundation, the Schwab Foundation, the Skoll Foundation (established by Jeffrey Skoll, founder of eBay) and the Gates Foundation (established by Microsoft founder Bill Gates and which increasingly receives support from financier Warren Buffett).

Video Clip of an interview with Simon Tucker of the Young Foundation giving examples of social innovation approaches is available on the Innovation Portal at **www.innovation-portal.info**

The Challenge of Social Entrepreneurship

While changing the world with social innovation is possible, it isn't easy. Just because there is no direct profit motive doesn't take the commercial challenges out of the equation. If anything, it becomes harder to be an entrepreneur when the challenge is not only to convince people that it can be done (and use all the tricks of the entrepreneur's trade to do so) but also to do so in a form that makes it commercially sustainable. Bringing a radio within reach of rural poor across Africa is a great idea – but someone still has to pay for raw materials, build and run a factory, arrange for distribution and collect the small money from the sales. None of this comes cheap, and setting up such a venture faces economic, political and business obstacles every bit as hard as a bright start-up company in medical devices or computer software working in a developed country environment.

Case Study of Lifeline Energy, a social innovation based on bringing communication and its accompanying benefits to children in the developing world, is available on the Innovation Portal at **www.innovation-portal.info**

Video Clip of an interview with Suzana Moreira, whose business is trying to use mobile communications to provide food and educational resources for families in rural southern Africa, is available on the Innovation Portal at **www.innovation-portal.info**

The problem isn't just the difficult one of finding resources. Table 19.1 lists some other examples of the difficulties social entrepreneurs face when trying to innovate for the greater good.

TABLE 19.1 Challenges in Social Innovation

Problem area	Challenges
Resources	Not easily available and may need to cast the net widely to secure funding and other support
Conflicts	While the overall goal may be to meet a social need, there can be conflicts in how this is to be balanced against the need to generate revenue. For example, Freeplay Energy wanted to provide simple communication devices for the developing world but it also wanted to provide employment to disabled people. The costs of the latter made the former difficult to achieve competitively and set up a major conflict for the management of the enterprise.
Voluntary nature	Many people involved in social innovation are there because of core values and beliefs and contribute their time and energy in a voluntary way. This means that 'traditional' forms of organization and motivation may not be available – posing a significant human resource management challenge
'Lumpy' funding	Unlike commercial businesses, where a stream of revenue can be used to fund innovation in a consistent fashion, many social enterprises rely on grants, donations and other sources which are intermittent and unpredictable
Scale of the challenge	The sheer size of many of the issues being addressed (e.g. how to provide clean drinking water, deliver reliable low-cost healthcare, combating illiteracy) mean that having a clear focus is essential. Without a targeted innovation strategy social enterprises risk dissipating their efforts

Enabling Social Innovation

We've seen throughout this book how innovation doesn't simply happen; it is a process which can be organized and managed. Figure 19.1 reminds us of the core model we have been using.

So how does this play out in the case of social innovation? The following section examines some examples of the challenges.

Challenges in Social Entrepreneurship

Search for opportunities

Many potential social entrepreneurs (SEs) have the passion to change something in the world – and there are plenty of targets to choose from, like poverty, access to education, health care and so on. But passion isn't enough; they also need the classic entrepreneur's skill of spotting an opportunity, a connection, a possibility which could develop. It's about searching for new ideas which may bring a different solution to an existing problem (e.g. the microfinance alternative to conventional banking or street-level money-lending).

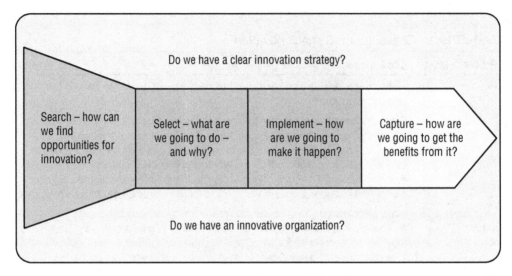

FIGURE 19.1   Core model of the innovation process

As we've seen elsewhere in this book, the skill is often not so much discovery (finding something completely new) as connection (making links between disparate things). In the SE field the gaps may be very wide (e.g. connecting rural farmers to high tech-international stock markets requires considerably more vision to bridge the gap than spotting the need for a new variant of futures' trading software). So SEs need both passion and vision, plus considerable broking and connecting skills.

Selection

Spotting an opportunity is one thing – but getting others to believe in it and, more importantly, back it is something else. Whether it's an inventor approaching a venture capitalist or an internal team pitching a new product idea to the strategic management in a large organization, the story of successful entrepreneurship is about convincing other people.

In the case of SE the problem is compounded by the fact that the targets for such a pitch may not be immediately apparent. Even if you can make a strong business case and have thought through the likely concerns and questions, who do you approach to try to get backing from? There are some foundations and non-profit organizations but in many cases one of the important skill sets of an SE is networking, the ability to chase down potential funders and backers and engage them in their project.

Even within an established organization, the presence of a structure may not be sufficient. For many SE projects the challenge is that they take the firm in very different directions, some of which fundamentally challenge its core business. For example, a proposal to make drugs cheaply available in the developing world may sound a wonderful idea from an SE perspective but it poses huge challenges to the structure and operations of a large pharmaceutical firm with complex economics around R&D funding, distribution and so on.

It is important to build coalitions of support – securing support for social innovation is very often a distributed process but power and resources are often not concentrated in the hands of a single decision-maker. There may also not be a board or venture capitalist to pitch the ideas to – instead it is a case of building momentum and groundswell.

It is also useful to provide practical demonstrations of what otherwise may be seen as idealistic pipedreams. The role of pilots which are then taken up and gather support is well proven (e.g. the Fair Trade model or microfinance).

Implementation

Social innovation requires extensive creativity in getting hold of the diverse resources to make things happen, especially since the funding base may be limited. Networking skills become critical here – engaging different players and aligning them with the core vision.

One of the most important elements in much social innovation is scaling up – taking what might be a good idea implemented by one person or in a local community and amplifying it so that it has widespread social impact.

Innovation strategy

Here the overall vision is critical – the passionate commitment to a clear vision can engage others – but SEs can also be accused of idealism and of having their head in the clouds. Consequently, there is a need for a clear plan to translate the vision step by step into reality.

Innovative organization/rich networking

Social innovation depends on loose and organic structures where the main linkages are through a sense of shared purpose. At the same time there is a need to ensure some degree of structure to allow for effective implementation. The history of many successful social innovations is essentially one of networking, mobilizing support and accessing diverse resources through rich networks. This places a premium on networking and broking skills.

> Case Study of Freeplay Energy detailing the difficulties in creating and growing a sustainable social innovation programme is available on the Innovation Portal at **www.innovation-portal.info**

Why Social Innovation?

> Social entrepreneurs are not content just to give a fish or teach how to fish. They will not rest until they have revolutionized the fishing industry.
> — *Bill Drayton, CEO, chair and founder of Ashoka, a global non-profit organization devoted to developing the profession of social entrepreneurship*

It's worth pausing for a moment to reflect on the underlying motivation for social innovation, whether we are talking about passionate individuals, enlightened corporations, public sector institutions or 'third sector' organizations.

At the Individual Level. . .

If we think about successful entrepreneurs, they are typically ambitious, mission driven, passionate, strategic (not just impulsive), resourceful and results oriented. And we can think of plenty of names to fit this frame: Bill Gates (Microsoft), Richard Branson (Virgin), James Dyson, Larry Page and Sergey Brin (Google) or Jeff Bezos (Amazon).

But we could also apply these terms to describe people like Florence Nightingale, Elizabeth Fry or Albert Schweizer. And while less famous than Gates or Bezos, there are some impressive individuals around today who have made a significant mark on the world through getting their ideas into action. As the Ashoka Foundation comments: 'Unlike traditional business entrepreneurs, social entrepreneurs primarily seek to generate "social value" rather than profits. And unlike the majority of non-profit organizations, their work is targeted not only towards immediate, small-scale effects, but sweeping, long-term change.'

Video Clip of a talk by Tad Golesworthy who developed and had implanted a novel design for a heart valve is available on the Innovation Portal at **www.innovation-portal.info**

Another important area where individuals have been a powerful source of social innovation comes from the world of 'user-innovators'. As we saw in Chapter 16, this class of innovator is increasingly important and has often been at the heart of major social change. Experiencing problems first-hand can often provide the trigger for change, for example in health care.

Why Organizations Do It

As we've seen, it isn't just individuals who undertake social innovation: it is increasingly part of the offering by all kinds of business organization. There are several reasons for this, and we will focus on three:

- social innovation as securing a 'licence to operate'
- social innovation as aligning values
- social innovation as a learning laboratory.

Licence to Operate

There is growing pressure on established businesses to work to a more socially responsible agenda – with many operating a key function around corporate social responsibility (CSR). The concept is simple: firms need to secure a 'licence to operate' from the stakeholders in the various constituencies in which they work. Unless they take notice of the concerns and values of those communities, they risk passive, and increasingly active, resistance and their operations can be severely affected. CSR goes beyond public relations in many cases with genuine efforts to ensure social value is created alongside economic value, and that stakeholders benefit as widely as possible and not simply as consumers. CSR thinking has led to the development of formal measures and frameworks like the 'triple bottom line', which many firms use as a way of expanding the traditional company reporting framework to take into account not just financial outcomes but also environmental and social performance.

INNOVATION IN ACTION 19.6

User-Led Social Innovation

One day Louis Plante – a sufferer from cystic fibrosis – had to leave a concert because of excessive coughing while sitting in proximity to a large speaker. Using his skills as an electronics technician, Louis developed a device that could generate the low frequency vibrations (Oliveira 2012). His primary goal was to develop a treatment he would benefit from but he realised that his efforts could be valuable for others and so he created a firm (Dymedso) to commercialize his solution.

Another CF affected person, Hanna Boguslawska, developed chest percussion with electrical percussion and founded a firm named eper ltd to commercialize it: 'My daughter, 26 with CF, depended for most of her life on us, her parents to do her chest physiotherapy. So her independence was constantly compromised and she hated it. On the other hand, we not always delivered the best physiotherapy; simply because we were tired, or didn't have all this time required, or were sick. Sure, you know all of this. [...] Many times I was thinking about a simple solution, which would deliver a good physiotherapy and wouldn't require a caregiver. And I am very happy I could do it. My daughter uses my eper 100 (stands for electrical percussor, and 100 symbolizes all my percussion ideas which were never realized) all the time. According to her it is much better than the human hand and she can do it alone.'

Source: Derived from Habicht, H., P. Oliveira and V. Scherbatuik (2012) User innovators: When patients set out to help themselves and end up helping many, *Die Unternehmung – Swiss Journal of Management Research*, **66** (3): 277–294.

INNOVATION IN ACTION 19.7

Different Types of Entrepreneurs

In an award-winning paper Emmanuelle Fauchart and Marc Gruber studied the motivations and underlying psychological drivers amongst entrepreneurial founders of businesses in the sports equipment sector. Their study used social identity theory to explore the underlying self-perceptions and aspirations and found three distinct types of role identity amongst their sample. 'Darwinians' were primarily concerned with competing and creating business success, whereas 'Communitarians' were much more concerned with social identities which related to participating in and contributing to a community. 'Missionaries' had a strong inner vision, a desire to change the world, and their entrepreneurial activity was an expression of this.

Source: Derived from Fauchart, E. and M. Gruber (2011) Darwinians, Communitarians, and Missionaries: The role of founder identity in entrepreneurship, *Academy of Management Journal*, **54** (5): 935–957.

It is easy to become cynical about CSR activity, seeing it as a cosmetic overlay on what are basically the same old business practices. But there is a growing recognition that pursuing social-entrepreneurship-linked goals may not be incompatible with developing a viable and commercially successful business.

This value is in both intangible domains like brand and reputation but increasingly in bottom line benefits like market share and product/service innovation. And the downside of a failure in CSR is that public perception of the organization can shift with a negative impact on brands, reputation and ultimately performance. Concern in the United Kingdom over the tax arrangements of Amazon, Starbucks and Google forced changes in their operating agenda while the backlash against fast-food meant that players like McDonald's and KFC had to rethink their approach.

Aligning Values

A second reason for engaging in social innovation on the part of organizations is the motivational effects they get from aligning their values with those of their staff. Most people want to work for organizations in which there is a positive benefit to society, and many see this as a way of fulfilling themselves. Think of the motives for working in health care or education and the sense is often one of vocation – a calling – rather than because of the more usual (financial) rewards.

Organizations which align with the values of their staff tend to have better retention and the chance to build on the ideas and suggestions of their staff – high-involvement innovation. This is also critical in those organizations which operate with a small core staff and a large number of volunteers, for example in the charity sector or in the case of social care.

Social Innovation as a Learning Laboratory

One other area where participating in social innovation may be valuable is in using it as an extension of innovation search possibilities. Social innovations often arise out of a combination of widespread and often urgent need *and* severe resource limitations. Existing solutions may not be viable in such situations and instead new solutions emerge which are better suited to the extreme conditions.

As we have seen, meeting the needs of a different group with very different characteristics to those of the mainstream population can provide a laboratory for the emergence of innovations which may well diffuse later to the wider population. There is a clear need for such innovation to meet the widespread demands for health care, education, sanitation, energy and food across populations which do not have the disposable income to purchase these goods and services via conventional routes.[4]

Humanitarian emergencies – such as earthquakes, tsunami, flood and drought, or man-made crises such as war and the consequent refugee problems – provide another example of urgent and widespread need which cannot be met through conventional routes. Instead, agencies working in this space are characterized by high rates of innovation, often improvising solutions which can then be shared across other agencies and provide radically different routes to innovation in logistics, communication and health care.

Learning from such experiments can lead to wider application of the underlying concepts, for example GE's bestselling portable ultrasound scanner emerged from a small project to meet the needs of midwives working in rural villages in India. Other examples include changing business models in banking (based on the Grameen experience) and resilient logistics using lessons originally learned in humanitarian crises.[5]

Case Studies of 'crisis driven' innovations which describe activities in the humanitarian aid sector are available on the Innovation Portal at **www.innovation-portal.info**

INNOVATION IN ACTION 19.8

Mobilizing Stakeholder Innovation

The Danish pharmaceutical firm Novo Nordisk is deploying stakeholder innovation through expansion and reframing of the role of its Corporate Stakeholder Relations (CSR) activities. It has been consistently highly rated on this, not least because it is a board-level strategic responsibility (specified in the company's articles of association) with significant resources committed to projects to sustain and enhance good practice. It was one of the first companies to introduce the concept of the 'triple bottom line' performance measurement, recognizing the need to take into account wider social and societal concerns and to be clear about its values.

But there is now growing recognition that this investment is also a powerful innovation resource which offers a way of complementing its mainstream R&D. For example, its DAWN (Diabetes Attitudes, Wishes and Needs) programme, initiated in 2001, tried to explore attitudes, wishes and needs of both diabetes sufferers and health care professionals to identify critical gaps in the overall care offering. Its findings showed in quantitative fashion how people with diabetes suffered from different types of emotional distress and poor psychological wellbeing, and that such factors were a major contributing factor to impaired health outcomes. Insights from the programme opened up new areas for innovation across the system. For example, a key focus was on the ways in which health care professionals presented therapeutic options involving a combination of insulin treatment and lifestyle elements – and on developing new approaches to this.

Søren Skovlund, senior adviser at Corporate Health Partnerships, saw the key element as 'the use of the DAWN study as a vehicle to get all the different people round the same table . . . to bring patients, health professionals, politicians, payers [and] the media together to find new ways to work more effectively together on the same task . . . You can't avoid getting some innovation because you're bringing together different baskets of knowledge in the room!'

DAWN provides an input to another set of activities operated by Novo Nordisk under the banner of National Diabetes Programmes (NDPs). This initiative began in 2001 when the company set about building a network of relationships in key geographical areas, helping devise and configure relevant holistic care programmes. Rather than a product focus, NDPs offer a range of inputs, for example supporting the education of health care professionals or establishing clinics for the treatment of diabetic ulcers. The CEO, Lars Rebien Sørensen, argues that 'only by offering and advocating the right solutions for diabetes care will we be seen as a responsible company. If we just say, "Drugs, drugs, drugs," they will say, "Give us a break!"' This is clearly

(continued)

good CSR practice – but the potential learning about new approaches to care, especially under resource-constrained conditions, also represents an important 'hidden R&D' investment.

For example, Tanzania was an early pilot. It was initially difficult to convince authorities there to take chronic diseases like diabetes into account since they had no budget for them and were already fighting hard with infectious diseases. With little likelihood of new investment, Novo Nordisk began working with local diabetes associations to establish demonstration projects. It set up clinics in hospitals and villages, trained staff and provided relevant equipment and materials. This gave visibility to the possibilities offered by a chronic disease management approach, for example before the programme someone with diabetes might have had to travel 200 km to the major hospital in Dar es Salaam, whereas now they could be dealt with locally. The value to the national health system was significant in terms of savings on the costs of treating complications such as blindness and amputations, which can be the tragic and expensive results of poor and delayed treatment. As a result the Ministry of Health was able to deal with diabetes management without the need for new investment in hospital capacity or recruitment of new doctors and nurses.

NDPs represent an experience-sharing network across over 40 countries. Much of the learning is about the context of different national health care systems and how to work within them to bring about significant change – essentially positioning the company for the co-evolution of novel models.

Summary

- Innovation is about creating value, and one important dimension of this is making change happen in a socially valuable direction.

- 'Social entrepreneurs' – individuals and organizations – recognize a social problem and organize an innovation process to enable social change.

- Just because there is no direct profit motive doesn't take the commercial challenges out of the equation. If anything, it becomes harder to be an entrepreneur when the challenge is not only to convince people that it can be done (and use all the tricks of the entrepreneur's trade to do so) but also to do so in a form that makes it commercially sustainable.

- Social entrepreneurship of this kind is also an increasingly important component of 'big business', as large organizations realize that they only secure a licence to operate if they can demonstrate some concern for the wider communities in which they are located.

- There are also benefits which emerge through aligning corporate values with those of employees within organizations.

- And there are significant learning opportunities through experiments in social innovation which may have impacts upon mainstream innovation.

- Making social entrepreneurship happen will require learning and absorbing a new set of skills to sit alongside our current ways of thinking about and managing innovation. How do we find opportunities which deliver social as well as economic benefits? How do we identify and engage a wide range of stakeholders – and understand and meet their very diverse expectations? How do we mobilize resources across networks? How do we build coalitions of support for socially valuable ideas?

Further Resources

There is a wealth of information about social entrepreneurship, including useful websites for the Ashoka Foundation (www.ashoka.org), the Skoll Foundation (www.skollfoundation. com) and the Institute for Social Entrepreneurs (www.socialent.org/). Stanford University's Entrepreneurs website has a number of resources, including videos of social entrepreneurs explaining their projects (http://edcorner.stanford.edu).

A number of books describing approaches and tools include Bornstein, D. *How to Change the World: Social entrepreneurs and the power of new ideas* (Oxford University Press, 2004), Brinckerhoff, P. *Social Entrepreneurship: The art of mission-based venture development* (John Wiley & Sons, Ltd, 2000), Dees, G., J. Emerson and P. Economy

Enterprising Nonprofits: A tool-kit for social entrepreneurs (John Wiley & Sons, Ltd, 2001), Murray, R., J. Caulier-Grice, and G. Mulgan *The Open Book of Social Innovation* (The Young Foundation, 2010).

    Case studies of projects like Grameen Bank (www.grameen-info.org) and the wind-up radio (www.freeplayenergy.com) also give insights into the process and the difficulties confronting social entrepreneurs.

References

1. Mulgan, G. (2007) *Ready or Not? Taking innovation in the public sector seriously*. London: NESTA.

2. Ramalingam, B., K. Scriven and C. Foley (2010) *Innovations in International Humanitarian Action*. London: ALNAP.

3. Bason, C. (2011) *Leading Public Sector Innovation*. London: Policy Press.

4. Prahalad, C. K. (2006) *The Fortune at the Bottom of the Pyramid*. Upper Saddle River, NJ: Wharton School Publishing.

5. Bessant, J., H. Rush and A. Trifilova (2012) Jumping the tracks: Crisis-driven social innovation and the development of novel trajectories, *Die Unternehmung – Swiss Journal of Business Research and Practice*, **66** (3): 221–242.

Deeper Dive explanations of innovation concepts and ideas are available on the Innovation Portal at **www.innovation-portal.info**

Quizzes to test yourself further are available online via the Innovation Portal at **www.innovation-portal.info**

Summary of online resources for Chapter 19 –
all material is available via the Innovation Portal at
www.innovation-portal.info

Cases	**Media**	**Tools**	**Activities**	**Deeper Dive**

Cases	Media	Tools	Activities	Deeper Dive
• Eastville Community Shop	• Suzana Moreira, moWoza	• Process mapping	• Social innovation	• Public sector innovation
• Aravind Eye Clinics	• Melissa Clark-Reynolds Minimonos	• Value engineering	• Frugal innovation	
• Lifeline Energy	• Simon Tucker, Young Foundation	• Frugal innovation		
• Crisis driven innovation	• Helle-Vibeke Carstensen			
• NHL Hospitals	• Lynne Maher			
• Lifespring Hospitals	• Tad Golesworthy (TED talk)			
• RED project				
• Open Door				
• Freeplay Energy				

Chapter 20

Innovation in Developing and Emerging Economies

LEARNING OBJECTIVES

By the end of this chapter you will understand:

- the idea of innovation as a global force and the increasingly important role played by emerging economies in that space
- the challenges faced and the opportunities offered by emerging markets
- the potential for new innovation trajectories arising from meeting needs at 'the bottom of the pyramid'.

Globalization and Innovation

In his best-selling book, *The World is Flat: The globalized world in the 21st century*, Thomas Friedman argues that developments in technology and trade, in particular information and communications technologies (ICTs), are spreading the benefits of globalization to the emerging economies, promoting their development and growth. While this may be a rather optimistic view, it does reflect the fact that recent developments have accelerated the globalization of innovation. For example, where R&D used to be the province of a relatively small number of industrialized countries (Japan, the US, Germany, the UK, Italy, etc.), it has now exploded and some of the biggest investments are being made by India and China. Even tiny economies like Singapore and Denmark are playing an increasingly important role in creating the knowledge on which future generations of innovation may be built. This doesn't mean that older economies and their R&D efforts are less important but rather that the whole game is getting much bigger and the stage on which it is being played much wider.

Frugal Innovation from Emerging Economies

An *Economist* Special Report argues that emerging economies are fast becoming sources of innovation, rather than simply relying on low-cost labour, and appears to support the popular belief that innovation is increasingly a global phenomenon.

The report estimates that there are more than 20 000 multinationals originating from the emerging economies, and that the firms in the *Financial Times'* 500 list from the BRIC economies – Brazil, Russia, India and China – more than quadrupled in 2006/08, from 15 to 62. The focus of innovation is not confined to technological breakthroughs, but typically incremental progress and product innovations, aimed at the middle or the bottom of the income pyramid, such as the $3000 car (£1800), $300 (£180) computer and $30 (£18) mobile phone, so-called frugal innovation.

For example, in India, Tata Consultancy Services (TCS) has developed a water filter which uses rice husks. It is simple, portable and relatively cheap, giving a large family an abundant supply of bacteria-free water for an initial investment of about $24 (£15) and around $4 (£2.50) every few months for a new filter. Similarly, General Electric's Bangalore R&D facility has developed a hand-held electrocardiogram (ECG) called the Mac 400. Through simplification, the Mac 400 can run on batteries and fit in a rucksack and sells for $800 (£500), instead of $2000 (£1200) for a conventional ECG, which reduces the cost of an ECG test to just $1 (60p) per patient. These innovations target two of India's most common health problems: contaminated water and heart disease, which cause millions of deaths each year.

Source: Derived from Adrian Wooldridge (2010) 'The World Turned Upside Down', *The Economist*, April 15 Special Report.

We also have to consider that it is not countries but firms which carry out much of the R&D – and their activities and locations are themselves becoming globalized. New players are joining the old established giants and playing an increasingly significant role in a world characterized by knowledge flow and open innovation.

And, of course, the demand side of innovation (the marketplace) has shifted out of all recognition in the past decade. First of all there are many more people on the planet – around seven billion and growing fast. But much of this population growth is in the regions of the world where economic growth is also accelerating, driving rising incomes and expectations and creating an explosion of market demand. These 'emerging markets' are often different in shape, size and segmentation, but they represent one of the major drivers for innovation in products and services.

We have already seen the growing importance of user-led innovation; so in a world where much of the growth is coming from very different places with different user characteristics, we should expect to see significant shifts in innovations which are aimed at meeting their needs.

This chapter explores briefly what we know about these changing conditions and particularly what that means for innovation management as an increasingly globally oriented skill and one which requires learning to act on an international stage.

Looking Back

The pattern of industrial development is a familiar one, with newcomer countries following the examples of longer-established economies and learning lessons from them before adding their own variations on the theme. This plays out in innovation. For example, the early days of industrialization saw massive innovation in Europe. Gradually, the lessons learnt through the Industrial Revolution diffused and found new application in the 'new' worlds of the United States and Japan, which rose to be significant powers in the early twentieth century. The period following the Second World War led to others – Korea, for example – picking up the baton, and later the 'Tiger' economies of East Asia, storming onto the world innovation stage through a strategy based on imitation and then self-generated development.

INNOVATION IN ACTION 20.2

Technology Strategies of Latecomer Firms in East Asia

The spectacular modernization in the past 25 years of the East Asian 'dragon' countries – Hong Kong, South Korea, Singapore and Taiwan – has led to lively debate about its causes. Michael Hobday has provided important new insights into how business firms in these countries succeeded in rapid learning and technological catch-up, in spite of underdeveloped domestic systems of science and technology, and of lack of technologically sophisticated domestic customers.

Government policies provided the favourable general economic climate: export orientation; basic and vocational education, with strong emphasis on industrial needs; and a stable economy, with low inflation and high savings. However, of major importance were the strategies and policies of specific business firms for the effective assimilation of foreign technology.

The main mechanism for catching up was the same in electronics, footwear, bicycles, sewing machines and automobiles, namely the 'OEM' (original equipment manufacture) system. OEM is a specific form of subcontracting, where firms in catching-up countries produce goods to the exact specification of a foreign transitional company (TNC) normally based in a richer and technologically more advanced country. For the TNC, the purpose is to cut costs, and to this end it offers assistance to the latecomer firms in quality control, choice of equipment, and engineering and management training. OEM began in the 1960s, and became more sophisticated in the 1970s. The next stage in the mid-1980s was ODM (own design and manufacture), where the latecomer firms learnt to design products for the buyer. The last stage is OBM (own brand manufacture), when latecomer firms market their own products under their own brand name (e.g. Samsung, Acer) and compete head-on with the leaders.

Source: Derived from Mike Hobday (1995) *Innovation in East Asia: The challenge to Japan.* Guildford: Edward Elgar.

Building BRICs: The Rise of New Players on the Innovation Stage

The current wave of innovation expansion has seen a focus on key countries known as the BRICs – Brazil, Russia, India and China – but there are many other smaller economies surging into the same space, for example Kazakhstan and South Africa. They share a mixture of rich resource endowments, relatively young populations, large potential domestic markets, reasonably developed infrastructure and a technological base which provides them with a platform for growing and building innovation capability to play on the wider global stage.

INNOVATION IN ACTION 20.3

Building BRICs – Capabilities in India

India has a population of around 1.1 billion, a large proportion of which is English-speaking, a relatively stable political and legal regime and a good national system of education, especially in science and engineering. It has some 250 universities and listed 1500 R&D centres (although care needs to be taken in the definitions used in both cases), and this has translated into international strengths in the fields of biotechnology, pharmaceuticals and software. As a result Indian firms have benefited greatly from the increasing international division of labour in some services and the support and development of software and services. India is now a global centre for outsourcing and offshoring. Until the mid-1980s, the software industry was dominated by government and public research organizations, but the introduction of export processing zones provided tax breaks and allowed the import of foreign computer technology for the first time. The market liberalization of 1991 accelerated development and inward investment, and in 2005 India attracted inward investment of $6 billion (£3.7) (significant, but still only around a tenth of that attracted by China). Since then the software and services industry in India has grown by around 50% each year to reach $8.3 billion (£5.1 billion) by 2000, and employing 400 000, second only to the United States. The industry is forecast to grow to $50 billion (£30 billion) by 2008. Unusually for India, which has historically pursued a policy of national self-reliance, the industry is very export-oriented, with around 70% of output being traded internationally.

There are three broad types of software firms in India. First, those that specialize in a specific sector or domain, for example accounting, gaming or film production, and these develop capabilities and relationships specific to those users. Second, those that develop methods and tools to provide low-cost and timely software support and solutions. The majority of the industry is in this lower-value-added part of the supply chain and is involved in low-level coding, maintenance and design, and relies on a large pool of English-speaking talent which costs around 10% of those in the United States or EU. However, a third segment of firms is emerging that are more involved with new product and service development.

India's version of Silicon Valley is around the southern city of Bangalore. This is home to a large number of firms from the United States, as well as indigenous Indian firms. Large employers include Infosys, and call and service centres here employ 250 000 operatives, including support services for firms such as Cisco, Microsoft and Dell. IBM, Intel, Motorola, Oracle, Sun Microsystems, Texas Instruments and GE all now have technology centres here. Texas Instruments was one of the few major foreign firms to start up a development unit in 1985, prior to the opening-up of the India economy in 1991. GE Medical Systems followed in the late 1980s, and established a development centre in Bangalore in 1990, which later resulted in a joint venture with the Indian firm Wipro Technologies. GE now employs 20 000 people in India, who generate sales of $500 million (£300 million). IBM was one of the first investors in India, but later withdrew because of onerous government policies and restrictions. It returned after the government liberalized the economy, and its Indian operations contributed $510 million (£312 million) in sales in 2005, employing 43 000 in India following the acquisition of the Indian outsourcing company Daksh in 2004. In 2006, it announced that it would triple its investment from $2 billion (£1.2 billion) to $6 billion (£3.6 billion) by 2009, including further service delivery centres to support computer networks worldwide and a new telecommunications research centre. Similarly, Adobe invested $50 million (£30 million) in India between 2009 and 2014, and recruited 300 software developers. Each year Adobe India contributes 10 of the 60 patents which Adobe files each year.

One of the challenges of the software and services industry in India is to increase value-added through product and service development. To date, the impressive growth has been based on winning more outsourcing business from overseas and employing more staff, rather than by increasing the value-added by new services and products. For example, the Indian software and service firm Tata increased the proportion of its revenue from new products from around 5% to 40%, to make it less reliant on low-cost human capital, which is likely to become more expensive, and more mobile. Ramco Systems developed an ERP system in the 1990s which cost a billion rupees to develop and involved 400 developers. By 2000, the company was profitable, with 150 customers, half overseas. It has established sales and support offices in the United States, Europe and Singapore. In 2006, the Indian outsourcing company Genpact (40% owned by GE of the US) launched a joint venture with New Delhi Television (NDTV) in digital video editing, post-production and archiving services to media firms. The industry is worth $1 trillion (£600 billion), and the majority of all media work is now digital.

Based on patent citations, Indian firms rely much more on linkages with the science base and technology from the developed countries, whereas China has a broader reliance, which includes its Asian neighbours, on other emerging economies, and specializes on more applied fields of technology. Indian firms rely on technologies from US firms mostly – about 60% of all patent citations, followed by (in order of importance) Japan, Germany, France and the United Kingdom. In many cases these linkages have been reinforced by inward investment by multinational corporations (MNCs), but in other cases they are the result of Indians trained or employed overseas who have returned to India to create new ventures.

Infosys was one of the first and now one of the largest software and IT services firms in India. It was created by the entrepreneur N. R. Narayana Murthy with six colleagues in 1981

(continued)

with only $250 (£150), but by 2006 it was worth $13.7 billion (£8.2 billion), with annual profits of $345 million (£210 million). Murthy believes that 'entrepreneurship is the only instrument for countries like India to solve the problem of its poverty . . . it is our responsibility to ensure that those who have not made that kind of money have an opportunity to do so'.

Sources: Derived from Forbes, N. and D. Wield (2002) *From Followers to Leaders: Managing technology and innovation.* London: Routledge; IEEE (2006) International Conference on Management of Innovation and Technology, Singapore; Friedman, T. L. (2007) *The World is Flat: The globalized world in the twenty-first century.* London: Penguin.

INNOVATION IN ACTION 20.4

Building BRICs – Capabilities in Russia

Industry in Russia is still dominated by heavy industry, including oil, gas, defence and aerospace. Consumer and service sectors are relatively poorly developed, reflecting national endowments and the legacy of the Communist, centrally planned era. For example, in 2001 oil and energy accounted for about 70% of all industrial output, and 40% of total GDP. Similarly, hydrocarbons account for more than half of exports, followed by metals, which make up about a quarter of overseas sales. Some higher-technology sectors have emerged from the earlier specialization of the Soviet economy, such as space-launches, aviation and lasers, but these remain relatively small niches. This absence of significant innovation is an interesting paradox, given the strong national emphasis given to investment and training in science and technology.

In 2000, Russia had more than 4000 formal organizations dedicated to science and technology, including 2600 public R&D centres employing almost a million qualified scientists and engineers. However, historically the focus of these numerous organizations has been on basic scientific research rather than technological or commercial innovation. The focus has been on 'big science' and the science-push model of innovation and growth, rather than a market or demand coupled model. On the supply side, the prestigious national Academy of Sciences dominates this system, and emphasizes traditional Soviet strengths in theoretical sciences such as mathematics, chemistry and physics. The Academy has never had the responsibility or role to commercialize scientific research, or to support the development of new processes or products. While overall investment in science and technology has declined in Russia, the investment in basic sciences has proportionally declined far less than investment in the applied sciences and technologies. On the demand side, the traditional, centrally planned and target-based structure did not provide incentives or resources for firms to develop or seek such innovations. Given this industrial structure and political legacy, the industrial research and design centres have failed to flourish: in 2000, there were fewer than 300 industrial R&D enterprises, and around 400 design organizations.

Russia also has an unusual industrial structure by the size of enterprise. Compared to other industrial economies, very large firms and very small enterprises are relatively under-represented. Instead, medium-sized firms are the most common and economically significant. In most advanced economies the very large firms are the main investors in formal R&D and development of commercially significant innovations, whereas the micro businesses provide a continuous outlet for more entrepreneurial behaviour. Typically, medium-sized enterprises are less important as they lack sufficient resources but suffer from most of the disadvantages of size. They are also less likely to participate in international joint ventures and alliances, or to receive foreign direct investment (FDI).

Unlike many other emerging economies, FDI and international joint ventures have played only a minor part in the development of the Russian economy. It accounts for only around 5% of total investment in Russia, compared to more than 20% in other former Soviet economies, such as Hungary, Poland and Romania. The main foreign investments and associated transfers of technological and managerial know-how have been in the oil industry, because of its significance to the Russian economy, and the food industry, which historically has been a low national priority and has performed poorly. However, in most manufacturing and service sectors there has been little foreign investment or influence, and little improvement or innovation. There are many reasons for this relative isolation from international investment and innovation, including problems of governance, including legal restrictions on ownership and the dominance of dynastic insiders in the main industries. Therefore, the institutional structure of Russia continues to constrain domestic and international innovation and entrepreneurship.

There are many cases of transfer of hard technologies in the oil and aerospace industries, both into and out of Russia, but these are usually rather conventional licensing agreements, with very little transfer or upgrading of critical managerial or commercial know-how. However, there are examples of successful innovation, often as a result of individual technical entrepreneurs or spin-offs from public research organizations, working with firms overseas. For example, the Moscow Centre for SPARC Technology, founded by Boris Babayan, is funded by Sun Microsystems and is active in the workstation market, but is based on supercomputer technology used in the Soviet space and nuclear industries. Similarly, ParaGraph, a Russian software company, is based on technology used by the military for pattern recognition, but worked with Apple to commercialize the technology.

Sources: Derived from Dyker, D. A. (2006) *Closing the EU East–West Productivity Gap.* London: Imperial College Press; (2004) *Catching Up and Falling Behind: Post-Communist transformation in historical perspective.* London: Imperial College Press.

Case Study of Spirit DSP, a leading provider of embedded voice and communication software products which originated in Moscow, is available on the Innovation Portal at **www.innovation-portal.info**

INNOVATION IN ACTION 20.5

Building BRICs – Capabilities in Brazil

In his research, Fernando Perini examined the structure and dynamics of the knowledge networks in the IT and telecommunications sectors in Brazil. The Brazilian government promoted the development of the industry between 1997 and 2003 by the 'ICT Law' which provided tax incentives for collaborative R&D, following the liberalization of the economy in the early 1990s and the unsuccessful period of import substitution. This policy promoted an overall private investment of more than $2 billion (£1.2 billion) in innovation supporting partnerships in innovation projects inside a network of 216 companies and 235 universities and research institutes, but the lasting effects on firm and national capabilities are more mixed. While the policy of tax incentives promoted a higher level of investments in innovation, it did not determine the direction or organization of innovation in the sector.

The study concludes that the effect of the tax incentives depends on the nature of the technology and industry structure. They were important in helping to create knowledge networks in system and software technologies where MNCs were key players, but much less successful in equipment, semiconductors, production process and hardware, where MNCs relied most on internal R&D and their own international networks. However, the MNCs did develop new partnerships in product development in IT systems and software, mainly with new private research institutes, rather than with established universities and research centres. Many of these private research institutes have become network integrators in the Brazilian ICT sector, and act as technological partners in activities such as training, technological services and research.

However, a small number of MNCs still dominate the Brazilian market. More than 70% of the total investments under the ICT Law were conducted by the top 15 MNC subsidiaries.

For example, Lucent entered Brazil through the acquisition of two main national telecom companies, Zetax and Batik. It benefited from the ICT Law incentives between 2000 and 2002, but now invests more than three times the amount required by the original legislation, and the laboratory in Brazil had around 105 employees in 2005. The lab has competencies in both hardware and software, but there has been a shift toward software because it is less influenced by the regulation of international trade. The lab includes a new group of 50 engineers created in 2004 to develop competences in optical access, specifically, an optical concentrator for public commutation networks. The interaction with the global R&D community is very strong, in particular through the exchange of personnel. For example, the new optical unit involved the exchange of 35 people for two months. In addition, Lucent has developed local supply and research networks, and approximately 85% of its external activities are out-sourced to FITEC. FITEC has facilities throughout Brazil, including Campinas, Belo Horizonte and Recife.

Siemens Mercosur has the longest and largest MNC presence in Brazil. The subsidiary has developed technological capabilities mainly in telecommunications, and since the ICT Law still invests more than twice that required by the legislation. R&D at the subsidiary is divided into six groups, the largest in Manaus, has 300 technical staff and specializes in Mobile Handsets that supply global markets. In addition, the Networks development group in Curitiba has around 120 engineers, and the Enterprise group 100 engineers. In relation to local technological partners, Siemens has focused on the upgrading of partnerships in the South, including two local universities (UTF-PR and PUC-PR) and one private institute (CITS), but the removal of public incentives and shifts in the technology have increased the importance of the partnership with the private research institute, CITS. However, the subsidiary has also invested in enabling institutes and postgraduate courses, for example, it helped to create a new postgraduate degree in Computer Science in Manaus. One recent development was the announcement in 2006 of a new 4 million euro development centre in Brazil, to develop digital TV technologies for the Brazilian market. Another initiative is the creation of an Innovation Portal to register and process innovative ideas from Brazilian companies and researchers.

Source: Derived from Perini, F. (2010) 'The Structure and Dynamics of the Knowledge Networks: Incentives to innovation and R&D spillovers in the Brazilian ICT sector', DPhil dissertation, SPRU, University of Sussex.

Case Study of Nokia IndT, a research institute originally established as a joint venture with the Brazilian government to work on a variety of solutions for both local and global needs in the ICT space, is available on the Innovation Portal at **www.innovation-portal.info**

Video Clip of an interview with Ana Sena discussing the work of Nokia IndT in its Living Lab, which aims to meet the needs of the largely rural population of Amazonas, is available on the Innovation Portal at **www.innovation-portal.info**

Case Study of Natura, a large cosmetics company in Brazil which uses a similar model to the Body Shop and aims to bring natural cosmetics and care products to a rapidly growing domestic and international market, is available on the Innovation Portal at **www.innovation-portal.info**

INNOVATION IN ACTION 20.6

Building BRICs – Capabilities in China

Since economic reform began in 1978, the Chinese economy has grown by about 9.5% each year, compared to 2–3% for the industrialized countries. As a result, its GDP overtook Italy's in 2004, France's and the United Kingdom's in 2005 and Germany's in 2008. China has a population of 1.3 billion, and an economy valued at $2.3 trillion (£1.4 trillion) in 2006 and over $8 trillion (£4.8 trillion) in 2012 and is now the world's second largest economy after the United States on a purchasing power basis.

The Chinese government has followed a twin-track policy of exporting relatively low-technology products while using various measures to protect its domestic economy, and providing subsidies to support selected state-owned firms to build technological capability. This activist technology policy was constrained with the completion of entry to the World Trade Organization, in 2005, and implementation of TRIPS (Trade Related Intellectual Property System), in 2006. These require stricter laws on intellectual property laws and their enforcement, and limit subsidies and interference with trade.

After two decades of providing the world economy with inexpensive labour, China is now starting to become a platform for innovation, research and development. The actual formal R&D expenditure is still comparatively small, about 1.3% of GDP (compared to an average of 2.3% of GDP in the advanced economies of the OECD, although Japan exceeds 3%), but the Chinese government aims to make China a scientific power by 2050. To facilitate this, it increased government funding in R&D in 2006 by 25% to $425 million (£260 million). It plans to increase R&D expenditure to 2.5% of GDP by 2020, in line with expenditure in developed economies. China's science and technology output is already increasing, and was ranked fifth globally in terms of science papers produced from 2002 to 2005, which is impressive given the language disadvantage.

China's policy has followed the east Asian model in which success has depended on technological and commercial investment by and collaboration with foreign firms. Typically, companies in the East Asian tiger economies such as South Korea and Taiwan developed technological capabilities on a foundation of manufacturing competence based on low-tech production, and developed higher levels of capability such as design and new product development, for example through OEM (own equipment manufacture) production for international firms. However, the flow of technology and the development of capabilities are not automatic. Economists refer to 'spillovers' of know-how from foreign investment and collaboration, but this demands a significant effort from domestic firms.

Most importantly, China has encouraged foreign MNCs to invest in China, and these are now also beginning to conduct some R&D in China. Motorola opened the first foreign R&D lab in 1992, and estimates indicate there were more than 700 R&D centres in China in 2005, although care needs to be taken in the definitions used. The transfer of technology to China, especially in the manufacturing sector, is considered a major contributor to its economic growth. Around 80% of China's inward FDI is 'technology' (hardware and software), and FDI inflows have continued to grow, to $72 billion

(£44 billion) in 2005 (for comparison, this is around 10 times that attracted by India, whereas some advanced economies continue to attract significant FDI, for example $165 billion (£100 billion) was invested in the United Kingdom in 2005). However, we must distinguish between technology transferred by foreign companies into their wholly or majority-owned subsidiaries in China versus the technology acquired by indigenous enterprises. It is only through the successful acquisition of technological capability by indigenous enterprises, many of which still remain state-owned, that China can become a really innovative and competitive economic power.

The import of foreign technology can have a positive impact on innovation, and for large enterprises the more foreign technology imported, the more conductive to its own patenting. However, for the small and medium-sized enterprises, this is not the case. This probably implies that larger enterprises possess certain absorptive capacity to take advantage of foreign technology, which in turn leads to an enhancement of innovation capacity, whereas the small-and medium-sized enterprises are more likely to rely on foreign technology because of the lack of appropriate absorptive capacity and the possibly huge gap between imported and own technology. Buying bundles of technology has been encouraged. These included 'embodied' and 'codified' technology: hardware and licences. If innovation expenditure is broken down by class of innovative activity, the costs of acquisition for *embodied* technology, such as machines and production equipment, account for about 58% of total innovation expenditure, compared with 17% internal R&D, 5% external R&D, 3% marketing, 2% training and 15% engineering and manufacturing start-up.

It is clear that the large foreign MNCs are the most active in patenting in China. Foreign patenting began in around 1995, and since 2000 patent applications have increased annually by around 50%. MNCs' patenting activities are highly correlated with total revenue, or the overall Chinese market size. This strongly supports the standpoint that foreign patents in China are largely driven by demand factors. China's specialization in patenting does not correspond to its export specialization. Automobiles, household durables, software, communication equipment, computer peripherals, semiconductors and telecommunication services are the primary areas. The semiconductor industry in 2005, for example, was granted as many as fourfold inventions of the previous year. Patents by foreign MNCs account for almost 90% of all patents in China, the most active being firms from Japan, the United States and South Korea. Thirty MNCs have been granted more than 1000 patents, and eight of these each have more than 5000: Samsung, Matsushita, Sony, LG, Mitsubishi, Hitachi, Toshiba and Siemens. Almost half of these patents are for the application of an existing technology, a fifth for inventions and the rest for industrial designs. Among the 18 000 patents for inventions with no prior overseas rights, only 924 originate from Chinese subsidiaries of these MNCs, accounting for only 0.75% of the total. The average lag between patenting in the home country and in China is more than three years, which is an indicator of the technology lag between China and MNCs.

One reason for this pattern is the very low level of industry-funded R&D, as opposed to publicly funded, but there has also been a failure of corporate governance in the large state-owned enterprises selected for support. When the economic reform programme began in 1978, it inherited the advantages and disadvantages of Maoist autarchy. China had enterprises producing across a very wide range of products, having spent heavily from the late 1950s to give itself a

(continued)

high degree of technological independence. The main disadvantage was that its technologies were out of date. The government promoted FDI through joint ventures, 51% owned by a 'national team' of about 120 large domestic state-owned enterprises. Pressures on and incentives for management in state-owned firms have encouraged them to rely on external sources of technology, rather than to develop their own internal capabilities. At the same time private Chinese firms have been constrained by a shortage of finance. However, in 2000, the government reviewed its policy and began to restructure the state-owned firms and to support the most successful private firms. There is a clear link between such restructuring and the development of capabilities.

Examples of companies which have gone through significant changes in governance or financial structure include Tianjin FAW Xiali, which was transformed into a joint venture with Toyota; TPCO, where debt funding was changed into equity and shareholding, which allowed higher investment in production capacity and technological development; and Tianjin Metal Forming, restructured to remove debt and in a stronger position to invest and be a more attractive candidate for foreign investment. Private firms like Lenovo, TCL, Ningbo Bird and Huawei have since prospered and, with belated government help, are successful overseas: Huawei, in 2004, gained 40% of its over $5 billion (£3 billion) revenues outside China; Haier has overseas revenues of over $1 billion (£600 million) from its home appliances; Lenovo bought IBM's PC division in 2005; TCL made itself the largest TV maker in the world by buying Thomson of France's TV division in 2004; Wanxiang, a motor components manufacturer started by a farmer's son as a bicycle repair shop made, by 2004, $2 billion (£1.2 billion) in annual sales.

However, there are significant differences of innovation and entrepreneurial activity in different areas of China. The eastern coastal region is higher than the other regions, especially in Shanghai, Beijing and Tianjin, whose entrepreneurial activity level is higher and continues to grow. Beijing and the Tianjin region, the Yangtze River Delta region (Shanghai, Jiangsu, Zhejiang) and the Zhu Jiang Delta region (Guangdong) are the most active regions. Shanghai ranks first in most surveys, followed by Beijing, but the disparity of the two areas has been expanding. For example, the local city government in Shanghai provides funds of $12 million (£7.3 million) each year to fund 'little giants', small high-technology firms which it hopes will contribute annual sales of $12 billion by 2010. In the middle and north-east regions, entrepreneurial activity is lower than the eastern coastal region, but it is increasing. The west and north-west regions are the lowest and least improving areas for entrepreneurial activity, and show little change. Econometric models indicate that the main determinants for entrepreneurial activity are explained by regional market demand, industrial structure, availability of financing, entrepreneurial culture and human capital. Technology innovation and rate of consumption growth have not had a significant effect on entrepreneurship in China.

Studies comparing successful and unsuccessful new ventures in China confirm the significance of entrepreneurial quality in explaining the success of new ventures, especially business and management skills, industrial experience and strength of social networks, the ubiquitous *guanxi*. However, there remain significant regulatory and institutional challenges with complex ownership structures, poor corporate governance and ambiguous intellectual property rights issues, especially with public research, former state enterprises and university spin-offs and academic-run enterprises.

Although just under 200 million Chinese still live on $1.25 (75p) a day, China is also the largest market in the world for luxury goods. In 2013, it was estimated to have well over a million millionaires (up from 300 000 only three years earlier) and more than 400 billionaires (there were only seven in 2010). Such disparities in income can create huge social and political tensions, and may result in a reaction against further growth unless governance and distribution are improved further.

Sources: Derived from Wang, Q., S. Collinson and X. Wu (eds) *International Journal of Innovation Management* (2010) Special Issue on Innovation in China, **14** (1); *East meets West: 15th International Conference on Management of Technology*, Beijing, May 2006.

Case Studies of large multinational firms and their efforts to introduce process innovations to improve environmental sustainability in their Chinese operations are available on the Innovation Portal at **www.innovation-portal.info**

Developing Countries

A characteristic of BRICs and other emerging economies is that they are simultaneously very advanced in terms of industrial and market development and often still at an early stage of development. India, for example, has satellite technology, a global pharmaceuticals industry and some market-leading corporations, but it also has huge problems of health care, illiteracy and basic infrastructure. And other countries – notably in Africa and much of Latin America – are still at a relatively early stage in their development of innovation capability.

But these conditions do not mean there is no scope for innovation. Indeed, there has been something of a revolution in thinking as we have come to realize that learning to meet the particular needs for goods and services in these spaces may actually offer radical new alternative pathways for innovation in more industrialized settings.

In his influential book *The Fortune at the Bottom of the Pyramid* Prahalad points out that most of the world's population – around four billion people – live close to or below the poverty line, with an average income of less than $2 (£1.20) a day.[1] It is easy to make assumptions about this group along the lines of 'they can't afford it so why innovate?' In fact, the challenge of meeting their basic needs for food, water, shelter and health care requires high levels of creativity, and beyond this social agenda lies a considerable innovation opportunity. But it requires a reframing of the 'normal' rules of the market game and a challenging of core assumptions. Table 20.1 gives some examples.

Solutions to meeting these needs will have to be highly innovative, but the prize is equally high: access to a high-volume, low-margin marketplace. For example, Unilever realized the

TABLE 20.1 Challenging Assumptions about the Bottom of the Pyramid

Assumption	Reality – and opportunity
The poor have no purchasing power and do not represent a viable market	Although low income, the sheer scale of this market makes it interesting. Additionally, the poor often pay a premium for access to many goods and services (e.g. borrowing money, clean water, telecommunications and basic medicines) because they cannot access mainstream channels like shops and banks. The innovation challenge is to offer low-cost, low-margin but high-quality goods and services across a potential market of four billion people.
The poor are not brand-conscious	Evidence suggests a high degree of brand and value consciousness – so if an entrepreneur can come up with a high-quality low-cost solution, it will be subject to hard testing in this market. Learning to deal with this can help migrate to other markets, essentially the classic pattern of 'disruptive innovation'.
The poor are hard to reach	By 2015, there are likely to be nearly 400 cities in the developing world with populations of over one million and 23 with over 10 million. Thirty to forty per cent of these people will be poor, so the potential market access is considerable. Innovative thinking around distribution – via new networks or agents (such as the women village entrepreneurs used by Hindustan Lever in India or the 'Avon ladies' in rural Brazil) – can open up untapped markets.
The poor are unable to use and not interested in advanced technology	Experience with PC kiosks, low-cost mobile phone sharing and access to the Internet suggests that rates of take-up and sophistication of use are extremely fast amongst this group.

potential of selling its shampoos and other cosmetic products not in 250 ml bottles, which were beyond the price range of most 'bottom of the pyramid' (BoP) customers, but in single sachets. The resulting market growth has been phenomenal, and examples like this are fuelling major activity amongst large corporations looking to adapt their products and services to serve the BoP market.

As G. Gilbert Cloyd, Chief Technology Officer, Procter and Gamble commented in a *Business Week* interview, 'We've put more emphasis on serving an even broader base of consumers. We have the goal of serving the majority of the world's consumers someday. Today, we probably serve about 2 billion-plus consumers around the globe, but there are 6 billion consumers out there. That has led us to put increased emphasis on low-end markets and in mid- and low-level pricing tiers in developed geographies. That has caused us to put a lot more attention on the cost aspects of our products.'

For example, in the Philippines there is little in the way of a formal banking system for the majority of people – and this has led to users creating very different applications for their mobile phones, where pay-as-you-go credits become a unit of currency to be transferred between people and used as currency for various goods and services. In Kenya, the M-PESA system is used to increase security: if a traveller wishes to move between cities, he or she will not take money but instead forward it via mobile phone in the form of credits which can then be collected from the phone recipient at the other end. This is only one of hundreds of new applications being developed in extreme conditions and by underserved users – and represents a powerful laboratory for new concepts which companies like Nokia and Vodafone are working closely to explore.

The potential exists to use this kind of extreme environment as a laboratory to test and develop concepts for wider application. For example, Citicorp has been experimenting with a design of ATMs based on biometrics for use with the illiterate population in rural India. The pilot involves some 50 000 people, but, as a spokesman for the company explained, 'We see this as having the potential for global application.'

Video Clip of an interview with Suzana Moreira, of Mowoza, discussing an example of 'bottom of the pyramid' social innovation using mobile phones is available on the Innovation Portal at **www.innovation-portal.info**

The BoP market covers the entire range of human wants and needs, from cosmetics and consumer goods through to basic health care and education. Prahalad's original book contains a wide range of case examples where this is beginning to happen and which indicate the huge potential of this group – but also the radical nature of the innovation challenge. Subsequently, there has been significant expansion of innovative activity in these emerging market areas, driven in part by a realization that the major growth in global markets will come from regions with a high BoP profile.

Importantly, many companies are actively using BoP markets as places to search for weak signals of potentially interesting new developments. For example, Nokia has been sending scouts to study how people in rural Africa and India are using mobile phones and the potential for new services which this may offer, while the pharmaceutical firm Novo Nordisk has been learning about low-cost provision of diabetes care in Tanzania as an input to a better understanding of how such models could be developed for different regions.

Meeting the needs of people at the bottom of the pyramid is not about charity but rather about a fundamental rethink of the business model – 'paradigm innovation' in the 4Ps model we looked at in Chapter 2 – to create sustainable alternative systems.

INNOVATION IN ACTION 20.7

Changing the Game at the Bottom of the Pyramid

Pretty high on anyone's list of wants is a quality home, but financing more than basic shelter is often beyond the means of most of the world's population. But CEMEX, the Mexican cement and building materials producer, has pioneered an innovative approach to changing this. Triggered by a domestic financial crisis in the mid-1990s, CEMEX saw a big drop in sales in Mexico. But closer inspection revealed that the market segment of do-it-yourself, especially

(continued)

amongst the less wealthy, had sustained demand levels. In fact, the market was worth a great deal (nearly a billion dollars a year) but was made up of many small purchases rather than large construction projects. Since over 60% of the Mexican population earn less than $5 (£3) a day, the challenge was to find ways to work with this market in the future.

The response was a novel financing approach, built on the fact that many communities operate a 'savings club' type of scheme to help finance major purchases – the tanda network. CEMEX set up Patrimonio Hoy – a version of the tanda system which allowed poor people to save and access credit for building projects. It relied on social networks, replacing traditional distributors with 'promoters' who worked on a commission but who also helped set up and run the tandas; significantly, 98% of these promoters were women. The scheme allowed access not just to materials but also to architects and other support services. It effectively changed the way a large segment of society could manage its own construction projects. Success with the home improvements area led to its extension to village infrastructure projects linked to drainage, lighting and other community facilities.

ITC is one of India's largest private sector firms, with a turnover of around $4 billion (£2.45 billion). It operates in a variety of markets including agri-trading, dealing with a variety of Indian commodities, including pepper, edible nuts and fruits and grains. It has been active in trying to improve its relationships with local farmers and pioneered the 'e-Choupal – village information centre – as a route for doing so. (*Choupal* is a Hindi word meaning 'traditional gathering place'.) Some 2000 computer kiosks have been located in villages and linked to a wider network across the country, allowing access to information about weather, prices, agricultural advice, etc. It helps ITC plan its logistics more effectively but also brings benefits to the farmers. E-Choupals allow them to find out about prices at local markets and reduce the high transaction costs which the traditional (and often corrupt) manual system of intermediaries and auctions carried. Uptake has been rapid and the farmers have quickly learnt to use the system to strengthen their position – indeed one group began not only looking at local markets but at the Chicago Stock Exchange to monitor soya bean prices and futures!

In addition, to direct benefits e-Choupals also provide villages with access to educational and information resources.

Audio Clip of interview with Girish Prabhu, a director of Srishti Labs in Bangalore which specializes in developing 'bottom of the pyramid' solutions, is available on the Innovation Portal at **www.innovation-portal.info**

Case Studies detailing innovative solutions to the major challenges posed by health care provision in India – Lifespring Hospitals, NHL and Aravind Eye Clinics – are available on the Innovation Portal at **www.innovation-portal.info**

Summary

- Recent developments have accelerated the globalization of innovation such that countries like India, Brazil and China are major players and even tiny economies like Singapore and Denmark are playing an increasingly important role in creating the knowledge on which future generations of innovation may be built.

- It is not countries but firms which carry out much of the R&D – and their activities and locations are themselves becoming globalized. New players are joining the old established giants and playing an increasingly significant role in a world characterized by knowledge flow and open innovation.

- On the demand side of innovation the pattern has shifted out of all recognition in the past decade. Most population growth is in the regions of the world where economic growth is also accelerating, driving rising incomes and expectations and creating an explosion of market demand. These 'emerging markets' are often different in shape, size and segmentation, but they represent one of the major drivers for innovation in products and services.

- We have already seen the growing importance of user-led innovation, so in a world where much of the growth is coming from very different places with different user characteristics, we should expect to see significant shifts in innovations which are aimed at meeting their needs.

Further Resources

There are a number of texts which describe and compare different systems of national innovation policy, including *National Innovation Systems* (Oxford University Press, 1993), edited by Richard Nelson; *National Systems of Innovation* (Pinter, 1992), edited by B.-A. Lundvall; and *Systems of Innovation: Technologies, Institutions and Organisations* (Pinter, 1997), edited by Charles Edquist. Michael Porter's *The Competitive Advantage of Nations* (Macmillan, 1990) provides a useful framework in which to examine the direct impact on corporate behaviour of innovation systems. At the other extreme, David Landes' *Wealth and Poverty of Nations* (Little Brown, 1998) takes a broad (and stimulating) historical and cultural perspective. The best overview is provided by the anthology of Chris Freeman's work in *Systems of Innovation* (Edward Elgar, 2008).

More relevant to firms from emerging economies is Naushad Forbes and David Wield's *From Followers to Leaders: Managing technology and innovation* (Routledge, 2002), which includes numerous case examples. Thomas Friedman's *The World is Flat* highlights the growing shift of economic force to the emerging economies while scholars like Mike Hobday[2] have worked to explain the 'how' of such growth. The work of C. K. Prahalad has opened up discussion of low-income developing countries as a source of innovation and this theme is picked up in the work of Jaideep Prabhu and colleagues[3] with their concept of *jugaad* innovation.

References

1. Prahalad, C. K. (2006) *The Fortune at the Bottom of the Pyramid*. Upper Saddle River, NJ: Wharton School Publishing.

2. Hobday, M. (1995) *Innovation in East Asia: The challenge to Japan*. Cheltenham: Edward Elgar.

3. Radjou, N., J. Prabhu and S. Ahuja (2012) *Jugaad Innovation: Think frugal, be flexible, generate breakthrough innovation*. San Francisco: Jossey-Bass.

 Deeper Dive explanations of innovation concepts and ideas are available on the Innovation Portal at **www.innovation-portal.info**

 Quizzes to test yourself further are available online via the Innovation Portal at **www.innovation-portal.info**

Summary of online resources for Chapter 20 – all material is available via the Innovation Portal at www.innovation-portal.info

Cases	Media	Tools	Activities	Deeper Dive
• Spirit DSP • Nokia Institute of Technology (IndT) • Natura • WWF Climate Savers in China • M-PESA • Lifespring Hospitals • Aravind Eye Clinics • NHL Hospitals	• Ana Sena, Nokia IndT • Suzana Moreira, moWoza • Girish Prabhu	• SWOT analysis • Rich pictures • Futures toolkit	• Global challenges	• Frugal innovation

Chapter 21

Sustainability

LEARNING OBJECTIVES

By the end of this chapter you will understand:

- the challenges which sustainability creates for innovation
- the different types of innovation which can contribute to improved sustainability
- a model framework for positioning sustainability-led innovation with three levels:
  - doing what we do better
  - opening up new opportunity at the enterprise level
  - system level change
- the key issues in the process of moving towards sustainability-led innovation
- how to use certain tools that will help with the journey.

The Challenge of Sustainability-led Innovation

The Threat: Running Out of Planet

It is clear that sustainability is becoming a major driver of innovation. For example, a report by the WWF suggests that lifestyles in the developed world at present require the resources of around two planets, and if emerging economies follow the same trajectory this will rise to 2.5 by 2050.[1] Many key energy and raw material resources are close to passing their 'peak' of availability and will become increasingly scarce.[2] At the same time, the dangers of global warming have moved centre stage and climate change – and how to deal with it – is an urgent political as well as economic issue. This translates to increasingly strong legislation forcing organizations to change their products and processes to reduce their carbon footprint, greenhouse gas emissions and energy consumption. Behind this is the growing challenge of environmental pollution and the concern not only to stop the increasing damage being done to the natural environment but also to reverse the impacts of earlier practices.[3]

. . . And the Opportunity

It's not necessarily all doom and gloom. Considerable opportunities are also opening up, both for process innovations which increase operating efficiencies and reduce costs, and for product innovations which exploit the huge potential market space represented by the 'green economy'. For example, the global market for green products and services was recently estimated as a $3.2 trillion (£1.9 trillion) business opportunity, while UK consumer spending on 'sustainable' products and services was last reported at more than £36 billion – bigger even than alcohol and tobacco sales combined.

The provision of alternative goods and services, more efficient approaches to resource and energy management, and new partnerships and ways of working could help unleash a new era of economic development. A PricewaterhouseCoopers report suggests significant market potential in the provision of green goods and services.[4] Its estimate was as high as 3% of global GDP. A United Nations (2011) report illustrates how 'greening the economy' is already becoming a powerful new engine of growth in the twenty-first century.[5] The World Business Council for Sustainable Development's (WBCSD) *Vision 2050* sets out new opportunities for businesses in responding to sustainability challenges, promoting whole-system perspectives.[6]

Significantly, investment in sustainability projects held up throughout the recent recession, suggesting a combination of enforced compliance with increasingly tough legislation and a perception of the major opportunities implicit in this agenda. (In a BCG/MIT survey of 2010, 60% of companies increased their investment with the 'embracers' in the survey sample, indicating plans to take this further, increasing investments by a further 24%.)[7] As the writer C. K. Prahalad puts it, 'sustainability is a mother lode of organizational and technological innovations that yield both bottom-line and top-line returns. Becoming environment-friendly lowers costs because companies end up reducing the inputs they use. In addition, the process generates additional revenues from better products or enables companies to create new businesses. In fact, because [growing the top and bottom lines] are the goals of corporate innovation, we find that smart companies now treat sustainability as innovation's new frontier.'[8]

Activity to help you explore the opportunities and challenges associated with sustainability – innovation challenges in sustainability – is available on the Innovation Portal at **www.innovation-portal.info**

INNOVATION IN ACTION 21.1

Sustainability-led Innovation at Interface

One of the 'success' stories in sustainability-led innovation (SLI) has been the growth of floor-ings business Interface, which has made radical changes to its business and operating model and secured significant business growth. Interface has cut greenhouse gas emissions by 82%, fossil fuel consumption by 60%, waste by 66% and water use by 75%, and increased sales by 66%, doubled earnings and raised profit margins. To quote Ray Anderson, founder and chairman: 'As we climb Mount Sustainability with the four sustainability principles on top, we are doing better than ever on bottom-line business. This is not at the cost of social or ecological systems, but at the cost of our competitors who still haven't got it.'

We've Seen This Before

Preoccupation with sustainability and the need for innovation to deal with it is, of course, not new. Back in the 1970s, an influential report entitled *The Limits to Growth* triggered a long-running and high-profile debate around these issues. This led to a continuing stream of research and advocacy around the need for change and the best ways to drive the innovation agenda.[9] Organizations such as WWF and Greenpeace emerged out of this and continue to play a key role in raising awareness, exploring issues and challenging policymakers and organizations to improve sustainability.

Whatever the perspective adopted, it is clear that change – innovation – will be needed. Growing concern of the kind described above is driving a combination of increasingly strong legislation, international environmental management standards, new sustainability metrics and reporting standards that will force business to adopt 'greener' approaches if they are to retain a licence to operate. At the same time the opportunities opened up for 'doing what we do better' (through 'lean, green' investments in improving efficiencies around resources, energy, logistics, etc.) and 'doing different' – radical new moves towards systems change – make it an increasingly significant item in strategic planning amongst progressive organizations of all sizes.

Evidence for this can be seen in their participation and active engagement with United Nations and business initiatives (such as the UN Global Compact and The Climate Group) and in networks like the Global Sustainability Forum. It is also reflected in strategic human resource development, for example the growth in job titles dealing explicitly with the sustainability agenda and of specialist training and education programmes such as WWF's One Planet MBA and One Planet Leaders.

Sustainability-led Innovation

This increasing evidence suggests that the adoption of sustainability targets as part of mainstream innovation strategy is accelerating. So what are organizations doing about this? Early activity centred on cosmetic activity (in which organizations sought to improve their image through high-profile activities designed to demonstrate their green credentials), but increasingly strong legislation now provides a degree of forced compliance. The frontier is now one along which leading organizations are seeking to exploit opportunities, as they recognize the need for innovation to deal with resource instability and scarcity, energy security and systemic efficiencies across their supply chains.

We can use the '4Ps' framework (see Chapter 2) to classify the kinds of activity going on around sustainability-led innovation (SLI). Table 21.1 gives some examples.

In the sustainability space a number of frameworks have been proposed to take account of this. For example, Prahalad and Nidumolo suggest five steps moving from 'viewing compliance as an opportunity' through 'making value chains sustainable' and 'designing sustainable products and services' to 'designing new business models'. Their fifth stage focuses on 'creating next practice platforms' – implying a system level change.[10] The consultancy Arthur D. Little has a similar model, while the Boston Consulting Group classifies SLI companies in terms of the extent to which they embrace such principles. They represent versions of what are termed 'maturity models', and we can synthesize them into a framework.[11]

We can see the 'journey' towards full sustainability as involving three dimensions which underpin a change in the overall approach, from treating the symptoms of a problem to eventually working with the system in which the problem originates (Figure 21.1).

Case Study of an extensive research project carried out with the Network for Business Sustainability, a Canadian organization working extensively with large companies and academic institutions, is available on the Innovation Portal at **www.innovation-portal.info**

TABLE 21.1 Examples of Sustainability-led Innovation

Innovation target	Examples
Product/service offering	'Green' products, design for greener manufacture and recycling, service models replacing consumption/ownership models
Process innovation	Improved and novel manufacturing processes, lean systems inside the organization and across supply chain, green logistics
Position innovation	Rebranding the organization as 'green', meeting needs of underserved communities, e.g. bottom of pyramid
Paradigm innovation – changing business models	System level change, multi-organization innovation, servitization (moving from manufacturing to service emphasis)

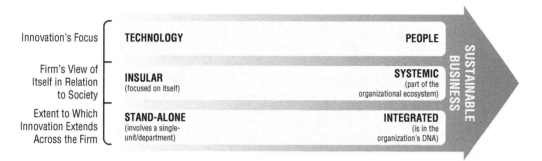

FIGURE 21.1 The journey towards sustainability-led innovation

In particular, we can think of three stages in the evolution of SLI, from simple compliance and 'doing what we do better' innovation through to a more radical exploration of new business opportunities. The third stage is all about system change, where significant effects can be achieved but which rely on cooperation and co-evolution of innovative solutions across a group of stakeholders.

Step 1 is 'Operational optimization' – essentially doing what we do but better. Table 21.2 gives some examples.

Step 2 is 'Organizational transformation' – essentially doing different at the level of the organization. Table 21.3 gives more detail.

> Case Studies of companies, such as TetraPak and Volvo, which have been working in China to improve their sustainability in relation to greenhouse gas emissions are available on the Innovation Portal at **www.innovation-portal.info**
>
>

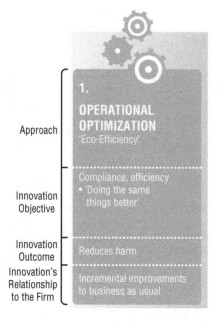

	1. OPERATIONAL OPTIMIZATION 'Eco-Efficiency'	2. ORGANIZATIONAL TRANSFORMATION 'New Market Opportunities'
Approach		
Innovation Objective	Compliance, efficiency • 'Doing the same things better'	Novel products, services or business models • 'Doing good by doing new things'
Innovation Outcome	Reduces harm	Creates shared value
Innovation's Relationship to the Firm	Incremental improvements to business as usual	Fundamental shift in firm purpose

TABLE 21.2   Operational Optimization

Definition	Characteristics	Examples
Compliance with regulations or optimized performance through increased efficiency	In the stage of Operational Optimization, the organization actively reduces its current environmental and social impacts without fundamentally changing its business model. In other words, an optimizer innovates in order to 'do less harm'. Innovations are typically incremental, addressing a single issue at a time. And they tend to favour the 'technofix', focusing on new technologies as ways to reduce impacts while maintaining business as usual. Innovation tends to be inward-focused in both development and outcome; at this stage, companies typically rely on internal resources to innovate, and the resulting innovations are company-centric: their intent is primarily to reduce costs or maximize profits	Pollution Controls Flexible Work Hours/Telecommuting Waste Diversion Shutting or Consolidating Facilities Energy-efficient Lighting Use of Renewable Energy Reduced Paper Consumption Reduced Packaging Decreased Use of Raw Materials Reduced Use/Elimination of Hazardous Materials Optimization of Product Size/Weight for Shipping Hybrid Electric Fleet Vehicles Delivery Boxes Redesigned from Single to Multi-Use

TABLE 21.3   Organizational Transformation

Definition	Characteristics	Examples
The creation of often disruptive new products and services by viewing sustainability as a market opportunity	Rather than focusing on 'doing less harm', Organizational Transformers believe their organization can benefit financially from 'doing good'. They see opportunities to serve new markets with novel, sustainable products, or they are new entrants with business models predicated on creating value by lifting people out of poverty or producing renewable energy. Organizational Transformers may focus less on creating products and more on delivering services, which	Disruptive new products that change consumption habits (e.g. a camp stove that turns any biomass into a hyper-efficient heat source and whose sales subsidize cheaper models distributed in developing countries) Disruptive new products that benefit people (e.g. portable, durable CT scanners that have minimum functionality, making them affordable and useful for health care providers in developing countries) *(continued)*

TABLE 21.3 *(Continued)*

Definition	Characteristics	Examples
	often have a lower environmental impact. They often produce innovations that are both technological and socio-technical – designed to improve quality of life for people inside or outside the firm. Transformers are still primarily internally focused in that they see their organization as an independent figure in the economy. However, they do work up and down the value chain and collaborate closely with external stakeholders. The move from Operational Optimization to Organizational Transformation requires a radical shift in mindset from doing things better to doing new things	Replacing products with services (e.g. leasing and maintaining carpets over a prescribed lifetime rather than selling them) Introducing car- and bike-sharing services in urban centres to reduce pollution caused by individual car ownership while increasing overall mobility Replacing physical services with electronic services (e.g. reducing paper consumption by delivering bills electronically rather than by mail) Services with social benefits (e.g. a smart phone app that rewards people with coupons for local merchants when they make charitable donations)

INNOVATION IN ACTION 21.2

Embedding Sustainability-led Innovation within Philips

Philips is a Dutch multinational corporation, founded in 1891, operating in over 100 countries and employing 118 000 people. It has a long-standing commitment to sustainability principles; for example, in the early twentieth century Philips' employees benefited from schools, housing and pension schemes. It has also been a key actor in several international sustainability initiatives; back in the early 1970s, Philips participated in the Club of Rome's 'The Limits to Growth' dialogue and in 1974 the first corporate environmental function was established. In 1992, it was one of 29 multinational companies participating in the World Council for Sustainable Business Development which developed 'Vision 2050': a roadmap for future development towards a more sustainable position.

Its own 'EcoVision' programmes were first launched in 1998, setting corporate-sustainability-related targets, and the first green innovation targets were introduced in 2007 in 'EcoVision4'. In parallel in 2003, the Philips Environmental Report (first published in 1999) was extended into a Sustainability Report. In 2009, this was integrated into the Philips Annual Report, signalling the full embedding of sustainability in Philips' business practices.

(continued)

Philips' 'EcoVision5'[12] programme for 2010–2015 establishes concrete targets for sustainable innovation:

- To bring care to 500 million people.
- To improve the energy efficiency of our overall portfolio by 50%.
- To double the amount of recycled materials in our products as well as to double the collection and recycling of Philips products.

Like many other long-lived corporations, Philips has adjusted its innovation approach several times, anticipating major changes in society. In recent decades this has resulted in the opening of an Experience Lab in Eindhoven and the extension of the traditional technology-driven product-creation process towards end-user driven innovation. 'Open innovation' has also changed the company's way of working. In the late 1990s, the former Research Laboratories were transformed into a vibrant High Tech Campus, now hosting over 80 non-Philips business entities. During the last decade, its focus was 'inside-out', based on teaming up, incubation and spin-outs and the emphasis is now on co-creating sustainable systems solutions.

With the launch of EcoVision4 Philips introduced a target on Green Innovation, spending a total of €1 billion (£830 million) on developing green products and processes. These are defined as offering significant environmental improvements in one or more Green Key Focal Areas: energy efficiency, packaging, hazardous substances, packaging, weight, recycling and disposal, and lifetime reliability. In 2010, green products accounted for 37.5% of Philips' sales. The target for 2015 is 50%.

For example, the Consumer Lifestyle division recently launched the first 'Cradle to Cradle' inspired products, such as the Performer EnergyCare vacuum cleaner, 50% made from post-industrial plastics and 25% from bio-based plastics. It is extremely energy-efficient, but it earns its designations as a Green Product primarily because it scores so highly in the focal area of recycling.

Another example is the award-winning Canova LED TV. This high-performance LED TV consumes 60% less power than its predecessor. Even the remote control is efficient: it is powered by solar energy. In addition, the TV is completely free of PVC and brominates flame-retardants, and 60% of the aluminium used in the set is recycled.

Case Study of Philips' activities over time to move from 'do better' to radical organizational transformation around the sustainability agenda is available on the Innovation Portal at **www.innovation-portal.info**

Case Study of Natura, a Brazilian cosmetics company which takes sustainability as a core foundation for its products, services and processes, is available on the Innovation Portal at **www.innovation-portal.info**

Step 3 is about changing the system, coevolving solutions with different stakeholders to create new and sustainable alternatives. Table 21.4 explores this in more detail.

3.

SYSTEMS BUILDING
'Societal Change'

Novel products, services or business models that are impossible to achieve alone
• 'Doing good by doing new things with others'

Creates net positive impact

Extends beyond the firm to drive institutional change

Case Study of Desso, and other organizations which are attempting to innovate across their supply networks and move towards a systems level approach – Green supply networks – is available on the Innovation Portal at **www.innovation-portal.info**

Case Study of Green Buildings, which outlines a total design approach to construction using a system perspective, is available on the Innovation Portal at **www.innovation-portal.info**

TABLE 21.4 Systems Building

Definition	Characteristics	Examples
The interdependent collaborations between many disparate organizations that create positive impacts on people and the planet	Systems Builders perceive their economic activity as being part of society, not distinct from it. Individually, almost every organization is unsustainable. But taken as a collective, systems can sustain each other. Systems Builders extend their thinking beyond the boundaries of the organization to include partners in previously unrelated areas or industries. Because the concept of Systems Building reflects an unconventional economic paradigm, very few organizations or industries occupy this realm The move from Organizational Transformation to Systems Building requires another radical shift in mindset – this time from doing new things and serving new markets to thinking beyond the firm	Industrial Symbiosis: Disparate organizations cooperate to create a 'circular economy' in which one firm's waste is another's resources. For example, a construction company uses other companies' glass waste: the synergies lead to environmental and economic benefits for all B Corporations: Conceived in the United States but now existing in dozens of countries worldwide, B Corporations are organizations legally obliged to deliver societal benefits. Well-known examples include ice cream producer Ben & Jerry's, e-commerce platform Etsy and cleaning product manufacturers Method and Seventh Generation

INNOVATION IN ACTION 21.3

An environmental Innovation Network for IKEA

The catalogue of IKEA has one if the world's highest circulations, with a print run of more than 100 million per year, needing 50 000 tonnes of high-quality paper each year. However, in the 1990s there were growing environmental concerns about the discharge of chlorinated compounds from the processes used to create the relatively high-quality paper used in such promotional materials, as well as the more general issue of paper recycling. In response to these concerns, in 1992 IKEA introduced two new goals for the production of its catalogue: to be printed on paper that was totally chlorine-free (TCF) and to include a high proportion of recycled paper.

However, these goals demanded significant innovation. No such paper product existed at the time, and the dominant industry suppliers believed that it would be impossible to combine chlorine-free materials with high levels of recycled pulp. To achieve the necessary paper brightness for catalogue printing, a minimum of 50% chlorine-dioxide-bleached pulp had been used. Chlorine had been used for 50 years as the bleaching agent for high-quality paper. Moreover, the high-quality paper used for such catalogues consisted of a very thin paper base, which is coated with clay, which makes the insertion of recycled fibre very difficult. The manager of R&D at Svenska Cellulosa Aktiebolaget (SCA), one of Europe's largest producers of high-quality paper, argued that 'the high-quality demands and the large volume of filling substances is the main reason that it is neither realistic nor necessary to use recycled fibre'. SCA reinforced this view with the decision to build a new SKr2.4 billion (£200 million) plant to produce conventional high-quality coated paper. At that time SCA was not a supplier to IKEA.

In Sweden, the paper manufacturer Aspa worked with the chemical firm Eka Nobel to develop an environmentally acceptable bleaching process with less damaging discharges, but this was still based on chlorine dioxide and failed to achieve the necessary brightness for use in high-quality paper, and was marketed as 'semi-bleached'. Following customer demand for a true TCF product, including a request from Greenpeace for TCF paper for production of its newsletter, Aspa was forced to develop a stable product with secure supplies. At this stage the pulp and fibre company Södra Cell became involved, and identified the need to reach full brightness to create a broader market for TCF paper. Södra worked with the German company Kværner to develop an alternative but equally effective bleaching process, and Kværner established a research project on ozone bleaching with Lenzing and Stora Billerud. The ozone bleaching process was adapted from an established process for water purification with the help of AGA Gas. However, the use of ozone in place of chlorine for bleaching required the quality of the pulpwood to be improved, so the harvesting system had to be changed to ensure that wood was better sorted and available within weeks of harvesting. To improve the brightness and strength of the paper, the impurities in the pulp from de-inked recycled paper had to be reduced, which required a new washing process. The changes in the chemistry of the pulp subsequently reduced the strength of the paper, which required changes in the paper production process. The printing processes had to be adapted to the characteristics of the new paper. Initially, Södra Cell supplied the new product to SCA through its relationship with Aspa, but also to the Italian paper producer Burgo, which provided the paper for the IKEA catalogue.

Thus, the organization evolved beyond a simple industrial supply relationship to an innovation network including customers, printers, paper manufacturers, pulp and fibre producers, forestry companies, research institutes and environmental lobby groups across many different countries. At the same time, the intended innovation shifted from a high-quality TCF clay-coated paper to a TCF uncoated fresh pulp and 10% de-inked recycled pulp product.

Source: Derived from Hakansson H. and A. Waluszewski (2003) *Managing Technological Development: IKEA, the environment and technology*. Routledge, London.

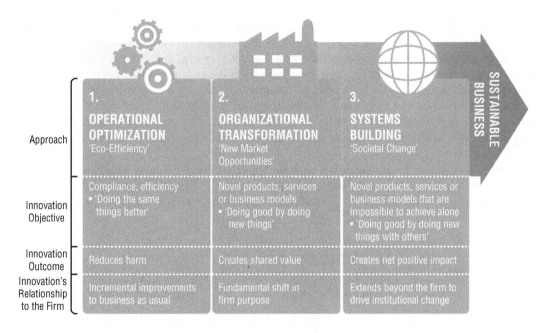

Managing the Innovation Process for Sustainability

While there is plenty of discussion about the need for innovation in the direction of sustainability, it is less clear *how* this process can be managed. What do these changes mean for the innovation process and how does consideration of sustainability change the routines we put in place for innovation management? Are our current models for handling the process sufficient or will the nature and pace of change be so disruptive that radically new approaches will be required? What kinds of innovation ecosystem may emerge and how will current players position themselves within it? What opportunities exist for entrepreneurs and how can they best frame their activities to ride the waves of radical change? What new skills will we need within, and between, our organizations? What tools, techniques and approaches will help equip established players and aspiring new entrants to manage effectively? In the face of radical change, what do we need to do more of, less of and differently in the ways we manage innovation?

We suggest that SLI highlights once again the challenge of 'dynamic capability' in that it forces firms to learn new approaches and let go of old ones around the core search, select and implement questions. By its nature SLI involves working with different knowledge components – new technologies, new markets, new environmental or regulatory conditions, etc. – and firms need to develop enhanced 'absorptive capacity' for handling this. In particular, they need capability (and enabling tools and methods) to acquire, assimilate and exploit new knowledge and to work at a systems level.

We can link this to our earlier model around the search and select challenges which we used in Chapters 7 and 9 (Figure 21.2).

Arguably, the 'do better' sustainability-linked activities belong in the 'exploit' space (zone 1) and many of the organizational transformation moves are in the 'bounded exploration' area (zone 2). The big challenge in SLI comes in 'reframing' to take into account the many different elements in this space – and to rethink the underlying knowledge architecture in the organization to work in it. In particular, as we move to the systems level change stage there is a need for working interactively with multiple stakeholders, essentially a complex system in which co-evolution of solutions is the model.

For example, zone 3 is associated with the 'eco-efficiency' concept, which involves finding new and more efficient ways of 'doing more with less'.[13] Eco-efficiency, with its famous '3 Rs' – reduce, reuse, recycle – has its roots in early industrialization but is now being

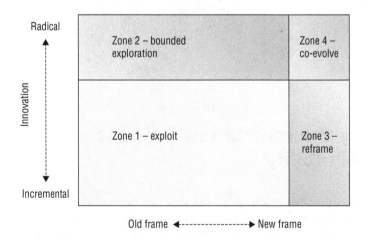

FIGURE 21.2   Sustainability-led innovation challenges

widely adopted by companies. Reducing carbon footprint through supply chain improvements or switching to less energy- or resource-intensive products and services which deliver equivalent value can generate significant savings. 3M, for example, saved nearly $1.4 billion (£860 million) over a 34-year period and prevented billions of pounds of pollutants entering the environment through its Pollution-Prevention-Pays (3P) programmes. GE Industrial saved $12.8 million (£7.8 million) per year by using high-efficiency lights in their plants. One of Alcoa's facilities in France achieved an 85% reduction in water consumption, leading to a $40 000 (£24 000) annual reduction in operating costs.[14]

Zone 4 involves significant 'system' level thinking around emergent and radically different solutions. Such system-level innovation has the capacity to generate positive social and environmental impacts rather than simply minimize negative ones, representing a shift from eco-efficiency to 'eco-effectiveness'. One aspect of this is the involvement of multiple players that have traditionally not worked together in co-creating system level change. For instance, Grameen Shakti, a rural renewable energy initiative in Bangladesh, fosters collaboration between the micro-finance sector, suppliers of solar energy equipment and consumers, enabling millions of poor households to leapfrog to new energy systems. It is generating new employment opportunities, increasing rural incomes, empowering women and reducing the use of environmentally polluting kerosene. Grameen Shakti is the largest and fastest-growing rural renewable energy company in the world.[15]

Unilever's Sustainable Living Plan, which builds partnerships with multiple stakeholders including suppliers, NGOs and consumers, aims to create a better future in which billions of

INNOVATION IN ACTION 21.4

Sustainability-led Innovation in Novo Nordisk

Novo Nordisk, a major Danish pharmaceuticals business, makes use of a company-wide scenario-based programme to explore radical futures around their core business. Its 'Diabetes 2020' process involved exploring radical alternative scenarios for chronic disease treatment and the roles which a player like Novo Nordisk could play. As part of the follow-up from this initiative, in 2003 the company helped set up the Oxford Health Alliance, a non-profit collaborative entity which brought together key stakeholders – medical scientists, doctors, patients and government officials – with views and perspectives which were sometimes quite widely separated. To make it happen, Novo Nordisk made clear that its goal was nothing less than the prevention or cure of diabetes – a goal which if it were achieved would potentially kill off the company's main line of business. As Lars Rebien Sørensen, the CEO of Novo Nordisk, explains:

> In moving from intervention to prevention – that's challenging the business model where the pharmaceuticals industry is deriving its revenues! . . . We believe that we can focus on some major global health issue – mainly diabetes – and at the same time create business opportunities for our company.

TABLE 21.5   Key Innovation Management Challenges Associated with Sustainability-linked Innovation

Innovation activity	Challenges in zone 3 and 4
Search	Peripheral vision – searching in unfamiliar fields (sectors, technologies, markets, etc.)
	Reframing
	Finding, forming, performing new networks
Selection	Resource allocation under high uncertainty
	Cognitive dissonance
	Not invented here
Implementation	Internal mobilization – new skills, structures, etc.
	Crossing the chasm and the diffusion problem
	New appropriate language
Innovation strategy	Need for a clear framework within which to locate search, select, implementation – a 'roadmap for the future'
	New corporate paradigm – criteria based on sustainability – people, profit, planet, etc.

people can increase their quality of life without increasing their environmental footprint. The new plan is fuelling innovation, generating markets and saving money.

Innovations can arise from developing unusual partnerships across sectors. For example, the GreenZone, in Umea, Sweden, designed by architect Anders Nyquist, is an early example of holistic planning. It involves a block of interconnected businesses, including a car dealership, a petrol station and carwash and a fast-food restaurant. The buildings are connected, allowing a recycling and sharing of heat.

Tool to help organizations work with sustainability-led innovation – SLI tools – is available on the Innovation Portal at **www.innovation-portal.info**

Table 21.5 highlights some of the emerging challenges to innovation management routines as organizations move into the sustainability space.

Responsible Innovation

One message from this theme of SLI is that we will need to look at some of the questions we ask during our innovation process. In particular, at the 'select' stage what criteria will we use to make sure that the project is worth pursuing? We saw in Chapter 9 that we needed to consider carefully whether to take possible innovation ideas forward, and the frameworks we introduced then dealt mainly with risks and rewards. In the public sector there is additional concern around the 'reliability' theme: will the changes we introduce have an impact on our ability to deliver the public services people depend on, like health care and education? But in this chapter we have seen that there are now urgent additional questions which we should bring into our decision-making process around the issues of sustainability and its wider impact.

Interestingly, much of the academic and policy-oriented innovation research tradition evolved around such concerns, riding on the back of the 'science and society' movement in the 1970s. This led to key institutes (like the Science Policy Research Unit (SPRU) at Sussex University) being established. Their concern – and the many tools which they developed – remained one of challenging the innovation process and particularly questioning the targets towards which it worked.

For example, although the global pharmaceutical industry has done much to improve health care through a highly efficient innovation process, there are questions which can be raised around it. Evidence suggests that 90% of its innovation efforts are devoted to the concerns of the richest 10% of the world's population. In similar fashion, questions can be asked about innovation systems which can produce impressive consumer electronics yet leave many people in the world short of clean water or without access to basic medical care.

The argument is that, despite the good intentions of individual researchers and corporations, innovation can sometimes be irresponsible. Well-publicized disasters – like DDT (developed as a powerful aid to controlling pests) or Thalidomide (a useful anti-nausea drug) – turned out to have unforeseen and seriously negative consequences, while others – like BSE – resulted from the pursuit of innovation without adequate safeguards. One of the major causes of the global financial crisis – with all the misery which that has brought – lay in irresponsible and sometimes reckless financial innovation around tools and techniques. And the current debates around genetically modified foods (GM) and reinvestment in nuclear power to cope with energy shortages remind us of the need to ask questions around innovation.

For these reasons, there is growing interest in developing frameworks which can bring a series of 'responsibility' questions into the innovation process and ensure that careful consideration takes place around major change programmes.[16]

Summary

- Sustainability is becoming a key factor in innovation, representing both a significant threat and an opportunity.

- Sustainability-led innovation (SLI) involves changes across the 'innovation space' – in products/services, in processes, in positions and in paradigms.

- SLI can involve incremental improvements – 'do better' – and more radical changes. We have explored a model which maps the nature of SLI into three areas:

  ○ Operational optimization
  ○ Organizational transformation
  ○ Systems building.

- SLI poses challenges across the innovation process model – how we search, select and implement. In particular, working at the higher levels of the model, towards organizational transformation and systems building will require developing new routines.

- Part of the dynamic capability challenge in dealing with SLI is to introduce some elements of a 'responsible innovation' framework to our decision-making around innovation selection and implementation.

Further Resources

For a general introduction to the key issues in sustainable development, our favourite text is *The Principles of Sustainability* by Simon Dresner (Earthscan, 2002). Unlike most of the literature on the subject, this treatment is well balanced and even includes some humour. Jennifer Elliott's *An Introduction to Sustainable Development* (Routledge, 2nd edition, 2005) is a more conventional academic approach, and focuses on the implications for developing nations. However, neither text is strong on the links between sustainability and innovation. The Special Issue of the *International Journal of Innovation Management* (2002) **6** (3) on 'Innovation for Sustainability' is a useful place to begin, and is edited by two leading scholars in the field, Frans Berkhout and Ken Green. Richard Adams and colleagues conducted an extensive literature review for the NBS report, which contains a wealth of useful resources.[17]

The Natural Advantage of Nations: Business opportunities, innovations and governance in the 21st century by Amory B. Lovins (Earthscan Publications, 2005) is a collection of papers by leading authors, including Michael Porter, and makes the business case for sustainable development, including technological, structural and social change. The book has a useful companion website. *Sustainable Business Development: Inventing the future through strategy, innovation, and leadership* by David L. Rainey (Cambridge University Press, 2006) provides a practical analysis of what sustainable business development (SBD) is and how companies do it, and includes many case studies from the United States, Europe, the Pacific Rim and South America. *Sustainable Innovation: The organisational, human and knowledge dimension* by Rene J. Jorna (Greenleaf Publishing, 2006) is a more theoretical and philosophical book, that deals with human, social and management challenges and responses to sustainable innovation.

Responsible innovation is a theme of increasing interest and the edited book of the same name by Richard Owen and colleagues is a good place to start exploring this theme (John Wiley & Sons, Ltd, 2013).

References

1. WWF (2010) *Living Planet Report: Biodiversity, biocapacity and development*. Gland, Switzerland: WWF International.

2. Brown, L. (2011) *World on the Edge: How to prevent environmental and economic collapse*. New York: Norton.

3. Heinberg, R. (2007) *Peak Everything: Waking up to the century of decline in Earth's resources*. London: Clairview.

4. PricewaterhouseCoopers (2010) Green products: Using sustainable attributes to drive growth and value, http://www.pwc.com/gx/en/sustainability/publications/.

5. UNEP (2011) Towards a green economy: Pathways to sustainable development and poverty eradication. United Nations Environment Programme: Online version, http://hqweb.unep.org/greeneconomy/Portals/88/documents/ger/GER_synthesis_en.pdf.

6. WBCSD (2010) *Vision 2050*. Geneva: World Business Council for Sustainable Development.

7. Haanaes, K., B. Balagopal, M. Teck Kong *et al.* (2011) New Sustainability Study: The 'embracers' seize advantage magazine: *Sloan Management Review*, http://sloanreview.mit.edu/article/new-sustainability-study-the-embracers-seize-advantage/.

8. Nidumolu, R., C. Prahalad and M. Rangaswami (2009) Why sustainability is the key driver of innovation, *Harvard Business Review*, 87 (9): 57–61.

9. Meadows, D. and J. Forrester (1972) *The Limits to Growth*. New York: Universe Books.

10. Nidumolu, R., C. Prahalad and M. Rangaswami (2009) Why sustainability is the key driver of innovation, *Harvard Business Review*, 87 (9): 57–61.

11. Adams, R., S Jeanrenaud, J. Bessant, P. Overy and D. Denyer (2012) *Innovating for Sustainability: A guide for executives*. London, Ontario: Network for Business Sustainability, www.nbs.net/knowledge.

12. More information can be found at: http://www.philips.com/about/sustainability/index.page.

13. WBCSD (2000) *Eco-efficiency: Doing more with less*. Geneva: World Business Council for Sustainable Development.

14. Senge, P., B. Smith, N. Kruschwitz, J. Laur and S. Schley (2008) *The Necessary Revolution: How individuals and organizations are working together to create a sustainable world*. New York: Doubleday.

15. Shakti, G. (2011) Grameen Shakti, available from: http://www.gshakti.org/.

16. Owen, R., J. Bessant and M. Heintz (eds) (2013) *Responsible Innovation*. Chichester: John Wiley & Sons, Ltd.

17. Adams, R., D. Denyer, S. Jeanrenaud, J. Bessant and R. Adams (2013) *Sustainability-Oriented Innovation: A systematic review of the literature*. Ottawa, Canada: Network for Business Sustainability, http://nbs.net/wp-content/uploads/NBS-Executive-Report-Innovation.pdf.

Deeper Dive explanations of innovation concepts and ideas are available on the Innovation Portal at **www.innovation-portal.info**

Quizzes to test yourself further are available online via the Innovation Portal at **www.innovation-portal.info**

Summary of online resources for Chapter 21 –
all material is available via the Innovation Portal at
www.innovation-portal.info

Cases

Media

Tools

Activities

Deeper Dive

- NBS report on Innovating for sustainability
- WWF Climate Savers in China
- Philips
- Natura
- Green supply networks
- Green buildings
- TetraPak
- Volvo

- Mike Pitts
- Melissa Clark-Reynolds, Minimonos

- Sustainability-led innovation toolkit (SLI)

- Innovation challenges in sustainability

- Peak Resources
- New energy models

Index

CPSIA information can be obtained
at www.ICGtesting.com
Printed in the USA
BVHW052247250121
598626BV00009B/290